A

REBEL WAR CLERK'S

DIARY

AT THE

CONFEDERATE STATES CAPITAL.

BY

J. B. JONES,

CLERK IN THE WAR DEPARTMENT OF THE CONFEDERATE STATES GOVERNMENT;
AUTHOR OF "WILD WESTERN SCENES," ETC. ETC.

VOL. II.

PHILADELPHIA:
J. B. LIPPINCOTT & CO.
1866.

Entered, according to Act of Congress, in the year 1866, by

J. B. LIPPINCOTT & CO.,

In the Clerk's Office of the District Court of the United States for the Eastern District of Pennsylvania.

A REBEL WAR CLERK'S DIARY.

CHAPTER XXIX.

Some desertion.—Lee falling back.—Men still foolishly look for foreign aid.—Speculators swarming.—God helps me to-day.—Conscripts.—Memminger shipping gold to Europe.—Our women and children making straw bonnets.—Attack on Charleston.—Robert Tyler as a financier.—Enemy throw large shells into Charleston, five and a half miles.—Diabolical scheme.—Gen. Lee has returned to the army.

AUGUST 1ST.—The President learns, by a dispatch from Gen. Hardee, of Mississippi, that information has reached him, which he considers authentic, that Gen. Taylor has beaten Banks in Louisiana, taking 6000 prisoners; but then it is said that Taylor has *fallen back*.

I see by Mr. Memminger's correspondence that he has been sending $1,000,000 in sterling exchange, with the concurrence of the President and the Secretary of War, to Gen. Johnston and Gov. Pettus. What can this mean? Perhaps he is buying stores, etc.

Gen. Pemberton, it is said, has proclaimed a thirty days' furlough to all his paroled army—a virtue of necessity, as they had all gone to their homes without leave.

Gen. Lee writes that fifty men deserted from Scale's Regiment, North Carolina (a small regiment), night before last, being incited thereto by the newspapers. He wants pickets placed at certain places to catch them, so that some examples may be made.

Gov. Vance urges the War Department to interdict speculation on the part of officers of the government and army, as it tempts them to embezzle the public funds, enhances prices, and enrages the community.

Peter V. Daniel, Jr., President of the Central Railroad, is anxious for the defense of the four bridges near Hanover Junction, which, if destroyed by the enemy, could not be replaced for months, and Lee would have to fall back to Richmond, if not farther, as all his supplies must be transported by the road. He indicates the places where troops should be stationed, and says from those places, if needed in battle, 10,000 men could be transported in twenty-four hours to either Fredericksburg or Richmond.

Gen. Bragg is hurt, because one of his captains has been given an independent command, without consulting him, to defend Atlanta, in his department. He says the captain has no merit, and Atlanta and Augusta are in great danger—the newspapers having informed the enemy of the practicability of taking them. He intimates an inclination to be relieved.

Mr. Plant, President of the Southern Express Company, was "allowed" to leave the Confederate States to-day by the Assistant Secretary of War, subject to the discretion of Gen. Whiting at Wilmington. I suppose his fortune is made.

AUGUST 2D.—We have warm, fair weather now; but the momentary gloom, hanging like the pall of death over our affairs, cannot be dispelled without a decisive victory somewhere, or news of speedy foreign intervention. The letters which I read at the department this morning, contain no news whatever. I have suggested to the government to prohibit the exchange of newspapers in the flag of truce boat; but I doubt if they will act upon it. It is a manifest injury to us.

The exchange of prisoners is practically resumed; the Federal boat delivering yesterday 750 of *our sick and wounded;* and we returned 600 of their sick and wounded.

AUGUST 3D.—The President issued a proclamation to-day, calling upon all absentees to return to the ranks without delay, etc.

Hon. D. M. Barringer writes from Raleigh, N. C., that the State is in a ferment of rage against the administration for appointing Marylanders and Virginians, if not Pennsylvanians, quartermasters, to collect the war tax within its limits, instead of native citizens.

Mr. W. H. Locke, living on the James River, at the Cement and Lime Works, writes that more than a thousand deserters from Lee's army have crossed at that place within the last fortnight. This is awful; and they are mainly North Carolinians.

AUGUST 4TH.—The partial gloom continues. It is now ascertained that Gen. Morgan is a prisoner; only some 250 of his men, out of 3000, having escaped.

Lee is falling back on this side of the Rappahannock. His army has been diminished by desertions; but he has been reinforced pretty considerably since leaving Pennsylvania. The President's address may reinforce him still more; and then it may be possible a portion of Bragg's and Johnston's armies may be ordered hither. If this should be done, the next battle may be fatal to Meade. Our people are thirsting for another victory; and may expect too much.

Confederate notes are now given for gold at the rate of $12 or $15 for $1. Flour is $40 per barrel; bacon, $1.75 per pound; coal, $25 per cart-load; and good wood, $30 per cord. Butter is selling at $3 per pound, etc. etc.

Nevertheless, most men look for relief in the foreign complications the United States are falling into. England *will not* prohibit the selling of steamers to the Confederate States, and the United States say it shall not be done; and France has taken possession of Mexico, erecting it into an Empire, upon the throne of which will be seated some European ruler. We think recognition of our government is not far behind these events; when we shall have powerful navies to open the blockade. We are used to wounds and death; but can hardly bear starvation and nakedness.

AUGUST 5TH.—A letter from Hon. W. Porcher Miles to the Secretary of War, received the 15th July, urging the government to send some long-range Brooke guns for the salvation of Charleston, and saying that the President had once promised him that they should be sent thither, being sent by the Secretary to the President, was, to-day, August 5th, returned by the President, with a paper from the Secretary of the Navy, showing that, at the time Mr. Miles says he was promised the Brooke guns, there *were really none on hand*. Thus Mr. Miles has been *caught* by the President, after the lapse of twenty days! It is not denied, even by the Secretary of the Navy, that long-range guns were on hand at the time—but there were no Brooke guns, simply. Thus, while Charleston's fate hangs trembling in the balance, and the guns are idle here, twenty days are fruitlessly spent. Mr. Miles appears to be a friend of Beauregard. Every letter that general sends to the department is sure to put twenty clerks at work in the effort to pick flaws in his accuracy of statement.

A report of the ordnance officers of Bragg's army shows that in the late retreat (without a battle) from Shelbyville to Chattanooga, the army lost some 6000 arms and between 200,000 and 300,000 cartridges!

Our naval commanders are writing that they cannot get seamen —and at Mobile half are on the sick list.

Lee writes that his men are in good fighting condition—if he only had enough of them. Of the three corps, one is near Fredericksburg (this side the river), one at Orange C. H., and one at Gordonsville. I doubt if there will be another battle for a month.

Meantime the Treasury notes continue to depreciate, and all the necessaries of life advance in price—but they do not rise in *proportion*.

The *Examiner* had a famous attack on the President to-day (from the pen, I think, of a military man, on Gen. Scott's staff, when Mr. Davis was Secretary of War), for alleged stubbornness and disregard of the popular voice; for appointing Pemberton, Holmes, Mallory, etc., with a side fling at Memminger.

AUGUST 6TH.—A dispatch from Gen. Lee shows that he is still falling back (this side the Rapidan), but gradually concentrating his forces. There *may* be another battle speedily—and if our army does not gain a *great* victory, there will be great disappointment.

There are some gun-boats in the James as high up as Aiken's Landing. Two torpedoes, badly ignited, failed to injure either of them.

Capt. Kay, of Mobile, in conjunction with several other parties, has a scheme for the destruction of the enemy in the Mississippi Valley. What it is, I know not—but I know large sums of money are asked for.

After all, it appears that twenty-two transports of Grant's troops have descended the Mississippi River—Mobile, no doubt, being their destination.

It is now believed that only a portion of Grant's army has been ordered here; also that Rosecrans's army will operate with Meade; the object being to besiege Richmond. Well, we shall, in that event, have Johnston and Bragg—altogether 200,000 men around the city, which *ought* to suffice for its safety. A grand battle may take place this fall, in which half a million of men may be engaged. That ought to be followed by a decisive result. Let it come!

The speculators have put up the price of flour to $50 per barrel. To the honor of Messrs. Warwick, they are selling it at their mills for $35—not permitting any family to have more than one barrel. This looks, however, like an approaching siege.

My good friend Dr. Powell, almost every week, brings my family cucumbers, or corn, or butter, or something edible from his farm. He is one in ten thousand! His son has been in sixteen battles—and yet the government refuses him a lieutenancy, because he is not quite twenty-one years of age. He is manly, well educated, brave, and every way qualified.

AUGUST 7TH.—Nothing new from Lee's army—only that his troops are eager for another battle, when they are resolved to gain the day. There will probably not be so many prisoners taken as usual, since the alleged cruel treatment of our men now taken at Gettysburg, and the sending of Gen. Morgan to the Ohio Penitentiary, and shaving his head, by order of Gen. Burnside.

A dispatch from Beauregard, to-day, states that the enemy are getting large reinforcements, and are at work on their island batteries. There was a slow firing—and but one man killed.

It is believed that Governor Letcher will, reluctantly, call the Legislature together; but he says the members will exhibit only the *bad spirit of the people they represent.* What that means, I know not.

The Governor elect—commonly called "Extra-Billy Smith"—has resigned his brigadiership. But he is a candidate for a major-generalship, until inauguration day, 1st January. He has had an interview with the President, and proposes to take command of the troops defending the city—that Gen. Elzey may take the field. Smith would undoubtedly have a strong motive in defending the capital—but then he knows nothing of military affairs, yet I think he will be appointed.

Gen. Wise's batteries crippled and drove off the enemy's monitor and gun-boats day before yesterday. The monitor was towed down the James River in a disabled condition.

To-day, for the third time since the war began, I derived some money from our farm. It was another interposition of Providence. Once before, on the very days that money was indispensable, a Mr. Evans, a blockade-runner to the Eastern Shore of Virginia, came unexpectedly with $100 obtained from my agent, who has had the management of the farm for many years, and who is reported to be a Union man. To-day, just when my income is wholly insufficient to pay rent on the house—$500 per annum and $500 rent for the furniture, besides subsisting the family—at the very moment when my wife was about to part with the last of her little store of gold, to buy a few articles of furniture at auction, and save a heavy expense ($40 per month), the same Evans came to me, saying that although he had no money from my agent, if I would give him an order on the agent for $300, he would advance that amount in Treasury notes. I accepted the sum on his conditions. This is the work of a beneficent Providence, thus manifested on three different occasions,—and to doubt it would be to deserve damnation!

AUGUST 8TH.—There is nothing new from any of the armies, except that my old friend, Gen. Rains, sent to Mississippi, stopped and stampeded Grant's army, after Johnston retreated from Jackson, with his "subterra batteries." It appears that hundreds of the enemy and their horses were killed and wounded by the shells planted by him beneath the surface of the earth, and which ignited under the pressure of their weight. They knew not where to go to avoid them, and so they retreated to Vicksburg. This invention may become a terror to all invading.

A letter received some days ago from a Mr. Bible, in Georgia, proposing to contribute one-quarter of his slaves as teamsters, cooks, etc. for the army, came back from the President, to-day, approved, with directions to quartermasters to employ in such capacities all that could be procured.

Col. Myers, the Quartermaster-General, who is charged with saying "Let them suffer," when the soldiers wanted blankets last winter, is to go out of office at last—to be succeeded by Brig.-Gen. Lawton.

Oak-wood is selling to-day for $35 per cord; coal, $25 per cartload; and flour, $45 per barrel. Mr. Warwick, however, sells any family one barrel for $34. I got one from him, and the promise of another for $33—from Commissary Warner; and I hope to get two loads of coal, under the navy contract, at $20 each. There is much excitement against the speculators in food and fuel—and some harsh proceeding may ensue.

The *Tribune* (New York) now says no terms will be listened to so long as we are in arms. We will not yield our arms but with life—and this insures independence.

AUGUST 9TH.—No news from the armies.

Mrs. ex-President Tyler, who has already been permitted to visit her native State, New York, once or twice during the war—and indeed her plantation has been within the enemy's lines—has applied for passage in a government steamer (the Lee) to Nassau, and to take with her "a few bales of cotton." I suppose it will be "allowed."

We have fine hot August weather now, and I hope my tomatoes will mature, and thus save me two dollars per day. My potatoes have, so far, failed; but as they are still green, perhaps they may produce a crop later in the season. The lima beans, trailed on the fence, promise an abundant crop; and the cabbages and peppers look well. Every inch of the ground is in cultivation—even the ash-heap, covered all over with tomato-vines.

AUGUST 10TH.—No army news of immediate importance.

South Carolina has set an example in the prices of supplies for the army, under the Impressment Act, fixed by the Commissioners. By this schedule (for August, and it will be less in succeeding months) bacon is to be from 65 to 75 cents per pound; beef, 25 cents; corn, $2 per bushel; flour $20; pork, 35 cents; hay, $1.50 per 100 pounds; oats, $2 per bushel; potatoes, $3; rice, 10 cents; sugar, 80 cents; soap, 40 cents; and wheat, $3.50 per bushel.

Gen. Lee writes that the railroad brings him but 1000 bushels of corn per day; not enough to bring up his exhausted cavalry and artillery horses; and he suggests that passenger cars be occasionally left behind for the purpose of supplying the army—an indispensable measure.

Gen. Lee also writes that he has 1700 unarmed men in his army; in two weeks there will be 5000, and in a month 10,000. He suggests that the troops for local defense here, and even the militia, be disarmed, to supply his men. This indicates that Lee is to have an *immense* army, and that Richmond is to be defended.

But the Central and Fredericksburg Railroads must be repaired immediately, and at any expense to the government, or else all will fail!

AUGUST 11TH.—After all the applications of the railroad companies when Gen. Lee was in Pennsylvania, and the enemy had withdrawn from this side of the Potomac, it appears that the fine iron on the road from Fredericksburg to Aquia Creek was not removed! Mr. Seddon's subordinates must answer for this. The iron was wanted more than anything else but men. The want of men cannot be alleged for not securing it, because the railroad companies would have procured negroes enough for its removal.

Well, the first of August has passed, and the grand scheme of the War Office at Washington of a general servile insurrection did not take place. On the contrary, a large army of slaves might be organized to fight for their masters.

To-day, it must be confessed, I saw some of the booty (if, indeed, it was not fairly bought) of the recent invasion of the North. A number of boxes of fine stationery, brought from Carlisle, Chambersburg, etc., were opened at the War Department.

There is a controversy between the Secretary of War, Assistant Secretary, and Attorney-General on one side, and the Commissary-General, Col. L. B. Northrop, on the other. It appears that one of the assistant commissaries exchanged sugar for flour and rice in Alabama with a merchant or speculator, and then, after the lapse of a month or so, *impressed the sugar*. The party got the Attorney-General's opinion in his behalf, which was approved by the Assistant Secretary of War, and the Secretary issued an order for the release of the sugar. In response to this, Col. N. rebuts the arguments of the whole three (lawyers) by saying it is not *good sense* to exempt anything, under any circumstances, from impressment, when needed to carry on the war; and that the way to success is to do justice to the whole country—and not to please the people. A palpable hit at the politicians. He says if the Secretary insists on the sugar being released, it will be done against his (N.'s) judgment.

AUGUST 12TH.—Letters from Georgia to-day assure the government that the grain crops of that State will afford a surplus sufficient for the army, cavalry and all, for 12 months.

Also one from P. Clayton, late Assistant Secretary of the Treasury, censuring the commissary agents in Georgia, who are sent thither from other States, who insult the farmers and encourage speculation.

Mr. Memminger is shipping gold from Wilmington, $20,000 by each steamer, to Bermuda and Nassau. Why is this? Cotton is quite as good as gold, and there are thousands of millions worth of that in the country, which Mr. Memminger might buy, certainly might have bought for Confederate notes, but, in his peculiar wisdom, he would not. And now, the *great financier* is shipping gold out of the country, thinking, perhaps, it may arrest the depreciation of paper money!

Col. Northrop, Commissary-General, is still urging a diminution of rations, and as our soldiers taken by the enemy fare badly in the North, and as the enemy make a point of destroying all the crops they can when they invade us, and even destroy our agricultural implements and teams, he proposes, in retaliation, to stop meat rations altogether to prisoners in our hands, and give them instead oat gruel, corn-meal gruel, and pea soup, soft hominy, and bread. This the Secretary will not agree to, because the law says they shall have the same as our troops.

I read to-day Gen. Lee's report of his operations (an outline) in June and July, embracing his campaign in Maryland and Pennsylvania.

The enemy could not be attacked advantageously opposite Fredericksburg, and hence he determined to draw him out of his position by relieving the lower valley of the Shenandoah, and, if practicable, transfer the scene of hostilities north of the Potomac.

The movement began on the 3d of June. The divisions of McLaws and Hood (Longstreet's) marched for Culpepper C. H. They were followed on the 4th and 5th by Ewell's corps, A. P. Hill's still occupying our lines at Fredericksburg.

When the enemy discovered the movement (on the 5th), he sent an army corps across the Rappahannock, but this did not arrest Longstreet and Ewell, who reached Culpepper C. H. on the 8th, where they found Gen. Stuart and his cavalry. On the 9th the enemy's cavalry and a strong force of infantry crossed the Rappahannock and attacked Gen. Stuart, but they were beaten back, after fighting all day, with heavy loss, including 400 prisoners, 3 pieces artillery, and several colors.

Gens. Jenkins and Imboden had been sent in advance, the latter against Romney, to cover the former's movement against Winchester, and both were in position when Ewell left Culpepper C. H. on the 16th.

Gen. Early stormed the enemy's works at Winchester on the 14th, and the whole army of Milroy was captured or dispersed.

Gen. Rhodes, on the same day, took Martinsburg, Va., capturing 700 prisoners, 5 pieces artillery, and a large supply of stores.

More than 4000 prisoners were taken at Winchester; 29 pieces artillery; 270 wagons and ambulances; 400 horses, besides a large amount of military stores.

Precisely at this time the enemy disappeared from Fredericksburg, seemingly designing to take a position to cover Washington.

Gen. Stuart, in several engagements, took 400 more prisoners, etc.

Meantime, Gen. Ewell, with Gen. Jenkins's cavalry, etc., penetrated Maryland, and Pennsylvania as far as Chambersburg.

On the 24th, Lt.-Gens. Longstreet and Hill marched to the Potomac, the former crossing at Williamsport and the latter at Shepherdstown, uniting at Hagerstown, Md., advancing into Pennsylvania, and encamping near Chambersburg on the 27th.

Ewell's corps advanced as far as York and Carlisle, to keep the enemy out of the mountains, and to keep our communications open.

Gen. Imboden destroyed all the important bridges of the Baltimore and Ohio Railroad from Martinsburg to Cumberland, damaging the Chesapeake and Ohio Canal.

Preparations were made to march upon Harrisburg, when information was received of the approach of the army of the enemy, menacing communications with the Potomac, necessitating a concentration of our army at Gettysburg.

Hill became engaged with a superior force of the enemy on the 1st July, but Ewell, coming up by the Harrisburg road, participated in the engagement, and the enemy were driven through Gettysburg with heavy loss, including about 5000 prisoners and several pieces of artillery.

The enemy retired to a high range of hills, south and east of the town.

On the 2d, Gen. Ewell occupied the left, Gen. Hill the center, and Gen. Longstreet the right.

Longstreet got possession of the enemy's position in front of his corps after a severe struggle; Ewell also carried some strong positions. The battle ceased at dark.

The next day, 3d July, our batteries were moved forward to the positions we had gained, and it was determined to renew the attack.

Meantime the enemy had strengthened his line. The battle raged with great violence in the afternoon, until sunset. We got possession of some of the enemy's batteries, but our ammunition failing, our troops were compelled to relinquish them, and fall back to their original position with severe loss.

Our troops (the general says) behaved well in the protracted and sanguinary conflict, accomplishing all that was practicable.

The strong position of the enemy, and reduction of his ammunition, rendered it inexpedient for Gen. Lee to continue longer where he was. Such of the wounded as could be moved, and part of the arms collected on the field, were ordered to Williamsport.

His army remained at Gettysburg during the 4th, and began to retire at night, taking with it about 4000 prisoners, nearly 2000 having been previously paroled. The enemy's wounded that fell into his hands were left behind.

He reached Williamsport without molestation, losing but few wagons, etc., and arrived at Hagerstown 7th July.

The Potomac was much swollen by recent rains, that had fallen incessantly ever since he had crossed it, and was unfordable.

The enemy had not yet appeared, until the 12th, when, instead of attacking, Meade fortified his lines.

On the 13th Gen. Lee crossed at Falling Waters, the river subsiding, by fords and a bridge, without loss, the enemy making no interruption. Only some stragglers, sleeping, fell into the hands of the enemy.

AUGUST 13TH.—No news. It turns out that Gen. Taylor got only 500 prisoners at Donaldsonville, La., instead of 4000.

A writer in the New York *Tribune* says the Northern troops burnt Jackson, Miss.

Lincoln has marked for close confinement and hostages three of our men for three free negroes taken on Morris Island.

The government here has, at last, indicated blockade-goods (U. S.) which are to be seized; also sent circular letters to the generals at Wilmington, Charleston, and Mobile to impose restrictions on blockade-running steamers belonging to private parties. The government must first have such articles as its necessities require, at fair prices, before the merchandise can be offered to the public, and the vessels must be freighted out partly with government cotton. This is a good arrangement, even if it is "locking the stable after the horse is stolen."

AUGUST 14TH.—The enemy is not idle. He knows the importance of following up his recent advantages, and making the utmost use of his veteran troops now in the field, because his new levies, if indeed the draft be submitted to, will not be fit for use this year, probably, if ever, for they will consist of the riff-raff of the Northern population. On the other hand, he suspects we will soon have larger armies in the field than ever before, and our accessions will consist of our bravest men, who will make efficient soldiers in a month. If our armies be not broken before October, no doubt the tide of success will turn again fully in our favor.

Major Wm. Norris, Signal Corps, reports that many transports and troops have been going down from Washington and Annapolis to Fortress Monroe during the whole week, and that 5000 men embarked at Fortress Monroe, on Monday, for (as they said themselves) Charleston. Among these was a negro regiment of 1300.

T. C. Reynolds, confidential agent of the government in the trans-Mississippi States, sends copy of a circular letter from Lieut.-Gen. Kirby Smith to the "representative men" of Missouri, Arkansas, Louisiana, and Texas, to meet him in convention, 15th August, at Marshall, Texas. Mr Reynolds says he and others will exert themselves to prevent the meeting from taking a dangerous political direction. Gen. Smith is popular, and opposed to the States named setting up for themselves, although he plainly says in the circular that they must now adopt self-sustaining measures, as they cannot look for aid from the East. Mr. Reynolds says something, not clearly understood by me, about an equipoise among the *political* generals. Has he been instructed on that point in reference to Gen. Price?

Letters from Mr. Crenshaw, in England, and the correspondence forwarded by him, might seem to implicate Major Caleb Huse, Col. J. Gorgas's ordnance agent, in some very ugly operations. It appears that Major H. has contracted for 50,000 muskets at $4 above the current price, leaving $200,000 commission for whom? And that he really seems to be throwing obstacles in the way of Mr. C., who is endeavoring to procure commissary stores in England. Mr. C. has purchased £40,000 worth of bacon, but Major Huse, he apprehends, is endeavoring to prevent its shipment. Can this be so?

The *Charleston Mercury* that came to-day contains an editorial broadside against the President, Mr. Benjamin, Mr. Mallory, and Commissary-General Northrop.

Mr. Gilmer, lawyer, remarked to me to-day that some grave men (!) really believed Davis and Lincoln had an understanding, and were playing into each other's hands to prolong the war, knowing that peace would be the destruction of both! I think there is more danger to both in war. The blood of a brave people could not be trifled with without the utmost danger. Let peace come, even if the politicians be shorn of all their power.

AUGUST 15TH.—I learn an order has been issued to conscribe all commissary and quartermasters' clerks liable to military service. There will be, and ought to be, some special cases of exemption, where men have lost everything in the war and have women and children depending on their salaries for subsistence; but if this order be extended to the ordnance and other bureaus, as it must be, or incur the odium of injustice, and the thousand and one A. A. G.'s, there will soon be a very important accession to the army.

Major Joseph B——, who was lately confined with over 1000 of our officers, prisoners, on Johnson Island, Lake Erie, proposes a plan to the Secretary of War whereby he is certain the island can be taken, and the prisoners liberated and conveyed to Canada. He proposes that a dozen men shall seize one of the enemy's steamers at Sandusky, and then overpower the guards, etc. It is wild, but not impracticable.

We hear nothing to-day from the enemy on the Rappahannock or at Fortress Monroe.

Our army in Western Louisiana captured some forty Yankee cotton-planters, who had taken possession of the plantations after driving their owners away. The account states that they were "sent to Texas." Were they not sent into eternity?

AUGUST 16TH.—The President rides out with some of the

female members of his family every afternoon, his aids no longer accompanying him. In this he evinces but little prudence, for it is incredible that he should be ignorant of the fact that he has some few deadly enemies in the city.

Everywhere the ladies and children may be seen plaiting straw and making bonnets and hats. Mrs. Davis and the ladies of her household are frequently seen sitting on the front porch engaged in this employment. Ostentation cannot be attributed to them, for only a few years ago the Howells were in humble condition and accustomed to work.

My wife borrowed $200 of Mr. Waterhouse, depositing $20 in gold as security—worth $260—which, with the $300 from Evans on account of rent, have been carefully applied to the purchase of sundry housekeeping articles. After the 1st September we shall cease to pay $40 per month rent on furniture, but that amount for house-rent, so that in the item of rent my expenses will be less than they were the preceding year. So far, with the exception of crockery-ware and chairs, the purchases (at auction) have been at low prices, and we have been fortunate in the time selected to provide indispensable articles.

I often wonder if, in the first struggle for independence, there was as much suffering and despondency among certain classes of the people as we now behold. Our rich men are the first to grow weary of the contest. Yesterday a letter was received by the Secretary of War from a Mr. Reanes, Jackson, Mississippi, advising the government to lose no time in making the best terms possible with the United States authorities, else all would be lost. He says but a short time ago he was worth $1,250,000, and now nothing is left him but a shelter, and that would have been destroyed if he had not made a pledge to remain. He says he is an old man, and was a zealous secessionist, and even now would give his life for the independence of his country. But that is impracticable—numbers must prevail—and he would preserve his wife and children from the horrors threatened, and inevitable if the war be prolonged He says the soldiers that were under Pemberton and Lovell will never serve under them again, for they denounce them as traitors and tyrants, while, as they allege, they were well treated by the enemy when they fell into their hands.

Yet it seems to me that, like the Israelites that passed through the Red Sea, and Shadrach and his brethren who escaped unscorched from the fiery furnace, my family have been miraculousl sustained. We have purchased no clothing for nearly three years, and had no superabundance to begin with, but still we have decent clothes, as if time made no appreciable change in them. I wear a hat bought four years ago, and shoes that cost me (government price then) $7.50 more than a year ago, and I suppose they would sell now for $10 ; new ones are bringing $50.

My tomatoes are maturing slowly, but there will be abundance, saving me $10 per week for ten weeks. My lima beans are very full, and some of them will be fit to pull in a few days. My potatoes are as green as grass, and I fear will produce nothing but vines; but I shall have cabbages and parsnips, and red peppers. No doubt the little garden, 25 by 50, will be worth $150 to me. Thank Providence, we still have health!

But the scarcity—or rather high prices, for there is really no scarcity of anything but meat—is felt by the cats, rats, etc., as well as by the people. I have not seen a rat or mouse for months, and lean cats are wandering past every day in quest of new homes.

What shall we do for sugar, now selling at $2 per pound? When the little supply this side of the Mississippi is still more reduced it will probably be $5! It has been more than a year since we had coffee or tea. Was it not thus in the trying times of the Revolution? If so, why can we not bear privation as well as our forefathers did? We must!

AUGUST 17TH.—No news, except that the bombardment at Charleston is getting hotter—but the casualties are few.

The chief ordnance officer of Gen. Lee's army writes that the ammunition from Richmond has always to be tested before they can venture to use it. The shells for the Parrott guns are often too large—and of course would be useless in the hour of battle!

The *Examiner* to-day has an attack on the President for removing A. C. Myers, the Quartermaster-General.

AUGUST 18TH.—There is heavy firing, day and night, on Wagner's battery and Fort Sumter. The enemy use 15-inch guns; but Sumter is 4000 yards distant, and it may be hoped will not be reduced.

After all, the enemy did not, durst not, shave the head of Gen. Morgan, and otherwise maltreat him, as was reported.

2*

The Secretary of War is, I believe, really in earnest in his determination to prevent future blockade-running on private account; and is resolved to send out cotton, tobacco, etc. by every steamer, so that funds and credit may be always available in Europe. The steamers go and come every week, in spite of the cruisers, and they bring munitions of war, equipments, provisions, iron, etc. etc. So long as this continues, the war can be maintained; and of late very few captures have been made by the enemy.

There are rumors of some manœuvres of Gen. Lee, which may indicate an approaching battle.

AUGUST 19TH.—A *scout*, from Washington, has reported to Major Norris, signal corps, that 10,000 New York troops have recently left Meade's army, their term of service having expired; and that 30,000 men have been sent from his army against Charleston. This accounts for the falling back of Meade—and the detachment never would have been made without.

This intelligence has been in the possession of the government four days; and if Charleston should fall now for want of men or material, there will be great culpability somewhere.

All the non-combatants have been requested to leave Charleston—and none are allowed to enter the city.

We have just got information from Charleston of a furious assault. So far the casualties are not very great, nor the Island batteries materially injured; but Sumter, it is feared, is badly shattered, yet is in no great danger. Much apprehension for the result is felt and manifested here. Six or eight large columbiads have been lying idle at the Petersburg depot for a month, although the prayers of the people of Charleston for heavy guns have been incessant!

Col. Preston, Chief of the Bureau of Conscription, sent in a long communication to-day, asking for enlarged powers and exclusive jurisdiction in the conscription business, and then, he says, he will have all the conscripts (not exempted) in the army in six months. But more are exempted than conscribed!

Robert Tyler publishes a long and hopeful letter on our finances.

If Mr. Memminger read and approved the manuscript, it is well; but if not, *good-by*, my friend! It is well done, however, even though *aspiring*. But it is incredible there should be no more Treasury notes in circulation—and no more indebtedness.

AUGUST 20TH.—A few weeks ago Gen. Cooper wrote to Bragg, suggesting that he advance into Middle Tennessee, reinforced by Gen. Johnston, and attack Rosecrans; Gen. Bragg replied (8th inst.) that with all the reinforcements he could get from Johnston, he would not have more than 40,000 effective men, while Rosecrans has 60,000, and will be reinforced by Burnside with 30,000 more—making 90,000 against 40,000—and as a true patriot he was opposed to throwing away our armies in enterprises sure to terminate disastrously. He said, moreover, that the enemy could starve him out, if he were to advance to the place designated, and thus destroy his army without a battle. Gen. Cooper sent this response to the President, asking if Bragg should not be *ordered* to fight under such circumstances. But the President paused, in following the guidance of this Northern man at the head of all our Southern generals—and to-day sent back the paper indorsed that "only a suggestion could be given to a commanding general to fight a battle; but to order him to fight when he predicted a failure in advance, would be unwise."

A paper from Beauregard intimates that even if batteries Wagner and Gregg should be taken by the enemy, he has constructed another which will render that part of Morris Island untenable. But he relied upon holding Sumter; and there is a vague rumor to-day that Sumter must surrender—if indeed it has not already been reduced.

Hon Wm. Porcher Miles writes another most urgent letter, demanding reinforcements of seasoned troops. He says Charleston was stripped of troops against the remonstrances of Beauregard to send to Mississippi—to no avail—which invited this attack; and now he asks that Jenkins's brigade of South Carolinians be sent to the defense; that South Carolinians are fighting in Virginia, but are not permitted to defend their native soil in the hour of extremity; and that if the enemy, with overwhelming numbers, should take James's Island, they would, from thence, be able to destroy the city. We are looking with anxiety for further news from Charleston.

Gen. Maury writes from Mobile that he has seized, in the hands of Steever (who is he?), receipts for 4000 bales of cotton—orders for 150 bonds, each £225 sterling, and two bags of coin, $10,000. The President indorses on the paper that the money had better be turned over to the Secretary of the Treasury. What is all this?

The Secretary sent a paper to the President relating to some novel action performed or proposed, asking his "instructions." The President returned it to-day indorsed, "The Secretary's advice invited." How in the mischief can such non-committalists ever arrive at a conclusion?

Hon. E. S. Dargan writes that if Pemberton be restored to command (as he understands this to be the government's purpose), our cause is ruined beyond redemption. I say so too. When he made up his mind to surrender, it is unpardonable that he did not destroy the 50,000 stand of arms before he made any overture. I shall never forgive him!

The signal officers report that three large ocean steamers passed down the Potomac day before yesterday, having on board 1000 men each; and that many large steamers are constantly going up —perhaps for more.

Brig.-Gen. Roger A. Pryor, after dancing attendance in the ante-rooms for six months, waiting assignment to a command, has resigned, and his resignation has been accepted. He says he can at least serve in the ranks as a private. The government don't like aspiring political generals. Yet Pryor was first a colonel, and member of Congress—resigned his seat—resigned his brigadier-generalship, and is now a private.

Our cause is dim in Europe, if it be true, as the Northern papers report, that the Confederate loan has sunken from par to 35 per cent. discount since the fall of Vicksburg.

AUGUST 21ST, FRIDAY.—This is a day appointed by the President for humiliation, fasting, and prayer. Yet the Marylanders in possession of the passport office report the following in the *Dispatch* of this date:

"*Passports.*—The passport office was besieged yesterday and last night by large crowds of persons soliciting permission to leave the city, in order that some relaxation might be had from its busy scenes. Among those who obtained them were His Excellency Jefferson Davis and his Honor Joseph Mayo, both designing to pay a short visit to the neighboring County of Chesterfield."

We fast, certainly—and feel greatly humiliated at the loss of New Orleans and Vicksburg—and we pray, daily.

Yesterday Fort Sumter suffered much from the enemy's batteries, and much apprehension is felt for its fate.

Gen. Lee, it is said, is not permitted to follow Meade, who is retrograding, being weakened by detachments. A few weeks hence the fall campaign will open in Virginia, when the very earth may tremble again with the thunders of war, and the rivulets may again spout human blood.

There were no letters to-day, for the reason that last night the clerks in the post-office resigned, their salaries not being sufficient to support them. I hope a force will be detailed, to-morrow, to distribute the letters.

I met Prof. A. T. Bledsoe to-day as he was ambling toward the passport office. He said he was just about to start for London, where he intended publishing his book—on slavery, I believe. He has a free passage on one of the government steamers, to sail from Wilmington. He asked me if I fasted to-day; I answered yes, as *usual!* He then bid me good-by, and at parting I told him I hoped he would not find us all hanged when he returned. I think it probable he has a mission from the President, as well as his book to publish.

August 22d.—All the guns of Fort Sumter on the south face have been silenced by the land batteries of the enemy on Morris Island; and this account is two days old. What has taken place since, none here but Gen. Cooper and the President know. But our battery, Wagner, dismounted one of the enemy's Parrott guns and blew up two magazines. It is rumored to-day that Sumter has been abandoned and blown up; also that 20,000 of *Grant's* men have been ordered to New York to quell a new *émeute*. Neither of these rumors are credited, however, by reflecting men. But they may be true, nevertheless.

Passengers from Bermuda say two monster guns were on the steamer, and were landed at Wilmington a few days ago, weighing each twenty-two tons; carriages, *sixty tons;* the balls, 15 inches in diameter, length not stated, weighing 700 pounds; the shells, not filled, weigh 480 pounds; and 40 pounds of powder are used at each discharge. They say these guns can be fired with accuracy and with immense effect seven miles. I wonder if the President will send them to Charleston? They might save the city.

The balls fired by the enemy are eight inches in diameter, and two feet in length; 2000 of these, solid and filled, have struck the southern face of Sumter.

It is now positively asserted that Morgan's head was shaved, when they put him in the penitentiary.

Night before last all the clerks in the city post-office resigned, because the government did not give them salaries sufficient to subsist them. As yet their places have not been filled, and the government gets no letters—some of which lying in the office may be of such importance as to involve the safety or ruin of the government. To-morrow is Sunday, and of course the mails will not be attended to before Monday—the letters lying here four days unopened! This really looks as if we had no Postmaster-General.

AUGUST 23D.—Dispatches from Charleston, yesterday, brought the melancholy intelligence that Fort Sumter is but little more than a pile of rubbish. The fall of this fort caused my wife a hearty cry—and she cried when Beauregard reduced it in 1861; not because he did it, but because it was the initiation of a terrible war. She hoped that the separation would be permitted to pass without bloodshed.

To-day we have a dispatch from Beauregard, stating the *extraordinary fact that the enemy's batteries, since the demolition of Sumter, have thrown shell, from their Parrott guns, into the city—a distance of five and a half miles!* This decides the fate of Charleston; for they are making regular approaches to batteries Wagner and Gregg, which, of course, will fall. The other batteries Beauregard provided to render the upper end of the island untenable, cannot withstand, I fear, the enginery of the enemy.

If the government had sent the long-range guns of large caliber when so urgently called for by Beauregard, and if it had *not* sent away the best troops against the remonstrances of Beauregard, the people are saying, no lodgment could have been made on Morris Island by the enemy, and Sumter and Charleston would have been saved for at least another year.

At all events, it is quite probable, now, that all the forts and cities on the seaboard (Mobile, Savannah, Wilmington, Richmond) must succumb to the mighty engines of the enemy; and our gunboats, built and in process of completion, will be lost. Richmond, it is apprehended, must fall when the enemy again approaches within four or five miles of it; and Wilmington can be taken from the rear, as well as by water, for no forts can withstand the Parrott guns.

Then there will be an end of blockade-running; and we must flee to the mountains, and such interior fastnesses as will be impracticable for the use of these long-range guns. Man must confront man in the deadly conflict, and the war can be protracted until the government of the North passes out of the hands of the Abolitionists. We shall suffer immensely; but in the end we shall be free.

AUGUST 24TH.—We have nothing further from Charleston, except that Beauregard threatened retaliation (how?) if Gilmore repeated the offense, against humanity and the rules of civilized war, of shelling the city before notice should be given the women and children to leave it. To-day, at 11 A.M., it is supposed the shelling was renewed.

This day week, I learn by a letter from Gen. Whiting, two 700-pounder Blakely guns arrived in the Gladiator. If these could only be transported to Charleston, what a *sensation* they would make among the turreted monitors! But I fear the railroad cannot transport them.

The Secretary of the Treasury asks transportation for 1000 bales of cotton to Wilmington. What for?

To-day I saw a copy of a dispatch from Gen. Johnston to the President, dated at Morton, Miss., 22d August, stating that he would send forward, the next day, two divisions to reinforce Gen. Bragg in Tennessee. This signifies battle.

The Secretary of the Treasury notified the Secretary of War, to-day, that the appropriation of fifty millions per month, for the expenditure of the War Department, was greatly exceeded; that already this month (August) the requisitions on hand amounted to over $70,000,000, and they could not be met—some must lie over; and large sums for contracts, pay of troops, etc. will not be paid, immediately.

Exchange on London, I learn by a letter written by Mr. Endus to his agent in London, detained by Gen. Whiting and sent to the Secretary of War, is selling in Richmond at a premium of fifteen hundred per cent.

The post-office clerks have returned to duty, the Postmaster-

General promising to recommend to Congress increased compensation.

AUGUST 25TH.—Hon. A. R. Boteler, after consultation with Gen. Stuart and Capt. Moseby, suggests that the Secretary of War send up some of Gen. Rains's subterra torpedoes, to place under the track of the Orange and Alexandria Railroad, in possession of the enemy. Gen. Stuart suggested that a man familiar with their use be sent along with them, as they are dangerous weapons.

We have a report, to-day, that our expedition from this city has succeeded in boarding and capturing two of the enemy's gun-boats in the Rappahannock.

AUGUST 26TH.—H. C. ———, a mad private, and Northern man, in a Georgia Regiment, writes to the President, proposing to take some 300 to 500 men of resolution and assassinate the leading public men of the United States—the war Abolitionists, I suppose. The President referred the paper, without notice, to the Secretary of War.

Gen. Whiting writes that Wilmington is in imminent danger from a *coup de main*, as he has but one regiment available in the vicinity. He says he gives the government fair warning, and full information of his condition; asking a small brigade, which would enable him to keep the enemy at bay until adequate reinforcements could arrive. He also wants two Whitworth guns to keep the blockaders at a more respectful distance, since they captured one steamer from us, recently, nine miles below the city, and blew up a ship which was aground. He says it is *tempting Providence* to suffer that (now) most important city in the Confederate States to remain a day liable to sudden capture, which would effectually cut us off from the rest of the world.

Gen. Beauregard telegraphs for a detail of 50 seamen for his iron-clads, which he intends shall support Sumter, if, as he anticipates, the enemy should make a sudden attempt to seize 'it—or rather its debris—where he still has some guns, *still under our flag*. None of his vessels have full crews. This paper was referred to the Secretary of the Navy, and he returned it with an emphatic *negative*, saying that the War Department had failed to make details from the army to the navy, in accordance with an act of Congress, and hence none of our war steamers had full crews.

AUGUST 27TH.—There is trouble in the Conscription Bureau.

Col. Preston, the new superintendent, finds it no bed of roses, made for him by Lieut.-Col. Lay—the lieutenant-colonel being absent in North Carolina, sent thither to *compose* the discontents; which may complicate matters further, for they don't want Virginians to meddle with North Carolina matters. However, the people he is sent to are supposed to be *disloyal*. Gen. Pillow has applied to have Georgia in the jurisdiction of his Bureau of Conscription, and the Governors of Georgia, Alabama, and Tennessee unite in the request; also Generals Johnston and Bragg. Gen. Pillow already has Mississippi, Tennessee, Alabama, etc.—a much larger jurisdiction than the bureau here. Col. Preston, of course, protests against all this, and I believe the Secretary sympathizes with him.

Prof. G. M. Richardson, of the Georgia Military Institute, sends some interesting statistics. That State has furnished the army 80,000, between the ages of eighteen and forty-five years. Still, the average number of men in each county between sixteen and eighteen and forty-five and sixty is 462, and there are 132 counties: total, 60,984. He deducts 30 per cent. for the infirm, etc. (18,689), leaving 42,689 men able to bear arms still at home. Thus, after putting some 500,000 in the field (if we could put them there), there would yet remain a reserve for home defense against raids, etc. in the Confederate States, of not less than 250,000 men.

Gen. Winder sent to the Secretary of War to-day for authority to appoint a clerk to attend exclusively to the mails to and from the United States—under Gen. Winder's sole direction.

Major Quantrel, a Missouri guerrilla chief, has dashed into Lawrence, Kansas, and burnt the city—killing and wounding 180. He had Gen. Jim Lane, but he escaped.

Gen. Floyd is dead; some attribute his decease to ill treatment by the government.

I saw Mr. Hunter yesterday, bronzed, but bright. He is a little thinner, which improves his appearance.

Gen. Lee is in town—looking well. When he returns, I think the fall campaign will open briskly.

A dispatch received to-day says that on Tuesday evening another assault on Battery Wagner was in progress—but as yet we have no result.

Lieut. Wood captured a third gun-boat in the Rappahannock, having eight guns.

The prisoners here selected to die, in retaliation for Burnside's execution of our officers taken while recruiting in Kentucky, will not be executed.

Nor will the officers taken on Morris Island, serving with the negroes, suffer death in accordance with the act of Congress and the President's proclamation. The Secretary referred the matter to the President for instruction, and the President invited the advice of the Secretary. The Secretary advised that they be held indefinitely, without being brought to trial, and in this the President acquiesces.

AUGUST 28TH.—Another letter, from Gen. Whiting, calls vehemently for reinforcements, artillery, cavalry, and infantry—or else the city and harbor are soon to be at the mercy of the enemy. He is importunate.

After all, Morgan's head was *not* shaved—but his beard, and that of his officers, was cut, and their hair made *short*. This I learn from a letter at the department from Morgan's Assistant Adjutant-General.

The tocsin was ringing in my ears when I awoke this morning. Custis packed his haversack, and, taking blanket, etc. etc., joined his department comrades, and they were all marched out the Brooke turnpike. Yesterday the enemy in considerable force came up the Peninsula and attacked the guard (70 men) at Bottom's Bridge, killing, so report says, Lieut. Jetu, of South Carolina, and some twelve or fifteen others. But I believe the attacking party have recrossed the Chickahominy. We shall know in a few hours. Gen. Lee is still here. Gen. Wise's brigade, with the militia, the department companies, and the convalescents from the hospitals, must number some 8000 men in this vicinity. If the enemy be in formidable numbers, we shall soon be reinforced.

We have nothing from Charleston since Tuesday evening, when, it is said, the "*first* assault" was repulsed. It is strange we get nothing later.

AUGUST 29TH.—After all, it appears that only a few hundred of the enemy's cavalry came up the Peninsula as far as Bottom's Bridge, from whence they quickly fell back again. And this alarm caused Gen. Elzey, or the government, to put in movement nearly

20,000 men! But something else may be behind this demonstration; it may be the purpose of the enemy to strike in another direction, perhaps at Hanover Junction—where, fortunately, we have nearly a division awaiting them.

The Hon. Mr. Dargan's letter, received at the department a few days ago, saying that the reinstatement of Gen. Pemberton in command would be the ruin of the cause, was referred by the Secretary to the President, with some strong remarks, to the effect that popular opinion was almost universal against Pemberton. It came back to-day, with the following indorsement of the President: "*The justice or injustice of the opinion will be tested by the investigation ordered.—J. D.*" If the President desires it, of course Pemberton will be exonerated. But even if he be honorably and fairly acquitted, the President ought not to forget that he is not a ruler by Divine right to administer justice merely, but the servant of the people to aid in the achievement of their independence; and that their opinions and wishes, right or wrong, must be respected, or they can deprive him of honor, and select another leader.

AUGUST 30TH.—The department companies and militia returned yesterday, through a heavy shower, from the wild-goose chase they were rushed into by Gen. Elzey's order.

Mr. Reagan, the Postmaster-General, informed me to-day (the government will not allow bad news to transpire) that at the *second* assault on Battery Wagner, Morris Island, the enemy captured and held the rifle-pits. This, perhaps, involves the loss of the battery itself—and indeed there is a report, generally believed, that it fell subsequently. I fear that the port of Charleston is closed finally—if indeed, as I hope, the city will be still held by Beauregard.

Letters from Wilmington, dated 21st instant, urgently ask the Secretary of War to have one of the Great Blakely guns for the defense of that city—and protesting against both being sent to Charleston. From this, I infer that one or both have been ordered to Beauregard.

Gen. Samuel Jones has had a small combat with the enemy in Western Virginia, achieving some success. His loss was about 200, that of the enemy much greater. This is a grain of victory to a pound of disaster.

The owners of several fast blockade-running steamers, in anticipation of the closing of all the ports, are already applying for letters of marque to operate against the commerce of the United States as privateers, or in the "volunteer navy"—still with an eye to gain.

Gen. Lee has returned to the Army of Northern Virginia—and we shall probably soon hear of interesting operations in the field. Governor Vance writes for a brigade of North Carolinians to collect deserters in the western counties of that State.

There must be two armies in Virginia this fall—one for defense, and one (under Lee) for the aggressive—150,000 men in all—or else the losses of the past will not be retrieved during the ensuing *terrible* campaign.

Some good may be anticipated from the furious and universal outcry in the Confederate States against the extortioners and speculators in food and fuel. Already some of the millers here are selling new flour at $27 to families; the speculators paid $35 for large amounts, which they expected to get $50 for! But meat is still too high for families of limited means. My tomatoes are now maturing—and my butter-beans are filling rapidly, and have already given us a dinner. What we shall do for clothing, the Lord knows—but we trust in Him.

August 31st.—Governor Vance writes that large bodies of deserters in the western counties of North Carolina are organized, with arms, and threaten to raise the Union flag at the courthouse of Wilkes County on next court-day. The Governor demands a brigade from Virginia to quell them. Lieut.-Col. Lay has been sent thither, by the new good-natured chief of the Bureau of Conscription, to cure the evil. We shall see what good this mission will effect. Col. Preston writes to the Secretary to-day that disorders among the conscripts and deserters are now occurring in South Carolina for the first time—and proposes shortly to visit them himself. The best thing that can be done is to abolish the Bureau of Conscription, and have the law enforced by the military commanders in the field.

I saw to-day a letter to the Secretary of War, written by Mr. Benjamin, Secretary of State, on the 18th inst., referring to a Mr. Jno. Robertson, an artist, whom the Secretary of War promised a free passage in a government steamer to Europe. Mr. B. says the promise was made in the President's room, and he asks if Mr. Seddon could not spare an hour in his office, for Mr. R. to take his portrait. He says Mr. R. has the heads of the President, all the heads of departments (except Mr. Seddon, I suppose), and the principal generals. It does not appear what was done by Mr. Seddon, but I presume everything asked for by Mr. Benjamin was granted. But this matter has not exalted the President and his "heads of departments" in my estimation. If it be not "fiddling while Rome is burning," it is certainly *egotizing* while the Confederacy is crumbling. On that day Sumter was falling to pieces, and some 40 locomotives and hundreds of cars were burning in Mississippi, and everywhere our territory passing into the hands of the invader!

Mr. Robertson, I believe, is a stranger and an Englishman, and a *free passage* in a government ship is equivalent to some $2000, Confederate States currency. Almost every day passages are denied to refugees, natives of the South, who have lost fortunes in the cause, and who were desirous to place their children and non-combatants in a place of security, while they fight for liberty and independence. The privileged passage is refused them, even when they are able and willing to pay for the passage, and this refusal is recommended by Col. Gorgas, a Northern man. They do not propose to immortalize "the President, the heads of departments, and the principal generals." But Mr. Benjamin has nothing else to do. Washington would accept no meed of praise until his great work was accomplished.

CHAPTER XXX.

Situation at Wilmington.—Situation at Charleston.—Lincoln thinks there is hope of our submission.—Market prices.—Ammunition turned over to the enemy at Vicksburg.—Attack on Sumter.—Stringent conscription order.—Disaffection in North Carolina.—Victory announced by Gen. Bragg.—Peril of Gen. Rosecrans.—Surrender of Cumberland Gap.—Rosecrans fortifying Chattanooga.—Mr Seward on flag-of-truce boat.—Burnside evacuating East Tennessee.—The trans-Mississippi army.—Meade sending troops to Rosecrans.—Pemberton in Richmond.—A suggestion concerning perishable tithes.

SEPTEMBER 1ST.—Another letter from Gen. Whiting, urging the government by every consideration, and with all the ingenuity and eloquence of language at his command, to save Wilmington by sending reinforcements thither, else it must be inevitably lost. He says it will not do to rely upon what now seems the merest stupidity of the enemy, for they already have sufficient forces and means at their command and within reach to capture the fort and city. He has but one regiment for its defense!

I saw to-day a telegraphic correspondence between the Secretary of War and Gen. Buckner in regard to the invasion of Kentucky, the general agreeing to it, being sure that with 10,000 men he could compel Rosecrans to fall back, etc. But I suppose the fall of Vicksburg, and the retreat from Pennsylvania, caused its abandonment.

Hon. Wm. Capeton, C. S. Senate, writes the Secretary on the subject of compelling those who have hired substitutes now to serve themselves, and he advocates it. He says the idea is expanding that the rich, for whose benefit the war is waged, have procured substitutes to fight for them, while the poor, who have no slaves to lose, have not been able to procure substitutes. All will be required to fight, else all will be engulfed in one common destruction. He will endeavor to get an expression of opinion from the Legislature, about to assemble, and after that he will advocate the measure in Congress, intimating that Congress should be convened at an early day.

SEPTEMBER 2D.—We have no news of any importance from any of the armies. Gen. Bragg, however, telegraphs, August 31st, that he is concentrating his forces to receive the enemy, reported to be on the eve of assailing his position. He says he has sent our paroled men to Atlanta (those taken at Vicksburg), and asks that arms be sent them by the *eastern road*. Col. Gorgas, Chief of Ordnance, says this is the first intimation he has had as to the disposition of the paroled prisoners. Does he understand that they are to fight before being exchanged?

Brig.-Gen. G. J. Rains writes from Charleston that the grenades reported by the enemy to have been so destructive in their repulse at Battery Wagner, were his subterra shells, there being no hand-grenades used.

The other night Beauregard sent a steamer out with a torpedo to destroy the *Ironsides*, the most formidable of the enemy's iron-clads. It ran within forty yards of the Ironsides, which, however, was saved by swinging round. The torpedo steamer's engine was so imperfect that it could not be worked when stopped, for several minutes, to readjust the arrangements for striking the enemy in his altered position. When hailed, "What steamer is that?" the reply was, "The Live Yankee," and our adventurers got off and back to the city without injury—and without inflicting any.

There has been much shelling the last few days, but Sumter and Battery Wagner are still under the Confederate flag. How long this will continue no one knows. But it is hoped the great Blakely guns are there by this time, and that Gen. Rains's torpedoes may avail something for the salvation of the city.

SEPTEMBER 3D.—Night before last the heavens were illuminated, it is said, by the terrific bombardment of the batteries and forts in the vicinity of Charleston, and earth and sea trembled with the mighty vibrations. Yet no material injury was done our works, and there were not more than a dozen casualties. On the side of the enemy there is no means of ascertaining the effect.

N. S. Walker, Confederate States agent, Bermuda, writes that the steamer R. E. Lee was chased, on her last trip out, twelve hours, and was compelled to throw 150 bales government cotton overboard. He says the British crown officers have decided that

British bottoms, with British owners of cargo, running out of blockaded ports, are liable to seizure anywhere on the high seas.

Some of the papers say Knoxville is in the hands of the enemy, and others deny it.

Hon. F. S. Lyon writes from Demopolis, Ala., that the Vicksburg army have not reported upon the expiration of the thirty days' leave, in large numbers, and that the men never can be reorganized to serve again under Pemberton.

Gen. Jos. E. Johnston writes from Morton, Miss., that he is disposing his force to oppose any raids of the enemy, and that he shall keep the Vicksburg troops (when exchanged) in Eastern Mississippi.

Gov. Jos. E. Brown telegraphs that the men (militia) in Georgia cannot be *compelled* to leave the State; but if the government will send them 5000 arms, he thinks he can *persuade* them to march out of it, provided he may name a commander. The President indorses on this: "If they are militia, I have no power to appoint; if C. S. troops, I have no power to delegate the authority to appoint."

Gen. Lee is still here (I thought he had departed), no doubt arranging the programme of the fall campaign, if, indeed, there be one. He rode out with the President yesterday evening, but neither were greeted with cheers. I suppose Gen. Lee has lost some popularity among idle street walkers by his retreat from Pennsylvania. The President seeks seclusion. A gentleman who breakfasted with him this morning, tells me the President complained of fatigue from his long ride with Gen. Lee.

SEPTEMBER 4TH.—There is a rumor that Gen. Lee (who is still here) is to take the most of his army out of Virginia, to recapture the Southern territory lost by Loring, Pemberton, and Bragg. I doubt this; for it might involve the loss of Richmond, and indeed of the whole State of Virginia. It would be a sad blow to the extortionate farmers, it is true; but we cannot afford to lose the whole country, and sacrifice the cause, to punish the speculators. It may be, however, that this is a *ruse*, and if so, Lee is preparing for another northern campaign.

The project of the Hon. Mr. Boteler to place Rains's subterra shells under the Orange and Alexandria Railroad used by the enemy, was referred by the Secretary to Col. J. Gorgas, the

Northern Chief of Ordnance, who says he can furnish the shells, but advises *against the use of them,* as they will "only irritate the enemy, and not intimidate them." For this presumptuous advice, which was entirely gratuitous, I do not learn that the Secretary has rebuked him.

Letters from Western North Carolina show that the defection is spreading. In Wilkes County, Gideon Smoot is the commander of the insurgents, and has raised the United States flag. I have not learned, yet, whether Lieut.-Col. Lay, of the Bureau of Conscription, reached that far; and I was amazed when the good nature of Col. Preston yielded to his solicitations to go thither. What possible good could he, a Virginian, and formerly an aid of Gen. Scott, effect in that quarter?

SEPTEMBER 5TH.—It is believed that Lee, with a large portion of his army, will proceed immediately to Tennessee against Rosecrans; and it is ascertained that Meade is sending reinforcements thither. But I fear for Virginia when Lee is away! Meade must have a large army left behind, else he would not send reinforcements to Rosecrans. This move will excite the fear of the extortionate farmers, at all events, and make them willing to sell their surplus produce. But if Richmond should fall, and the State be overrun, it is possible it would secede from the Confederacy, which would be a virtual dissolution of it. She would then form alliances with other Southern States on a new basis, and create a new provisional government, and postpone the formation of a permanent one until independence be achieved. However, I am incredulous about the abandonment of Virginia.

Meantime, I hope France will intervene, and that Mexico will recognize the independence of the Southern Government.

Another letter from Hon. Mr. Miles, of Charleston, in reply, as it seems, to a pretty severe rebuke by the Secretary of War, for asking Jenkins's brigade of South Carolinians for the defense of South Carolina, was received to-day. Knowing the honorable gentleman's intimate relations with Beauregard, the Secretary criticises the conduct of the general in permitting the enemy to establish himself on the lower end of Morris Island—allowing a grove to remain, concealing the erection of batteries, etc. etc. Mr. Miles in reply asserts the fact that Gen. B. did the utmost that could be accomplished with the force and means left at his disposal by the government; and that the grove would have been felled, if he had been authorized to impress labor, etc. It is sad to read these criminations and recriminations at such a time as this; but every Secretary of War is apt to come in conflict with Beauregard.

Gen. Whiting asks, as second in command, Brig.-Gen. Herbert, and reiterates his demand for troops, else Wilmington will be lost. This letter came open—having been broken on the way. If a spy did it, which is probable, the army will soon learn what an easy conquest awaits them.

Mr. C. C. Thayer, clerk in the Treasury Department, leaves on the 9th, with $15,000,000 for the trans-Mississippi Department; another clerk has already gone with $10,000,000.

After all, I am inclined to think our papers have been lying about the barbarous conduct of the enemy. A letter was received to-day from C. N. Hubbard, a respectable farmer of James City County, stating that when Gen. Keyes came up the Peninsula about the 1st of July, he sent guards for the protection of the property of the people living along the line of march; and they remained, faithfully performing that duty, until the army retired. Mr. H. complains that these guards were made prisoners by our troops, and, if exchanges be demanded for them, he fears the next time the hostile army approaches Richmond, their request for a guard will be refused. What answer the Secretary will make to this, I have no means of conjecturing; but Mr. Hubbard recommends him to come to some understanding with the enemy for the mutual protection of the persons and property of non-combating civilians; and he desires an answer directed to the care of Col. Shingler, who, indeed, captured the guard. The Secretary consented to the exchange.

SEPTEMBER 6TH.—Northern papers received yesterday evening contain a letter from Mr. Lincoln to the Illinois Convention of Republicans, in which I am told (I have not seen it yet) he says if the Southern people will first lay down their arms, he will then listen to what they may have to say. Evidently he has been reading of the submission of Jack Cade's followers, who were required to signify their submission with ropes about their necks.

This morning I saw dispatches from Atlanta, Ga., stating that in one of the northern counties the deserters and tories had defeated the Home Guard which attempted to arrest them. In Tennessee, North Carolina, Mississippi, and Georgia, we have accounts of much and growing defection, and the embodying of large numbers of deserters. Indeed, all our armies seem to be melting away by desertion faster than they are enlarged by conscription. They will return when there is fighting to do!

A letter from Col. Lay, dated North Carolina, to the Chief of the Bureau of Conscription, recommends the promotion of a lieutenant to a captaincy. The colonel is *great* in operations of this nature; and Col. Preston is sufficiently good natured to recommend the recommendation to the Secretary of War, who, good easy man, will not inquire into his age, etc.

Gold is worth from 1000 to 1500 per cent. premium; and yet one who has gold can buy supplies of anything, by first converting it into Confederate notes at low prices. For instance, coal at $30 is really bought for $3 per load. A fine horse at $1000 for $100. Bacon, at $2 per pound is only 20 cents; boots at $100 is only $10, and so on.

Thank Heaven! the little furniture, etc. we now have is our own —costing less to buy it than the rent we paid for that belonging to others up to the beginning of the month. A history of the household goods we possess would, no doubt, if it could be written, be interesting to haberdashers. I think we have articles belonging in their time to twenty families.

The following list of prices is cut from yesterday's paper:

"*Produce, provisions, etc.*—Apples, $30 to $35 per barrel; bacon is firm at $2 to $2.10 for hoground. Butter is advancing; we quote at $2.50 to $3 by the package. Cheese has advanced, and now sells at $1 50 to $2 per pound; corn, $8 to $9 per bushel; corn-meal, $9 per bushel, in better supply. Flour, at the Gallego Mills, new superfine, uninspected, is sold at $25 per barrel; at commission houses and in second hands, the price of new superfine is from $35 to $40; onions, $40 to $50 per barrel; Irish potatoes, $5 to $6 per bushel, according to quality; oats firm at $6 per bushel. Wheat—the supply coming in is quite limited. The millers refuse to compete with the government, and are consequently paying $5 per bushel. It is intimated, however, that outside parties are buying on speculation at $6 to $6.50, taking the risk of impressment. Lard, $1.70 to $1.75 per pound; eggs, $1.25

to $1.50 per dozen; seeds, timothy, $8 to $10; clover, $40 to $45 per bushel.

"*Groceries.*—Sugars: the market is active; we hear of sales of prime brown at $2 to $2.15; coffee, $4.25 to $4.75 per pound; molasses, $15 per gallon; rice, 25 cents per pound; salt, 45 cents per pound; soap, 50 cents to 80 cents, as to quality; candles, $2.75 to $3 per pound.

"*Liquors.*—We quote corn whisky at $20 to $25 per gallon; rye whisky, $38 to $40, according to quality; apple brandy, $25 to $30; rum, $28 per gallon."

SEPTEMBER 7TH —Batteries Wagner and Gregg and Fort Sumter have been evacuated! But this is not *yet* the capture of Charleston. Gen. Beauregard telegraphed yesterday that he was preparing (after thirty-six hours' incessant bombardment) to evacuate Morris Island; which was done, I suppose, last night. He feared the loss of the garrisons, if he delayed longer; and he said Sumter was silenced. Well, it is understood the great Blakely is in position on Charleston wharf. If the enemy have no knowledge of its presence, perhaps we shall soon have reports from it.

Gen. Lee, it is said, takes *two corps d'armée* to Tennessee, leaving *one* in Virginia. But this can be swelled to 50,000 men by the militia, conscripts, etc., which ought to enable us to stand a protracted *siege*, provided we can get subsistence. Fortune is against us now.

Lieut.-Col. Lay reports great defection in North Carolina, and even says half of *Raleigh* is against "the Davis Government."

The Secretary of War has called upon the Governor *for all the available slave labor in the State, to work on the defenses, etc.*

The United States flag of truce boat came up to City Point last night, *bringing no prisoners*, and nothing else except some dispatches, the nature of which has not yet transpired.

SEPTEMBER 8TH.—We have nothing further from Charleston, to-day, except that the enemy is not yet in possession of Sumter.

Mr. Seddon, Secretary of War, said to Mr. Lyons, M. C., yesterday, that he had heard nothing of Gen. Lee's orders to march a portion of his army to Tennessee. That may be very true; but, nevertheless, 18,000 of Lee's troops (a corps) is already marching thitherward.

A report on the condition of the military prisons, sent in to-day, shows that there is no typhoid fever, or many cases of other diseases, among the prisoners of war. Everything is kept in cleanliness about them, and they have abundance of food, wholesome and palatable. The prisoners themselves admit these facts, and denounce their own government for the treatment alleged to be inflicted on our men confined at Fort Delaware and other places.

An extra session of the legislature is now sitting. The Governor's message is defiant, as no terms are offered; but he denounces as unjust the apportionment of slaves, in several of the counties, to be impressed to work on the defenses, etc.

SEPTEMBER 9TH —Troops were arriving all night and to-day (Hood's division), and are proceeding Southward, per railroad, it is said for Tennessee, via Georgia Road. It may be deemed impracticable to send troops by the western route, as the enemy possesses the Knoxville Road. The weather is excessively dry and dusty again.

Gen. Jos. E. Johnston, Morton, Miss., writes that such is the facility of giving information to the enemy, that it is impossible to keep up a ferry at any point on the Mississippi; but he will be able to keep up communications, by trusty messengers with small parcels, with Lieut.-Gen. E. Kirby Smith's trans-Mississippi Department. He says if he had another cavalry brigade, he could make the navigation too dangerous for merchant steamers between Grand Gulf and Natchez.

Two letters were received to-day from privates in North Carolina regiments, demanding to be transferred to artillery companies in the forts of North Carolina, or else they would *serve no more*. This is very reckless!

Ordnance officer J. Brice transmitted to the Secretary to-day, through the Ordnance Bureau, an OFFICIAL account of the ammunition, etc. at Vicksburg during the siege and at the evacuation. He says all the ordnance stores at Jackson were hastily removed to Vicksburg, and of which he was unable, in the confusion, to get an accurate account, although he accompanied it. He detained and held 9000 arms destined for the trans-Mississippi Department, and issued 120 rounds to each man in the army, before the battle of Baker's Creek. Much *ammunition* was destroyed on the battlefield, by order of Gen. Pemberton, to keep it, as he alleged, from falling into the hands of the enemy. During the siege, he got

250,000 percussion caps from Gen. Johnston's scouts, and 150,000 *from the enemy's pickets,* for a *consideration.* There was abundance of powder. The ammunition and small arms turned over to the enemy, on the surrender, consisted as follows: 36,000 cartridges for Belgian rifles; 3600 Brunswick cartridges; 75,000 rounds British rifled muskets; 9000 shot-gun cartridges; 1300 Maynard cartridges; 5000 Hall's carbine cartridges; 1200 holster pistol cartridges; 35,000 percussion caps; 19,000 pounds of cannon powder.

All this was in the ordnance depots, and exclusive of that in the hands of the troops and in the ordnance wagons, doubtless a large amount. He says 8000 defective arms were destroyed by fires during the bombardment. The troops delivered to the enemy, on marching out, 27,000 arms.

The Governor demanded the State magazine to-day of the War Department, in whose custody it has been for a long time. What does this mean? The Governor says the State has urgent use for it.

Gen. Cooper visited the President *twice* to-day, the Secretary not *once*. The *Enquirer*, yesterday, attacked and ridiculed the Secretary of War on his passport system in Richmond.

The Northern papers contain the following letter from President Lincoln to Gen. Grant:

"Executive Mansion,
"Washington, July 13th, 1863.
"Major-General Grant.

"My dear General:—I do not remember that you and I ever met personally. I write this now as a grateful acknowledgment for the almost inestimable service you have done the country. I wish to say a word further. When you first reached the vicinity of Vicksburg I thought you should do what you finally did—march the troops across the neck, run the batteries with the transports, and thus go below; and I never had any faith, except a general hope that you knew better than I, that the Yazoo Pass expedition and the like could succeed. When you got below and took Port Gibson, Grand Gulf, and vicinity, I thought you should go down the river and join Gen. Banks; and when you turned northward, east of the Big Black, I feared it was a mistake. I now wish to make the personal acknowledgment that you were right and I was wrong. A. Lincoln."

If Pemberton had acted differently, if the movement northward had been followed by disaster, then what would Mr. Lincoln have written to Grant? Success is the only standard of merit in a general.

SEPTEMBER 10TH.—A Mr. J. C. Jones has addressed a letter to the President asking permission to run the blockade to confer with Mr. Bates, of President Lincoln's cabinet, on terms of peace, with, I believe, authority to assure him that none of the Northwestern States, or any other free States, will be admitted into the Confederacy. Mr. J. says he has been on intimate terms with Mr. B., and has conceived the idea that the United States would cease the war, and acknowledge the independence of the South, if it were not for the apprehension of the Northwestern States seceding from the Union. If his request be not granted, he intends to enter the army immediately. He is a refugee from Missouri. He assures the President he is his friend, and that a "concentration of power" in his hands is essential, etc. The President refers this paper, with a gracious indorsement, to the Secretary of War, recommending him either to see Mr. Jones, or else to institute inquiries, etc.

S. Wyatt, Augusta, Ga., writes in favor of appeals to the patriotism of the people to counteract what Mr. Toombs has done. What has he done? But he advises the President, to whom he professes to be very friendly, to order a discontinuance of seizures, etc.

A. Cohen (Jew name), purser of the blockade-running steamer "Arabia" at Wilmington, has submitted a notable scheme to Gen. Winder, who submits it to the Secretary of War, establishing a police agency at *Nassau*. Gen. W. to send some of his detectives thither to examine persons coming into the Confederate States, and if found "all right," to give them passports. It was only yesterday that a letter was received from Gen. Whiting, asking authority to send out a secret agent on the "Arabia," to see what disposition would be made of her cargo, having strong suspicions of the loyalty of the owners and officers of that vessel.

Gov. Z. B. Vance complains indignantly of Marylanders and Virginians appointed to office in that State, to the exclusion of natives; he says they have not yet been recalled, as he had a right to expect, after his recent interview with the President. He says he is disgusted with such treatment, both of his State and of himself. Alas! what is behind?

Night before last some thirty of the enemy's barges, filled with men, attempted to take the ruins of Sumter by assault. This had been anticipated by Beauregard, and every preparation had been made accordingly. So the batteries at Forts Moultrie, Bee, etc. opened terrifically with shell and grape; the amount of execution by them is not ascertained: but a number of the barges reached the debris of Sumter, where a battalion of infantry awaited them, and where 115 of the Yankees, including more than a dozen officers, begged for quarters and were taken prisoners. No doubt the casualties on the side of the assailants must have been many, while the garrison sustained no loss. This is substantially the purport of a dispatch from Beauregard to Gen. Cooper, which, however, was published very awkwardly—without any of the niceties of punctuation a fastidious general would have desired. Nevertheless, Beauregard's name is on every tongue.

The clerks in the departments were startled to-day by having read to them an order from Brig.-Gen. Custis Lee (son of Gen. R. E. Lee), an order to the captains of companies to imprison or otherwise punish all who failed to be present at the drills. These young gentlemen, not being removable, according to the Constitution, and exempted from conscription by an act of Congress, volunteered some months ago for "local defense and special service," never supposing that regular drilling would be obligatory except when called into actual service by the direction of the President, in the terms of an act of Congress, which provided that such organizations were not to receive pay for military service, unless summoned to the field by the President in an emergency. They receive no pay now—but yet the impression prevails that this order has the approbation of the President, as Gen. G. W. Custis Lee is one of his special aids, with the rank and pay of a colonel of cavalry. As an aid of the President, he signs himself colonel; as commander of the city brigade, he signs himself brigadier-general, and has been so commissioned by the President. How it can be compatible to hold both positions and commissions, I do not understand—but perhaps the President does, as he is well versed in the rules and regulations of the service. Some of the clerks, it is said, regard the threat as unauthorized by law, and will resist what they deem a usurpation, at the hazard of suffering its penalties. I know not what the result will be, but I fear "no good will come of it." They are all willing to fight, when the enemy comes (a probable thing); but they dislike being *forced* out to drill, under threats of "punishment." This measure will not add to the popularity of Col. (or Gen.) Lee.

SEPTEMBER 11TH.—A dispatch from Raleigh informs us of a mob yesterday in that city. Some soldiers broke into and partially destroyed the office of the *Standard*, alleged to be a disloyal paper; after that, and when the soldiers had been dispersed by a speech from Governor Vance, the citizens broke into and partially destroyed the *Journal*, an ultra-secession paper. These were likewise dispersed by a speech from the Governor.

Gen. Whiting writes that the enemy is making demonstrations against Lockwood's Folly, 23 miles from Wilmington. He says if 3000 were to pass it, the forts and harbor would be lost, as he has but one regiment—and it is employed on picket service. He says in ten nights the enemy can come from Charleston—and that Wilmington was never so destitute of troops since the beginning of the war, and yet it was never in such great peril. It is the only port remaining—and to lose it after such repeated warning would be the grossest culpability.

The officers of the signal corps report that Gen. Meade has been ordered to advance, for it is already known in Washington that a large number of troops are marching out of Virginia. Lee, however, it is now believed, will not go to Tennessee. They also report that a Federal army of 6400—perhaps they mean 64,000—is to march from Arkansas to the Rio Grande, Texas. If they do, they will be lost.

The engineer corps are to fortify Lynchburg immediately.

The clerks of the Post-office Department have petitioned the Secretary of War to allow them (such as have families) commissary stores at government prices, else they will soon be almost in a state of starvation. Their salaries are utterly inadequate for their support. The clerks in all the departments are in precisely the same predicament. The Postmaster-General approves this measure of relief—as relief must come before Congress meets—and he fears the loss of his subordinates.

It is said by western men that the enemy is organizing a force of 25,000 mounted men at Memphis, destined to penetrate Georgia and South Carolina, as far as Charleston! If this be so—and it may be so—they will probably fall in with Longstreet's corps of 20,000 now passing through this city.

SEPTEMBER 12TH.—Lieut.-Col. Lay, "Inspector," reports from North Carolina that some twenty counties in that State are "disaffected;" that the deserters and "recusants" are organized and brigaded; armed, and have raised the flag of the United States. This is bad enough to cause the President some loss of sleep, if any one would show it to him.

Gen. Wise, it is said, is ordered away from the defense of Richmond with his brigade. I saw him to-day (looking remarkably well), and he said he did not know where he was going—waiting orders, I suppose.

C. J. McRae, agent of the loan in Europe, writes July 24th, 1863, that the bad news of Lee's failure in Pennsylvania and retreat across the Potomac, caused the loan to recede $3\frac{1}{2}$ per cent., and unless better news soon reaches him, he can do nothing whatever with Confederate credits. He says Capt. Bullock has contracted for the building of two "iron-clads" in France, and that disbursements on account of the navy, hereafter, will be mostly in France. I fear the reports about a whole fleet of Confederate gun-boats having been built or bought in England are not well founded. Major Ferguson has also (several have done so before him) made charges against Major Huse, the agent of Col. Gorgas, Chief of Ordnance. Mr. McRae thinks the charges cannot be substantiated.

We have tidings of the bursting of the Blakely gun at Charleston. I fear this involves the fall of Charleston. Still Beauregard is there.

Gen. Pickett's division (decimated at Gettysburg) is to remain in this vicinity—and Jenkins's and Wise's brigades will leave. The hour now seems a dark one. But we must conquer or die.

It is said a deserter has already gone over from our lines and given information to the enemy of the large number of troops detached from the Army of Virginia. No doubt Gen. Meade will take advantage of their absence, and advance on Richmond again. Yet I am told the very *name* of Richmond is a terror to the foe.

SEPTEMBER 13TH.—A letter from Gen. J. E. Johnston, Atlanta—whither he had repaired to attend a Court of Inquiry relating to

Pemberton's operations, but which has been postponed under the present peril—repels indignantly the charge which seems to have been made in a letter from the Secretary of War, that in executing the law of conscription in his command, he had acted hastily, without sufficient attention to the rights of exemption under the provisions of the act. He says the law was a dead letter when he charged Gen. Pillow with its execution; that Gen. Pillow has now just got his preparations made for its enforcement; and, of course, no appeals have as yet come before him. He hopes that the Secretary will re-examine the grounds of his charge, etc. He is amazed, evidently, with the subject, and no doubt the "Bureau" here will strain every nerve to monopolize the business—providing as usual for its favorites, and having appointed to snug places a new batch of A. A. G.'s—men who ought to be conscribed themselves.

Col Preston, under the manipulations of Lieut.-Col. Lay, is getting on swimmingly, and to-day makes a requisition for arms and equipments of 2500 cavalry to *force* out conscripts, arrest deserters, etc. I think they had better popularize the army, and strive to reinspire the enthusiasm that characterized it at the beginning; and the only way to do this is to restore to its ranks the wealthy and educated class, which has abandoned the field for easier employments. I doubt the policy of shooting deserters in this war—better shoot the traitors in high positions. The indigent men of the South will fight, shoulder to shoulder with the wealthy, for Southern independence; but when the attempt is made to debase them to a servile condition, they will hesitate.

Gen. Pickett's division, just marching through the city, wears a different aspect from that exhibited last winter. Then it had 12,000 men—now 6000; and they are dirty, tattered and torn.

The great Blakely gun has failed.

We have reports of the evacuation of Cumberland Gap. This was to be looked for, when the Virginia and Tennessee Railroad was suffered to fall into the enemy's hands. When will this year's calamities end?

Gen. Lee is at Orange Court House, and probably will not leave Virginia. He will still have an army of 50,000 men to oppose Meade; and Richmond may possibly be held another winter.

Congress will not be called, I think; and the Legislature, now in session, I am told, will accomplish no good. It will not be likely to interfere with the supreme power which resolves to "rule or ruin,"—at least this seems to be the case in the eyes of men who merely watch the current of events.

SEPTEMBER 14TH.—The report from Lt.-Col. Lay of the condition of affairs in North Carolina, received some days ago, was indorsed by Judge Campbell, Assistant Secretary of War, and father-in-law of Col. Lay, that the destruction of the government was imminently menaced, does not seem to have alarmed the President; on the contrary, he sends the paper back to the Secretary, Mr. Seddon, suggesting that he had better correspond with Gov. Vance on the subject, and if military force should be required, he might call in the aid of Brig.-Gen. Hoke, thus ending hopes of a conscription officer here obtaining a command.

And so with rumors from Eastern Tennessee; the President takes matters coolly, saying the "locals," meaning home guards, or companies for local defense, should be on the alert against raiders. If large bodies of the enemy come in, Jenkins's brigade, and one from Pickett's division, might be temporarily detached to punish them.

Bragg is falling back toward Atlanta, and Burnside says, officially, that he has taken Cumberland Gap, 1200 prisoners, with 14 guns, without a fight. All of Tennessee is now held by the enemy.

There has been another fight (cavalry) at Brandy Station, and our men, for want of numbers, "fell back." When will these things cease?

SEPTEMBER 13TH.—Gov. Vance writes that he has reliable information that the 30,000 troops in New York, ostensibly to enforce the draft, are intended for a descent on North Corolina, and Gen. Whiting has said repeatedly that 3000 could take Wilmington. The Governor says if North Carolina be occupied by the enemy, Virginia and the whole Confederacy will be lost, for all communication now, by rail, is through that State.

Gen. Sam. Jones writes from Abingdon, Va., that from his information he does not doubt Cumberland Gap and its garrison capitulated on the 9th inst. He calls lustily for reinforcements, and fears the loss of everything, including the salt works, if he be not reinforced. Well, he *will* be reinforced!

Gov. (just elected) R. L. Caruthers (of Tennessee) begs that 20,000 men from Lee's army be sent out on Rosecrans's left flank to save Tennessee, which alone can save the Confederacy. Well, they *have* been sent!

There must be a "fight or a foot-race" soon in Northern Georgia, and also in Virginia, on the Rappahannock. May God defend the right! If we deserve independence, I think we shall achieve it. If God be not for us, we must submit to His will.

Major Huse is buying and shipping 2000 tons saltpetre, besides millions of dollars worth of arms and stores. If we can keep Wilmington, we can send out cotton and bring in supplies without limit.

SEPTEMBER 16TH.—The enemy advanced yesterday, and, our forces being unequal in numbers, captured Culpepper C. H. Our cavalry fell back several miles, and a battle is looked for immediately, near Orange C. H., where Gen. Lee awaits the foe in an advantageous position.

From the Southwest also a battle is momentarily looked for. If the enemy be beaten in these battles, they will suffer more by defeat than we would.

Gov. Vance has written a pointed letter to the President in regard to the mob violence in Raleigh. He says, when the office of the *Standard* was sacked, the evil was partially counterbalanced by the sacking of the *Journal*,—the first, moderate Union, the last, ultra-secessionist. He demands the punishment of the officers present and consenting to the assault on the *Standard* office, part of a Georgia brigade, and avers that another such outrage will bring back the North Carolina troops from the army for the defense of their State.

From Morton, Miss., Gen. Hardee says, after sending reinforcements to Bragg, only three brigades of infantry remain in his department. Upon this the President made the following indorsement and sent it to the Secretary of War:

"The danger to Atlanta has probably passed."

While the army of Gen. Taylor threatens the southwestern part of Louisiana, troops will not probably leave New Orleans. The movement to White River is more serious at this time than the preparations against Mobile.

"Efforts should be made to prevent the navigation of the Mississippi by commercial steamers, and especially to sink transports."

The letter of Gov. Vance in relation to the 30,000 men destined for North Carolina being referred to the President, he sent it back indorsed as follows:

"Gov. V.'s vigilance will discover the fact if this supposition be true, and in the mean time it serves to increase the demand for active exertions, as well to fill up the ranks of the army as to organize 'local defense' troops."

The letter of Lt.-Col. Lay, Inspector of Conscripts, etc., was likewise referred to the President, who suggests that a general officer be located with a brigade near where the States of North Carolina, South Carolina, etc. meet.

And the President indorses on Gen. Whiting's earnest calls for aid at Wilmington, that Gen. Martin be sent him, with the "locals," as he calls them, and a brigade from Pickett's division, *when filled up.* But suppose that should be too late? He says Ransom's troops should also be in position, for it is important to hold Wilmington.

Calico is selling now for $10 per yard; and a small, dirty, dingy, dilapidated house, not near as large as the one I occupy, rents for $800. This one would bring $1200 now; I pay $500, which must be considered low. Where are we drifting? I know not; unless we have a crop of victories immediately.

SEPTEMBER 17TH.—Lee and Meade have their armies daily drawn up in battle array, and an engagement may be expected.

It is said the enemy is evacuating East Tennessee; concentrating, I suspect, for battle with Bragg.

It is now said that Brigadier and Col. Lee, A. D. C. to the President, etc. etc., is going to call out the civil officers of the government who volunteered to fight in defense of the city, and encamp them in the country. This will make trouble.

A Mr. Mendenhall, New Garden, N. C., Quaker, complains of the treatment two of his young Friends are receiving at Kinston from the troops. They won't fight, because they believe it wrong, and they won't pay the tax (war) of $500, because they cannot do it conscientiously. And Gov. Vance says the treatment referred to will not be tolerated.

SEPTEMBER 18TH.—Nothing new from the Rappahannock, but

a battle is looked for soon. Rosecrans, who had advanced into Georgia, has fallen back on Chattanooga, which he is fortifying. If he be not driven from thence, we shall lose our mines, and the best country for commissary supplies. But Bragg had from 60,000 to 70,000 men on the 5th inst., when he had not fallen back far from Chattanooga; since then he has received more reinforcements from Mississippi, and Longstreet's corps, arrived by this time, will swell his army to 90,000 men, perhaps. Johnston will probably take command, for Bragg is becoming unpopular. But Bragg will fight!

The equinoctial storm has commenced, and the monitors are not in view of Charleston, having sought quiet waters.

The *Enquirer* has again assailed Mr. Benjamin, particularly on account of the retention of Mr. Spence, financial agent in England (appointed by Mr. Memminger), an anti-slavery author, whose books advocate Southern independence. To-day a letter was sent to the Secretary of War, from Mr. Benjamin, stating the fact that the President had changed the whole financial programme for Europe. Frazer, Trenholm, & Co., Liverpool, are to be the custodians of the treasure in England, and Mr. McRae, in France, etc., and they would keep all the accounts of disbursements by the agents of departments, thus superseding Mr. Spence. I think this arrangement will somewhat affect the operations of Major Huse (who is a little censured in the letter, purporting to be dictated by the President, but really written by the President) and Col. Gorgas.

If Wilmington continues in our possession, the transactions in Europe will be large, and the government will derive more of its supplies from thence.

SEPTEMBER 19TH.—The reports from Western North Carolina indicate that much bad feeling prevails there still; and it is really something more than a military trick to obtain a command. But I think the government had better keep out of the field its assistant adjutant-generals, and especially those in the Bureau of Conscription, unless they are put in subordinate positions. Some of them have sought their present positions to keep aloof from the fatigues and dangers of the field; and they have contributed no little to the disaffection in North Carolina. Gen. Whiting suggests that one of Gen. Pickett's brigades be sent to Weldon; and then, with Ransom's brigade, he will soon put down the deserters and tories. The Governor approves this plan, and I hope it will be adopted.

The Northern papers say President Lincoln, by proclamation, has suspended the writ of *habeas corpus* throughout the United States. This is good news for the South; for the people there will strike back through the secret ballot-box.

They also say an expedition is about to sail up the Rio Grande, where it will come in collision with the French, now occupying Matamoras.

And it appears that Lord John Russell will *not* prevent the sailing of our monitor-rams from British ports without evidence of an intention to use them against the United States. He will do nothing on suspicion; but must have affidavits, etc.

A young lady, Miss Heiskell, applied yesterday, through the Hon. A. H. H. Stuart, for a passport to Philadelphia, to be married to a young merchant of that city. Her father was a merchant of that city, though a native of Virginia. I believe it was granted.

The country is indignant at the surrender of Cumberland Gap by Brig.-Gen. Frazier, without firing a gun, when his force was nearly as strong as Burnside's. It was too bad! There must be some examples of generals as well as of deserting poor men, whose families, during their absence, are preyed upon by the extortioners, who contrive to purchase exemption from military service. The country did not know there was such a general until his name became famous by this ignominious surrender. Where did Gen. Cooper find him?

SEPTEMBER 20TH.—We have nothing to-day from any of the seats of war; but I saw several hundred head of cattle driven through the city this morning, marked "C. S.," which I learned had come from Essex and King and Queen Counties, which may indicate either a raid from the Lower Rappahannock, or another advance on Richmond.

There was a meeting called for mechanics, etc. last night, to consider the grievance of the times. I have not learned what was done, or rather said; but I hear citizens on the street to-day talking about subverting the government. I believe they have no *plan;* and as yet it amounts to nothing.

SEPTEMBER 21ST.—The President was called out of church yesterday, and was for three hours closeted with the Secretary of War and Gen. Cooper. It appears that the enemy were occupying Bristol, on the line between Virginia and Tennessee, with seven regiments, and Carse's brigade was ordered (by telegraph) to reinforce Gen. S. Jones. But to-day a dispatch from Gen. Jones states that the enemy had been driven back at Zollicoffer, which is beyond Bristol. This dispatch was dated yesterday. It is unintelligible.

But to-day we have a dispatch from Gen. Bragg, announcing a great battle on the 19th and 20th insts. He says, "after two days' engagement, we have driven the enemy, after a desperate resistance, from several positions; we hold the field, but the enemy still confronts us. The losses on both sides are heavy, and especially so among our officers. We have taken more than twenty guns, and 2500 prisoners." We await the sequel—with fear and trembling, after the sad experience of Western victories. The Secretary of War thinks Longstreet's corps had not yet reached Bragg; then why should he have commenced the attack before the reinforcements arrived? We must await further dispatches. If Bragg beats Rosecrans utterly, the consequences will be momentous. If beaten by him, he sinks to rise no more. Both generals are aware of the consequences of failure, and no doubt it is a sanguinary field. Whether it is in Georgia or over the line in Tennessee is not yet ascertained.

SEPTEMBER 22D.—Another dispatch from Bragg, received at a late hour last night, says the *victory* is *complete*. This announcement has lifted a heavy load from the spirits of our people; and as successive dispatches come from Gov. Harris and others on the battle-field to-day, there is a great change in the recent elongated faces of many we meet in the streets. So far we learn that the enemy has been beaten back and pursued some eleven miles; that we have from 5000 to 6000 prisoners, some 40 guns, besides small arms and stores in vast quantities. But Gen. Hood, whom I saw at the department but a fortnight ago, is said to be dead! and some half dozen of our brigadier-generals have been killed and wounded. The loss of the enemy, however, has been still greater than ours. At last accounts (this morning) the battle was still raging—the enemy having made a stand (temporarily, I presume) on a ridge, to protect their retreat. They burnt many commissary stores, which they may need soon. Yet, this is from the West.

The effects of this great victory will be electrical. The whole South will be filled again with patriotic fervor, and in the North there will be a corresponding depression. Rosecrans's position is now one of great peril; for his army, being away from the protection of gun-boats, may be utterly destroyed, and then Tennessee and Southern Kentucky may fall into our hands again. To-morrow the papers will be filled with accounts from the field of battle, and we shall have a more distinct knowledge of the magnitude of it. There must have been at least 150,000 men engaged; and no doubt the killed and wounded on both sides amounted to tens of thousands!

Surely the Government of the United States must now see the impossibility of subjugating the Southern people, spread over such a vast extent of territory; and the European governments ought now to interpose to put an end to this cruel waste of blood and treasure.

My little garden has been a great comfort to me, and has afforded vegetables every day for a month past. My potatoes, however, which occupied about half the ground, did not turn out well. There were not more than a dozen quarts—worth $10, though—in consequence of the drought in June and July; but I have abundance of tomatoes, and every week several quarts of the speckled lima bean, which I trailed up the plank fence and on the side of the wood-house—just seven hills in all. I do not think I planted more than a gill of beans; and yet I must have already pulled some ten quarts, and will get nearly as many more, which will make a yield of more than 300-fold! I shall save some of the seed. The cabbages do not head, but we use them freely when we get a little bacon. The okra flourishes finely, and gives a flavor to the soup, when we succeed in getting a shin-bone. The red peppers are flourishing luxuriantly, and the bright red pods are really beautiful. The parsnips look well, but I have not yet pulled any. I shall sow turnip seed, where the potatoes failed, for spring salad. On the whole, the little garden has compensated me for my labor in substantial returns, as well as in distraction from painful meditations during a season of calamity.

SEPTEMBER 23D.—We have nothing additional up to three P.M.

to-day; but there is an untraceable rumor on the street of some undefinable disaster somewhere, and perhaps it is the invention of the enemy. We still pause for the sequel of the battle; for Rosecrans has fallen back to a strong position; and at this distance we know not whether it be practicable to flank him or to cut his communications. It is said Gen. Breckinridge commanded only 1600 men, losing 1300 of them! Gen. Cooper and the Secretary of War have not been permitted to fill up his division; the first probably having no desire to replenish the dilapidated command of an aspiring "political general."

A Mr. G. Preston Williams, of Eden, Chatham County, Ga., writes to the President, Sept. 7th, 1863, saying he has lost three sons in the war, freely given for independence. His fourth son is at home on furlough, but he shall not return unless the President gives up his *obstinacy*, and his favorites—*Bragg*, Pemberton, Lovell, etc. He charges the President with incapacity, if not wickedness, and says our independence would have been won ere this, but for the obstacles thrown by him in the way. He threatens revolution within a revolution, when Congress meets, unless the President reforms, which will cause him to lose his office, and perhaps his *head*. To which the President replies thus, in an indorsement on the envelope:

"SECRETARY OF WAR.—This is referred to you without any knowledge of the writer. If it be a genuine signature, you have revealed to you a deserter, and a man who harbors him, as well as *incites* to desertion, and opposition to the efforts of the government for public defense. Sept. 19th, 1863.—J. D."

The indorsement was written to-day, since hearing of Bragg's victory.

SEPTEMBER 24TH.—A dispatch from Gen. Bragg, received to-day, three miles from Chattanooga, and dated yesterday, says the enemy occupies a strong position, and confronts him in great force, but he is sending troops round his flanks. No doubt he will cross the river as soon as possible. Only a small portion of Longstreet's corps has been engaged, so Bragg will have a fresh force to hurl against the invader. We learn to-day that Gen. Hood is not dead, and will recover.

The President sent over to the Secretary of War to-day some extracts from a letter he has just received from Mobile, stating that a large trade is going on with the enemy at New Orleans. A number of vessels, laden with cotton, had sailed from Pascagoula Bay, for that destination. Some one or two had been stopped by the people, as the traffic is expressly prohibited by an act of Congress. But upon inquiry it was ascertained that the trade was authorized by authority from Richmond—the War Department. I doubt whether Mr. Seddon authorized it. Who then? Perhaps it will be ascertained upon investigation.

Mr. Kean, the young Chief of the Bureau, is a most fastidious civil officer, for he rebukes older men than himself for mistaking an illegible K for an R, and puts *his* warning on record in pencil marks. Mr. K. came in with Mr. Randolph, but declined to follow his patron any further.

SEPTEMBER 25TH.—The latest dispatch from Gen. Bragg states that he has 7000 prisoners (2000 of them wounded), 36 cannon, 15,000 of the enemy's small arms, and 25 colors. After the victory, he issued the following address to his army:

"HEADQUARTERS ARMY OF TENNESSEE,
"FIELD OF CHICKAMAUGA, Sept. 22, 1863.

"It has pleased Almighty God to reward the valor and endurance of our troops by giving our arms a complete victory over the enemy's superior numbers. Thanks are due and are rendered unto Him who giveth not the battle to the strong.

"Soldiers! after days of severe battle, preceded by heavy and important outpost affairs, you have stormed the barricades and breastworks of the enemy and driven him before you in confusion, and destroyed an army largely superior in numbers, and whose constant theme was your demoralization and whose constant boast was your defeat. Your patient endurance under privations, your fortitude, and your valor, displayed at all times and under all trials, have been meetly rewarded. Your commander acknowledges his obligations, and promises to you in advance the country's gratitude.

"But our task is not ended. We must drop a soldier's tear upon the graves of the noble men who have fallen by our sides, and move forward. Much has been accomplished—more remains to be done, before we can enjoy the blessings of peace and freedom.

"(Signed) BRAXTON BRAGG."

The President has received an official report of Gen. Frazer's surrender of Cumberland Gap, from Major McDowell, who escaped. It comprised 2100 men, 8 guns, 160 beef cattle, 12,000 pounds of bacon, 1800 bushels of wheat, and 15 days' rations. The President indorsed his opinion on it as follows:

"This report presents a shameful abandonment of duty, and is so extraordinary as to suggest that more than was known to the major must have existed to cause such a result.—J. D. Sept. 24."

The quartermasters in Texas are suggesting the impressment of the cotton in that State. The President indorses as follows on the paper which he returned to the Secretary of War:

"I have never been willing to employ such means except as a last resort.—J. D."

The Secretary of War is falling into the old United States fashion. He has brought into the department two broad-shouldered young relatives, one of whom might serve the country in the field, and I believe they are both possessed of sufficient wealth to subsist upon without $1500 clerkships.

SEPTEMBER 26TH.—Nothing additional has been received from Gen. Bragg, but there is reason to believe Rosecrans is fortifying Chattanooga, preparatory to crossing the river and retreating northward with all possible expedition.

From the Upper Rappahannock there is much skirmishing, the usual preliminary to a battle; and Kemper's brigade, of Pickett's division, went up thither last night, and it may be probable that a battle is imminent. Lee is apt to fight when the enemy is present facing him. The victory of Bragg has lifted a mountain from the spirits of the people, and another victory would cast the North into the "slough of despond."

Gen. C. J. McRae, and another gentleman, have been directed to investigate the accounts of Major Caleb Huse, the friend and agent of Col. Gorgas, Chief of Ordnance. Gen. McR. writes from Folkestone, England, to Col. G. that the other gentleman not having appeared, he is undertaking the work himself, and, so far, the accounts are all right. Messrs Isaac, Campbell & Co. (Jews), with whom the Ordnance Bureau has had large transactions, have afforded (so far) every facility, etc.

SEPTEMBER 27TH.—Nothing additional has been heard from

either Bragg's or Lee's army. But the positions of both seem quite satisfactory to our government and people. How Rosecrans can get off without the loss of half his army, stores, etc., military authorities are unable to perceive; and if Meade advances, there is a universal conviction that he will be beaten.

But there *is* an excitement in the city. It is reported that the United States flag of truce steamer is down the river, having on board no less a personage than Mr. Seward, United States Secretary of State, and that Mr. Benjamin, and other dignitaries of the Confederate States, are going off this morning to meet him. Of course it is conjectured that terms of peace will be discussed, and an infinite variety of opinions are expressed in relation to them. Some suppose the mission grows out of foreign complications, of which, as yet, we can have no knowledge, and that, to maintain the vantage ground of France or England, or both, Mr. Seward may have a scheme of recognition and alliance, etc., looking to the control of affairs on this continent by the United States and Confederate States in conjunction, with commercial arrangements, etc. Both Seward and Benjamin are regarded by their uncharitable enemies as alike destitute of principle, and of moral or physical courage, and hence that they would have no hesitation in agreeing to any terms likely to be mutually advantageous—to themselves. They are certainly men of great intellectual power, and if they are not strictly honest, as much may be said of the greatest diplomats who have played conspicuous parts in the field of diplomacy during the last century. They may sacrifice men, and castles, etc., as skillful players do chessmen, with no particle of feeling for the pieces lost, for equivalents, etc. Nevertheless, nothing can be finally consummated without the concurrence of all the co-ordinate branches of both governments, and the acquiescence of the people. But these gentlemen are fully aware of the anxiety of both peoples (if so they may be called) for peace, and they may, if they choose, strike a bargain which will put an end to the manslaughter which is deluging the land with blood. Then both governments can go into bankruptcy. It may be a humbug.

SEPTEMBER 28TH.—All is reported quiet on the Rappahannock, the enemy seeming to be staggered, if not stupefied, by the stunning blows dealt Rosecrans in the West.

Burnside's detachment is evacuating East Tennessee; we have

Jonesborough, and are pursuing the enemy, at last accounts, toward Knoxville. Between that and Chattanooga he may be intercepted by the right wing of Bragg.

The President had his cabinet with him nearly all day. It is not yet ascertained, precisely, whether Mr. Seward was really on the flag of truce steamer yesterday, but it is pretty certain that Mr. Benjamin went down the river. Of course the public is not likely to know what transpired there—if anything.

The trans-Mississippi army is getting large amounts of stores, etc., on the Rio Grande River. Major Hart, Quartermaster, writes from San Antonio, Texas, on the 13th of July, that three large English steamers, "Sea Queen," "Sir Wm. Peel," and the "Gladiator," had arrived, were discharging, etc. Also that two large schooners were hourly expected with 20,000 Enfield rifles on board. He says Gen. Magruder is impressing cotton to freight these vessels.

So far, 260 Quakers, non-combatants, have been reported, mostly in North Carolina. A few cannot pay the $500—conscientiously.

The papers begin to give the details of the great battle of Chickamauga—the "*river of death.*"

SEPTEMBER 29TH.—We have nothing additional from Bragg, except confirmation of his victory from Northern journals; and it is reported that Meade is sending two more army corps to the Southwest, for the purpose of extricating Rosecrans from his perilous predicament. It is believed our cavalry is in his rear, and that we have the road below Chattanooga, cutting him off from his supplies.

The President sent for the Secretary of War and Gen. Cooper just before 3 P.M. to-day, having, it is supposed, some recent intelligence of the movements of the enemy. It is possible we shall send troops, etc., with all possible expedition, to reinforce Bragg, for the purpose of insuring the destruction of Rosecrans's army, and thus to Tennessee may be transferred the principal military operations of the fall campaign.

Young Mr. Kean has taken friend Jacques's place at the door of the Secretary, and put him to abstracting the recorded letters containing decisions, the plan I suggested to the President, but which was claimed as the invention of the Assistant Secretary of War.

Some one has written a flaming article on the injurious manner in which impressments have been conducted in Mississippi—the President's State—and sent it to him. This being referred to Col. Northrop, the Commissary-General, the latter splutters over it in his angular chirography at a furious rate, saying he did not authorize it, he doubted if it were done, and lastly, if done, he was sure it was done by agents of the Quartermaster-General.

SEPTEMBER 30TH.—Still nothing additional from Lee's or Bragg's army; but from abroad we learn that the British Government has prevented the rams built for us from leaving the Mersey.

Gen. Pemberton is here, and was closeted for several hours to-day with the Secretary of War.

Capt. J. H. Wright, 56th Georgia, gives another version of the surrender of Cumberland Gap. He is the friend of Gen. Frazer, and says he was induced to that step by the fear that the North Carolina regiments (62d and 63d) could not be relied on. Did he try them?

A Mr. Blair, Columbus, Miss., applies for permission to bring drugs from *Memphis*, and refers, for respectability, to President Davis and Gov. Letcher. His letter gives a list of prices of medicines in the Confederate States. I select the following: Quinine, per oz., $100; calomel, $20; blue mass, $20; Opium, $100; S. N. bismuth, $100; soda, $5; borax, $14; oil of bergamot, per lb., $100; indigo, $35; blue-stone, $10.

Boots are selling in this city at $100 per pair, and common shoes for $60. Shuck mattresses, $40. Blankets, $40 each; and sheets, cotton, $25 each. Wood is $40 per cord.

I submitted a proposition to the Secretary (of a quartermaster) to use some idle government wagons and some negro prisoners, to get in wood for the civil officers of the government, which could be done for $8 per cord; but the quartermasters opposed it.

But to-day I sent a letter to the President, suggesting that the perishable tithes (potatoes, meal, etc.) be sold at reasonable rates to the civil officers and the people, when in excess of the demand of the army, and that transportation be allowed, and that a government store be opened in Richmond. I told him plainly, that without some speedy measure of relief there would be much discontent, for half the families here are neither half-fed nor half-clad. The measure, if adopted in all the cities, would be a beneficent one, and would give popular strength to the government, while it would be a death-blow to the speculators and extortioners. It will be seen what heed the government will give it.

Gen. Wise has his brigade in South Carolina.

"*The markets.*—The quantity of produce in our markets continues large, and of good quality, but the prices remain as high as ever, as the following quotations will show: butter, $4; bacon, $2.75 to $3 per pound; lard, $2.25 per pound; beef, $1 to $1.25; lamb, $1 to $1.25; veal, $1 to $1.50; shote, $1.25 to $1.75; sausage, $1; chickens, $2.50 to $7 per pair; ducks, $5 per pair; salt herrings, $4 per dozen; cabbage, $1 to $1.50; green corn, $1.50 to $2 per dozen; sweet potatoes, $21 to $26 per bushel; Irish potatoes, 50 to 75 cts. per quart; snaps, $1 per quart; peas, 75 cts. to $1.25 per quart; butter-beans, $1 to $1.50 per quart; onions, $1.25 per quart; egg-plant, $1 to $2 a piece; tomatoes, 50 cts. to $1 per quart; country soap, $1 to $1.50 per pound."

CHAPTER XXXI.

Suffering of our wounded at Gettysburg.—Prisoners from the battle of Chickamauga.—Charleston.—Policy in the Southwest.—From Gen. Bragg. —Letter from President Davis.—Religious revival.—Departure of the President for the Southwest. — About General Bragg. — Movement of mechanics and non-producers.—About "French" tobacco.—The markets.—Outrage in Missouri.—Speculations of government agents.—From Gen. Lee.—Judge Hastings's scheme.—Visit to our prisons.—Letter from Gen. Kirby Smith.—President Davis at Selma.—Gen. Winder's passports.—The markets.—Campbellites and Methodists.—From Gen. Lee.— From the Southwest.

OCTOBER 1ST.—We have a rumor to-day that Meade is sending heavy masses of troops to the West to extricate Rosecrans, and that Gen. Hooker is to menace Richmond from the Peninsula, with 25,000 men, to keep Lee from crossing the Potomac.

We have absolutely nothing from Bragg; but a dispatch from Gen. S. Jones, East Tennessee, of this date, says he has sent Gen. Ranseur after the rear guard of the enemy, near Knoxville.

A letter from W. G. M. Davis, describes St. Andrew's Bay, Florida, as practicable for exporting and importing purposes. It may be required, if Charleston and Wilmington fall—which is not improbable.

Nevertheless, Bragg's victory has given us a respite in the East, and soon the bad roads will put an end to the marching of armies until next year. I doubt whether the Yankees will desire another winter campaign in Virginia.

The papers contain the following account of sufferings at Gettysburg, and in the Federal prisons:

"A lady from the vicinity of Gettysburg writes: 'July 18th—We have been visiting the battle-field, and have done all we can for the wounded there. Since then we have sent another party, who came upon a camp of wounded Confederates in a wood between the hills. Through this wood quite a large creek runs. This camp contained between 200 and 300 wounded men, in every stage of suffering; two well men among them as nurses. Most of them had frightful wounds. A few evenings ago the rain, sudden and violent, swelled the creek, and 35 of the unfortunates were swept away; 35 died of starvation. No one had been to visit them since they were carried off the battle-field; they had no food of any kind; they were crying all the time "bread, bread! water, water!" One boy without beard was stretched out dead, quite naked, a piece of blanket thrown over his emaciated form, a rag over his face, and his small, thin hands laid over his breast. Of the dead none knew their names, and it breaks my heart to think of the mothers waiting and watching for the sons laid in the lonely grave on that fearful battle-field. All of those men in the woods were nearly naked, and when ladies approached they tried to cover themselves with the filthy rags they had cast aside. The wounds themselves, unwashed and untouched, were full of worms. God only knows what they suffered.

"'Not one word of complaint passed their lips, not a murmur; their only words were "Bread, bread! water, water!" Except when they saw some of our ladies much affected, they said, "Oh, ladies, don't cry; we are used to this." We are doing all we can; we served all day yesterday, though it was Sunday.' This lady adds: 'There were two brothers—one a colonel, the other a captain—lying side by side, and both wounded. They had a Bible between them.' Another letter from Philadelphia says: 'There are over 8000 on the island (Fort Delaware), the hospitals crowded, and between 300 and 400 men on the bare floor of the barracks; not even a straw mattress under them. The surgeon says the hundred pillows and other things sent from here were a God-send. Everything except gray clothing will be thankfully received, and can be fully disposed of. It is very difficult to get money here. I write to you in the hope that you may be able to send some comforts for these suffering men. Some two or three thousand have been sent to an island in the East River, most of them South Carolinians, and all in great destitution. Your hearts would ache as mine does if you knew all I hear and know is true of the sufferings of our poor people.'

"Another writes: Philadelphia, July 20th, 1863. 'I mentioned in my last the large number of Southern prisoners now in the hands of the Federal Government in Fort Delaware, near this city. There are 8000, a large portion of whom are sick and wounded; all are suffering most seriously for the want of a thousand things. Those in the city who are by birth or association connected with Southern people, and who feel a sympathy for the sufferings of these prisoners, are but few in number, and upon these have been increasing calls for aid. Their powers of contribution are now exhausted. I thought it my duty to acquaint you and others in Europe of this state of things, that you might raise something to relieve the sufferings of these prisoners. I believe the government has decided that any contributions for them may be delivered to them. There is scarcely a man among them, officers or privates, who has any money or any clothes beyond those in which they stood when they were captured on the battle-field. You can, therefore, imagine their situation. In the hospitals the government gives them nothing beyond medicines and soldier's rations. Sick men require much more, or they perish; and these people are dying by scores. I think it a matter in which their friends on the other side should take prompt and ample action.'"

OCTOBER 2D.—Our 5000 prisoners taken at the battle of Chickamauga have arrived in this city, and it is ascertained that more are on the way hither. Gen. Bragg said he had 5000 besides the wounded, and as none of the wounded have arrived, more must have been taken since his dispatch. Every effort is being made on our part to capture the army of Rosecrans—and everything possible is done by the enemy to extricate him, and to reinforce him to such an extent that he may resume offensive operations. Without this be done, the campaign must close disastrously in the West, and then the peace party of the North will have a new inspiration of vitality.

It is now said that Gen. Lee, despairing of being attacked in his chosen position, has resolved to attack Meade, or at least to advance somewhere. It is possible (if Meade has really sent two corps of his army to the West) that he will cross the Potomac again—at least on a foraging expedition. If he meets with only conscripts and militia he may penetrate as far as Harrisburg, and then let Europe perpend! The Union will be as difficult of reconstruction, as would have been the celebrated Campo Formio vase shivered by Napoleon. It is much easier to destroy than to construct. The emancipation and confiscation measures rendered reconstruction impracticable—unless, indeed, at a future day, the Abolitionists of the United States should be annihilated and Abolitionism abolished.

To-day I got an excellent pair of winter shoes from a quartermaster here for $13—the retail price for as good an article, in the stores, is $75; fine boots have risen to $200!

The enemy's batteries on Morris Island are firing away again at Sumter's ruins, and at Moultrie—but they have not yet opened on the city.

The newspapers continue to give accounts of the Chickamauga battle.

OCTOBER 3D.—Nothing from the armies; but from Charleston it is ascertained that the enemy's batteries on Morris Island have some of the guns pointing *seaward*. This indicates a provision against attack from that quarter, and suggests a purpose to withdraw the monitors, perhaps to use them against Wilmington. I suppose the opposite guns in the batteries will soon open on Charleston.

Thomas Jackson, Augusta, Ga., writes that he can prove the president of the Southern Express Company, who recently obtained a passport to visit Europe, really embarked for the United States, taking a large sum in gold; that another of the same company (which is nothing more than a branch of Adams's Express Company of New York) will leave soon with more gold. He says this company has enough men detailed from the army, and conscripts exempted, to make two regiments.

J. M. Williams writes from Morton, Miss., that his negroes have been permitted to return to his plantation, near Baton Rouge, and place themselves under his overseer. During their absence some ten or twelve died. This is really wonderful policy on the part of the enemy—a policy which, if persisted in, might ruin us. Mr. Williams asks permission to sell some *fifty bales of cotton to the enemy for the support of his slaves.* He says the enemy is getting all the cotton in that section of country—and it may be inferred that all the planters are getting back their slaves. The moment any relaxation occurs in the rigorous measures of the enemy, that moment our planters cease to be united in resistance.

OCTOBER 4TH.—The major-quartermasters and the acting quartermaster-generals (during the illness or absence of Gen. Lawton) are buffeting the project some of us set on foot to obtain wood at cost, $8, instead of paying the extortioners $40 per cord. All the wagons and teams of Longstreet's corps are here idle, while the corps itself is with Bragg—and the horses are fed by the government of course. These wagons and teams might bring into the city thousands of cords of wood. The quartermasters at first said there were no drivers; but I pointed out the free Yankee negroes in the prisons, who beg employment. Now Col. Cole, the quartermaster in charge of transportation, says there is a prospect of getting teamsters—but that hauling should be done exclusively for the army—and the quartermaster-general (acting) indorses on the paper that if the Secretary will *designate the class of clerks* to be benefited, some little wood might be delivered them. This concession was obtained, because the Secretary himself sent my *second* paper to the quartermaster-general—the *first* never having been seen by him, having passed from the hands of the Assistant Secretary to the file-tomb.

Another paper I addressed to the President, suggesting the opening of government stores for the sale of perishable tithes,—being a blow at the extortioners, and a measure of relief to the non-producers, and calculated to prevent a riot in the city,—was referred by him yesterday to the Secretary of War, for his special notice, and for *conference*, which may result in good, if they adopt the plan submitted. That paper the Assistant Secretary *cannot* withhold, having the President's mark on it.

OCTOBER 5TH.—It is now said that Meade's army has not retired, and that two corps of it have not been sent to Rosecrans. Well, we shall know more soon, for Lee is preparing for a movement. It may occur this week.

In the West it is said Gen. Johnston is working his way, with a few brigades, from Meridian towards *Nashville*.

Lieut.-Gen. E. Kirby Smith writes for authority to make appointments and promotions in the trans-Mississippi Army, as its "communications with Richmond are permanently interrupted." The President indorses that he has no authority to delegate the power of appointing, as that is fixed by the constitution; but he will do anything in his power to facilitate the wishes of the general. The general writes that such delegation is a "military necessity."

The *Enquirer* and the *Dispatch* have come out in opposition to the fixing of maximum prices for articles of necessity, by either the Legislature of the State or by Congress. It is charged against these papers, with what justice I know not, that the proprietors of both are realizing profits from speculation.

To-day I got a fine shin-bone (for soup) for $1. I obtained it at the government shop; in the market I was asked $5.50 for one. We had a good dinner, and something left over for to-morrow.

OCTOBER 6TH.—Gen. Bragg and others recommend Gen. Hood for promotion to a lieutenant-generalcy; but the President says it is impossible, as the number authorized by Congress is full. And Gen. Bragg also gives timely notice to the Commissary-General that the supplies at Atlanta will suffice for but a few weeks longer. This, Commissary-General Northrop took in high dudgeon, indorsing on the paper that there was no necessity for such a message to him; that Bragg knew very well that every effort had been and would be made to subsist the army; and that when he evacuated Tennessee, the great source of supplies was abandoned. In short, the only hope of obtaining ample supplies was for Gen. Bragg to recover Tennessee, and drive Rosecrans out of the country.

AT THE CONFEDERATE STATES CAPITAL. 63

The President has at last consented to send troops for the protection of Wilmington—Martin's brigade; and also Clingman's, from Charleston, if the enemy should appear before Wilmington.

I read to-day an interesting report from one of our secret agents —Mr. A. Superviele—of his diplomatic operations in Mexico, which convinces me that the French authorities there favor the Confederate States cause, and anticipate closer relations before long. When he parted with Almonte, the latter assured him that his sympathies were with the South, and that if he held any position in the new government (which he does now) he might say to President Davis that his influence would be exerted for the recognition of our independence.

Mr. Jeptha Fowlkes, of Aberdeen, Miss., sends a proposition to supply our army with 200,000 suits of clothing, 50,000 pairs of shoes, etc. etc. from the United States, provided he be allowed to give cotton in return. Mr. Randolph made a contract with him last year, of this nature, which our government revoked afterward. We shall see what will be done now.

It is positively asserted that Gen. Bragg has arrested Lieut.-Gen. (Bishop) Polk and Brig.-Gen. Hindman, for disobedience of orders in the battle of Chickamauga.

LETTER FROM PRESIDENT DAVIS —The Mobile papers publish the following letter from President Davis to the "Confederate Society," of Enterprise, Miss.:

"RICHMOND, VA., Sept. 17th, 1863.

"J. W. HARMON, ESQ , SECRETARY OF THE CONFEDERATE SOCIETY, ENTERPRISE, MISS.

"SIR:—I have received your letter of the 22d ult., inclosing a copy of an address to the people of the Confederate States, calling upon them to unite in an effort to restore and maintain the par value of the currency with gold by forming societies of citizens who will engage to sell and buy only at reduced prices. The object of the address is most laudable, and I sincerely hope for it great success in arousing the people to concerted action upon a subject of the deepest importance. The passion for speculation has become a gigantic evil. It has seemed to take possession of the whole country, and has seduced citizens of all classes from a determined prosecution of the war to a sordid effort to amass money. It destroys enthusiasm and weakens public confidence.

It injures the efficiency of every measure which demands the zealous co-operation of the people in repelling the public enemy, and threatens to bring upon us every calamity which can befall freemen struggling for independence.

"The united exertions of societies like those you propose should accomplish much toward abating this evil, and infusing a new spirit into the community.

"I trust, therefore, that you will continue your labors until their good effect becomes apparent everywhere.

"Please accept my thanks for the comforting tone of your patriotic letter. It is a relief to receive such a communication at this time, when earnest effort is demanded, and when I am burdened by the complaining and despondent letters of many who have stood all the day idle, and now blame anybody but themselves for reverses which have come and dangers which threaten.

"Very respectfully,
"Your fellow-citizen,
"JEFFERSON DAVIS."

There is a revival in the city among the Methodists; and that suggests a recent expiring. In my young days I saw much of these sensational excitements, and partook of them; for how can the young resist them? But it is the Cæsarean method of being born again, violating reason, and perhaps outraging nature. There was one gratifying deduction derived from my observation to-night, at the Clay Street meeting-house—the absence of allusion to the war. I had supposed the attempt would be made by the exhorters to appeal to the fears of the soldiery, composing more than half the congregation, and the terrors of death be held up before them. But they knew better; they knew that every one of them had made up his mind to die, and that most of them expected either death or wounds in this mortal struggle for independence. The fact is they are familiar with death in all its phases, and there is not a coward among them. They look upon danger with the most perfect indifference, and fear not to die. Hence there was no allusion to the battle-field, which has become a scene divested of novelty. But the appeals were made to their sympathies, and reliance was placed on the force of example, and the contagion of ungovernable emotions.

OCTOBER 7TH.—We have not a particle of news from the army to-day. It may be an ominous calm.

A Mr. Livingstone, from Georgia I believe, has been extensively engaged in financial transactions during the last week. He drew upon the house of North & Co., Savannah, and purchased some $35,000 in gold. After obtaining some $350,000 from the brokers here, he obtained a passport (of course !) and fled into the enemy's lines.

OCTOBER 8TH.—The President, accompanied by two of his aids, set off quietly day before yesterday for the Southwest—to Bragg's army, no doubt, where it is understood dissensions have arisen among the chieftains.

By telegraph we learn that one of Bragg's batteries, on Lookout Mountain, opened fire on the Federals in Chattanooga on the 5th inst., which was replied to briskly.

Night before last an attempt was made to destroy the enemy's steamer Ironsides at Charleston, but failed. The torpedo, however, may have done it some injury.

From Lee and Meade we have nothing.

A rather startling letter was read by the Secretary of War to-day from ———, Lieut.-Gen. Bragg's ———d in command. It was dated the 26th of September, and stated that Chickamauga was one of the most complete victories of the war, but has not been "followed up." On the 21st (day after the battle), Gen. Bragg asked Gen. ———'s advice, which was promptly given : " that he should immediately strike Burnside a blow; or if Burnside escaped, then to march on Rosecrans's communications in the rear of Nashville." Gen. Bragg seemed to adopt the plan, and gave orders accordingly. But the right wing had not marched more than eight or ten miles the next day, before it was halted, and ordered to march toward Chattanooga, after giving the enemy two and a half days to strengthen the fortifications. Bragg's army remains in front of the enemy's defenses, with orders not to assault him. The only thing Bragg has done well (says Gen. ———) was to order the attack on the 19th of September ; everything else has been wrong : and now only God can save us or help us—while Bragg commands. He begs that Gen. Lee be sent there, while the Army of Virginia remains on the defensive, to prosecute offensive measures against Rosecrans. He says Bragg's army has neither organization nor mobility; and B. cannot remedy the evil. He cannot adopt or adhere to any course, and he invokes the government to interpose speedily. This letter is on file in the archives.

The question now is, who is right? If it be ———, Bragg ought certainly to be relieved without delay; and the President cannot arrive in the field a moment too soon. As it is, while others are exulting in the conviction that Rosecrans will be speedily destroyed, *I* am filled with alarm for the fate of Bragg's army, and for the cause! I am reluctant to attribute the weakness of personal pique or professional jealousy to ———; yet I still hope that events will speedily prove that Bragg's plan was the best, and that he had really adopted and advised to the wisest course.

OCTOBER 9TH.—From the West we have only unreliable reports of movements, etc.; but something definite and decisive must occur shortly.

Gen. Lee's army crossed the Rapidan yesterday, and a battle may be looked for in that direction any day. It is said Meade has only 40,000 or 50,000 men; and, if this be so, Lee is strong enough to assume the offensive.

To-morrow the departments will be closed for a review of the clerks, etc., a piece of nonsense, as civil officers are under no obligation to march except to fight, when the city is menaced.

The mechanics and non-producers have made a unanimous call (in placards) for a mass meeting at the City Hall to-morrow evening. The ostensible object is to instruct Mr. Randolph and other members of the Legislature (now in session) to vote for the bill, fixing maximum prices of commodities essential to life, or else to resign. Mr. Randolph has said he would not vote for it, unless so instructed to do. It is apprehended that these men, or the authors of the movement, have ulterior objects in view; and as some ten or twelve hundred of them belong to the militia, and have muskets in their possession, mischief may grow out of it. Mr. Secretary Seddon ought to act at once on the plan suggested for the sale of the perishable tithes, since the government is blamed very much, and perhaps very justly, for preventing transportation of meat and bread to the city, or for impressing it in transitu.

Capt. Warner, who feeds the prisoners of war, and who is my good "friend in need," sent me yesterday 20 odd pounds of bacon sides at the government price. This is not exactly according to law and order, but the government loses nothing, and my family have a substitute for butter.

OCTOBER 10TH.—The enemy is undoubtedly falling back on the Rappahannock, and our army is pursuing. We have about 40,000 in Lee's army, and it is reported that Meade has 50,000, of whom many are conscripts, altogether unreliable. We may look for stirring news soon.

About 2500 of the "local" troops were reviewed to-day. The companies were not more than half filled; so, in an emergency, we could raise 5000 fighting men, at a moment's warning, for the defense of the capital. In the absence of Custis Lee, Col. Brown, the English aid of the President, commanded the brigade, much to the disgust of many of the men, and the whole were reviewed by Gen. Elzey, still more to the chagrin of the ultra Southern men.

The Secretary seems unable to avert the storm brewing against the extortioners; but permits impressments of provisions coming to the city.

It is said the President and cabinet have a large special fund in Europe. If they should fall into the hands of Lincoln, they might suffer death; so in the event of subjugation, it is surmised they have provided for their subsistence in foreign lands. But there is no necessity for such provision, provided they perform their duty here. I cut the following from the papers:

"The Vicomte de St. Romain has been sent by the French Government to ours to negotiate for the exportation of the tobacco bought for France by French agents.

"The Confederate States Government has at last consented to allow the tobacco to leave the country, provided the French Government will send its own vessels for it.

"The latter *will* send French ships, accompanied by armed convoys.

"To this the United States Government objects *in toto*.

"Vicomte de St. Romain is now making his way to New York to send the result of his mission, through the French Consul, to the Emperor.

"The French frigates in New York are there on this errand."

OCTOBER 11TH.—I attended a meeting of "mechanics" and citizens at the City Hall last night. The prime mover of this organization is E. B. Robinson, some twenty years ago one of my printers in the *Madisonian* office. It was fully attended, and although not so boisterous as might have been expected, was, nevertheless, earnest and determined in its spirit. Resolutions instructing Mr. Randolph (State Senator, and late Secretary of War) to vote for a bill before the General Assembly reducing and fixing the prices of the necessities of life, were passed unanimously; also one demanding his resignation, in the event of his hesitating to obey. He was bitterly denounced by the speakers.

I understood yesterday, from the butchers, that they have been buying beef cattle, not from the producers, but from a Mr. Moffitt (they say a commissary agent), at from 45 to 55 cents gross; and hence they are compelled to retail it (net) at from 75 cents to $1.25 per pound to the people. If this be so, and the commissary buys at government prices, 18 to 22 cents, a great profit is realized by the government or its agent at the expense of a suffering people. How long will the people suffer thus? This community is even now in an inflammable condition, and may be ignited by a single spark. The flames of insurrection may at any moment wrap this slumbering government in its destructive folds; and yet the cabinet cannot be awakened to a sense of the danger. Mr. Seddon (who may be better informed than others), deeply sunken in his easy chair, seems perfectly composed; but he cannot know that his agents are permitted to prey upon the people: and the complaints and charges sent to him are acted upon by his subordinates, who have orders not to permit business of secondary importance to engage his attention; and his door-keepers have instructions to refuse admittance to persons below a certain rank.

Nothing but the generous and brave men in the army could have saved us from destruction long ago, and nothing else can save us hereafter. If our independence shall be achieved, it will be done in *spite* of the obstructions with which the cause has been burdened by the stupidity or mismanagement of incompetent or dishonest men.

"THE SUFFERINGS OF THE BORDER MISSOURIANS.—The people of Missouri, on the Kansas border, are being slaughtered without mercy under the authority of the Yankee commander of that department, Schofield. A letter to the St. Louis *Republican* (Yankee) says:

"On Sunday last the desire for blood manifested itself in the southeastern part of Jackson County, not far from the village of Lone Jack. Although it was Sunday, the people of that region, alarmed and terror-stricken by threats from Kansas, and cruel edicts from headquarters of the district, were hard at work straining every nerve to get ready to leave their homes before this memorable 9th day of September, 1863.

"One party of these unfortunate victims of a cruel order had almost completed their preparations, and within half an hour's time would have commenced their weary wanderings in search of a home. It consisted of Benjamin Potter, aged seventy-five; John S. Cave, aged fifty; William Hunter, aged forty-seven; David Hunter, aged thirty-five; William C. Tate, aged thirty; Andrew Owsley, aged seventeen; and Martin Rice and his son. While thus engaged in loading their wagons with such effects as they supposed would be most useful to them, a detachment of Kansas troops (said to be part of the Kansas 9th, though this may be a mistake), under command of Lieut.-Col. Clark and Capt. Coleman, came up and took them all prisoners.

"After a little parleying, Mr. Rice and his son were released and ordered to leave; which they did, of course. They had not gone much over three-fourths of a mile before they heard firing at the point at which they had left the soldiers with the remaining prisoners. In a short time the command moved on, and the wives and other relatives of the prisoners rushed up to ascertain their fate. It was a horrid spectacle.

"There lay six lifeless forms—mangled corpses—so shockingly mangled that it was difficult, my informant stated, to identify some of them. They were buried where they were murdered, without coffins, by a few friends who had expected to join them on that day, with their families, and journey in search of a home.

"These are the unvarnished facts with reference to an isolated transaction. There are many, very many others of a similar character that I might mention, but I will not. The unwritten and secret history of our border would amaze the civilized world, and would stagger the faith of the most credulous. In the case just mentioned, we find an old man who had passed his threescore and ten, and a youth who had not yet reached his score, falling victims to this thirsty cry for blood.

"The world will doubtless be told that six more bushwhackers have been cut off, etc. But believe it not, sir; it is not true. These six men never were in arms, neither in the bush or elsewhere, I have been told by one who has known them for years past. The widows and orphans of some of them passed through this city yesterday, heart-broken, homeless wanderers."

OCTOBER 12TH.—Hon. G. A. Henry, Senator from Tennessee, writes to the Secretary that it is rumored that Gen. Pemberton is to command Gen. Polk's corps in Tennessee. He says if this be true, it will be disastrous; that the Tennessee troops will not serve under him, but will mutiny and desert.

It is reported to-day by Gen. Elzey (on what information I know not) that Meade's army has been reduced to 30,000 or 40,000 men, by the heavy reinforcements sent to extricate Rosecrans. Be this as it may, there is no longer any doubt that Lee is advancing toward the Potomac, and the enemy is retreating. This must soon culminate in something of interest.

I saw Commissary-General Northrop to-day, and he acknowledges that Mr. Moffitt, who sells beef (gross) to the butchers at from 45 to 55 cents, is one of his agents, employed by Major Ruffin, to purchase beef for the army! The schedule price is from 16 to 20 cents, and he pays no more, for the government—and if he buys for himself, it is not likely he pays more—and so we have a government agent a speculator in meat, and co-operating with speculators! Will Mr. Secretary Seddon permit this?

OCTOBER 13TH.—Gen. Lee's cavalry are picking up some prisoners, several hundreds having already been sent to Richmond. It is said the advance of his army has been delayed several weeks for want of commissary stores, while Commissary-General Northrop's or Major Ruffin's agent Moffitt, it is alleged, has been selling beef (gross) to the butchers at 50 cents per pound, after buying or impressing at from 16 to 20 cents.

Gen. Lee writes that a scout (from Washington?) informs him that Gen. Gilmore has been ordered to take Charleston at all hazards, and, failing in the attempt, to make a flank movement and seize upon Branchville; which he (Gen. Lee) deems an unlikely feat.

What a change! The young professors and tutors who shouldered their pens and became clerks in the departments are now resigning, and seeking employment in country schools remote from the horrid sounds of war so prevalent in the vicinity of the Capitol, and since they were ordered to volunteer in the local companies, which will probably have some sharp practice in the field. They are intent, however, on "teaching the young *idea* how to shoot." The young chiefs of bureaus, being fixed "for life," did not *volunteer*.

OCTOBER 14TH.—A letter from Gen. Lee to the Secretary of War, dated 11th inst. at Madison C. H., complains of the injury done by the newspapers of Richmond, which contain early accounts of his movements, and are taken quickly (by flag of truce? or Gen. Winder's corps of rogues and cut-throats?) to the enemy. He says he is endeavoring to strike at Meade, and has already captured, this week, some 600 of the enemy (cavalry), including that number of horses. The Secretary sent the requisite notice to the editors.

Gen. Gilmer, at Charleston, suggests the removal of the guns on the boats in that harbor to land batteries, to be commanded by officers of the navy.

An order has been sent to Gen. S. Jones, West Virginia, for the 8th and 14th Regiments Virginia Cavalry.

OCTOBER 15TH.—To-day, at 12 M., I saw a common leather-wing bat flying over the War Department. What this portends I do not pretend to say, perhaps nothing. It may have been dislodged by the workmen building chimneys to the offices of the department.

The order of the government conscribing all foreign residents who have acquired homes in this country, and the expulsion of the British consuls, will immediately be followed by another exodus of that class of residents. Already passports are daily applied for, and invariably granted by Mr. Assistant Secretary Campbell. The enemy, of course, will reap great benefit from the information conveyed by these people, and the innumerable brood of blockade-runners.

Gen. Lee has sent down between 600 and 700 prisoners captured in recent cavalry engagements. He took their horses and equipments also. And there is an account of an engagement in the West, near Memphis, in which the Confederate troops inflicted injury on the enemy, besides destroying the railroad in several places.

OCTOBER 16TH.—No battle had occurred in Northern Virginia up to 10 o'clock yesterday morning, although there is a constant stream of prisoners being sent to this city daily, taken by our cavalry. At last accounts Meade's army was retreating toward Washington City, hotly pursued by Lee. They were near Manassas, the first battle-field of the war.

There is nothing new from the West, except some skirmishing of cavalry in Central and Western Tennessee, wherein our men have had the advantage, though sometimes falling back before superior numbers.

At Charleston a brisk cannonading is kept up between the batteries; and it is said more hostile transports are arriving, which may indicate active operations on land. Our 700-pounder Blakely No. 2 is there.

Judge Campbell is giving passports rapidly, sometimes binding the Jews not to engage in private operations, but to confine themselves, while in the United States, to the purchase of supplies for the Confederate States service! Some, however, are willing to go on these terms to avoid conscription, but will realize profit by selling information to the enemy.

Judge Hastings, of California, proposes to return thither and publish a pamphlet describing newly discovered gold mines, and organizing companies to work them, which shall be secessionists; and when organized, he will fall upon and destroy the United States troops, march into Arizona, and from thence pour reinforcements into Texas. The Secretary, in the absence of the President, sends a copy of this scheme to Lieut.-Gen. E. K. Smith, trans-Mississippi Department, and gives some encouragement to the judge; abstaining, however, for the present, from devoting any money to the project.

OCTOBER 17TH.—We hear to-day that a battle has taken place near Manassas, and that Lee has taken some 9000 prisoners and many wagons. At 3 P.M. there was no official intelligence of this event, and it was not generally credited.

Gen. Wise writes from Charleston, that it is understood by the French and Spanish Consuls there that the city will not be bombarded.

In Eastern North Carolina the people have taken the oath of allegiance to the United States, to be binding only so long as they are within the military jurisdiction of the enemy; and they ask to be exempt from the Confederate States tithe tax, for if they pay it, the enemy will despoil them of all that remains.

OCTOBER 18TH.—No authentic information of a battle near Manassas has been received at the War Department, although it is certain there has been some heavy skirmishing on the Rappahannock. We have several brigadier-generals wounded, and lost five guns; but, being reinforced, continued the pursuit of the enemy, picking up many prisoners—they say 1500. The pursuit was retarded by the swelling of the streams.

A letter from Major-Gen. Jones, at Dublin Depot, Va., Oct. 14th, leads me to think danger is apprehended in that quarter, the objective point being the Salt Works; and it may be inferred, from the fact that Burnside is still there, that Rosecrans is considered safe, by reason of the heavy reinforcements sent from other quarters.

While I write, the government is having the tocsin sounded for volunteers from the militia to go to the rescue of the Salt Works, which is absurd, as the enemy will either have them before aid can be received from Richmond, or else he will have been driven off by the local troops near that vicinity.

Captain Warner took me in his buggy this morning to the military prisons. He did not lead me into the crowded rooms above, where he said I would be in danger of vermin, but exhibited his cooking apparatus, etc.—which was ample and cleanly. Everywhere I saw the captives peeping through the bars; they occupy quite a number of large buildings—warehouses—and some exhibited vengeful countenances. They have half a pound of beef per day, and plenty of good bread and water—besides vegetables and other matters furnished by themselves. Several new furnaces are in process of erection, and most of the laborers are Federal prisoners, who agree to work (for their own convenience) and are paid for it the usual wages. There are baths to the prisons; and the conduits for venting, etc. have cost some $10,000. To-day the weather is as warm as summer, and no doubt the prisoners sigh for the open air (although all the buildings are well ventilated), and their distant homes in the West—most of them being from the field of Chickamauga.

OCTOBER 19TH.—After all the rumors from Northern Virginia,

I have seen nothing official. I incline to the belief that we have achieved no success further than an advance toward Washington, and a corresponding retreat of the enemy. It is to be yet seen whether Lee captured more prisoners than Meade captured. It is said we lost *seven* guns. But how can Lee achieve anything when the enemy is ever kept informed not only of his movements in progress, but of his probable intentions? I observe that just about the time Lee purposes a movement, several Jews and others of conscript age are seen to apply for passports through the lines, for ordnance and medical stores, and Judge Campbell is certain to "allow" them. The letter-book, for they are now recorded, shows this. These men bring supplies from Maryland, if they ever return, in saddle-bags, while the same kind are landed every week at Wilmington by the cargo!

A recent letter from Lieut.-Gen. E. Kirby Smith, trans-Mississippi, fills me with alarm. He says the property-holders in Arkansas and Louisiana—which States we are evacuating—are willing to return to their allegiance to the United States if that government should modify its policy. He says we have but 32,500 in Texas, Louisiana, and Arkansas—all told—and the enemy twice that number.

Gen. D. H. Hill has been relieved in the West, and ordered to report in this city to Gen. Cooper. It was necessary perhaps to have a scape-goat. Bragg will *probably* be sustained by the President—but then what will become of ———, who is so inimical to Bragg?

The President has published, in the West, an eloquent address to the soldiers.

It appears from Gen. K. Smith's letter that the French captured a vessel having on board, for the Confederate States, 12,000 stand of arms, which were taken to Vera Cruz. It is presumed that the French commander supposed these arms were sent over for the use of the Mexicans, probably by the United States. If this be so, it is reasonable to suppose they will be restored us, and so far I do not learn that this government has taken umbrage at the capture. It may be that they were taken to keep them from falling into the possession of the United States cruisers. There are one or two French war steamers now at Charleston, interchanging courtesies with the Confederate States authorities there. It also appears by Gen. Smith's letter that a large amount of arms for the trans-Mississippi Department were deposited at Vicksburg, and fell into the hands of the enemy. The President indorsed on the back of the letter that this was a blunder, and asks by whose order the deposit was made. Col. Gorgas must answer.

OCTOBER 20TH.—Nothing definite from Lee. I fear his little campaign from the Rapidan to Bull Run was not a glorious one, although Meade did run to the fortifications at Centreville. He may possibly have had a counter-plot, which is not yet developed. Our papers are rejoicing over thousands of prisoners "picked up;" but Captain Warner, who furnishes the prisoners their rations, assures me that they have not yet arrived; while our papers acknowledge we lost 1000 men, killed and wounded, besides several guns.

The Secretary of War received a dispatch to-day from Gen. Barton, Kinston, N. C., stating that a number of Federal regiments were embarking for (he thinks) South Carolina. This, the Secretary, of course, sends to Gen. Beauregard, but doubts, however, the destination of the troops. He thinks they are to menace Richmond again, and says there are indications of this purpose on the York River. Is Hooker really there? The public knows nothing, as yet, of what is going on down that river. What if Meade retreated to entice Lee away from Richmond, having in preparation an expedition against this city? I should not wonder at anything, since so many equivocal characters are obtaining passports to the United States. Gen. Winder and Judge Campbell are busy signing passports—one granted by the latter yesterday (recorded) also allows the bearer to take with him 2000 pounds tobacco!

A letter was received to-day from the President, ordering certain concessions to Governor Brown, relating to exemptions and details.

Letters have been received justifying the belief (notwithstanding the forebodings of Lieut.-Gen. E. K. Smith) that we have taken Little Rock, Ark., again. This is Price's work; also that Quantrell and other bold raiders in Missouri have collected some thousands of desperate men, and *killed* several regiments of the enemy. They have burned a number of towns (Union), and taken the large town of Boonville. These are the men against whom

Kansas Abolitionists have sworn vengeance—no quarter is to be granted them. I suspect they are granting no quarter!

Yesterday I saw a Captain Commissary on Broad Street give his dog a piece of beef for which I would have given a dollar. Many little children of soldiers stood by with empty baskets. He would not sell a shank!

Dispatch from Alabama:

"SELMA, October 18th, 1863.

"President Davis arrived here this evening, and was welcomed by the citizens *en masse*. An immense crowd gathered in front of the hotel. The President congratulated the people on meeting them under such favorable circumstances, and spoke in glowing terms of the gallantry of Alabamians on every battle-field. He said if the non-conscripts of Alabama would gather their guns and go to the rescue, by guarding Courtland and other points, thereby relieving regular soldiers who are now, from necessity, discharging that sort of duty, such blows would be dealt the enemy as he would find it difficult to recover from. In this way most effective aid could be given the gallant men and officers who are carrying out the plans of the noble Longstreet, under the supervision of the heroic Bragg.

"In this way the President was confident that Rosecrans could be crushed to dust. It was only by force of arms that the Yankees could be brought to reason and their plans for our subjugation defeated. Self-reliance and energy were now our only duty. We should not look to Europe for aid, for such is not to be expected now. Our only alternative was to sustain ourselves with renewed energy and determination, and a little more sacrifice upon the part of the people, and the President firmly believed that next spring would see the invader driven from our borders. Then farmers, who are now refugees, could return to their families and pursue their business undisturbed as heretofore. In fact, he believed that the defeat of Rosecrans would practically end the war."

Mr. Randolph has signified his purpose to vote for the bill reducing prices, rather than resign; but Mr. Wyndham Robertson, the delegate, has resigned. Nearly all the papers have taken ground against the "Maximum Bill." To-night a mass meeting is called, to urge the passage of the bill.

The "mass meeting" to-night was a small affair. Mr. Robinson, my old compositor, made a speech, abusing the editors; but the editors have succeeded in putting down for the present the cry for bread. I fear, however, it is but the work of Sisyphus, and it may destroy them; for, if the measure fails before the Legislature, the prices will be sure to advance, and then the people will attribute their woes to those who were instrumental in the defeat of the plan of relief. It is a dangerous thing to array one's self against a famishing people, even when the remedy they demand is not calculated to alleviate their distresses. I saw flour sell at auction to-day for $61 per barrel. This, too, when there is an abundant crop of new grain but recently harvested. It is the result of the depreciation of a redundant currency, and not of an ascertained scarcity. Timber and coal are as abundant as ever they were; and the one sells at $32 per cord, and the other at $30 per load of 25 bushels. And cotton is abundant, while brown domestic is bringing $3.00 per yard. Many are becoming very shabby in appearance; and I can get no clothes for myself or my family, unless the government shall very materially increase our salaries.

OCTOBER 21ST.— Gen. Lee telegraphed last night that our cavalry had routed the enemy's horse on Monday, capturing some 200, etc. etc.

The Legislature passed a series of resolutions yesterday, requesting the Secretary of War to impress free negroes for the public works; to detail the 2d class militia (over 45); and to order into the ranks the thousands of detailed soldiers and conscripts seen everywhere. The report of a committee states that conscripts and soldiers pay bonuses to contractors to have them detailed, and then they furnish negroes as substitutes to perform the work, engaging themselves in speculation. Also that one-third of the conscripts of one county have been detailed to get wood for certain iron works which have a year's supply on hand! Surely the Secretary will attend to this.

There is a row about passports. It appears that Judge Campbell and Gen. Winder are competitors in the business. Judge C. yesterday remarked that, at Gen. Winder's office, he understood a passport could be bought for $100; and this was repeated by Mr. Kean, the young Chief of the Bureau, and it somehow reached the ears of Gen. Winder. Perhaps Judge C. reported the fact of his belief to Mr. Secretary Seddon, who had ceased to grant any himself (to the United States), and of course was not aware of the great number his assistant, much less Gen. W., issued; and if so, it is probable he called Gen. W. to an account. The general, in a rage, charged Mr. Kean with the propagation of a damaging report. Mr. K. said he heard Mr. Chapman (a clerk) say so—and so off they started in pursuit of Chapman, who could not be found up to 3 P.M. By to-morrow Gen. W. may hear of Judge Campbell's remarks and agency, and a pretty kettle of fish they will have, if Judge C.'s record be brought to the notice of the Secretary! It is all wrong, and if the business be not better regulated or terminated, it will terminate the government. Gen. Lee's reputation as a great captain will be ruined, if the blockade-runners be allowed to continue to give information to the enemy of all his movements.

OCTOBER 22D.—Gen. Wheeler has taken 700 of the enemy's cavalry in East Tennessee, 6 cannon, 50 wagons, commissary stores, etc. *Per contra*, the steamer Venus, with bacon, from Nassau, got aground trying to enter the port of Wilmington, and ship and cargo were lost. There is a rumor that Gen. Taylor, trans-Mississippi, has captured Gen. Banks, his staff, and sixteen regiments. This, I fear, is not well authenticated.

A poor woman yesterday applied to a merchant in Carey Street to purchase a barrel of flour. The price he demanded was $70.

"My God!" exclaimed she, "how can I pay such prices? I have seven children; what shall I do?"

"I don't know, madam," said he, coolly, "unless you eat your children."

Such is the power of cupidity—it transforms men into demons. And if this spirit prevails throughout the country, a just God will bring calamities upon the land, which will reach these cormorants, but which, it may be feared, will involve all classes in a common ruin.

Beef, to-day, sold in market at $1.50 per pound. There is no bacon for sale, or corn-meal. But we shall not starve, if we have faith in a beneficent Providence. Our daughter Anne, teaching in Appomattox County, writes that she will send us a barrel of potatoes, some persimmons, etc. next Wednesday. And we had a good dinner to-day : a piece of fat shoulder Capt. Warner let me have at $1 per pound—it is selling for $2.50—and cabbage from my garden, which my neighbor's cow overlooked when she broke through the gate last Sunday. Although we scarcely know what we shall have to-morrow, we are merry and patriotic to-day.

Last night I went to hear Rev. Dr. Hobson, Reformed Baptist, or Campbellite, preach. He is certainly an orator (from Kentucky) and a man of great energy and fertility of mind. There is a revival in his congregation too, as well as among the Methodists, but he was very severe in his condemnation of the emotional or sensational practices of the latter. He said, what was never before known by me, that the word pardon is not in the New Testament, but remission was. His point against the Methodists was their fallacy of believing that conversion was sudden and miraculous, and accompanied by a happy feeling. Happy feeling, he said, would naturally *follow* a consciousness of remission of sins, but was no evidence of conversion, for it might be produced by other things. It was the efficacy of the Word, of the promise of God, which obliterated the sins of all who believed, repented, and were baptized. He had no spasmodic extravagances over his converts; but, simply taking them by the hand, asked if they believed, repented, and would be baptized. If the answers were in the affirmative, they resumed their seats, and were soon after *immersed* in a pool made for the purpose in the church.

I pray sincerely that this general revival in the churches will soften the hearts of the extortioners, for this class is specifically denounced in the Scriptures. There is abundance in the land, but "man's inhumanity to man makes countless thousands mourn." I hope the extortioners may all go to heaven, first ceasing to be extortioners.

The Legislature has broken up the gambling establishments, for the time being, and the furniture of their gorgeous saloons is being sold at auction. Some idea of the number of these establishments may be formed from an estimate (in the *Examiner*) of the cost of the entertainment prepared for visitors being not less than $10,000 daily. Their agents bought the best articles offered for sale in the markets, and never hesitated to pay the most exorbitant prices. I hope now the absence of such customers may have a good effect. But I fear the currency, so redundant, is past remedy.

OCTOBER 23D.—Gen. Lee has retired to the south side of the Rappahannock again, while Meade remains in the intrenchments at Centreville. Gen. Imboden occupies Winchester.

From the West we have only newspaper reports, which may not be true.

OCTOBER 24TH.—To-day we have a cold northwest storm of wind and rain, and we have our first fire in the parlor.

The elections in Ohio and Pennsylvania have gone for the Republican (War) candidates. We rely on ourselves, under God, for independence. It is said Gen. Lee learned that 15,000 Republican voters were sent from Meade's army into Pennsylvania to vote, and hence he advanced and drove back the Federal army. Yet he says that Meade's army is more numerous than his. It is not known what our losses have been, but the following dispatch from Lee gives an accurate account of the enemy's loss in prisoners.

"HEADQUARTERS ARMY NORTHERN VIRGINIA,
"October 23d, 1863.

"GEN. S. COOPER, A. and I. General.

"Gen. Imboden, on the 18th, attacked the garrison at Charlestown, Shenandoah Valley, captured 434 prisoners, with their arms, transportation, and stores. To these, add prisoners already forwarded, makes 2462.

"(Signed) R. E. LEE.

"Official: JOHN WITHERS, A. A. General."

And Capt. Warner says he is now feeding them.

Gen. Lee writes on the 19th inst., that it is doubtful whether Gen. Meade will remain where he is, behind his fortifications along Bull Run, or make another movement on Richmond. A few days will decide this matter. He says Meade has superior numbers. If he remains, Gen. Lee will advance again, provided he can get quartermaster supplies for his army. But at present, thousands of his men are barefooted, without overcoats, blankets, etc. He says it was the sublimest spectacle of the war to see men in such condition move forward with such cheerfulness and alacrity, in the recent pursuit of the enemy. He deprecates sending any of his regiments to West Virginia and East Tennessee, and thinks Gen. Sam Jones has not evinced sufficient energy and judgment in that quarter. He says it would be better to send reinforcements to Chattanooga, where it is practicable to conduct a winter campaign. He could drive the enemy from the Peninsula, Gloucester Point, Williamsburg, and Yorktown, but to keep them away Lee would have to station an army there. If North Carolina be menaced, he advises that the troops at Richmond and Petersburg be sent thither, and he will replace them with troops from his army. He thinks it the best policy not to disperse troops in Virginia.

From this letter it is easy to perceive that the Secretary of War, in the absence of the President, has been making suggestions to Gen. Lee, none of which does he deem it good policy to adopt, the Secretary not being versed in military matters.

A private note from Gen. Lee, dated the 13th inst., which I saw to-day, informs the Secretary of War that much of the benefits he anticipated from his movement, then in progress, must be lost, from the fact that the enemy had been informed of his purposes. This it was the duty of the government to prevent, but Mr. Seddon, like his predecessors, cannot be convinced that the rogues and cut-throats employed by Gen. Winder as detectives, have it in their power to inflict injury on the cause and the country. The cleaning of the Augean stables here is the work which should engage the attention of the Secretary of War, rather than directing the movements of armies in the field, of which matter he knows nothing whatever.

The Secretary of War wrote a long and rather rebuking letter to-day to Mr. Sheffey, chairman of the Committee on Confederate Relations, of the General Assembly, who communicated a report and resolutions of the House of Delegates, in relation to details of conscripts, and the employment in civil offices of robust young men capable of military service, and urging the department to appoint men over forty-five years of age to perform such services, and to impress free negroes to do the labor that soldiers are detailed for. The Secretary thinks the Confederate Government knows its duties, and ought not to be meddled with by State Governments. It touched Mr. Seddon nearly.

By the last Northern papers I see President Lincoln has issued a proclamation calling for 300,000 more volunteers, and if they "do not come when he calls for them," that number will be *drafted* in January. This is very significant; either the draft has already failed, or else about a million of men per annum are concerned in the work of suppressing this "rebellion." We find, just at the time fixed for the subjugation of the South, Rosecrans is defeated, and Meade is driven back upon Washington!

OCTOBER 25TH.—We have nothing new this morning; but letters to the department from North and South Carolina indicate that while the troops in Virginia are almost perishing for food, the farmers are anxious to deliver the tithes, but the quartermaster and commissary agents are negligent or designedly remiss in their duty. The consequence will be the loss of the greater portion of these supplies, and the enhancement of the price of the remainder in the hands of the monopolists and speculators.

The *Southern* Express Co. has monopolized the railroads, delivering cotton for speculators, who send it to the United States, while the Confederate States cannot place enough money in Europe to pay for the supplies needed for the army.

OCTOBER 26TH.—No news from our armies. The President was in Mobile two days ago.

Gen. Rosecrans has been removed from his command, and Grant put in his place. Meade, it is said in Northern papers, will also be decapitated, for letting Lee get back without loss. Also Dalgren, at Charleston, has been relieved. And yet the Northern papers announce that Richmond will soon and suddenly be taken, and an unexpected joy be spread throughout the North, and a corresponding despondency throughout the South.

The weather is cloudy and cold. The papers announce that all clerks appointed since October 11th, 1862, by order of the Secretary of War, are liable to conscription. This cannot be true; for I know a Secretary who has just appointed two of his cousins to the best clerkships in the department—both of conscript age. But Secretaries know how to evade the law, and "whip the devil round the stump."

How long will it be after peace before the sectional hatred intensified by this war can abate? A lady near by, the other night, while surveying her dilapidated shoes, and the tattered sleeping-gowns of her children, burst forth as follows: "I pray that I may live to see the United States involved in a war with some foreign power, which will make refugees of her people, and lay her cities in ashes! I want the people ruined who would ruin the South. It will be a just retribution!"

OCTOBER 27TH.—Nothing from the North or West to-day. But Beauregard telegraphs that the enemy's batteries and monitors opened this morning heavily on his forts and batteries, but, as yet, there were no casualties.

The Commissary-General to-day, in a communication to the department, relating to the necessity of impressment to subsist our armies, says "the armies in Virginia muster 150,000 men." If this be so, then let Meade come! It may be possible that instead of exaggerating, a policy may have been adopted calculated to conceal the actual strength of armies.

Nevertheless, it is understood that one of the cabinet is offering his estates, lands, and negroes for sale. Will he convert the money into European funds? If so, he should not let it be known, else it will engender the terrible idea that our affairs are in a desperate condition. The operations of the next thirty days may be decisive of our fate. Hundreds of thousands of Southern men have yet to die before subjugation can be effected; and quite that number of invaders must fall to accomplish it!

OCTOBER 28TH.—No news from the army. We have some 13,000 prisoners here, hungry; for there is not sufficient meat for them.

Mr. Memminger, Secretary of the Treasury, is said to be transporting his private fortune (very large) to Europe.

OCTOBER 29TH.—Gen. Lee writes (a few days since), from Brandy Station, that Meade seems determined to advance again; that troops are going up the Potomac to Washington, and that volunteers from New York have been ordered thither. He asks the Secretary to ascertain if there be really any Federal force in the York River; for if the report be correct of hostile troops being there, it may be the enemy's intention to make another raid on the railroad. The general says we have troops enough in Southwestern Virginia; but they are not skillfully commanded.

After all, I fear we shall not get the iron from the Aquia Creek Railroad. In the summer the government was too slow, and now it is probably too slow again, as the enemy are said to be landing there. It might have been removed long ago, if we had had a faster Secretary.

Major S. Hart, San Antonio, Texas, writes that the 10,000 (the number altered again) superior rifles captured by the French off the Rio Grande last summer, were about to fall into the hands of United States cruisers; and he has sent for them, hoping the French will turn them over to us.

Gen. Winder writes the Secretary that the Commissary-General will let him have no meat for the 13,000 prisoners; and he will not be answerable for their safe keeping without it. The Quartermaster-General writes that the duty of providing for them is in dispute between the two bureaus, and he wants the Secretary to decide between them. If the Secretary should be very *slow*, the prisoners will suffer.

Yesterday a set (six) of cups and saucers, white, and not china, sold at auction for $50.

Mr. Henry, Senator from Tennessee, writes the Secretary that if Ewell were sent into East Tennessee with a corps, and Gen. Johnston were to penetrate into Middle Tennessee, forming a junction north of Chattanooga, it would end the war in three months.

OCTOBER 30TH.—We have nothing new to-day, except the continued bombardment of Charleston. That city has been besieged over one hundred days.

OCTOBER 31ST.—Letters came to-day from the President (or rather *copies* in his own handwriting), relieving Lieut.-Gen. Hardee, in Mississippi, and assigning him to a command under Gen. Bragg. He also writes a friendly letter (from Meridian, Miss.) to Gen. Bragg, informing him that Gen. Hardee had been ordered to report to him without delay, and that two brigades might go with him, if needed. This indicates that the President means to sustain Bragg, nothwithstanding the clamor against him; and that Bragg must have an immense army. Lieut.-Gen. Polk (whom the President will always sustain) is assigned to the Mississippi Department.

The latest accounts from Chattanooga show that the enemy are stirring a little, and trying to flank Bragg's left wing.

The bombardment at Charleston is still without decisive result.

CHAPTER XXXII.

Letters from various sections.—The President and Gen. Bragg.—State of the markets.—Causes of the President's tour.—Gen. Duff Green —Return of the President.—Loss of Hoke's and Haye's brigades.—Letter from Gen. Howell Cobb.—Dispatch from Gen. Lee.—State of the markets.—Letter from A. Moseley.—Mrs. Todd in Richmond.—Vice-President Stephens on furloughs.—About Gen. Bragg and the battle of Lookout Mountain.

NOVEMBER 1ST.—No news from any of the armies this morning. But Gen. Whiting writes that he is deficient in ordnance to protect our steamers and to defend the port. If Wilmington should fall by the neglect of the government, it will be another stunning blow.

However, our armies are augmenting, from conscription, and if we had honest officers to conduct this important business, some four or five hundred thousand men could be kept in the field, and subjugation would be an impossibility. But exemptions and details afford a tempting opportunity to make money, as substitutes are selling for $6000 each; and the rage for speculation is universal.

The President is looked for to-morrow, and it is to be hoped that he has learned something of importance during his tour. He will at once set about his message, which will no doubt be an interesting one this year.

How we sigh for peace, on this beautiful Sabbath day! But the suffering we have endured for nearly three years is no more than was experienced by our forefathers of the Revolution. We must bear it to the end, for it is the price of liberty. Yet we sigh for peace—God knows I do—while at the same time we will endure the ordeal for years to come, rather than succumb to the rule of an oppressor. We must be free, be the cost what it may. Oh, if the spirit of fanaticism had been kept down by the good sense of the people of the United States, the Union would have been preserved, and we should have taken the highest position among the great powers of the earth. It is too late now. Neither government may, for a long series of years, aspire to lead the civilized nations of the earth. Ambition, hatred, caprice and folly have combined to snap the silken cord, and break the golden bowl. These are the consequences of a persistency in sectional strife and domination, foreseen and foretold by me in the *"Southern Monitor,"* published in Philadelphia; no one regarded the warning. Now hundreds of thousands are weeping in sackcloth and ashes over the untimely end of hundreds of thousands slain in battle! And thousands yet must fall, before the strife be ended.

NOVEMBER 2D.—A refugee from Portsmouth reports the arrival of 6000 Federal troops at Newport News, and that Richmond is to be menaced again.

Brig.-Gen. H. W. Allen, Alexandria, La., reports 8000 deserters and skulking conscripts in that vicinity, and a bad state of things generally.

Gen. Lee has written three letters to the department, dated 30th and 31st October. 1st, complaining of the tardiness of the Bureau of Examination, and the want of efficient officers; 2d, complaining of the furloughs given Georgia officers as members of the legislature, causing a brigade to be commanded by a lieutenant-colonel, etc.; 3d, relating to an order from the Secretary to respite certain deserters, condemned to execution. He says executions are necessary to keep the army together, but he *feels* the painfulness of the sad necessity.

Mr. H. D. Whitcomb, Superintendent Central Railroad, applied for and obtained passports for his mother and sister to return to the United States. He is a Northern man.

Brig.-Gen. S. A. Meredith (United States) writes from Fortress Monroe, proposing that prisoners west of the Mississippi be exchanged at Galveston. Mr. Ould, our agent of exchange, indorses on it that there is no necessity for immediate action, for the United States are not exchanging any prisoners at all at this time.

Mr. Memminger writes for troops to be sent to Ashville, West North Carolina, which is menaced by the traitors, tories, and Federals. His family is there, having fled from South Carolina. Hon. Jas. Farron also writes that a bad state of things exists in that section, and communication is kept open with the enemy in East Tennessee.

From St. Helena Parish, Ark., we have letters stating that all restraint is thrown off, and everybody almost is trading with the enemy. Some 1500 bales of cotton per week is taken to the Yankees from that region. They say most of the parties have permits from the government or from commanding generals to trade with the enemy.

Gen. Whiting writes that his men are suffering for shoes, and as 15,000 pairs are in that town, asks if he shall not impress them. The Secretary is reluctant to do this, and asks the Quartermaster-General what he shall do. The Quartermaster-General advises that the shoes be bought at a fair price, and paid for in cotton. He says blankets may be had in the same way.

NOVEMBER 3D.—Gen. Lee writes that he will endeavor to protect the workmen while removing the iron at Aquia Creek, but he fears the work has been too long delayed. The government has been too slow.

Gen. Sam Jones writes from Abingdon that his cavalry was at Jonesborough on the 30th ult., although the enemy's raiding parties were on this side. He says if he had a little more infantry, he could soon clear East Tennessee of the foe; and asks that an order from Gen. Cooper (A. and I. G.), calling for two of his best regiments of cavalry, be revoked.

In Gen. Lee's recent campaign beyond the Rappahannock, our losses in killed, wounded, and missing amounted to 1740; the enemy's losses must have been three times that number.

The President made a speech in Charleston on the 1st instant. We have copies from him to day of his correspondence with Gen. Bragg since he left Chickamauga field. Gen. B. says he will immediately call for Hardee's brigades, promised him, and without delay commence operations on the enemy's left (it is too wet on the right), and drive Burnside out of East Tennessee. But he complains of Gen. Buckner, who assumes to have an independent command in East Tennessee and West Virginia. The President replies that neither Bragg nor Buckner has jurisdiction over Gen. Jones in West Virginia, but that he gets his orders from Richmond. He does not promise to remove Buckner, whom he deems only *impatient*, but says he must be subject to Bragg's orders, etc.

Gen. Bragg has applied for Gen. Forrest (who went some time since to Mobile and tendered his resignation, in a pet with Gen.

Bragg) to command a cavalry force in North Mississippi and West Tennessee. In short, the President is resolved to sustain Gen. Bragg at the head of the army in Tennessee in spite of the tremendous prejudice against him in and out of the army. And unless Gen. Bragg does something more for the cause before Congress meets a month hence, we shall have more clamor against the government than ever. But he has quashed the charges (of Bragg) against Gen. Polk, and assigned him, without an investigation, to an important command.

NOVEMBER 4TH.—Mr. M———, Major Ruffin's commissary agent, denies selling *government* beef to the butchers; of course it was his own. But he has been ordered not to sell any more, while buying for the government.

Mr. Rouss, of Winchester, merchant, has succeeded in getting some brown cotton from the manufacturer, in Georgia, at cost, which he sells for cost and carriage to refugees. My wife got 20 yards to-day for $20. It is brown seven-eighth cotton, and brings in other stores $3 per yard. This is a saving of $40. And I bought 24 pounds of bacon of Capt. Warner, Commissary, at $1 per pound. The retail price is $2.50—and this is a saving of $36. Without such "short cuts" as these, occasionally, it would be impossible to maintain my family on the salaries my son Custis and myself get from the government, $3000.

How often have I and thousands in our youth expressed the wish to have lived during the first Revolution, or rather to have partaken of the excitements of war! Such is the romance or "enchantment" which "distance lends" "to the view." Now we see and feel the horrors of war, and we are unanimous in the wish, if we survive to behold again the balmy sunshine of peace, that neither we nor our posterity may ever more be spectators of or participants in another war. And yet we know not how soon we might plunge into it, if an adequate necessity should arise. Henceforth, in all probability, we shall be a military people. But I shall seek the peaceful haunts of quiet seclusion, for which I sigh with great earnestness. O for a garden, a vine and fig-tree, and my library!

Among the strange events of this war, not the least is the position on slavery (approving it) maintained by the Bishop of Vermont.

NOVEMBER 5TH.—The President has not yet returned, but was inspecting the defenses of Charleston. The Legislature has adjourned without fixing a maximum of prices. *Every night troops from Lee's army are passing through the city.* Probably they have been ordered to Bragg.

Yesterday flour sold at auction at $100 per barrel; to-day it sells for $120 ! There are 40,000 bushels of sweet potatoes, taken by the government as tithes, rotting at the depots between Richmond and Wilmington. If the government would wake up, and have them brought hither and sold, the people would be relieved, and flour and meal would decline in price. But a lethargy has seized upon the government, and no one may foretell the consequences of official supineness.

The enemy at Chattanooga have got an advantageous position on Bragg's left, and there is much apprehension that our army will lose the ground gained by the late victory.

The Commissary-General (Northrop) has sent in his estimate for the ensuing year, $210,000,000, of which $50,000,000 is for sugar, exclusively for the hospitals. It no longer forms part of the rations. He estimates for 400,000 men, and takes no account of the tithes, or tax in kind, nor is it apparent that he estimates for the army beyond the Mississippi.

A communication was received to-day from Gen. Meredith, the Federal Commissioner of Exchange, inclosing a letter from Gov. Todd and Gen. Mason, as well as copies of letters from some of Morgan's officers, stating that the heads of Morgan and his men are *not* shaved, and that they are well fed and comfortable.

NOVEMBER 6TH.—The President was to have returned to-day, but did not.

Various conjectures are made as to the object of his month's tour of speech-making. Some deem the cause very desperate, others that the President's condition is desperate. If the first, they say his purpose was to reanimate the people by his presence, and to cultivate a renewal of lost friendships, and hence he lingered longest at Charleston, in social intercourse with Gens. Beauregard and Wise, who had become estranged. The latter is the oldest brigadier-general in the service, and still they have failed to promote him. The President's power is felt in the army, and his patronage being almost unlimited, it was natural, they say, that he should be received with cheers. From a lieutenant up to a general, all are dependent on his favor for promotion. At all events, his austerity and inflexibility have been relaxed, and he has made popular speeches wherever he has gone. I hope good fruits will ensue. But he returns to find the people here almost in a state of starvation in the midst of plenty, brought on by the knavery or incompetency of government agents.

What is remarkable is the estimate of $50,000,000 by the Commissary-General for the purchase of sugar, exclusively for the sick and wounded in hospitals, the soldiers in the field being refused any more. One-fourth of the whole estimates ($210,000,000) for sugar, and not an ounce to go to the army! And this, too, when it is understood nearly all the sugar in the Confederacy has been impressed by his agents at from 50 cts. to $1 per pound. It is worth $2.50 now, and it is apprehended that a large proportion of the *fifty millions* asked for will go into the pockets of commissaries. No account whatever is taken of the *tithe* in the Commissary-General's estimates.

Flour sold at $125 per barrel to-day. There must be an explosion of some sort soon. Certainly Confederate notes have fallen very low indeed.

Another solution of the President's tour, by the uncharitable or suspicious, is a preparatory or a preliminary move to assuming all power in his own hands. They say the people are reduced by distress to such an extremity that, if he will only order rations to be served them, they will not quarrel with him if he assumes dictatorial powers. Legislation has failed to furnish remedies for the evils afflicting the community; and, really, if the evils themselves were not imputed to the government, and the President were ambitious—and is he not?—he might now, perhaps, play a successful Cromwellian rôle. But can he control the State governments? The government of *this* State seems like potter's clay in his hands, the Legislature being as subservient as the Congresses have hitherto been. It is observed—independence *first*—then let Cromwells or Washingtons come.

My wife, to-day, presented me with an excellent under-shirt, made of one of her dilapidated petticoats. A new shirt would cost $30. Common brown cotton (and in a cotton country!) sells for $3 per yard. I saw common cotton shirts sell at auction to-day for $40 per pair. Beef is $1.50 per pound, and pork $2. But these prices are paid in Confederate Treasury notes, and they mark the rapid depreciation of paper money.

The enemy, however, in spreading over the Southern territory, are not completing the work of subjugation. It would require a million of bayonets to keep this people in subjection, and the indications are that the United States will have difficulty in keeping their great armies up. It is a question of endurance.

NOVEMBER 7TH.—No news from any quarter, except the continued bombardment of the debris of Fort Sumter, and the killing and wounding of some 10 or 12 men there—but that is not news.

There is a pause,—a sort of holding of the breath of the people, as if some event of note was expected. The prices of food and fuel are far above the purses of all except speculators, and an explosion must happen soon, of some sort. People will not perish for food in the midst of plenty.

The press, a portion rather, praises the President for his carefulness in making a tour of the armies and ports south of us; but as he retained Gen. Bragg in command, how soon the tune would change if Bragg should meet with disaster!

Night before last some of the prisoners on Belle Isle (we have some 13,000 altogether in and near the city) were overheard by the guard to say they must escape immediately, or else it would be too late, as cannon were to be planted around them. Our authorities took the alarm, and increasing the guard, did plant cannon so as to rake them in every direction in the event of their breaking out of their prison bounds. It is suspected that this was a preconcerted affair, as a full division of the enemy has been sent to Newport News, probably to co-operate with the prisoners. Any attempt now must fail, unless, indeed, there should be a large number of Union sympathizers in the city to assist them.

Several weeks ago it was predicted in the Northern papers that Richmond would be taken in some mysterious manner, and that there was a plan for the prisoners of war to seize it by a *coup de main*, may be probable. But the scheme was impracticable. What may be the condition of the city, and the action of the people a few weeks hence, if relief be not afforded by the government, I am afraid to conjecture. The croakers say five millions of "greenbacks," and cargoes of provisions, might be more effectual in expelling the Confederate Government and restoring that of the United States than all of Meade's army. And this, too, they allege, when there is abundance in the country. Many seem to place no value on the only money we have in circulation. The grasping farmers refuse to get out their grain, saying they have as much Confederate money as they want, and the government seems determined to permit the perishable tithes to perish rather than allow the famishing people to consume them. Surely, say the croakers, such a policy cannot achieve independence. No, it must be speedily changed, or else worse calamities await us than any we have experienced.

Old Gen. Duff Green, after making many fortunes and losing them, it seems, is to die poor at last, and he is now nearly eighty years old. Last year he made a large contract to furnish the government with iron, his works being in Tennessee, whence he has been driven by the enemy. And now he says the depreciation of the money will make the cost of producing the iron twice as much as he will get for it. And worse, he has bought a large lot of sugar which would have realized a large profit, but the commissary agent has impressed it, and will not pay him cost for it. All he can do is to get a small portion of it back for the consumption of his employees, provided he returns to Tennessee and fulfills his iron contract.

NOVEMBER 8TH.—At this late day the Secretary of War is informed by Col. Gorgas that, in consequence of the enemy's possessing the coal mines in Tennessee, he shall not be able to supply orders for heavy shot, etc., for the defense of Charleston harbor, if the fleet of monitors were to pass the forts. Why, this has been daily looked for any time during the last three months! And information from the Western army indicates that only about one shell in twenty, furnished by Col. Gorgas, will explode. This reminds me of the doubts expressed by Gen. Cobb of the fitness of Col. G. for his position.

This is a bleak November day, after some days of pleasant autumnal sunshine. I still gather a few tomatoes from the little garden; a bushel of green ones on the vines will never mature. The young turnips look well, and I hope there may be abundance of salad in the spring.

Yesterday two tons of Northern anthracite coal in this city sold for $500 per ton, to a church! We hope for relief when Congress meets, a month hence; but what can Congress do? The money is hopelessly depreciated. Even victories and peace could not restore it to par.

NOVEMBER 9TH.—The President returned Saturday evening, looking pretty well. Yesterday, Sunday, he was under the necesity of reading a dispatch from Gen. Lee, *announcing the surprise and capture of two brigades on the Rappahannock!*

This is a dark and gloomy day, spitting snow; while not a few are despondent from the recent disasters to our arms. It is supposed that we lost 3000 or 4000 men on Saturday. A day or two before, Gen. Echols had his brigade cut up at Lewisburg! *Per contra,* Brig.-Gen. W. E. Jones captured, on Saturday, at Rogerville, 850 prisoners, 4 pieces of artillery, 2 stands of colors, 60 wagons, and 1000 animals. Our loss, 2 killed and 8 wounded. So reads a dispatch from "R. Ransom, Major-Gen."

There is some excitement in the city now, perhaps more than at any former period. The disaster to the "Old Guard" has put in the mouths of the croakers the famous words of Napoleon at Waterloo: "*Sauve qui peut.*" We have out our last reserves, and the enemy still advances. They are advancing on North Carolina, and there was some danger of the President being intercepted at Weldon. Thousands believe that Gen. Bragg is about to retire from before Grant's army at Chattanooga. And to-day bread is selling at 50 cents per loaf—small loaf!

And now the Assistant Secretary of War, Judge Campbell, is "allowing" men to pass to Maryland, through our lines. First, is a Rev. Mr. A. S. Sloat, a chaplain in the army. He was degraded for some offense by his own church, and his wife and children having preceded him (all being Northern born), as stated in his letter on file, he is allowed a passport to follow them. Recommended by Mr. S. R. Tucker. Second, Mr. J. L. White and Mr. Forrester are "allowed" passports to go to Maryland for ordnance stores. Recommended by Col. Gorgas. Third and lastly, "Tom Wash. Smith" is "allowed," by the Assistant Secretary, to take fifteen boxes of tobacco to Maryland, and promises to bring back "medical stores." Recommended by B. G. Williams, one of Gen. Winder's detectives, and by Capt. Winder, one of the general's sons. They bring in stores, when they return, in saddle-bags, while whole cargoes are landed at Wilmington!

NOVEMBER 10TH.—It is supposed our loss in the surprise on Saturday did not exceed 1500, killed, wounded, and taken. It is thought that a battle will occur immediately, if it be not already in progress.

There is no news of moment from any quarter, except the loss of our steamer Cornubia, taken by the blockaders at Wilmington. She was laden with government stores. For months nearly all ships with arms or ammunition have been taken, while those having *merchandise on board get in safely.* These bribe their way through!

Col. Gorgas gave notice to-day that our supply of saltpeter will be exhausted in January, unless we can import a large quantity.

Another blue day!

NOVEMBER 11TH.—No news. I saw, to-day, Gen. Lee's letter of the 7th instant, simply announcing the capture of Hoke's and Haye's brigades. They were on the north side of the river, guarding the *pont de tete.* There is no excuse, no palliation. He said it was likely Meade's entire army would cross. This had been sent by the Secretary to the President, who indorsed upon it as follows: "If it be possible to reinforce, it should be done promptly. Can any militia or local defense men be made available?—J. D."

Gen. Whiting writes that he has refused to permit Mr. Crenshaw's correspondence with Collie & Co. to pass uninspected, from a knowledge of the nature of previous correspondence seen by him.

The Northern papers state that Mr. Seward has authorized them to publish the fact that the French Government has seized the Confederate rams building in the ports of France.

I have written Custis Lee, the President's aid, that but one alternative now remains: for the President, or some *one* else, to assume all power, temporarily, and crush the speculators. This I think is the only chance of independence. I may be mistaken—but we shall see.

Capt. Warner, who feeds the 13,000 prisoners here, when he has the means of doing so, says Col. Northrop, the Commissary, does not respond to his requisitions for meat. He fears the prisoners will take or destroy the city, and talks of sending his family out of it.

I condemned the reign of martial law in this city, in 1862, as it was not then necessary, and because its execution was intrusted to improper and obnoxious men. But now I am inclined to think it necessary not only here, but everywhere in the Confederacy. Many farmers refuse to get out their grain, or to sell their meat, because they say they have enough Confederate money! money for the redemption of which their last negro and last acre are responsible. So, if they be permitted to maintain this position, neither the army nor the non-producing class of the population can be subsisted; and, of course, all classes must be involved in a common ruin. A Dictator might prevent the people from destroying themselves, and it seems that nothing short of extreme measures can prevent it. But, again, suppose the Federal Government were to propose a sweeping amnesty, and exemption from confiscation to all who should subscribe to a reconstruction of the Union—and this, too, at a time of suffering and despondency—and so large a body were to embrace the terms as to render a prolongation of the war impracticable? What would the money the farmers now possess be worth? And what would become of the slaves, especially in Virginia, Tennessee, Kentucky, and Missouri?

NOVEMBER 12TH.—No accounts of any fighting, but plenty of battles looked for.

A. A. Little writes to the Secretary of War from Fredericksburg, that the attempt to remove the iron from the Aquia Railroad by the government having failed, now is the time for private enterprise to effect it. If the Secretary "will say the word," it can be done. He says the iron is worth "millions, its weight in gold!" Will Mr. Seddon let it be saved? Yes, indeed.

Mr. Heyliger, agent at Nassau, writes on the 3d instant (just a week ago), that he is shipping bacon by every steamer (three or four per week), leather, percussion caps, and a large amount of quartermaster's stores. But the supply of lead and saltpeter is exhausted, and he hopes the agents in Europe will soon send more. About one in every four steamers is captured by the enemy. We can afford that.

The President sent over to-day, for the perusal of the Secretary of War, a long letter from Gen. Howell Cobb, dated at Atlanta, on the 7th instant. He had just returned from a visit to Bragg's army, and reports that there is a better feeling among the officers for Gen. Bragg, who is regaining their confidence. However, he says it is to be wished that more cordiality subsisted between Generals Bragg and ——, his —— in command. He thinks Generals B—— and C—— might be relieved without detriment to the service, if they cannot be reconciled to Bragg. He hints at some important movement, and suggests co-operation from Virginia by a demonstration in East Tennessee.

It is generally believed that France has followed the example of England, by seizing our rams. Thus the whole world seems combined against us. And Mr. Seward has made a speech, breathing fire and destruction unless we submit to Lincoln as our President. He says he was fairly elected President for four years of the whole United States, and there can be no peace until he is President of all the States, to which he is justly entitled. A war for the President!

NOVEMBER 13TH.—No news of battles yet. But we have a rumor of the burning of the fine government steamer R. E. Lee, chased by the blockaders. That makes two this week.

Gen. Lee dispatched the President, yesterday, as follows:

"Orange C. H., Nov. 12th.—For the last five days we have only received three pounds of corn per horse, from Richmond, per day. We depend on Richmond for corn. At this rate, the horses will die, and cannot do hard work. The enemy is very active, and we must be prepared for hard work any day.—R. E. LEE."

On the back of which the President indorsed: "Have the forage sent up in preference to anything else. The necessity is so absolute as to call for every possible exertion.—JEFFERSON DAVIS."

Perhaps this may rouse the department. Horses starving in the midst of corn-fields ready for gathering! Alas, what mismanagement!

I cut the following from the *Dispatch:*

"FLOUR.—We heard yesterday of sales of flour at $110 per barrel. We do not, however, give this as the standard price; for, if the article was in market, we believe that even a higher figure would be reached. A few days since a load of flour was sent to an auction-house on Cary Street to be sold at auction. The proprietors of the house very properly declined to receive it, refusing to dispose of breadstuffs under the hammer, where men of money, and destitute of souls, would have an opportunity of buying it up and withdrawing it from market.

"CORN-MEAL.—This article is bringing from $18 to $20 per bushel, and scarce at that.

"COUNTRY PRODUCE AND VEGETABLES.—We give the following as the wholesale rates: Bacon, hoground, $2.75 to $3; lard, $2.25 to $2.30; butter, $3.75 to $4; eggs, $2 to $2.25; Irish potatoes, $7.50 to $8; sweet potatoes, $10.50 to $12; tallow candles, $4 per pound; salt, 45 cents per pound.

"GROCERIES.—Coffee—wholesale, $9 per pound, retail, $10; sugar, $2.85 to $3.25; sorghum molasses, wholesale, $10, and $14 to $15 at retail; rice, 30 to 35 cents.

"LIQUORS.—Whisky, $55 to $70 per gallon, according to quality, apple brandy, $50; high proof rum, $50; French brandy, $80 to $100.

"In the city markets fresh meats are worth $1.25 to $1.50 for beef and mutton, and $2 for pork; chickens, $6 to $8 per pair; ducks, $7 to $8 per pair; butter, $4.50 to $5 per pound; sweet potatoes, $2.50 per half peck; Irish potatoes, $2 per half peck.

"LEATHER.—Sole leather, $6.50 to $7.50 per pound; upper leather, $7.50 to $8; harness leather, $5.50 to $6; hides are quoted at $2.50 to $2.75 for dry, and $1.50 for salted green; tanners' oil, $4 to $5 per gallon.

"TOBACCO.—Common article, not sound, $1 to $1.25; medium, pounds, dark, $1.30 to $2; good medium bright, $2 to $2.75; fine bright, $2 to $4; sweet 5's and 10's scarce and in demand, with an advance."

My friend Capt. Jackson Warner sent me, to-day, two bushels of meal at government price, $5 per bushel. The price in market is $20. Also nine pounds of good beef, and a shank—for which he charged nothing, it being part of a present to him from a butcher.

NOVEMBER 14TH.—Some skirmishing between Chattanooga and Knoxville. From prisoners we learn that the enemy at both those places are on half rations, and that Grant intends to attack Bragg soon at Lookout Mountain. Either Grant or Bragg must retire, as the present relative positions cannot long be held.

Mr. A. Moseley, formerly editor of the *Whig*, writes, in response to a letter from the Secretary of War, that he deems our affairs in a rather critical condition. He is perfectly willing to resume his labor, but can see no good to be effected by him. He thinks, however, that the best solution for the financial question would be to cancel the indebtedness of the government to all except foreigners, and call it ($800,000,000) a contribution to the wars—and the sacrifices would be pretty equally distributed. He suggests the formation of an army, quietly, this winter, to invade Pennsylvania next spring, leaving Lee still with his army on this side of the Potomac. Nevertheless, he advises that no time should be lost in securing foreign aid, while we are still able to offer some equivalents, and before the enemy gets us more in his power. Rather submit to terms with France and England, or with either, than submission to the United States. Such are the opinions of a sagacious and experienced editor.

Another letter from Brig.-Gen. Meredith, Fortress Monroe, was received to-day, with a report of an agent on the condition of the prisoners at Fort Delaware. By this report it appears our men get meat three times a day—coffee, tea, molasses, chicken soup, fried mush, etc. But it is not stated *how much* they get. The agent says they confess themselves satisfied. Clothing, it would appear, is also issued them, and they have comfortable sleeping beds, etc. He says several of our surgeons propose taking the oath of allegiance, first resigning, provided they are permitted to visit their families. Gen. M. asks for a similar report of the rations, etc. served the Federal prisoners here, with an avowed purpose of retaliation, provided the accounts of their condition be true. I know not what response will be made; but our surgeon-general recommends an inspection and report. They are getting sweet potatoes now, and generally they get bread and beef daily, when our Commissary-General Northrop has them. But sometimes they have little or no meat for a day or so at a time—and occasionally they have bread only once a day. It is difficult to feed them, and I hope they will be exchanged soon. But Northrop says our own soldiers must soon learn to do without meat; and but few of us have little prospect of getting enough to eat this winter. My family had a fine dinner to-day—the only one for months. As for clothes, we are as shabby as Italian lazzaronis—with no prospect whatever of replenished wardrobe, unless some European power will come and take us, as the French have done Mexico.

NOVEMBER 15TH.—After a fine rain all night, it cleared away

beautifully this morning, cool, but not unseasonable. There is no news of importance. The Governor of Georgia recommends, in his message, that the Legislature instruct their representatives in Congress to vote for a repeal of the law allowing substitutes, and also to put the enrolling officers in the ranks, leaving the States to send conscripts to the army. The Georgia Legislature have passed a resolution, unanimously, asking the Secretary of War to revoke the appointments of all impressing agents in that State, and appoint none but civilians and citizens. I hope the Secretary will act upon this hint. But will he?

The papers contain the following:

"*Arrived in Richmond.*—Mrs. Todd, of Kentucky, the mother of Mrs. Lincoln, arrived in this city on the steamer Schultz, Thursday night, having come to City Point on a flag of truce boat. She goes South to visit her daughter, Mrs. Helm, widow of Surgeon-General Helm, who fell at Chickamauga. Mrs. Todd is about to take up her residence in the South, all her daughters being here, except the wife of Lincoln, who is in Washington, and Mrs. Kellogg, who is at present in Paris."

"To the Poor.—C. Baumhard, 259 Main Street, between Seventh and Eighth, has received a large quantity of freshly-ground corn-meal, which he will sell to poor families at the following rates: one bushel, $16; half bushel, $8; one peck, $4; half peck, $2."

November 16th.—Governor Brown, Georgia, writes the Secretary that he is opposed to impressments, and that the government should pay the market price—whatever that is. And the Rhett politicians of South Carolina are opposed to raising funds to pay with, by taxing land and negroes. So indicates the *Mercury.*

We have news to-day of the crossing of the Rapidan River by Meade's army. A battle, immediately, seems inevitable.

November 17th.—A cold, dark day. No news. It was a mistake about the enemy crossing the Rapidan—only one brigade (cavalry) came over, and it was beaten back without delay.

Vice-President Stephens writes a long letter to the Secretary, opposing the routine policy of furloughs, and extension of furloughs; suggesting that in each district some·one should have authority to grant them. He says many thousands have died by being hastened back to the army uncured of their wounds, etc.—preferring death to being advertised as deserters.

Captain Warner sent me a bag of sweet potatoes to-day, received from North Carolina. We had an excellent dinner.

NOVEMBER 18TH.—We have no news whatever, except some damage reported at Charleston, done to two monitors yesterday. The bombardment has assumed no new phase.

A letter from Gen. J. E. Johnston, Meridian, Miss., indicates that the Secretary has been writing him and saying that he was responsible for the outrages of the impressing agents in his department. Gen. J. disclaims the responsibility, inasmuch as the agents referred to act under orders from the Commissary-General or Secretary of War.

NOVEMBER 19TH.—Miss Harriet H. Fort, of Baltimore, has arrived via Accomac and Northampton Counties, with a complete drawing of all the defenses of Baltimore.

The Medical Purveyor's Guards have petitioned the Secretary for higher pay. They get now $1500 per annum, and say the city watchmen get $2300.

Gens. Banks and Taylor in the West are corresponding and wrangling about the exchange of prisoners—and the cartel is to be abrogated, probably.

The Governor of Mississippi (Clark) telegraphs the President that the Legislature (in session) is indignant at the military authorities for impressing slaves. The President telegraphs back that the order was to prevent them falling into the lines of the enemy, and none others were to be disturbed.

NOVEMBER 20TH.—We have reports of some successes to-day. Gen. Hampton, it appears, surprised and captured several companies of the enemy's cavalry, a day or two since, near Culpepper Court House. And Gen. Wheeler has captured several hundred of the enemy in East Tennessee, driving the rest into the fortications of Knoxville. Gen. Longstreet, at last accounts, was near Knoxville with the infantry. We shall not be long kept in suspense—as Longstreet will not delay his action; and Burnside may find himself in a "predicament."

A private soldier writes the Secretary to-day that his mother is in danger of starving—as she failed to get flour in Richmond, at $100 per barrel. He says if the government has no remedy for this, he and his comrades will throw down their arms and fly to some other country with their families, where a subsistence may be obtained.

Every night robberies of poultry, salt meats, and even of cows and hogs are occurring. Many are desperate.

NOVEMBER 21ST.—We have further reports from the West, confirming the success of Longstreet. It is said he has taken 2200 prisoners, and is probably at Knoxville.

The President left the city this morning for Orange Court House, on a visit to Gen. Lee and the Army of Northern Virginia.

We are a shabby-looking people now—gaunt, and many in rags. But there is food enough, and cloth enough, if we had a Roman Dictator to order an equitable distribution.

The Secretary of War is destined to have an uncomfortable time. After assuring the Legislature and the people that provisions in *transitu* would not be impressed, it is ascertained that the agents of the Commissary-General are impressing such supplies, and the Secretary is reluctant to interfere, the Commissary-General being understood to have the support of the President.

A committee of the Grand Jury yesterday submitted a paper to the President, on the subject of provisions—indicating the proximity of famine, and deprecating impressments. The President sent it to the Secretary, saying Mr. Seddon would no doubt take measures to keep the people of Richmond from starving; and directing the Secretary to "confer" with him. But to-day he is off to the army, and perhaps some may starve before any relief can be afforded.

A genteel suit of clothes cannot be had now for less than $700. A pair of boots, $200—if good. I saw to-day, suspended from a window, an opossum dressed for cooking, with a card in its mouth, marked "price, $10." It weighed about four pounds. I luxuriated on parsnips to-day, from my own little garden.

A dollar in gold sold for $18 Confederate money, to-day. Our paper is constantly depreciating; and I think it is past redemption, unless we adopt Mr. Moseley's plan, and cause some six or eight hundred millions to be canceled, and fix a maximum price for all commodities necessary for the support of life. Congress will never agree upon any measure of relief. But if the paper money be repudiated, nevertheless we shall have our independence, unless the Southern people should become mad, divided among themselves. Subjugation of a united people, such as ours, occupying such a vast extent of territory, is impossible. The tenure of its occupation by an invading army would always be uncertain, and a million would be required to hold it.

A hard rain commenced falling this evening, and continued in the night. This, I suppose, will put an end to operations in Virginia, and we shall have another respite, and hold Richmond at least another winter. But such weather must cause severe suffering among the prisoners on Belle Isle, where there are not tents enough for so large a body of men. Their government may, however, now consent to an exchange. Day before yesterday some 40,000 rations were sent them by the United States flag-boat—which will suffice for three days, by which time I hope many will be taken away. Our Commissary-General Northrop has but little meat and bread for them, or for our own soldiers in the field. It must be confessed they have but small fare, and, indeed, all of us who have not been "picking and stealing," fare badly. Yet we have quite as good health, and much better appetites than when we had sumptuous living.

November 22d.—We have nothing additional to-day, except another attempt to take Fort Sumter by assault, which was discovered before the crews of the boats landed, and of course it was defeated. Since then some shells have been thrown into the city of Charleston, doing little damage.

This morning was bright and warm, the clouds having passed away in the night.

November 23d.—Nothing of moment from the armies, although great events are anticipated soon.

On Saturday, Gen. Winder's or Major Griswold's head of the passport office, Lieut. Kirk, was arrested on the charge of selling passports at $100 per man to a Mr. Wolf and a Mr. Head, who transported passengers to the Potomac. W. and H. were in prison, and made the charge or confession. This passport business has been our bane ever since Gen. Winder got control of it under Mr. Benjamin. Lieut. K. is from Louisiana, but originally from New York.

Mr. Benjamin sent over to-day extracts from dispatches from

Mr. Slidell and a Mr. Hotze, agent, showing how the government is swindled in Europe by the purchasing agents of the bureaus here. One, named Chiles, in the purchase of $650,000, Mr. Slidell says, was to realize $300,000 profit! And Mr. Hotze (who is he?) says the character and credit of the government are ruined abroad by its own agents! Mr. Secretary Seddon will soon see into this matter.

Capt. Warner says the Federal prisoners here have had no meat for three days, Commissary-General Northrop having none, probably, to issue. One hundred tons rations, however, came up for them yesterday on the flag boat.

Exchange on London sells at $1 for $18.50, and gold brings about the same. Our paper money, I fear, has sunk beyond *redemption*. We have lost *five* steamers lately; and it is likely the port of Wilmington (our last one) will be hermetically sealed. Then we shall soon be destitute of ammunition, unless we retake the mineral country from the enemy.

Mr. Memminger has sent a press to the trans-Mississippi country, to issue paper money there.

Mr. Slidell writes that all our shipments to and from Matamoras ought to be under the French flag. There may be something in this.

The President was expected back to-day; and perhaps came in the evening. He is about to write his message to Congress, which assembles early in December, and perhaps he desired to consult Gen. Lee.

Everywhere the people are clamorous against the sweeping impressments of crops, horses, etc. And at the same time we have accounts of corn, and hay, and potatoes rotting at various depots! Such is the management of the bureaus.

The clerks are in great excitement, having learned that a proposition will be brought forward to put all men under forty-five years of age in the army. It will be hard to carry it; for the heads of departments generally have nephews, cousins, and pets in office, young and rich, who care not so much for the salaries (though they get the best) as for exemption from service in the field. And the editors will oppose it, as they are mostly of conscript age. And the youthful members of Congress could not escape odium if they exempted themselves, unless disabled by wounds.

NOVEMBER 24TH.—The President is expected back to-day. A letter from Gen. Lee indicates that the Commissary-General has been suggesting that he (the general) should impress supplies for his army. This the general deprecates, and suggests that if supplies cannot be purchased, they should be impressed by the agents of the Commissary Department; and that the burden should be laid on the farmers equally, in all the States. Gen. Lee does not covet the odium. But it is plain, now, that the extortionate farmers, who were willing to see us non-producing people starve, unless we paid them ten prices for their surplus products, will be likely to get only the comparatively low schedule price fixed by the government. Instead of $20 per bushel for potatoes, they will receive only $2 or $3. This will be a good enough maximum law. But the government *must* sell to us at cost, or I know not what may be the consequences.

NOVEMBER 25TH.—We have an unintelligible dispatch from Gen. Bragg, saying he had, yesterday, a prolonged contest with the enemy for the possession of Lookout Mountain, during which one of his divisions suffered severely, and that the manœuvring of the hostile army was for position. This was the purport, and the language, as well as I remember. There is no indication of the probable result—no intimation whether the position was gained. But the belief is general that Bragg will retreat, and that the enemy may, if he will, penetrate the heart of the South! To us it *seems* as if Bragg has been in a fog ever since the battle of the 20th of September. He refused to permit —— to move on the enemy's left for nearly two months, and finally consented to it when the enemy had been reinforced by 30,000 from Meade, and by Sherman's army from Memphis, of 20,000, just when he could not spare a large detachment! In other words, lying inert before a defeated army, when concentrated; and dispersing his forces when the enemy was reinforced and concentrated! If disaster ensues, the government will suffer the terrible consequences, for it assumed the responsibility of retaining him in command when the whole country (as the press says) demanded his removal.

From letters received the last few days at the department, I perceive that the agents of the government are impressing everywhere —horses, wagons, hogs, cattle, grain, potatoes, etc. etc.—leaving the farmers only enough for their own subsistence. This will insure subsistence for the army, and I hope it will be a death-blow to speculation, as government pays less than one-fourth the prices demanded in market. Let the government next sell to non-producers, and every man of fighting age will repair to the field, and perhaps the invader may be driven back.

We have the speech of the French Emperor, which gives *us* no encouragement, but foreshadows war with Russia, and perhaps a general war in Europe.

We have rain again. This may drive the armies in Virginia into winter quarters, as the roads will be impracticable for artillery.

The next battle will be terrific; not many men on either side will be easily taken prisoners, *as exchanges have ceased.*

Dr. Powell brought us a bushel of meal to-day, and some persimmons.

NOVEMBER 26TH.—The weather is clear and bright again; but, oh, how dark and somber the faces of the croakers!

The following dispatches have been received:

[BATTLE AT LOOKOUT MOUNTAIN.]

(OFFICIAL DISPATCH.)

"MISSION RIDGE, Nov. 24th, 1863.

"To GEN. S. COOPER.

"We have had a prolonged struggle for Lookout Mountain to-day, and sustained considerable loss in one division. Elsewhere the enemy has only manœuvred for position.

"[Signed] BRAXTON BRAGG, *General.*"

The Latest—Official.

"CHICKAMAUGA, Nov. 25th, 1863.

"GEN. S. COOPER, A. AND I. GENERAL.

"After several unsuccessful assaults on our lines to-day, the enemy carried the left center about four o'clock. The whole left soon gave way in considerable disorder. The right maintained its ground, repelling every assault. I am withdrawing all to this point.

"[Signed] BRAXTON BRAGG.

" Official—JOHN WITHERS, A. A. G."

All agree in the conviction that the enemy has been defeated—perhaps badly beaten.

Hon. H. S. Foote, just arrived from the vicinity of the field, says Bragg has only some 20,000 or 30,000 men, while Grant has 90,000, and he infers that incalculable disaster will ensue.

And Meade is steadily advancing. Gen. Pickett, at Petersburg, has been ordered to send some of his troops north of Richmond, for the defense of the railroad in Hanover County.

Miss Stevenson, sister of Major-Gen. Stevenson, has written the President for employment in one of the departments. He referred it to Mr. Memminger, who indorsed on it, coldly, as usual, there were no vacancies, and a hundred applications. The President sent it to the Secretary of War. He will be more polite.

Another letter to-day from Mr. Memminger, requesting that a company, commanded by a son of his friend, Trenholm, of Charleston, be stationed at Ashville, where his family is staying.

Lieut.-Gen. D. H. Hill has applied for a copy of Gen. Bragg's letter asking his removal from his army. The President sends a copy to the Secretary, who will probably comply, and there may be a personal affair, for Bragg's strictures on Hill as a general were pretty severe.

There are rumors of a break in the cabinet, a majority, it is said, having been in favor of Bragg's removal.

Bragg's disaster so shocked my son Custis that, at dinner, when asked for rice, he poured water into his sister's plate, the pitcher being near.

NOVEMBER 27TH.—Dark and gloomy. At 10 o'clock Gov. Vance, of North Carolina, telegraphed the Secretary of War, asking if anything additional had been heard from Bragg. The Secretary straightened in his chair, and answered that he knew nothing but what was published in the papers.

At 1 o'clock P.M. a dispatch was received from Bragg, dated at *Ringgold, Ga.*, some thirty miles from the battle-field of the day before. Here, however, it is thought he will make a stand. But if he could not hold his mountain position, what can he do in the plain? We know not yet what proportion of his army, guns, and stores he got away—but he must have retreated rapidly.

Meade is advancing, and another battle seems imminent.

To-day a countryman brought a game-cock into the department.

Upon being asked what he intended to do with it, he said it was his purpose to send its left wing to Bragg!

NOVEMBER 28TH.—It rained last night. To-day there is an expectation of a battle near Chancellorville, the battle-ground of June last. Meade is certainly advancing, and Pickett's division, on the south side of the James River, at Chaffin's Farm, is ordered to march toward Lee, guarding the railroad, and the local defense men are ordered out.

My son Custis goes with his battalion to Chaffin's Farm in the morning.

There are rumors of six or eight thousand of the enemy marching up the line of the James River against Petersburg, etc. We have also a rumor of Gen. Rosser having captured the wagon train of two divisions of the enemy in Culpepper County.

From Bragg not a word since his dispatch from Ringgold, Ga., and nothing from Longstreet.

Gen. Whiting writes that a large number of Jews and others with gold, having put in substitutes, and made their fortunes, are applying for passage out of the country. They fear their substitutes will no longer keep them out of the army. Gen. W. says they have passports from Richmond, and that the spy who published in the North an account of the defenses of Wilmington, had a passport from Richmond. The government will never realize the injury of the loose passport system until it is ruined.

Never have I known such confusion. On the 26th inst. the Secretary ordered Gen. Pickett, whose headquarters were at Petersburg, to send a portion of his division to Hanover Junction, it being apprehended that a raid might be made in Lee's rear. Gen. P. telegraphs that the French steam frigate was coming up the river (what for?), and that two Federal regiments and three companies of cavalry menaced our lines on the south side of the river. The Secretary sent this to Gen. Elzey, on this side of the river, asking if his pickets and scouts could not get information of the movements of the enemy. To-day Gen. E. sends back the paper, saying his scouts could not cross the river and get within the enemy's lines. So the government is in a fog—and if the enemy knew it, and it may, the whole government might be taken before any dispositions for defense could be made. Incompetency in Richmond will some day lose it.

Three o'clock P.M. The weather is clear, and Lee and Meade may fight, and it may be a decisive battle.

I met Mr. Foote, of Tennessee, to-day. He asked me if I did not think our affairs were in a desperate condition. I replied that I did not know that they were not, and that when one in my position did not know, they must be bad enough.

NOVEMBER 29TH.—The clerks were marched out into the muddy street this morning in a cold rain, and stood there for hours, while the officers were making up their minds when to start for the boat to convey them to Drewry's Bluff, whence they are to march to Chaffin's Farm, provided the officers don't change their minds.

There are reports of a repulse of the enemy by Lee yesterday, and also of a victory by Bragg, but they are not traceable to authentic sources.

At 3 o'clock P.M. it is cold, but has ceased to rain.

The want of men is our greatest want, and I think it probable Congress will repeal the Substitute Law, and perhaps the Exemption Act. Something must be done to put more men in the ranks, or all will be lost. The rich have contrived to get out, or to keep out, and there are not poor men enough to win our independence. All, with very few exceptions, between the ages of 18 and 45, must fight for freedom, else we may not win it.

NOVEMBER 30TH.—It is clear and cold. The boat in which my son and the battalion of clerks went down the river yesterday, sunk, from being overloaded, just as it got to the landing. It is said some of the boys had to wade ashore; but none were lost—thank God!

This morning early, Lee and Meade confronted each other in battle array, and no one doubts a battle is in progress to-day this side of the Rapidan. Lee is outnumbered some two to one, but Meade has a swollen river in his rear. It is an awful moment.

I took my remaining son to the office this morning, to aid me in Custis's absence.

At night. Nothing has yet been heard from the battle, if indeed it occurred to-day. It is said that Meade is *ordered* to fight. They know at Washington it is too late in the season, in the event of Meade's defeat, for Lee to menace that city, or to invade Pennsylvania. It is a desperate effort to crush the "rebellion," as they suppose, by advancing all their armies. And indeed it seems that

Meade is quite as near to Richmond as Lee; for he seems to be below the latter on the Rappahannock, with his back to Fredericksburg, and Lee's face toward it. If Meade should gain the victory, he might possibly cut off Lee from this city. Nevertheless, these positions are the result of Lee's manœuvres, and it is to be supposed he understands his business. He has no fear of Meade's advance in this direction with his communications cut behind him.

Captain Warner has sold me two pieces of bacon again, out of his own smoke-house, at $1 per pound, while it is selling in the market at $3.50 per pound—and he has given us another bushel of sweet potatoes. Had it not been for this kind friend, my little revenue would not have sufficed for subsistence.

While the soldiers are famishing for food, what is called "red tapeism" prevents the consummation of contracts to supply them. Captains Montgomery and Leathers, old steamboat captains, with ample capital, and owning the only steamboats in certain waters of Florida, have just proposed to furnish the government with a million pounds salt beef, on the main line of railroad in Florida, at a reduced price. The cattle are exposed to incursions of the enemy, and have to be transported by steamboats. They endeavored to make a proposal directly to the Secretary, which was so expressed in the communication I prepared for them—as they were unwilling to treat with Col. Northrop, the Commissary-General, who has become extremely obnoxious. But it was intercepted, and referred to the Commissary-General. Learning this, the captains abandoned their purpose and left the city—the Secretary never having seen their proposal. Our soldiers will not get the beef, and probably the enemy will.

CHAPTER XXXIII.

Assembling of Congress.—President's message.—The markets.—No hope for the Confederate currency.—Averill's raid.—Letter from Gov. Vance.—Christmas.—Persons having furnished substitutes still liable to military duty.

DECEMBER 1ST.—This morning the ground is frozen hard. There was no battle yesterday, only heavy skirmishing. Both armies were drawn up in line of battle, and the front lines slept on their arms. Some froze to death. This morning the enemy opened with artillery—but no battle ensued that we are aware of.

At the last accounts from Bragg he was still retiring, near Dalton. His army must be nearly broken up.

Bragg, it is rumored to-day, has been relieved.

DECEMBER 2D.—No battle yet, though still hourly expected on the old field near the Rappahannock. And we have nothing definite from the West.

The appointment of Beauregard to succeed Bragg is not officially announced; and the programme may be changed.

DECEMBER 3D —Meade recrossed the Rapidan last night! This is a greater relief to us than the enemy has any idea of. I hope the campaign is over for the winter.

And we have authentic advices of a terrible check given the enemy at Ringgold, Ga.; their killed and wounded being estimated at 2000, which caused Grant to recoil, and retire to Chickamauga, where he is intrenching.

After all, it is doubted whether Beauregard is to succeed Bragg. Lieut.-Gen. Hardee is in command, temporarily, and it may be permanently. Bragg was relieved at his own request. I know he requested the same thing many months ago. A full general should command there.

DECEMBER 4TH.—The only thing new to-day is a dispatch from Gen. Longstreet, before Knoxville, stating that he had been repulsed in an assault upon the place, and calling for reinforcements, which, alas! cannot be sent him.

Hon. Mr. Henry, from Tennessee, estimates our loss in prisoners in Bragg's defeat at but little over 1000, and 30 guns. We captured 800 prisoners.

We have intelligence to day of the escape of Brig.-Gen. Jno. H. Morgan from the penitentiary in Ohio, where the enemy had confined him.

DECEMBER 5TH.—It has begun to rain again; and yet the clerks are kept at Chaffin's Bluff, although the roads are impracticable, and no approach of the enemy reported.

There is not a word of news from the armies on the Rapidan or in Georgia.

A collision between the Confederate and State authorities in Georgia is imminent, on the question of "just compensation" for sugar seized by the agents of the Commissary-General—whose estimates for the ensuing year embrace an item of $50,000,000 to be paid for sugar. The Supreme Court of Georgia has decided that if taken, it must be paid for at a fair valuation, and not at a price to suit the Commissary-General. It is the belief of many, that these seizures involve many frauds, to enrich the Commissaries.

DECEMBER 6TH.—It is clear and cold again. Custis came home last evening, after a week's sojourn at Chaffin's Bluff, where, however, there were tents. Some 1500 local troops, or "National Guards," had been sent there to relieve Pickett's division, recalled by Lee; but when Meade recrossed the Rapidan, there was no longer any necessity for the "Guards" to remain on duty. A brigade of regulars goes down to-day. Custis says it was the third day before ammunition was issued! Yesterday he heard shelling down the river, by the enemy's gun-boats.

I had a conversation with Col. Northrop, Commissary-General, to-day. He anticipates a collision between the Confederate and State authorities on the impressment question. He says the law was intended to secure subsistence for both the people and the army; but there is not sufficient grain in the States. Therefore the army must have what there is, and the people must go without. I differed with him, and maintained if a proper distribution were made there would be enough for all.

To-morrow Congress assembles. It is to be apprehended that a conflict with the Executive will ensue—instead of unanimity against the common enemy—and no one living can foretell the issue, because no one knows the extent of capacity and courage on either side.

The President has made his cabinet a unit.

DECEMBER 7TH.—Cold and clear. Gen. Longstreet telegraphs to-day from Rutledge, Tenn., some fifty miles northeast of Knoxville, and says he will soon need railroad facilities. He is flying from superior numbers, and may be gathering up supplies.

Governor Vance writes distressfully concerning the scarcity of provisions in certain counties of North Carolina, and the rudeness of impressing agents.

Lieut.-Gen. Hardee telegraphs from Dalton that 5000 cavalry, besides two brigades of Buckner's command, are with Longstreet, and that other troops ought to be sent him (H.) to compensate for these detachments.

Mr. L. S. White obtained another passport yesterday to go to Maryland, on the recommendation of Col. Gorgas, Chief of Ordnance.

There was a quorum in Congress to-day; but the message was not sent in.

A five-dollar gold piece sold at auction on Saturday for $140—$28 in Confederate notes for one of gold.

DECEMBER 8TH.—The President's message was sent to Congress to-day. I was not present, but my son Custis, who heard it read, says the President dwells largely on the conduct of foreign powers. To diminish the currency, he recommends compulsory funding and large taxation, and some process of diminishing the volume of Treasury notes. In other words, a *suspension* of such clauses of the Constitution as stand in the way of a successful prosecution of the war. He suggests the repeal of the Substitute law, and a modification of the Exemption act, etc. To-morrow I shall read it myself.

DECEMBER 9TH.—The President's message is not regarded with much favor by the croakers. The long complaint against foreign powers for not recognizing us is thought in bad taste, since all the points nearly had been made in a previous message. They say it is like abusing a society for not admitting one within its circle as well as another. The President specifies no plan to cure the redundancy of the currency. He is opposed to increasing the pay of the soldiers, and absolutely reproaches the soldiers of the left wing of Bragg's army with not performing their whole duty in the late battle.

Mr. Foote denounced the President to day. He said he had striven to keep silent, but could not restrain himself while his State was bleeding—our disasters being all attributable by him to the President, who retained incompetent or unworthy men in command, etc.

DECEMBER 10th.—No news from any of the armies, except that Longstreet has reached Bristol, Va.

Yesterday, in Congress, Mr. Foote denounced the President as the author of all the calamities; and he arraigned Col. Northrop, the Commissary-General, as a monster, incompetent, etc.—and cited * * * *

I saw Gen. Bragg's dispatch to-day, dated 29th ult., asking to be relieved, and acknowledging his defeat. He says he must still fall back, if the enemy presses vigorously. It is well the enemy did not know it, for at that moment Grant was falling back on Chattanooga! Mr. Memminger has sent to Congress an impracticable plan of remedying the currency difficulty.

To-day I saw copies of orders given a year ago by Gen. Pemberton to Col. Mariquy and others, to barter cotton with the enemy for certain army and other stores.

It is the opinion of many that the currency must go the way of the old Continental paper, the French assignats, etc., and that speedily.

Passports are again being issued in profusion to persons going to the United States. Judge Campbell, who has been absent some weeks, returned yesterday.

The following prices are quoted in to-day's papers:

"The specie market has still an upward tendency. The brokers are now paying $18 for gold and selling it at $21; silver is bought at $14 and sold at $18.

"GRAIN.—Wheat may be quoted at $15 to $18 per bushel, according to quality. Corn is bringing from $14 to $15 per bushel.

"FLOUR.—Superfine, $100 to $105; Extra, $105 to $110.

"CORN-MEAL.—From $15 to $16 per bushel.

"COUNTRY PRODUCE AND VEGETABLES.—Bacon, hoground, $3

to $3.25 per pound; lard, $3.25 to $3.50; beef, 80 cents to $1; venison, $2 to $2.25; poultry, $1.25 to $1.50; butter, $4 to $4.50; apples, $65 to $80 per barrel; onions, $30 to $35 per bushel; Irish potatoes, $8 to $10 per bushel; sweet potatoes, $12 to $15, and scarce; turnips, $5 to $6 per bushel. These are the wholesale rates.

"GROCERIES.—Brown sugars firm at $3 to $3.25; clarified, $4.50; English crushed, $4.60 to $5; sorghum molasses, $13 to $14 per gallon; rice, 30 to 32 cents per pound; salt, 35 to 40 cents; black pepper, $8 to $10.

"LIQUORS.—Whisky, $55 to $75 per gallon; apple brandy, $45 to $50; rum, proof, $55; gin, $60; French brandy, $80 to $125; old Hennessy, $180; Scotch whisky, $90; champagne (extra), $350 per dozen; claret (quarts), $90 to $100; gin, $150 per case; Alsop's ale (quarts), $110; pints, $60."

DECEMBER 12TH.—There was a rumor that Chattanooga had been evacuated; but it turns out that the enemy are fortifying it, and mean to keep it, while operating in East Tennessee. It is said Gen. Grant is to bring 30,000 men to Virginia, and assume command of the Army of the Potomac, superseding Meade. He may be ordered to take Richmond next—if he can. Hardee is yet commanding Bragg's army.

I saw to-day a project, in Mr. Benjamin's handwriting, for a Bureau of Export and Import.

Mr. G. A. Myers got a passport to-day for a Mr. Pappenheimer, a rich Jew; it was "allowed" by the Assistant Secretary of War. And a Mr. Kerchner (another Jew, I suppose) got one on the recommendation of Col. J. Gorgas, Chief of Ordnance, to bring back stores in his saddle-bags.

Orders to-day were given that no more supplies from the United States should be received by the Federal prisoners here. It seems that our men in their hands are not even allowed the visits of their friends.

DECEMBER 13TH.—Rained last night—and this morning we have warm April weather and bright sunshine.

It is getting to be the general belief among men capable of reflection, that no jugglery can save the Confederate States currency. As well might one lift himself from the earth by seizing his feet, as to legislate a remedy. Whatever scheme may be devised to increase the value of the Confederate States paper money, the obligor is the same. For the redemption of the currency (now worth about five cents in specie to the dollar), every citizen, and every description of property, has been pledged; and as the same citizens and the same property must be pledged for the redemption of any newly created currency, there is no reason to suppose it would not likewise run the same career of depreciation. Nor can bonds be worth more than notes. Success in the field, only, can appreciate either; for none will or can be paid, if we fail to achieve independence.

The weather, this afternoon, is warm, calm, and clear; but the roads are too soft for military operations.

I am reading the Memoirs of Bishop Doane, by his son, Rev. William Croswell Doane. He was the great bishop truly; and his son proves an admirable biographer. I knew the bishop personally, and much of his personal history; and hence this work is to me, and must be to many others, very interesting. The coming year is to be an eventful one. We shall be able (I hope) to put 400,000 effective men in the field; and these, well handled, might resist a million of assailants from without. We have the center, they the circumference; let them beware of 1864—when the United States shall find herself in the throes of an embittered Presidential contest!

DECEMBER 14TH.—We have President Lincoln's message to-day, and his proclamation of amnesty to all who take an oath of allegiance, etc., and advocate emancipation. There are some whom he exempts, of course. It is regarded here as an electioneering document, to procure a renomination for the Presidency in the radical Abolition Convention to assemble in a few months. But it will add 100,000 men to our armies; and next year will be the bloody year.

Congress spent much of the day in secret session.

A Baltimorean, last week, seeing a steamer there loading with goods of various kinds for the Federal prisoners here, bought a box of merchandise for $300, and put it on board, marked as if it contained stores for the prisoners. He ran the blockade so as to meet the steamer here; and obtained his box, worth, perhaps, $15,000. But all this is forbidden hereafter.

DECEMBER 15TH.—Bright, beautiful day—but, alas! the news

continues dark. Two companies of cavalry were surprised and taken on the Peninsula day before yesterday; and there are rumors of disaster in Western Virginia.

Foote still keeps up a fire on the President in the House; but he is not well seconded by the rest of the members, and it is probable the President will regain his control. It is thought, however, the cabinet will go by the board.

DECEMBER 16TH.—The *Examiner* to-day discovers that if the President's project of enrolling all men, and detailing for civil pursuits such as the Executive may designate, be adopted, that he will then be constituted a DICTATOR—the best thing, possibly, that could happen in the opinion of many; though the *Examiner* don't think so. It is probable the President will have what he wants.

Per contra, the proposition of Senator Johnson, of Arkansas, requiring members of the cabinet to be renominated at the expiration of every two years, if passed, would be a virtual seizure of Executive powers by that body. But it won't pass.

DECEMBER 17TH.—Averill (Federal) made a raid a day or two since to Salem (Roanoke County, Va.), cutting the Virginia and Tennessee Railroad, destroying the depot, bridges, court-house, etc.

Gen. J. E. Johnston has been ordered to take command of Bragg's army.

I saw a communication from Lieut.-Col. Ruffin (Commissary Bureau), suggesting the trade of cotton to the enemy in New Orleans for supplies, meat, etc., a Mr. Pollard, of St. Louis, having proposed to barter meat for cotton, which Col. Ruffin seems to discourage.

Gen. Halleck has proposed a plan of exchange of prisoners, so far as those we hold go. We have 15,000; they, 40,000.

A letter from Mr. Underwood, of Rome, Ga., says our people fly from our own cavalry, as they devastate the country as much as the enemy.

We have a cold rain to-day. The bill prohibiting the employment of substitutes has passed both Houses of Congress. When the Conscription act is enlarged, all substitutes now in the army will have to serve for themselves, and their employers will also be liable.

DECEMBER 18TH.—Yesterday evening the battalion of clerks

was to leave for Western Virginia to meet the *raiders*. After keeping them in waiting till midnight, the order was countermanded. It is said now that Gen. Lee has sent three brigades after Averill and his 3000 men, and hopes are entertained that the enemy may be captured.

It is bright and cold to-day.

DECEMBER 19TH.—Bright and cold. A resolution passed Congress, calling on the President to report the number of men of conscript age removed from the Quartermaster's and Commissary's Departments, in compliance with the act of last session. The Commissary-General, in response, refers only to *clerks*—none of whom, however, it seems have been removed.

Capt. Alexander, an officer under Gen. Winder, in charge of Castle Thunder (prison), has been relieved and arrested for malfeasance, etc.

Gen. C. J. McRae, charged with the investigation of the accounts of Isaacs, Campbell & Co., London, with Major Huse, the purchasing agent of Col. J. Gorgas, Chief of Ordnance, reports irregularities, overcharges, etc., and recommends retention of gold and cotton in this country belonging to I., C. & Co.

Mr. —— informed me to-day that he signed a contract with the Commissary-General last night to furnish meat on the Mississippi in Tennessee, in exchange for cotton. He told me that the proposition was made by the Federal officers, and will have their connivance, if not the connivance of Federal functionaries in Washington, interested in the speculation. Lieut.-Col. Ruffin prefers trading with the enemy at New Orleans.

It is rumored that Mr. Seddon will resign, and be succeeded by Gov. Letcher; notwithstanding Hon. James Lyons asserted in public (and it appears in the *Examiner* to-day) that Gov. L. told Gen. J. R. Anderson last year, subsequent to the fall of Donelson, "he was still in favor of the Union."

DECEMBER 20TH.—We have nothing new yet from Averill's raiders; but it is said Gen. Lee has set a trap for them. From East Tennessee there is a report that a battle has taken place somewhere in that region, but with what result is not yet known.

There is much consternation among the Jews and other speculators here, who have put in substitutes and made money. They fear that their substitutes will be made liable by legislative action, and then the principals will be called for. Some have contributed money to prevent the passage of such a law, and others have spent money to get permission to leave the country. Messrs. Gilmer and Myers, lawyers, have their hands full.

The Confederate States Tax act of last session of Congress is a failure, in a great measure, in Virginia. It is said only 30,000 bushels of wheat have been received! But the Governor of Alabama writes that over 5,000,000 pounds of bacon will be paid by that State.

DECEMBER 21ST.—We have dispatches to-day from Western Virginia, giving hope of the capture of Averill and his raiders.

Such is the scarcity of provisions, that rats and mice have mostly disappeared, and the cats can hardly be kept off the table.

DECEMBER 22D.—Averill has escaped, it is feared. But it is said one of his regiments and all his wagons will be lost.

Gen. Longstreet writes (16th instant) that he must suspend active operations for the want of shoes and clothing. The Quartermaster-General says he sent him 3500 blankets a few days since.

There are fifty-one quartermasters and assistant quartermasters stationed in this city!

Pound cakes, size of a small Dutch oven, sell at $100. Turkeys, from $10 to $40.

DECEMBER 23D.—Nothing further from the West. But we have reliable information of the burning (accidentally, I suppose) of the enemy's magazine at Yorktown, destroying all the houses, etc.

I learn to-day that the Secretary of War revoked the order confiscating blockade goods brought from the enemy's country.

DECEMBER 24TH.—Another interposition of Providence in behalf of my family. The bookseller who purchased the edition of the first volume of my "Wild Western Scenes—new series," since Mr. Malsby's departure from the country, paid me $300 to-day, copyright, and promises more very soon. I immediately bought a load of coal, $31.50, and a half cord of wood for $19. I must now secure some food for next month.

Among the papers sent in by the President, to-day, was one from Gen. Whiting, who, from information received by him, believes there will be an attack on Wilmington before long, and asks reinforcements.

One from Gen. Beauregard, intimating that he cannot spare any of his troops for the West, or for North Carolina. The President notes on this, however, that the troops may be sent where they may seem to be actually needed.

Also an application to permit one of Gen. Sterling Price's sons to visit the Confederate States, which the President is not disposed to grant.

The lower house of Congress yesterday passed a bill putting into the army all who have hitherto kept out of it by employing substitutes. I think the Senate will also pass it. There is great consternation among the speculators.

DECEMBER 25TH.—No war news to-day. But a letter, an impassioned one, from Gov. Vance, complains of outrages perpetrated by detached bodies of Confederate States cavalry, in certain counties, as being worse than any of the plagues of Egypt: and says that if any such scourge had been sent upon the land, the children of Israel would not have been followed to the Red Sea. In short, he informs the Secretary of War, if no other remedy be applied, he will collect his militia and levy war against the Confederate States troops! I placed that letter on the Secretary's table, for his Christmas dinner. As I came out, I met Mr. Hunter, President of the Senate, to whom I mentioned the subject. He said, phlegmatically, that many in North Carolina were "prone to act in opposition to the Confederate States Government."

Yesterday the President sent over a newspaper, from Alabama, containing an article marked by him, in which he was very severely castigated for hesitating to appoint Gen. J. E Johnston to the command of the western army. *Why* he sent this I can hardly conjecture, for I believe Johnston has been assigned to that command; but I placed the paper in the hands of the Secretary.

My son Custis, yesterday, distributed proposals for a night-school (classical), and has some applications already. He is resolved to do all he can to aid in the support of the family in these cruel times.

It is a sad Christmas; cold, and threatening snow. My two youngest children, however, have decked the parlor with evergreens, crosses, stars, etc. They have a cedar Christmas-tree, but it is not burdened. Candy is held at $8 per pound. My two sons rose at 5 A.M. and repaired to the canal to meet their sister Anne, who has been teaching Latin and French in the country; but she was not among the passengers, and this has cast a shade of disappointment over the family.

A few pistols and crackers are fired by the boys in the streets—and only a few. I am alone; all the rest being at church. It would not be safe to leave the house unoccupied. Robberies and murders are daily perpetrated.

I shall have no turkey to-day, and do not covet one. It is no time for feasting.

DECEMBER 26TH.—No army news. No papers. No merriment this Christmas. Occasionally an *exempt*, who has speculated, may be seen drunk; but a somber heaviness is in the countenances of men, as well as in the sky above. Congress has adjourned over to Monday.

DECEMBER 27TH.—From Charleston we learn that on Christmas night the enemy's shells destroyed a number of buildings. It is raining to-day: better than snow.

To-day, Sunday, Mr. Hunter is locked up with Mr. Seddon, at the war office. No doubt he is endeavoring to persuade the Secretary not to relinquish office. Mr. S. is the only Secretary of War over whom Mr. Hunter could ever exercise a wholesome influence. Mr. Stephens, the Vice-President, is still absent; and Mr. H. is president of the Senate.

Mr. Hunter is also a member of the Committee on Finance, and the protracted consultations may refer mainly to that subject—and a difficult one it is. Besides, if this revolution be doomed by Providence to failure, Mr. Hunter would be the most potent negotiator in the business of reconstruction. He has great interests at stake, and would save his property—and of course his life.

Another letter from Gov. Vance demands the return of some 300 bales of cotton loaned the Confederate States. He likewise applies for the extension of a detail of a North Carolina soldier, "for satisfactory reasons."

DECEMBER 28TH.—Averill has escaped, losing a few hundred men, and his wagons, etc. The Chesapeake, that sailed out of New York, and was subsequently taken by the passengers (Confederates), was hotly followed to Canada, where it was surrendered to the British authorities by the United States officers, after being abandoned.

DECEMBER 29TH.—A letter from the President, for the Secretary of War, marked "private," came in to-day at 2 P.M. Can it be an acceptance of his resignation?

A resolution has been introduced in the House of Representatives to inquire into the fact of commissioned officers doing clerical duties in Richmond receiving "allowances," which, with their pay, make their compensation enormous. A colonel, here, gets more compensation monthly than Gen. Lee, or even a member of the cabinet!

Mr. Ould, agent of exchange, has sent down some 500 prisoners, in exchange for a like number sent up by the enemy. But he has been instructed by the President not to hold correspondence with Gen. Butler, called "the Beast," who is in command at Fortress Monroe.

My daughters have plaited and sold several hats, etc., and to-day they had a large cake (costing $10) from their savings. And a neighbor sent in some egg-nog to my daughter Anne, just arrived from the country.

Gen. Winder reported to the Secretary, to-day, that there were no guards at the bridges, the militia refusing to act longer under his orders.

DECEMBER 30TH.—A memorial from the army has been presented in both houses of Congress.

The speech of Mr. Foote, relative to a Dictator, has produced some sensation in the city, and may produce more.

A great many Jews and speculators are still endeavoring to get out of the country with their gains.

To-day Mr. Davies paid me $350 more, the whole amount of copyright on the 5000 copies of the first volume of new "Wild Western Scenes," published by Malsby. He proposes to publish the second volume as soon as he can procure the necessary paper.

DECEMBER 31ST.—Yesterday the Senate passed the following bill, it having previously passed the House:

"*A Bill to be entitled An Act to put an end to the exemption from military service of those who have heretofore furnished substitutes.*

"Whereas, in the present circumstances of the country, it requires the aid of all who are able to bear arms, the Congress of the Confederate States of America do enact, That no person shall be exempted from military service by reason of his having furnished a substitute; but this act shall not be so construed as to affect persons who, though not liable to render military service, have, nevertheless, put in substitutes."

It was preceded by discussion, yet only two votes were cast in the negative. Mr. Wigfall, it is said, was strangely indisposed; however that might be, his speech is represented as being one of the best ever delivered by him.

To-morrow the President throws open his house for a public reception: his enemies allege that this is with a view to recovering popularity!

It rained during the whole of this day. Nevertheless, the Jews have been fleeing to the woods with their gold, resolved to take up their abode in the United States rather than fight for the Confederate States, where they leave in the ranks the substitutes hired by them.

CHAPTER XXXIV.

Hospitalities of the city to Gen. Morgan.—Call for a Dictator.—Letter from Gen. Lee.—Letters from Gov. Vance.—Accusation against Gen. Winder.—Treatment of Confederate prisoners (from the *Chicago Times*).—Change of Federal policy.—Efforts to remove Col. Northrop.—Breach between the President and Congress.—Destitution of our prisoners.—Appeal of Gen. Lee to the army.—New Conscription Act.—Letter from Gen. Cobb.

JANUARY 1ST, 1864.—A bright windy day, and not cold. The President has a reception to-day, and the City Councils have voted the hospitalities of the city to Brig.-Gen. J. H. Morgan, whose arrival is expected. If he comes, he will be the hero, and will have a larger crowd of admirers around him than the President. The Councils have also voted a *sword* to ex-Gov. Letcher, whose term of service ended yesterday. Gov. Wm. Smith—nicknamed Extra-Billy—is to be inaugurated to-day.

Flour is now held at $150 per barrel. Capt. Warner has just sold me two bushels of meal at $5 per bushel; the price in market is $16 per bushel.

I did not go to any of the receptions to-day; but remained at home, transplanting lettuce-plants, which have so far withstood the frost, and a couple of fig-bushes I bought yesterday. I am also breaking up some warm beds, for early vegetables, and spreading manure over my little garden: preparing for the siege and famine looked for in May and June, when the enemy encompasses the city. I bought some tripe and liver in the market at the low price of $1 per pound. Engaged to pay $250 hire for our servant this year.

JANUARY 2D.—Gen. Longstreet writes that it will be well to winter in East Tennessee (Rogersville), unless there should be a pressing necessity for him elsewhere. But his corps ought to be at least 20,000. He says provisions may be got in that section; and if they be collected, the enemy may be forced to leave.

The Secretary of the Navy has requested the Secretary of War to open the obstructions at Drewry's Bluff, so that the iron-clads, Richmond and Fredericksburg, may pass out. This he deems necessary for the defense of Richmond, as our iron-clads may prevent the enemy from coming up the river and landing near the city.

The *Lynchburg Virginian* has come out for a dictator, and names Gen. Lee.

The Raleigh (N. C.) *Progress* says we must have peace on any terms, or starvation. I think we can put some 200,000 additional men in the field next year, and they can be fed also.

JANUARY 2D.—Yesterday was the coldest day of the winter, and last night was a bitter one. This morning it is bright and clear, and moderating. We have had no snow yet.

There is much talk everywhere on the subject of a dictator, and many think a strong government is required to abate the evils we suffer. The President has temporarily lost some popularity.

The speculators and extortioners who hired substitutes are in consternation—some flying the country since the passage of the bill putting them in the army, and the army is delighted with the measure. The petition from so many generals in the field intimidated Congress, and it was believed that the Western army would have melted away in thirty days, if no response had been accorded to its demands by government. Herculean preparations will now be made for the next campaign, which is, as usual, looked forward to as the final one.

JANUARY 4TH.—On Saturday, resolutions were unanimously adopted by the Senate complimenting Gen. Lee. This is his opportunity, if he be ambitious,—and who can see his heart? What man ever neglected such an opportunity?

The weather is dark and threatening. Again the rumor is circulated that ex-Gov. Letcher is to be Secretary of War. I don't believe that.

Major Tachman claims $5000 in gold and $1600 paper, because after raising two regiments in 1861 he was not made a brigadier-general. He says he expended that much money. I thought this Polish adventurer would give the government trouble.

Custis commenced his school to-night, with three scholars,—small beginnings, etc.

JANUARY 5TH.—Bright, pleasant day. I saw a letter from Gen. Elzey to-day, stating that his command will probably soon be called out from the city on important service. What can this mean? And our iron-clads are to go below the obstructions if they can get out.

Yesterday Mr. Good offered a resolution declaring the unalterable purpose of Congress to prosecute the war until independence is attained. What significance is in this? Why declare such a purpose at this day?

Mr. Benjamin, Gen. Myers, Col. Preston, and Mr. Seddon are to partake of a feast on Thursday. A feast in time of famine!

JANUARY 6TH.—Yesterday Mr. Moffitt, Lieut.-Col. Ruffin's agent (commissary), was in the market buying beef for Gen. Lee's army! And this same Moffitt was in September selling beef to the same butchers (as they say) at from 40 to 50 cts. gross, the impressing price in the country being 20 cts.

On the 2d inst. Gen. Lee wrote the President that he had just heard of two droves of cattle from the West, destined for his army, being ordered to Richmond. [He does not say by whom, or for what purpose. He knew not.] He says he has but one day's meat rations, and he fears he will not be able to retain the army in the field. The President sent a copy of this to the Commissary-General, with a few mild remarks, suggesting that he shall get such orders from the Secretary of War as are necessary in such an emergency. In response to this the Commissary-General makes a chronological list of his letters to Gen. Lee and others, pretending that if certain things were not done, the army, some day, would come to want, and taking great credit for his foresight, etc. This table of contents he ran first to the department with, but not finding the Secretary, he carried it to the President, who returned it without comment to Col. N. yesterday, and to-day the Secretary got it, not having seen it before. Well, if Col. N. had contracted with Capt. Montgomery for the 1,000,000 pounds of salt beef, it would have been delivered ere this. But the Secretary never saw Capt. M.'s offer at all!

JANUARY 7TH.—Gen. J. E. Johnston dispatches from the West that the meat is so indifferent, the soldiers must have an additional quantity of rice.

Beef sells to-day at $1.25 per pound by the quarter. And yet an Englishman at the best hotel yesterday remarked that he never lived so cheaply in any country, his board being only three shillings (in specie) per diem, or about $20 Confederate States notes.

A dozen china cups and saucers sold at auction to-day for $160. Col. Preston, Conscription Bureau, several members of the cabinet, etc. feasted at a cost of $2000! It is said that the Jack was turned up and *Jeff* turned down in a witticism, and smiled at *nem. con.* But I don't believe that.

We have a light snow, the first time the earth has been white this winter.

I am reminded daily of the privations I used to read of in the Revolutionary War. Then thorns were used, now we use pins, for buttons. My waistbands of pantaloons and drawers are pinned instead of buttoned.

Gen. Jno. H. Morgan arrived this evening, and enjoyed a fine reception, as a multitude of admirers were at the depot.

About the same hour the President rode past my house alone, to indulge his thoughts in solitude in the suburbs of the city.

JANUARY 8TH.—Dispatches from both Beauregard and Whiting indicate a belief of an intention on the part of the enemy to attempt the capture of Charleston and Wilmington this winter. The President directs the Secretary to keep another brigade near Petersburg, that it may be available in an emergency.

It snowed again last night, but cleared off to-day, and is bitter cold.

A memorial was received to-day from the officers of Gen. Longstreet's army, asking that all men capable of performing military service, including those who have hired substitutes, be placed in the army.

To-day I bought a barrel of good potatoes (Irish) for $25, and one of superior quality and size for $30. This is providing for an anticipated season of famine.

Gen. Morgan received the congratulations of a vast multitude to-day. One woman kissed his hand. Gov. Smith advertises a reception to-night.

Yesterday a committee was appointed to investigate the report that a certain member of Congress obtained passports for several absconding Jews, for a bribe.

JANUARY 9TH.—Cold and clear. Gen. Longstreet has preferred charges against Major-Gen. McLaws and another general of his command, and also asks to be relieved, unless he has an independent command, as Gen. Johnston's headquarters are too far off, etc. The Secretary is willing to relieve him, but the President intimates that a successor ought to be designated first.

Beef was held at $2.50 per pound in market to-day—and I got none; but I bought 25 pounds of rice at 40 cts., which, with the meal and potatoes, will keep us alive a month at least. The rich rogues and rascals, however, in the city, are living sumptuously, and spending Confederate States notes as if they supposed they would soon be valueless.

JANUARY 10TH.—Letters from Governor Vance received to-day show that he has been making extensive arrangements to clothe and subsist North Carolina troops. His agents have purchased abroad some 40,000 blankets, as many shoes, bacon, etc., most of which is now at Bermuda and Nassau. He has also purchased an interest in several steamers; but, it appears, a recent regulation of the Confederate States Government forbids the import and export of goods except, almost exclusively, for the government itself. The governor desires to know if his State is to be put on the same footing with private speculators.

He also demands some thousands of bales of cotton, loaned the government—and which the government cannot now replace at Wilmington—and his complaints against the government are bitter. Is it his intention to assume an independent attitude, and call the North Carolina troops to the rescue? A few weeks will develop his intentions.

Mr. Hunter is in the Secretary's room every Sunday morning. Is there some grand political egg to be hatched?

If the government had excluded private speculators from the ports at an early date, we might have had clothes and meat for the army in abundance—as well as other stores. But a great duty was neglected!

Sunday as it is, trains of government wagons are going incessantly past my door laden with ice—for the hospitals next summer, if we keep Richmond.

JANUARY 11TH.—The snow has nearly vanished—the weather bright and pleasant, for midwinter; but the basin is still frozen over.

Gen. E. S. Jones has captured several hundred of the enemy in Southwest Virginia, and Moseby's men are picking them up by scores in Northern Virginia.

Congress recommitted the new Conscript bill on Saturday, intimidated by the menaces of the press, the editors being in danger of falling within reach of conscription.

A dwelling-house near us rented to-day for $6000.

JANUARY 12TH.—Hundreds were skating on the ice in the basin this morning; but it thawed all day, and now looks like rain.

Yesterday the President vetoed a bill appropriating a million dollars to clothe the Kentucky troops. The vote in the Senate, in an effort to pass it nevertheless, was 12 to 10, not two-thirds. The President is unyielding. If the new Conscription act before the House should become a law, the President will have nearly all power in his hands. The act suspending the writ of *habeas corpus*, before the Senate, if passed, will sufficiently complete the Dictatorship.

Gen. Jos. E. Johnston writes in opposition to the organization of more cavalry.

Mr. J. E. Murral, Mobile, Ala., writes Judge Campbell that a party there has authority from the United States authorities to trade anything but arms and ammunition for cotton.

Gen. Winder being directed to send Mr. Hirsh, a rich Jew, to the conscript camp, says he gave him a passport to leave the Confederate States some days ago, on the order of Judge Campbell, A. S. W. Col. Northrop says supplies of meat have failed.

JANUARY 13TH.—There was firing yesterday near Georgetown, S. C., the nature and result of which is not yet known.

Yesterday the Senate passed a bill allowing increased pay to civil officers in the departments; but Senator Brown, of Miss., proposed a *proviso*, which was adopted, allowing the increased compensation only to those who are not liable to perform military duty, and unable to bear arms.

The auctions are crowded—the people seeming anxious to get rid of their money by paying the most extravagant prices for all articles exposed for sale. An old pair of boots, with large holes in them, sold to-day for $7.00—it costs $125 to foot a pair of boots.

JANUARY 14TH.—Mr. A. ——, editor of the ——, recommends the Secretary of War to get Congress to pass, in secret session, a resolution looking to a reconstruction of the Union on the old basis, and send Commissioners to the Northern Governors. Meantime, let the government organize an army of invasion, and march into Pennsylvania. The object being to sow dissension among the parties of the North.

A letter from a Mr. Stephens, Columbia, S. C., to the President, says it is in his power to remove one of the evils which is bringing the administration into disrepute, and causing universal indignation—Gen. Winder. The writer says Winder drinks excessively, is brutish to all but Marylanders, and habitually receives bribes, etc. The President indorsed on it that he did not know the writer, and the absence of specifications usually rendered action unnecessary. But perhaps the Secretary may find Mr. S.'s character such as to deserve attention.

Captain Warner says it is believed there will be a riot, perhaps, when Col. Northrop, the Commissary-General, may be immolated by the mob. Flour sold to-day at $200 per barrel; butter, $8 per pound; and meat from $2 to $4. This cannot continue long without a remedy.

The President has another reception to-night.

"A YANKEE ACCOUNT OF THE TREATMENT OF CONFEDERATE PRISONERS.—The *Chicago Times* gives the account which follows of the treatment of our soldiers at Camp Douglas.

"It is said that about four weeks ago one of the prisoners was kindling his fire, which act he had a right to perform, when one of the guard accosted him with, 'Here, what are you doing there?' The prisoner replied, 'That is not your business,' when the guard instantly drew his musket and shot the fellow dead. It is said also that a mulatto boy, a servant of one of the Confederate captains, and, of course, a prisoner of war, who was well known to have a pass to go anywhere within the lines, was walking inside the guard limits about a day after the above occurrence, when the guard commanded him to halt. He did not stop, and was instantly killed by a bullet.

"It is also charged that, at the time the discovery was made of an attempt on the part of some of the prisoners to escape, a party of three or four hundred was huddled together and surrounded by a guard; that one of them was pushed by a comrade and fell to the ground, and that instantly the unfortunate man was shot, and that three or four others were wounded. It is further stated that it is no uncommon thing for a soldier to fire on the barracks without any provocation whatever, and that two men were thus shot while sleeping in their bunks a week or two ago, no inquiry being made into the matter. No court-martial has been held, no arrest has been made, though within the past month ten or twelve of the prisoners have been thus put out of the way. Another instance need only be given: one of the prisoners asked the guard for a chew of tobacco, and he received the bayonet in his breast without a word."

JANUARY 15TH.—We have no news. But there is a feverish anxiety in the city on the question of subsistence, and there is fear of an outbreak. Congress is in secret session on the subject of the currency, and the new Conscription bill. The press generally is opposed to calling out all men of fighting age, which they say would interfere with the freedom of the press, and would be unconstitutional.

JANUARY 16TH.—General good spirits prevail since Northern arrivals show that the House of Representatives at Washington has passed a resolution that 1,000,000 men, including members of Congress under 50, volunteer to deliver the prisoners of war out of our hands. This produces a general smile, as indicative of the exhaustion of the available military force of the United States

—and all believe it to be the merest bravado and unmitigated humbug. Every preparation will be made by the Confederate States Government for the most stupendous campaign of the war.

There are indications of disorganization (political) in North Carolina—but it is too late. The Confederate States Executive is too strong, so long as Congress remains obedient, for any formidable demonstration of that character to occur in any of the States. We shall probably have martial law everywhere.

I bought some garden seeds to-day, fresh from New York! This people are too improvident, even to sow their own seeds.

JANUARY 17TH.—There is nothing new to-day. The weather is pleasant for the season, the snow being all gone.

Custis has succeeded in getting ten pupils for his night-school, and this will add $100 per month to our income—if they pay him. But with flour at $200 per barrel; meal, $20 per bushel, and meat from $2 to $5 per pound, what income would suffice? Captain Warner (I suppose in return for some writing which Custis did for him) sent us yesterday two bushels of potatoes, and, afterwards, a turkey! This is the first turkey we have had during our housekeeping in Richmond.

I rarely see Robert Tyler nowadays. He used to visit me at my office. His brother John I believe is in the trans-Mississippi Department. My friend Jacques is about town occasionally.

JANUARY 18TH.—A flag of truce boat came up, but no one on board was authorized to negotiate for an exchange of prisoners but Gen. Butler, outlawed. It returns without anything being effected. Congress has passed a bill for the reduction of the currency, in secret session. We know not yet what are its main features. The Senate bill increasing the compensation of civil officers has not yet been acted on in the House, and many families are suffering for food.

Anne writes us that Lieut. Minor has returned from his Canada expedition, which failed, in consequence of the gratuitous action of Lord Lyons, the British Minister at Washington, who has been secured in the interest of the Federal Government, it is said, by bribes. Lieut. M. brought his family a dozen cups and saucers, dresses, shoes, etc., almost unattainable here.

The President receives company every Tuesday evening.

Among the letters referred by the Commissary-General to the Secretary of War to-day for instructions, was one from our honest commissary in North Carolina, stating that there were several million pounds of bacon and pork in Chowan and one or two other counties, liable to the incursions of the enemy, which the people were anxious to sell the government, but were afraid to bring out themselves, lest the enemy should ravage their farms, etc., and suggesting that a military force be sent thither with wagons. The Commissary-General stated none of these facts in his indorsement; but I did, so that the Secretary must be cognizant of the nature of the paper.

The enemy made a brief raid in Westmoreland and Richmond counties a few days ago, and destroyed 60,000 pounds of meat in one of the Commissary-General's depots! A gentleman writing from that section, says it is a pity the President's heart is not in his head; for then he would not ruin the country by retaining his friend, Col. Northrop, the Commissary-General, in office.

It appears that Gen. Meade has changed the Federal policy in the Northern Neck, by securing our people within his lines from molestation; and even by allowing them to buy food, clothing, etc. from Northern traders, on a pledge of strict neutrality. The object is to prevent the people from conveying intelligence to Moseby, who has harassed his flanks and exposed detachments very much. It is a more dangerous policy for us than the old habit of scourging the non-combatants that fall in their power.

JANUARY 19TH.—A furious storm of wind and rain occurred last night, and it is rapidly turning cold to-day.

The prisoners here have had no meat during the last four days, and fears are felt that they will break out of confinement.

Yesterday Senator Orr waited upon the President, to induce him to remove Col. Northrop, the obnoxious Commissary-General. The President, it is said, told him that Col. N. was one of the greatest geniuses in the South, and that, if he had the physical capacity he would put him at the head of an army.

A letter from Mrs. Polk, widow of President Polk, dated at Nashville, expresses regret that a portion of her cotton in Mississippi was burnt by the military authorities (according to law), and demanding remuneration. She also asks permission to have the remainder sent to Memphis, now held by the enemy. The Secretary will not refuse.

I bought a pretty good pair of second-hand shoes at auction today for $17.50; but they were too large. I will have them sold again, without fear of loss.

A majority of the Judiciary Committee, to whom the subject was referred, have reported a bill in the Senate vacating the offices of all the members of the cabinet at the expiration of every two years, or of every Congress. This is a blow at Mr. Benjamin, Mr. Memminger, etc., and, as the President conceives, at himself. It will not pass, probably; but it looks like war between the Senate and the Executive. Some of the Secretaries *may* resign on the 18th of February, when this Congress expires. *Nous verrons.*

JANUARY 20TH.—The Senate bill to give increased compensation to the civil officers of the government in Richmond was *tabled* in the House yesterday, on the motion of Mr. Smith, of North Carolina, who spoke against it.

Major-Gen. Gilmer, Chief of the Engineer Bureau, writes that the time has arrived when no more iron should be used by the Navy Department; that no iron-clads have effected any good, or are likely to effect any; and that all the iron should be used to repair the roads, else we shall soon be fatally deficient in the means of transportation. And Col. Northrop, Commissary-General, says he has been trying to concentrate a reserve supply of grain in Richmond, for eight months; and such has been the deficiency in means of transportation, that the effort has failed.

Gov. Milton, of Florida, writes that the fact of quartermasters and commissaries, and their agents, being of conscript age, and being speculators all, produces great demoralization. If the rich will not fight for their property, the poor will not fight for them.

Col. Northrop recommends that each commissary and quartermaster be allowed a confidential clerk of conscript age. That would deprive the army of several regiments of men.

The weather is bright again, but cool.

JANUARY 21ST.—Gen. Longstreet reports some small captures of the enemy's detached foraging parties.

The prisoners here have now been six days without meat; and Capt. Warner has been ordered by the Quartermaster-General to purchase supplies for them, relying no longer on the Commissary-General.

Last night an attempt was made (by his servants, it is supposed) to burn the President's mansion. It was discovered that fire had been kindled in the wood-pile in the basement. The smoke led to the discovery, else the family might have been consumed with the house. One or two of the servants have absconded.

At the sale of a Jew to-day an *etegere* brought $6000; a barrel of flour, $220; and meal, $25 per bushel. All else in proportion. He is a jeweler, and intends leaving the country. He will succeed, because he is rich.

Yesterday the House passed the Senate bill, adjourning Congress on the 18th of February, to meet again in April. Mr. Barksdale, the President's organ in the House, moved a reconsideration, and it will probably be reconsidered and defeated, although it passed by two to one.

Major Griswold being required by resolution of the Legislature to give the origin of the passport office, came to me to-day to write it for him. I did so. There was no law for it.

JANUARY 22D.—Troops, a few regiments, have been passing down from Lee's army, and going toward North Carolina. A dispatch, in cipher, from Petersburg, was received to-day at 3 P.M. It is probable the enemy threaten the Weldon and Wilmington Railroad. We shall hear soon.

It is thought the negroes that attempted to burn the President's house (they had heaped combustibles under it) were instigated by Yankees who have been released upon taking the oath of allegiance. But I think it quite as probable his enemies here (citizens) instigated it. They have one of the servants of the War Department under arrest, as participating in it.

The weather is delightful, and I seek distraction by spading in my garden.

Judge Campbell is still "allowing" men to pass out of the Confederate States; and they will invite the enemy in!

JANUARY 23D.—The Secretary of War has authorized Mr. Boute, President of the Chatham Railroad, to exchange tobacco through the enemy's lines for bacon. And in the West he has given authority to exchange cotton with the enemy for meat. It is supposed certain men in high position in Washington, as well as the military authorities, wink at this traffic, and share its profits. I hope we may get bacon, without strychnine.

Congress has passed a bill prohibiting, under severe penalties, the traffic in Federal money. But neither the currency bill, the tax bill, nor the repeal of the exemption act has been effected yet, and the existence of the present Congress shortly expires. A *permanent* government is a cumbersome one.

The weather is fine, and I am spading up my little garden.

JANUARY 24TH.—For some cause, we had no mail to-day. Fine, bright, and pleasant weather. Yesterday Mr. Lyons called up the bill for increased compensation to civil officers, and made an eloquent speech in favor of the measure. I believe it was referred to a special committee, and hope it may pass soon.

It is said the tax bill under consideration in Congress will produce $500,000,000 revenue! If this be so, and compulsory funding be adopted, there will soon be no redundancy of paper money, and a magical change of values will take place. We who live on salaries may have better times than even the extortioners—who cannot inherit the kingdom of Heaven. And relief cannot come too soon: for we who have families are shabby enough in our raiment, and lean and lank in our persons. Nevertheless, we have health and never-failing appetites. Roasted potatoes and salt are eaten with a keen relish.

JANUARY 25TH.—The breach seems to widen between the President and Congress, especially the Senate. A majority of the Committee on Military Affairs have reported that Col. A. C. Myers (relieved last August) is still the Quartermaster-General of the armies, and that Gen. Lawton, who has been acting as Quartermaster-General since then, is not the duly authorized Quartermaster-General: not having given bond, and his appointment not having been consented to by the Senate. They say all the hundreds of millions disbursed by his direction have been expended in violation of law.

For the last few nights Col. Browne, one of the President's A. D. C.'s, and an unnaturalized Englishman, has ordered a guard (department clerks) to protect the President. Capt. Manico (an Englishman) ordered my son Custis to go on guard to-night; but I obtained from the Secretary a countermand of the order, and also an exemption from drills, etc. It will not do for him to neglect his night-school, else we shall starve.

I noticed, to-day, eight slaughtered deer in one shop; and they are seen hanging at the doors in every street. The price is $3 per pound. Wild turkies, geese, ducks, partridges, etc. are also exposed for sale, at enormous prices, and may mitigate the famine now upon us. The war has caused an enormous increase of wild game. But ammunition is difficult to be obtained. I see some perch, chubb, and other fish, but all are selling at famine prices.

The weather is charming, which is something in the item of fuel. I sowed a bed of early York cabbage, to-day, in a sheltered part of the garden, and I planted twenty-four grains of early-sweet corn, some cabbage seed, tomatoes, beets, and egg-plants in my little hot-bed—a flour barrel sawed in two, which I can bring into the house when the weather is cold. I pray God the season may continue mild, else there must be much suffering. *And yet no beggars are seen in the streets.* What another month will develope, I know not; the fortitude of the people, so far, is wonderful.

Major-Gen. Sam. Jones, Dublin, Va., is at loggerheads with Lieut.-Gen. Longstreet about some regiments the latter keeps in East Tennessee. Gen. J. says Averill is preparing to make another raid on the Virginia and Tennessee Railroad, the salt-works, the mines, etc.; and if he is charged with the defense, he must have at least all his regiments. He gets his orders from Gen. Cooper, A. and I. G., who will probably give him what he wants.

JANUARY 26TH.—Gen. Lee recommends the formation of several more brigades of cavalry, mostly from regiments and companies in South Carolina, and to this he anticipates objections on the part of the generals and governors along the Southern seaboard; but he deems it necessary, as the enemy facing him has a vastly superior cavalry force.

The prisoners on Belle Isle (8000) have had no meat for eleven days. The Secretary says the Commissary-General informs him that they fare as well as our armies, and so he refused the commissary (Capt. Warner) of the prisoners a permit to buy and bring to the city cattle he might be able to find. An outbreak of the prisoners is apprehended : and if they were to rise, it is feared some of the inhabitants of the city would join them, for they, too, have no meat—many of them—or bread either. They believe the famine is owing to the imbecility, or worse, of the government. A riot would be a dangerous occurrence, now: the city battalion would not fire on the people—and if they did, the army might break up, and avenge their slaughtered kindred. It is a perilous time.

My wife paid $12, to-day, for a half bushel of meal; meantime I got an order for two bushels, from Capt. Warner, at $10 per bushel.

The President receives visitors to-night; and, for the first time, I think I will go.

Mr. Foote, yesterday, offered a resolution that the Commissary-General ought to be removed; which was defeated by a decided vote, twenty in the affirmative. Twenty he relied on failed him. Letters from all quarters denounce the Commissary-General and his agents.

JANUARY 27TH.—Last night, the weather being very pleasant, the President's house was pretty well filled with gentlemen and ladies. I cannot imagine how they continue to dress so magnificently, unless it be their old finery, which looks well amid the general aspect of shabby mendicity. But the statures of the men, and the beauty and grace of the ladies, surpass any I have seen elsewhere, in America or Europe. There is high character in almost every face, and fixed resolve in every eye.

The President was very courteous, saying to each, "I am glad to meet you here to-night." He questioned me so much in regard to my health, that I told him I was not very well; and if his lady (to whom he introduced us all) had not been so close (at his elbow), I might have assigned the cause. When we parted, he said, "*We* have met before." Mrs. Davis was in black—for her father. And many of the ladies were in mourning for those slain in battle.

Gen. Lee has published the following to his army:

"HEADQUARTERS ARMY OF NORTHERN VIRGINIA,
"January 22d, 1864.

"GENERAL ORDERS No 7.

"The Commanding General considers it due to the army to state that the temporary reduction of rations has been caused by circumstances beyond the control of those charged with its support. Its welfare and comfort are the objects of his constant and earnest solicitude; and no effort has been spared to provide for its wants. It is hoped that the exertions now being made will render the necessity but of short duration: but the history of the army has shown that the country can require no sacrifice too great for its patriotic devotion.

"Soldiers! you tread, with no unequal steps, the road by which your fathers marched through suffering, privation, and blood to independence!

"Continue to emulate in the future, as you have in the past, their valor in arms, their patient endurance of hardships, their high resolve to be free, which no trial could shake, no bribe seduce, no danger appal: and be assured that the just God, who crowned their efforts with success, will, in His own good time, send down His blessings upon yours.

"(Signed) R. E. LEE, *General.*"

An eloquent and stirring appeal!

It is rumored that the writ of *habeas corpus* has been suspended —as the President has been allowed to suspend it—by Congress, in secret session. But Congress passed a resolution, yesterday, that after it adjourns on the 18th February, it will assemble again on the first Monday in May.

Mr. Lyons, chairman of the Committee on Increased Compensation to the civil officers, had an interview with the Secretary of War yesterday. The Secretary told him, it is said, that unless Congress voted the increase, he would take the responsibility of ordering them rations, etc. etc. And Mr. Smith, of North Carolina, told me, to-day, that something would be done. He it was who moved to lay the bill on the table. He said it would have been defeated, if the vote had been taken on the bill.

Gov. Smith sent to the Legislature a message, yesterday, rebuking the members for doing so little, and urging the passage of a bill putting into the State service all between the ages of sixteen and eighteen and over forty-five. The Legislature considered his lecture an insult, and the House of Delegates contemptuously laid it on the table by an almost unanimous vote. So he has war with the Legislature, while the President is in conflict with the Confederate States Senate.

JANUARY 28TH.—The beautiful, pleasant weather continues.

It is said Congress passed, last night, in secret session, the bill allowing increased compensation to civil officers and employees.

Mr. Davidson, of fifty years of age, resigned, to-day, his clerkship in the War Department, having been offered $5000 by one of the incorporated companies to travel and buy supplies for it.

Mr. Hubbard, of Alabama, suggests to the Secretary to buy 500,000 slaves, and give one to every soldier enlisting from beyond our present lines, at the end of the war. He thinks many from the border free States would enlist on our side. The Secretary does not favor the project.

Gen. Whiting writes for an order for two locomotive boilers, at Montgomery, Ala., for his torpedo-boats, now nearly completed. He says he intends to attack the blockading squadron off Wilmington.

The weather is still warm and beautiful. The buds are swelling.

JANUARY 30TH.—The Senate has passed a new Conscription Act, putting all residents between the ages of eighteen and fifty-five in the military service for the war. Those over forty-five to be detailed by the President as commissary quartermasters, Nitre Bureau agents, provost guards, clerks, etc. This would make up the enormous number of 1,500,000 men! The express companies are to have no detail of men fit for the field, but the President may exempt a certain class for agricultural purposes, which, of course, can be revoked whenever a farmer refuses to sell at schedule prices, or engages in speculation or extortion. Thus the President becomes almost absolute, and the Confederacy a military nation. The House will pass it with some modifications. Already the *Examiner* denounces it, for it allows only one owner or editor to a paper, and just sufficient printers,— no assistant editors, no reporters, no clerks, etc. This will save us, and hasten a peace.

Mr. G. A. Myers, the little old lawyer, always potential with the successive Secretaries of War, proposes, in a long letter, that the Department allows 30 to 40 foreigners (Jews) to leave the Confederate States, *via* Maryland, every week!

Mr. Goodman, President of the Mississippi Railroad, proposes to send cotton to the Yankees in exchange for implements, etc., to repair the road, and Lieut.-Gen. (Bishop) Polk favors the scheme.

Commissary-General Northrop likewise sent in a proposal from an agent of his in Mississippi, to barter cotton with the Yankees for subsistence, and he indorses an approval on it. I trust we shall be independent this summer.

To-day it is cool and cloudy, but Custis has had no use for fire in his school-room of nights for a week—and that in January. The warm weather saved us a dollar per day in coal. Custis's scholars are paying him $95 the first month.

I shall hope for better times now. We shall have men enough, if the Secretary and conscription officers do not strain the meshes of the seine too much, and the currency will be reduced. The speculators and extortioners, in great measure, will be circumvented, for the new conscription will take them from their occupations, and they will not find transportation for their wares.

The 2000 barrels of corn destroyed by the enemy on the Peninsula, a few days ago, belonged to a relative of Col. Ruffin, Assistant Commissary-General! He would not impress that—and lo! it is gone! Many here are glad of it.

JANUARY 31ST.—It rained moderately last night, and is cooler this morning. But the worst portion of the winter is over. The pigeons of my neighbor are busy hunting straws in my yard for their nests. They do no injury to the garden, as they never scratch. The shower causes my turnips to present a fresher appearance, for they were suffering for moisture. The buds of the cherry trees have perceptibly swollen during the warm weather.

A letter from Gen. Cobb (Georgia) indicates that the Secretary of War has refused to allow men having employed substitutes to form new organizations, and he combats the decision. He says they will now appeal to the courts, contending that the law putting them in the service is unconstitutional, and some will escape from the country, or otherwise evade the law. They cannot go into old companies and be sneered at by the veterans, and commanded by their inferiors in fortune, standing, etc. He says the decision will lose the service 2000 men in Georgia.

The Jews are fleeing from Richmond with the money they have made.

CHAPTER XXXV.

Gen. Lovell applies for a command.—Auspicious opening of 1864.—Mr. Wright's resolutions.—Rumored approach of Gen. Butler.—Letter from Gov. Brown.—Letter from Gen. Lee.—Dispatches from Gen. Beauregard. —President Davis's negroes.—Controversy between Gen. Winder and Mr. Ould.—Robbery of Mr. Lewis Hayman.—Promotion of Gen. Bragg, and the *Examiner* thereon.—Scarcity of provisions in the army.—Congress and the President.

FEBRUARY 1ST.—Hazy, misty weather. Gen. Lovell (who lost New Orleans) has applied for a command in the West, and Gen. Johnston approves it strongly. He designs dividing his army into three corps, giving one (3d division) to Gen. Hardee; one (2d division) to Gen. Hindman; and one (1st division) to Lovell. But the Secretary of War (wide awake) indorses a disapproval, saying, in his opinion, it would be injudicious to place a corps under the command of Gen. Lovell, and it would not give confidence to the army. This being sent to the President, came back indorsed, "opinion concurred in.—J. D."

Gen. Pillow has applied for the command of two brigades for operations between Gen. Johnston's and Gen. Polk's armies, protecting the flanks of both, and guarding the coal mines, iron works, etc. in Middle Alabama. This is strongly approved by Generals Johnston, Polk, Gov. Watts & Co. But the President has not yet decided the matter.

The Commissary-General is appointing many ladies to clerkships. Old men, disabled soldiers, and ladies are to be relied on for clerical duty, nearly all others to take the field. But every ingenuity is resorted to by those having in substitutes to evade military service.

There is a great pressure of foreigners (mostly Irish) for passes to leave the country.

FEBRUARY 2D.—So lax has become Gen. Winder's rule, or deficient, or worse, the vigilance of his detectives,—the rogues and cut-throats,—one of them keeps a mistress in a house the rent of which is more than his salary, that five Jews, the other day, cleared out in a schooner laden with tobacco, professedly for Petersburg, but sailed directly to the enemy. They had with them some $10,000 in gold; and as they absconded to avoid military service in the Confederate States, no doubt they imparted all the information they could to the enemy.

Mr. Benjamin, Secretary of State, asked the Secretary of War to-day to make such arrangements as would supply the State Department with regular files of Northern papers. They sometimes have in them important diplomatic correspondence, and the perusal of this is about all the Secretary of State has to do.

It is rumored that the Hon. Robert Toombs has been arrested in Georgia for treason. I cannot believe it, but I know he is inimical to the President.

The British papers again seem to sympathise with us.

Senator Orr writes to the Secretary that a resolution of the Senate, asking for copies of Gen. Beauregard's orders in 1862 for the fortification of Vicksburg (he was the first to plan the works which made such a glorious defense), and also a resolution calling for a copy of Gen. B.'s charges against Col. ——, had not been responded to by the President. He asks that these matters may be brought to the President's attention.

The weather is beautiful and spring-like again, and we may soon have some news both from Tennessee and North Carolina. From the latter I hope we shall get some of the meat endangered by the proximity of the enemy.

FEBRUARY 3D.—The following dispatch indicates the prestige of success for the year 1864, and it is probable it will be followed by a succession of successes, for the administration at Washington will find, this year, constant antagonisms everywhere, in the North as well as in the South, and in the army there will be opposing parties—Republicans and Democrats. On the part of the South, we have experienced the great agony of 1863, and have become so familiar with horrors that we shall fight with a fearful desperation. But the dispatch:

"Glorious news! The whole Yankee force, about 150, are our prisoners, and their gun-boat 'Smith Briggs,' destroyed.

"No one hurt on our side. Four Yankees killed and two or three wounded.

"The prisoners are now at Broad Water. Send down a train for them to-morrow."

We learn that this Yankee force was commissioned to destroy a large factory at Smithfield, in Isle of Wight County. We do not know the size or composition of our command which achieved the results noticed above, but understand that it contained two companies of the Thirty-first North Carolina Regiment.

Congress has not yet finally acted on the Tax bill, nor on the new Conscription bill.

The Secretary of War said to-day that he would not allow the increased pay to any of his civil officers who were young and able to bear arms—and this after urging Congress to increase their compensation. It will be very hard on some who are refugees, having families dependent on them. Others, who board, must be forced into the army (the design), for their expenses per month will be some fifty per cent. more than their income.

The weather is clear but colder.

FEBRUARY 4TH.—Clear and pretty cold. We have news of another brilliant affair at Kinston, N. C., where Gen. Pickett has beaten the enemy, killing and wounding and taking some 500 men, besides capturing another gun-boat! Thus the campaign of 1864 opens auspiciously.

And Gen. Early has beaten the foe in Hardy County, Northwest Virginia, capturing, it is said, some 800.

It is supposed that Gen. Pickett will push on to Newbern, and probably capture the town. At all events we shall get large supplies from the tide-water counties of North Carolina. General Lee planned the enterprise, sending some 15,000 men on the expedition.

Yesterday the Senate Committee reported *against* the House bill modifying the act making all men liable to conscription who have hired substitutes. But they are debating a new exemption bill in the House.

It is true Mr. Toombs was arrested at Savannah, or was ejected from the cars because he would not procure a passport.

To-day Mr. Kean, the young Chief of the Bureau of War, has registered all the clerks, the dates of their appointments, their age, and the number of children they have. He will make such remarks as suits him in each case, and submit the list to the Secretary for his action regarding the increased compensation. Will he intimate that his own services are so indispensable that he had better remain out of the field?

The following "political card" for the Northern Democrats was played yesterday. I think it a good one, if nothing more be said about it here. It will give the Abolitionists trouble in the rear while we assail them in the front.

The following extraordinary resolutions were, yesterday, introduced in the House of Representatives by Mr. Wright of Georgia. The House went into secret session before taking any action upon them.

"WHEREAS: The President of the United States, in a late public communication, did declare that no propositions for peace had been made to that government by the Confederate States, when, in truth, such propositions were prevented from being made by the President of the United States, in that he refused to hear, or even to receive, two commissioners, appointed to treat expressly of the preservation of amicable relations between the two governments.

"Nevertheless, that the Confederate States may stand justified in the sight of the conservative men of the North of all parties, and that the world may know which of the two governments it is that urges on a war unparalleled for the fierceness of the conflict, and intensifying into a sectional hatred unsurpassed in the annals of mankind. Therefore,

"*Resolved*, That the Confederate States invite the United States, through their government at Washington, to meet them by representatives equal to their representatives and senators in their respective Congress at ——, on the —— day of —— next, to consider,

"*First:* Whether they cannot agree upon the recognition of the Confederate States of America.

"*Second:* In the event of such recognition, whether they cannot agree upon the formation of a new government, founded upon the equality and sovereignty of the States; but if this cannot be done, to consider

"*Third:* Whether they cannot agree upon treaties, offensive, defensive, and commercial.

"*Resolved,* In the event of the passage of these resolutions, the President be requested to communicate the same to the Government at Washington, in such manner as he shall deem most in accordance with the usages of nations; and, in the event of their acceptance by that government, he do issue his proclamation of election of delegates, under such regulations as he may deem expedient."

Eighteen car loads of coffee went up to the army to-day. I have not tasted coffee or tea for more than a year.

FEBRUARY 5TH.—Bright frosty morning, but warmer and hazy later in the day. From dispatches from North Carolina, it would seem that our generals are taking advantage of the fine roads, and improving the opportunity, while the enemy are considering the plan of the next campaign at Washington.

FEBRUARY 6TH.—Major-Gen. Breckinridge, it is said, is to command in Southwestern Virginia near the Kentucky line, relieving Major-Gen. Sam Jones.

Yesterday the cabinet decided to divide the clerks into three classes. Those under eighteen and over forty-five, to have the increased compensation; those between those ages, who shall be pronounced unable for field service, also to have it; and all others the Secretaries may certify to be necessary, etc. This will cover all their cousins, nephews, and pets, and exclude many young men whose refugee mothers and sisters are dependent on their salaries for subsistence. Such is the unvarying history of public functionaries.

Gen. Pickett, finding Newbern impregnable, has fallen back, getting off his prisoners, etc. But more troops are going to North Carolina.

FEBRUARY 7TH, SUNDAY.—*The tocsin is sounding at* 9 A.M. It appears that Gen. Butler is marching up the Peninsula (I have not heard the estimated number of his army) toward Richmond. But, being in the Secretary's room for a moment, I heard him say to Gen. Elzey that the "local defense men" must be relied on to defend Richmond. These men are mainly clerks and employees of the departments, who have just been *insulted* by the government, being informed that no increased compensation will be allowed them because they are able to bear arms. In other words, they must famish for subsistence, and their families with them, because they happen to be of fighting age, and have been patriotic enough to volunteer for the defense of the government, and have drilled, and paraded, and marched, until they are pronounced good

AT THE CONFEDERATE STATES CAPITAL. 145

soldiers. Under these circumstances, the Secretary of War says they must be relied upon to defend the government. In my opinion, many of them are *not* reliable. Why were they appointed contrary to law? Who is to blame but the Secretaries themselves? Ah! but the Secretaries had pets and relatives of fighting age they must provide for; and *these*, although not dependent on their salaries, will get the increased compensation, and will also be exempted from aiding in the defense of the city—at least such has been the practice heretofore. These things being known to the proscribed local troops (clerks, etc.), I repeat my doubts of their reliability at any critical moment.

We have good news from the Rappahannock. It is said Gen. Rosser yesterday captured several hundred prisoners, 1200 beeves, 350 mules, wagons of stores, etc. etc.

Nevertheless, there is some uneasiness felt in the city, there being nearly 12,000 prisoners here, and all the veteran troops of Gen. Elzey's division are being sent to North Carolina.

FEBRUARY 8TH.—The air is filled with rumors—none reliable.

It is said Gen. Lee is much provoked at the alarm and excitement in the city, which thwarted a plan of his to capture the enemy on the Peninsula; and the militia and the Department Battalions were kept yesterday and to-day under arms standing in the cold, the officers blowing their nails, and "waiting orders," which came not. Perhaps they were looking for the "conspirators;" a new hoax to get "martial law."

A Union meeting has been held in Greensborough, N. C. An intelligent writer to the department says the burden of the speakers, mostly lawyers, was the terrorism of Gen. Winder and his corps of rogues and cut-throats, Marylanders, whose operations, it seems, have spread into most of the States. Mr. Sloan, the writer, says, however, a vast majority of the people are loyal.

It is said Congress is finally about to authorize martial law.

My cabbages are coming up in my little hot-bed—half barrel.

Gen. Maury writes from Mobile that he cannot be able to obtain any information leading to the belief of an intention on the part of the enemy to attack Mobile. He says it would require 40,000 men, after three months' preparation, to take it.

Gov. Brown, of Georgia, says the Confederate States Government has kept bad faith with the Georgia six months' men; and hence they cannot be relied on to relieve Gen. Beauregard, etc. (It is said the enemy are about to raise the siege of Charleston.) Gov. B. says the State Guard are already disbanded. He says, moreover, that the government here, if it understood its duty, would not seize and put producers in the field, but would stop details, and order the many thousand young officers everywhere swelling in the cars and hotels, and basking idly in every village, to the ranks. He is disgusted with the policy here. What are we coming to?

Everywhere our troops in the field, whose terms of three years will expire this spring, are re-enlisting for the war. This is an effect produced by President Lincoln's proclamation; that to be *permitted* to return to the Union, all men must first take an oath to abolish slavery!

FEBRUARY 9TH.—A letter from Gen. Johnston says he received the "confidential instructions" of the President, from the Secretary of War, and succeeded in getting Gen. Cleburn to lay aside his "memorial," the nature of which is not stated; but I suspect the President was getting alarmed at the disposition of the armies to dictate measures to the government.

Hon. Mr. Johnson, Senator, and Hon. Mr. Bell, Representative from Missouri, called on me to-day, with a voluminous correspondence, and "charges and specifications" against Lieut.-Gen. Holmes, by my nephew, Lieut.-Col. R. H. Musser. They desired me to read the papers and submit my views. I have read them, and shall advise them not to proceed in the matter. Gen. Holmes is rendered unfit, by broken health, for the command of a Western Department, and his conviction at this time would neither benefit the cause nor aid Lieut.-Col. Musser in his aspirations. It is true he had my nephew tried for disobedience of orders; but he was honorably acquitted. Missouri will some day rise like a giant, and deal death and destruction on her oppressors.

Col. Gorgas, Chief of Ordnance, says the enemy have taken more guns from us than we from them—exclusive of siege artillery —but I don't think so.

Our people are becoming more hopeful since we have achieved some successes. The enemy cannot get men again except by dragging them out, unless they should go to war with France—a not improbable event.

FEBRUARY 10TH.—Gen. Lee wrote to the Secretary of War, on

the 22d of January, that his army was not fed well enough to fit them for the exertions of the spring campaign; and recommended the discontinuance of the rule of the Commissary-General allowing officers at Richmond, Petersburg, and many other towns, to purchase government meat, etc. etc. for the subsistence of their families, at schedule prices. He says the salaries of these officers ought to be sufficient compensation for their services; that such allowances deprived the officers and soldiers *in the field* of necessary subsistence, and encouraged able-bodied men to seek such easy positions; it offended the people who paid tithes, to see them consumed by these non-combating colonels, majors, etc., instead of going to feed the army; and it demoralized the officers and soldiers in the field.

This letter was referred to the Commissary-General, who, after the usual delay, returned it with a long argument to show that Gen. Lee was in "*error*," and that the practice was necessary, etc.

To this the Secretary responded by a peremptory *order*, restricting the city officers in the item of meat.

Again the Commissary-General sends it back, recommending the *suspension* of the order until it be seen what Congress will do! Here are twenty days gone, and the Commissary-General has his own way still. He don't hesitate to bully the Secretary and the highest generals in the field. Meantime the Commissary-General's pet officers and clerks are living sumptuously while the soldiers are on hard fare. But, fortunately, Gen. Lee has captured 1200 beeves from the enemy since his letter was written.

And Gen. Cobb writes an encouraging letter from Georgia. He says there is more meat in that State than any one supposed; and men too. Many thousands of recruits can be sent forward, and meat enough to feed them.

The President has issued a stirring address to the army.

The weather is still clear, and the roads are not only good, but dusty—yet it is cold.

They say Gen. Butler, on the Peninsula, has given orders to his troops to respect private property—and not to molest non-combatants.

FEBRUARY 11TH.—Night before last 109 Federal prisoners, all commissioned officers, made their escape from prison—and only three or four have been retaken!

The letter of Mr. Sloan, of North Carolina, only produced a reply from the Secretary that there was not the slightest suspicion against Gen. W., and that the people of North Carolina would not be satisfied with anybody.

Eight thousand men of Johnston's army are without bayonets, and yet Col. Gorgas has abundance.

Governor Milton, of Florida, calls lustily for 5000 men—else he fears all is lost in his State.

To-day bacon is selling for $6 per pound, and all other things in proportion. A negro (for his master) asked me, to-day, $40 for an old, tough turkey gobbler. I passed on very briskly.

We shall soon have martial law, it is thought, which, judiciously administered, might remedy some of the grievous evils we labor under. I shall have no meat for dinner to-morrow.

FEBRUARY 12TH.—It is warm to-day, and cloudy; but there was ice early in the morning. We have recaptured twenty-odd of the escaped prisoners.

A bill has passed Congress placing an embargo on many imported articles; and these articles are rising rapidly in price. Sugar sold to-day at auction in large quantity for $8.00 per pound; rice, 85 cents, etc.

There is a rumor that Gen. Finnegan has captured the enemy in Florida.

Gen. Lee says his army is rapidly re-enlisting for the war.

FEBRUARY 13TH.—Bright, beautiful weather, with frosty nights.

The dispatches I cut from the papers to-day are interesting. Gen. Wise, it appears, has met the enemy at last, and gained a brilliant success—and so has Gen. Finnegan. But the correspondence between the President and Gen. Johnston, last spring and summer, indicates constant dissensions between the Executive and the generals. And the President is under the necessity of defending *Northern* born generals, while Southern born ones are without trusts, etc.

INTERESTING FROM FLORIDA.

OFFICIAL DISPATCH.

"CHARLESTON, February 11th, 1864.

"To GEN. S. COOPER.

"Gen Finnegan has repulsed the enemy's force at Lake City—details not known.

"(Signed) G. T. BEAUREGARD."

SECOND DISPATCH.

"CHARLESTON, February 11th—11 A.M.
"To GEN. S. COOPER.

"Gen. Finnegan's success yesterday was very creditable—the enemy's force being much superior to his own. His reinforcements had not reached here, owing to delays on the road. Losses not yet reported.

"(Signed) G. T. BEAUREGARD."

REPULSE OF THE ENEMY NEAR CHARLESTON.

OFFICIAL DISPATCH.

"CHARLESTON, February 12th, 1864.

"Gen. Wise gallantly repulsed the enemy last evening on John's Island. He is, to-day, in pursuit. Our loss very trifling. The force of the enemy is about 2000; ours about one-half.

"(Signed) G. T. BEAUREGARD."

Every day we recapture some of the escaped Federal officers. So far we have 34 of the 109.

The President sent over a "confidential" sealed letter to the Secretary to-day. I handed it to the Secretary, who was looking pensive.

Dr. McClure, of this city, who has been embalming the dead, and going about the country with his coffins, has been detected taking Jews and others through the lines. Several *live men* have been found in his coffins.

Again it is reported that the enemy are advancing up the Peninsula in force, and, to-morrow being Sunday, the local troops may be called out. But Gen. Rhodes is near with his division, so no serious danger will be felt, unless more than 20,000 attack us. Even that number would not accomplish much—for the city is fortified strongly.

It is rumored by blockade-runners that gold in the North is selling at from 200 to 500 per cent. premium. If this be *true*, our day of deliverance is not distant.

FEBRUARY 14TH.—Clear and windy. There is nothing new that I have heard of; but great apprehensions are felt for the fate of Mississippi—said to be penetrated to its center by an overwhelming force of the enemy. It is defended, however, or it is to be, by Gen. (Bishop) Polk.

I hear of more of the escaped Federal officers being brought in to-day.

The correspondence between the President and Gen. Johnston is causing some remark. The whole is not given. Letters were received from Gen. J. to which no allusion is made, which passed through my hands, and I think the fact is noted in this diary. He intimated, I think, that the position assigned him was equivocal and unpleasant in Tennessee. He did not feel inclined to push Bragg out of the field, and the President, it seems, would not relieve Bragg.

Mr. Secretary Seddon, it is now said, is resolved to remain in office.

FEBRUARY 15TH.—We have over forty of the escaped Federal officers. Nothing more from Gens. Wise and Finnegan. The enemy have retreated again on the Peninsula. It is said Meade's army is falling back on Washington.

We have a snow storm to-day.

The President is unfortunate with his servants, as the following from the *Dispatch* would seem:

"*Another of President Davis's Negroes run away.* — On Saturday night last the police were informed of the fact that Cornelius, a negro man in the employ of President Davis, had run away. Having received some clew of his whereabouts, they succeeded in finding him in a few hours after receiving the information of his escape, and lodged him in the upper station house. When caught, there was found on his person snack enough, consisting of cold chicken, ham, preserves, bread, etc., to last him for a long journey, and a large sum of money he had stolen from his master. Some time after being locked up, he called to the keeper of the prison to give him some water, and as that gentleman incautiously opened the door of his cell to wait on him, Cornelius knocked him down and again made his escape. Mr. Peter Everett, the only watchman present, put off after him; but before running many steps stumbled and fell, injuring himself severely."

FEBRUARY 16TH.—A plan of invasion. Gen. Longstreet telegraphs that he has no corn, and cannot stay where he is, unless supplied by the Quartermaster-General. This, the President says, is impossible, for want of transportation. The railroads can do no more than supply grain for the horses of Lee's army—all being brought from Alabama, Georgia, South Carolina, etc. But the President says Longstreet might extricate himself from the exigency by marching into Middle Tennessee or Kentucky, or both.

Soon after this document came in, another followed from the Tennessee and Kentucky members of Congress, inclosing an elaborate plan from Col. Dibrell, of the Army of Tennessee, of taking Nashville, and getting forage, etc. in certain counties not yet devastated, in Tennessee and Kentucky. Only 10,000 additional men will be requisite. They are to set out with eight days' rations; and if Grant leaves Chattanooga to interfere with the plan, Gen. Johnston is to follow and fall upon his rear, etc. Gen. Longstreet approves the plan—is eager for it, I infer from his dispatch about corn; and the members of Congress are in favor of it. If practicable, it ought to be begun immediately; and I think it will be.

A bright windy day—snow gone.

The Federal General Sherman, with 30,000 men, was, at the last dates, still marching southeast of Jackson, Miss. It is predicted that he is rushing on his destruction. Gen. Polk is retreating before him, while our cavalry is in his rear. He cannot keep open his communications.

FEBRUARY 17TH.—Bright and very cold—freezing all day. Col. Myers has written a letter to the Secretary, in reply to our ordering him to report to the Quartermaster-General, stating that he considers himself the Quartermaster-General—as the Senate has so declared. This being referred to the President, he indorses on it that Col. Myers served long enough in the United States army to know his status and duty, without any such discussion with the Secretary as he seems to invite.

Yesterday Congress consummated several measures of such magnitude as will attract universal attention, and which must have, perhaps, a decisive influence in our struggle for independence.

Gen. Sherman, with 30,000 or 40,000 men, is still advancing deeper into Mississippi, and the Governor of Alabama has ordered the non-combatants to leave Mobile, announcing that it is to be attacked. If Sherman *should go on*, and succeed, it would be the most brilliant operation of the war. If he goes on and fails, it will be the most disastrous—and his surrender would be, probably, like the surrender of Lord Cornwallis at Yorktown. He ought certainly to be annihilated.

I have advised Senator Johnson to let my nephew's purpose to bring Gen. Holmes before a court-martial lie over, and I have the papers in my drawer. The President will probably promote Col. Clark to a brigadiership, and then my nephew will succeed to the colonelcy; which will be a sufficient rebuke to Gen. H., and a cataplasm for my nephew's wounded honor.

The *Examiner* has whipped Congress into a modification of the clause putting assistant editors and other employees of newspaper proprietors into the army. They want the press to give them the meed of praise for their bold measures, and to reconcile the people to the tax, militia, and currency acts. This is the year of crises, and I think we'll win.

We are now sending 400 Federal prisoners to Georgia daily; and I hope we shall have more food in the city when they are all gone.

FEBRUARY 18TH.—This was the coldest morning of the winter. There was ice in the wash-basins in our bed chambers, the first we have seen there. I fear my cabbage, beets, etc. now coming up, in my half barrel hot-bed, although in the house, are killed.

The topic of discussion everywhere, now, is the effect likely to be produced by the Currency bill. Mr. Lyons denounces it, and says the people will be starved. I have heard (not seen) that some holders of Treasury notes have burnt them to spite the government! I hope for the best, even if the worst is to come. Some future Shakspeare will depict the times we live in in striking colors. The wars of "The Roses" bore no comparison to these campaigns between the rival sections. Everywhere our troops are re-enlisting for the war; one regiment re-enlisted, the other day, for forty years!

The President has discontinued his Tuesday evening receptions. The Legislature has a bill before it to suppress theatrical amusements during the war. What would Shakspeare think of that?

Sugar has risen to $10 and $12 per pound.

FEBRUARY 19TH.—Cold and clear. Congress adjourned yesterday, having passed the bill suspending the writ of *habeas corpus* for six months at least. Now the President is clothed with DICTATORIAL POWERS, to all intents and purposes, so far as the war is concerned.

The first effect of the Currency bill is to inflate prices yet more. But as the volume of Treasury notes flows into the Treasury, we shall see prices fall. And soon there will be a great rush to fund the notes, for fear the holders may be *too late*, and have to submit to a discount of 33½ per cent.

Dispatches from Gen. Polk state that Sherman has paused at Meridian.

FEBRUARY 20TH.—Bright, calm, but still cold—slightly moderating. Roads firm and dusty. Trains of army wagons still go by our house laden with ice.

Brig.-Gen. Wm. Preston has been sent to Mexico, with authority to recognize and treat with the new Emperor Maximilian.

I see, by a letter from Mr. Benjamin, that he is intrusted by the President with the custody of the "secret service" money.

Late papers from the United States show that they have a money panic, and that gold is rising in price. In Lowell not a spindle is turning, and 30,000 operatives are thrown out of employment!

From England we learn that the mass of the population are memorializing government to put an end to the war!

I saw a *ham* sell to-day for $350; it weighed fifty pounds, at $7 per pound.

FEBRUARY 21ST.—Cold, clear, and calm, but moderating.

Mr. Benjamin sent over, this morning, extracts from dispatches received from his commercial agent in London, dated December 26th and January 16th, recommending, what had already been suggested by Mr. McRae, in Paris, a government monopoly in the export of cotton, and in the importation of necessaries, etc.

This measure has already been adopted by Congress, which clearly shows that the President can have any measure passed he pleases; and this is a good one.

So complete is the Executive master of the "situation," that, in advance of the action of Congress on the Currency bill, the Secretary of the Treasury had prepared plates, etc. for the new issue of notes before the bill passed calling in the old.

Some forty of the members of the Congress just ended failed to be re-elected, and of these a large proportion are already seeking office or exemption.

The fear is now, that, from a plethora of paper money, we shall soon be without a sufficiency for a circulating medium. There are $750,000,000 in circulation; and the tax bills, etc. will call in, it is estimated, $800,000,000! Well, I am willing to abide the result. Speculators have had their day; and it will be hoped we shall have a season of low prices, if scarcity of money always reduces prices. There are grave lessons for our edification daily arising in such times as these.

I know my ribs stick out, being covered by skin only, for the want of sufficient food; and this is the case with many thousands of non-producers, while there is enough for all, if it were equally distributed.

The Secretary of War has nothing new from Gen. Polk; and Sherman is supposed to be still at Meridian.

There is war between Gen. Winder and Mr. Ould, agent for exchange of prisoners, about the custody and distribution to prisoners, Federal and Confederate. It appears that parents, etc. writing to our prisoners in the enemy's country, for want of three cent stamps, are in the habit of inclosing five or ten cent pieces, and the perquisites of the office amounts to several hundred dollars per month—and the struggle is really between the clerks in the two offices. A Mr. Higgens, from Maryland, is in Winder's office, and has got the general to propose to the Secretary that he shall have the exclusive handling of the letters; but Mr. Ould, it appears, detected a letter, of an alleged treasonable character, on its way to the enemy's country, written by this Higgens, and reported it to the Secretary. But as the Secretary was much absorbed, and as Winder will indorse Higgens, it is doubtful how the contest for the perquisites will terminate.

The Secretary was aroused yesterday. The cold weather burst the water-pipe in his office, or over it, and drove him off to the Spottswood Hotel.

FEBRUARY 22D —The offices are closed, to-day, in honor of Washington's birth-day. But it is a *fast* day; meal selling for $40 per bushel. Money will not be so abundant a month hence! All my turnip-greens were killed by the frost. The mercury was, on Friday, 5° above zero; to-day it is 40°. Sowed a small bed of curled Savoy cabbage; and saved the early York in my half barrel hot-bed by bringing it into the parlor, where there was fire.

A letter from Lieut.-Col. R. A. Alston, Decatur, Ga., says Capt. —— ——, one of Gen. Morgan's secret agents, has just arrived there, after spending several months in the North, and reports that Lincoln cannot recruit his armies by draft, or any other mode, unless they achieve some signal success in the spring campaign. He says, moreover, that there is a perfect organization, all over the North, for the purpose of revolution and the expulsion or death of the Abolitionists and free negroes; and of this organization Generals ——, ——, and —— —— —— are the military leaders. Col. A. asks permission of the Secretary of War to go into Southern Illinois, where, he is confident, if he cannot contribute to precipitate civil war, he can, at least, bring out thousands of men who will fight for the Southern cause.

Dispatches from Gen. Lee show that nearly every regiment in his army has re-enlisted for the war.

The body guard of the President has been dispersed.

Here is the sequel to the history of the Jew whose goods brought such fabulous prices at auction a few weeks ago:

"*A Heavy Robbery —A former citizen of Richmond stripped of all his goods and chattels.*—A few weeks ago, Mr. Lewis Hyman, who had for some years carried on a successful and profitable trade in jewelry in the City of Richmond, disposed of his effects with a view of quitting the Confederacy and finding a home in some land where his services were less likely to be required in the tented field. Having settled up his business affairs to his own satisfaction, he applied for and obtained a passport from the Assistant Secretary of War, to enable him to pass our lines. He first took the Southern route, hoping to run out from Wilmington to Nassau; but delays occurring, he returned to Richmond. From this point he went to Staunton, determined to make his exit from the country by the Valley route. All went on smoothly enough until he had passed Woodstock, in Shenandoah County. Between that point and Strasburg he was attacked by a band of robbers and stripped of everything he possessed of value, embracing a heavy amount of money and a large and valuable assortment of jewelry. We have heard his loss estimated at from $175,000 to $200,000. His passport was not taken from him, and after the robbery he was allowed to proceed on his journey—minus the essential means of traveling. It is stated that some of the jewelry taken from him has already made its appearance in the Richmond market.

"P. S.—Since writing the above, we have had an interview with Mr. Jacob Ezekiel, who states that the party of Mr. Hyman consisted of Lewis Hyman, wife and child, Madam Son and husband, and H. C. Ezekiel; and the presumption is that if one was robbed, all shared the same fate. Mr. E. thinks that the amount in possession of the whole party would not exceed $100,000. On Friday last two men called upon Mr. Ezekiel, at his place of business in this city, and exhibited a parchment, in Hebrew characters, which they represented was captured on a train on the Baltimore and Ohio Railroad. This story, Mr. Ezekiel thinks, is incorrect, from the fact that he received a letter from his son, then at Woodstock, dated subsequent to the capture of the train on that road; and he is satisfied that the articles shown him belonged to some of the parties above mentioned."

FEBRUARY 23D.—Bright and pleasant.

A letter from Gen. Maury indicates now that Mobile is surely to be attacked. He says they may force a passage at Grant's Pass, which is thirty miles distant; and the fleet may pass the forts and reach the lower bay. Gen. M. has 10,000 effective men, and subsistence for 20,000 for six months. He asks 6000 or 7000 more men. He has also food for 4000 horses for six months. But he has only 200 rounds for his cannon, and 250 for his siege guns, and 200 for each musket.

Meal is the only food now attainable, except by the rich. We look for a healthy year, everything being so cleanly consumed that no garbage or filth can accumulate. We are all good scavengers now, and there is no need of buzzards in the streets. Even the pigeons can scarcely find a grain to eat.

Gold brought $30 for $1, Saturday. Nevertheless, we have only good news from the armies, and we have had a victory in Florida.

FEBRUARY 24TH.—Bright and pleasant. Intelligence from the West is of an interesting character. The column of Federal cavalry from Memphis, destined to co-operate with Gen. Sherman, has been intercepted and a junction prevented. And both Sherman and the cavalry are now in full retreat—running out of the country faster than they advanced into it. The desert they made as they traversed the interior of Mississippi they have now to repass, if they can, in the weary retreat, with no supplies but those they brought with them. Many will never get back.

And a dispatch from Beauregard confirms Finnegan's victory in Florida. He captured all the enemy's artillery, stores, etc., and for three miles his dead and wounded were found strewn on the ground. Thus the military operations of 1864 are, so far, decidedly favorable. And we shall probably soon have news from Longstreet. If Meade advances, Lee will meet him—and let him beware!

Gold is still mounting up—and so with everything exposed for sale. When, when will prices come down?

But we shall probably end the war this year—and independence will compensate for all. The whole male population, pretty much, will be in the field this year, and our armies will be strong. So far we have the prestige of success, and our men are resolved to keep it, if the dissensions of the leaders do not interfere with the general purpose.

FEBRUARY 25TH.—The President has certainly conferred on Bragg the position once (1862) occupied by Lee, as the following official announcement, in all the papers to-day, demonstrates:

"WAR DEPARTMENT,
"ADJUTANT AND INSPECTOR GENERAL'S OFFICE,
"RICHMOND, February 24th, 1864.

"GENERAL ORDERS No. 23.

"Gen. Braxton Bragg is assigned to duty at the seat of government, and, under direction of the President, is charged with the conduct of military operations in the armies of the Confederacy.

"By order of the Secretary of War.

"S. COOPER,
"Adjutant and Inspector General."

No doubt Bragg can give the President valuable counsel—nor can there be any doubt that he enjoys a secret satisfaction in triumphing thus over popular sentiment, which just at this time is much averse to Gen. Bragg. The President is naturally a little oppugnant.

He has just appointed a clerk, in the Department of War, a military judge, with rank and pay of colonel of cavalry—one whom he never saw; but the clerk once had a street fight with Mr. Pollard, who has published a pamphlet against the President. Mr. Pollard sees his enemy with three golden stars on each side of his collar.

The retreat of Sherman seems to be confirmed.

Gen. Beauregard sends the following dispatch:

"CHARLESTON, February 23d—2 15 P.M.
"To GEN. S. COOPER.

" The latest reports from Gen. Finnegan give no particulars of the victory at Occum Pond, except that he has taken all of the enemy's artillery, some 500 or 600 stand of small arms already collected, and that the roads for three miles are strewn with the enemy's dead and wounded.

"(Signed) G. T. BEAUREGARD."

The *Examiner* has the following remarks on the appointment of Bragg:

"The judicious and opportune appointment of Gen. Bragg to the post of Commander-in-Chief of the Confederate Armies, will be appreciated as an illustration of that strong common sense which forms the basis of the President's character, that regard for the opinions and feelings of the country, that respect for the Senate, which are the keys to all that is mysterious in the conduct of our public affairs. The Confederate armies cannot fail to be well pleased. Every soldier's heart feels that merit is the true title to promotion, and that glorious service should insure a splendid reward. From Lookout Mountain, a step to the highest military honor and power is natural and inevitable. Johnston, Lee, and Beauregard learn with grateful emotions that the conqueror of Kentucky and Tennessee has been elevated to a position which his superiority deserves. Finally this happy announcement should enliven the fires of confidence and enthusiasm, reviving among the people like a bucket of water on a newly kindled grate."

The day before his appointment, the *Enquirer* had a long editorial article denouncing in advance his assignment to any prominent position, and severely criticised his conduct in the West. To-day *it hails his appointment as Commander-in-Chief with joy and enthusiasm!* This reminds one of the *Moniteur* when Napoleon was returning from Elba. The *Enquirer's* notion is to prevent discord—and hence it is patriotic.

The weather is still bright, pleasant, but dusty. We have had only one rain since the 18th of December, and one light snow. My garden is too dry for planting.

We have not only the negroes arrayed against us, but it appears that recruiting for the Federal army from Ireland has been carried on to a large extent.

FEBRUARY 26TH.—Cool, bright, but windy and dusty.

Dispatches announce heavy skirmishing in the vicinity of Dalton —and Gen. Johnston's army was in line of battle. It may be merely a feint of the enemy to aid in the extrication of Sherman.

Gen. Lee is here in consultation with the President. They decided that over 1000 men be transferred from the army to the navy—so that something may be soon heard from our ironclads.

Pork is selling at $3 per pound to-day.

Writings upon the walls of the houses at the corners of the streets were observed this morning, indicating a riot, if there be no amelioration of the famine.

FEBRUARY 27TH.—Bright and pleasant—dusty. But one rain during the winter!

The "associated press" publishes an unofficial dispatch, giving almost incredible accounts of Gen. Forrest's defeat of Grierson's cavalry, 10,000 strong, with only 2000. It is said the enemy were cut up and routed, losing all his guns, etc.

Sugar is $20 per pound; new bacon, $8; and chickens, $12 per pair. Soon we look for a money panic, when a few hundred millions of the paper money is funded, and as many more collected by the tax collectors. Congress struck the speculators a hard blow. One man, eager to invest his money, gave $100,000 for a house and lot, and he now pays $5000 tax on it; the interest is $6000 more—$11,000 total. His next door neighbor, who bought his house in 1860 for $10,000, similar in every respect, pays $500 tax (valued at date of sale), interest $600; total, $1100 per annum. The speculator pays $10,000 per annum more than his patriotic neighbor, who refused to sell his house for $100,000.

FEBRUARY 28TH.—Bright, cool, and dusty. No war news; nor denial or confirmation of the wonderful victory of Forrest in Mississippi. That he captured the enemy's artillery and drove them back, is official.

Longstreet has retired from before Knoxville; perhaps to assault Nashville, or to penetrate Kentucky.

Yesterday the Secretary ordered Col. Northrop to allow full rations of meal to the engineer corps; to-day he returns the order, saying: "There is not sufficient transportation for full rations to the troops in the field."

Last night the Secretary sent for Mr. Ould, exchange agent, and it is thought an exchange of prisoners will be effected, and with Butler. A confidential communication *may* have been received from Butler, who is a politician, and it may be that he has offered *secret* inducements, etc. He would like to establish a *trade* with us for tobacco, as he did for cotton and sugar when he was in New Orleans. No doubt some of the high officials at Washington would *wink* at it for a share of the profits.

The Southern Express Company (Yankee) has made an arrangement with the Quartermaster-General to transport private contributions of supplies to the army—anything to monopolize the railroads, and make private fortunes. Well, "all's well that ends well,"—and our armies may be *forced* to forage on the enemy.

I copy this advertisement from a morning paper:

"NOTICE.—Owing to the heavy advance of feed, we are compelled to charge the following rates for boarding horses on and after the 1st of March:

  Board per month...$300.00
   " " day.. 15.00
  Single feed... 5.00

"*Virginia Stables.*   JAMES C. JOHNSON,
                W. H. SUTHERLAND,
                B. W. GREEN."

Congress and the President parted at the adjournment in bad temper. It is true everything was passed by Congress asked for by the Executive as necessary in the present exigency—a new military bill, putting into the service several hundred thousand more men, comprising the entire male population between the ages of 17 and 50; the tax and currency bills, calculated to realize $600,000,000 or $300,000,000; and the suspension of the writ of *habeas corpus*. These were conceded, say the members, for the sake of the country, and not as concessions to the Executive. But the Commissary-General's nomination, and hundreds of others, were not sent into the Senate, in derogation of the Constitution; and hundreds that were sent in, have not been acted on by the Senate, and such officers now act in violation of the Constitution.

Dill's Government Bakery, Clay Street, is now in flames—supposed to be the work of an incendiary. Loss not likely to be heavy.

FEBRUARY 29TH.—Raining moderately.

There is a rumor that Frederick's Hall, between this city and Fredericksburg, was taken to-day by a detachment of the enemy's cavalry, an hour after Gen. Lee passed on his way to the army. This is only rumor, however.

A dispatch from Gen. Lee's Chief Commissary, received to-day, says the army has only bread enough to last till the 1st of March, to-morrow! and that meat is getting scarce again. Col. Northrop, the Commissary-General, indorses on this, that he *foresaw* and frequently *foretold* that such a crisis would come. He says transportation sufficient cannot be had, and that he has just heard of an accident to the Wilmington Railroad, which will diminish the transportation of corn one-half; and he says a similar accident to the Charlotte Road would be fatal. Comfortable! And when I saw him afterward, his face was lit up with triumph, as if he had gained a victory! He *predicted* it, because they would not let him impress all the food in the country. And now he has no remedy for the pressing need. But the soldiers won't starve, in spite of him.

CHAPTER XXXVI

Attempt to capture Richmond.—Governor Vance and Judge Pearson—Preparations to blow up the "Libby" prisoners.—Letter from General Lee.—Proposal to execute Dahlgren's raiders.—General Butler on the Eastern Shore.—Colonel Dahlgren's body.—Destitution of the army.—Strength of the Southwestern army.—Destitution of my family.—Protest from South Carolina.—Difficulty with P. Milmo & Co.—Hon. J. W. Wall.

MARCH 1ST.—Dark and raining.

As the morning progressed, the city was a little startled by the sound of artillery in a northern direction, and not very distant. Couriers and horsemen from the country announced the approach of the enemy *within* the outer fortifications; a column of 5000 cavalry. Then Hon. James Lyons came in, reporting that the enemy were shelling his house, one and a half miles from the city. And Gen. Elzey (in command) said, at the department, that a fight was in progress; and that Brig.-Gen. Custis Lee was directing it in person. But an hour or so after the report of artillery ceased, and the excitement died away. Yet the local troops and militia are marching out as I write; and a caisson that came in an hour ago has just passed our door, returning to the field. Of course the city is full of rumors, and no one yet knows what has occurred. I presume it was only distant shelling, as no wounded men have been brought in.

It is reported that the enemy captured Mr. Seddon's family twenty-five miles distant,—also Gen. Wise's. To-morrow we shall know more; but no *uneasiness* is felt as to the result. In a few hours we can muster men enough to defend the city against 25,000.

A letter from Gen. Whiting suggests that martial law be proclaimed in North Carolina, as a Judge Pearson—a traitor, he thinks—is discharging men who have in conscripts as substitutes, on the ground that the act of Congress is unconstitutional. The President suggest a General Order, etc., complying with Gen. W.'s request.

Col. A. C. Myers, late Quartermaster-General, writes again, indignantly resenting the President's indorsement, etc. as unfounded and injurious, etc.

The President indorses this letter as follows: "Unless this letter is designed to ask whether Col. M. is still in the army, or discharged by the appointment of a successor, I find nothing which changes the case since my indorsement referred to, as causing resentment and calling for vindication. Your orders were certainly official communications. Not having seen them, I can express no opinion upon their terms.—JEFFERSON DAVIS."

MARCH 2D.—A slight snow on the ground this morning—but bright and cool. Last night, after I had retired to bed, we heard a brisk cannonading, and volleys of musketry, a few miles distant.

This morning an excitement, but no alarm, pervaded the city. It was certainly a formidable attempt to take the city by surprise. From the number of disgraceful failures heretofore, the last very recently, the enemy must have come to the desperate resolution to storm the city this time at all hazards. And indeed the coming upon it was sudden, and if there had been a column of 15,000 bold men in the assault, they might have penetrated it. But now, twenty-four hours subsequently, 30,000 would fail in the attempt.

The Department Clerks were in action in the evening in five minutes after they were formed in line. Capt. Ellery, Chief Clerk of 2d Auditor, was killed, and several were wounded. It rained fast all the time, and it was very dark. The enemy's cavalry charged upon them, firing as they came; they were ordered to lie flat on the ground. This they did, until the enemy came within fifteen yards of them, when they rose and fired, sending the assailants to the right and left, helter-skelter. How many fell is not yet known.

To-day Gen. Hampton sent in 77 prisoners, taken six miles above town—one lieutenant-colonel among them; and Yankee horses, etc. are coming in every hour.

Gov. Vance writes that inasmuch as Judge Pearson still grants the writ of *habeas corpus*, and discharges all who have put substitutes in the army, on the ground of the unconstitutionality of the act of Congress, he is bound by his oath to sustain the judge, even to the summoning the military force of the State to resist the Confederate States authorities. But to avoid such a fatal collision, he is willing to abide the decision of the Supreme Court, to assemble in June; the substitute men, meantime, to be left unmolested. We shall soon see the President's decision, which will probably be martial law.

Last night, when it was supposed probable that the prisoners of war at the Libby might attempt to break out, Gen. Winder ordered that a large amount of powder be placed under the building, with instructions to blow them up, if the attempt were made. He was persuaded, however, to consult the Secretary of War first, and get his approbation. The Secretary would give no such order, but said the prisoners must not be permitted to escape under any circumstances, which was considered sanction enough. Capt. —— obtained an order for, and procured several hundred pounds of gunpowder, which were placed in readiness. Whether the prisoners were advised of this I know not; but I told Capt. —— it could not be justifiable to spring such a mine in the absence of their knowledge of the fate awaiting them, in the event of their attempt to break out,—because such prisoners are not to be condemned for striving to regain their liberty. Indeed, it is the *duty* of a prisoner of war to escape if he can.

Gen. Winder addressed me in a friendly manner to-day, the first time in two years.

The President was in a bad humor yesterday, when the enemy's guns were heard even in his office.

The last dispatch from Gen. Lee informs us that Meade, who had advanced, had fallen back again. But communications are cut between us and Lee; and we have no intelligence since Monday.

Gen. Wilcox is organizing an impromptu brigade here, formed of the furloughed officers and men found everywhere in the streets and at the hotels. This looks as if the danger were not yet regarded as over.

The Secretary of War was locked up with the Quartermaster and Commissary-Generals and other bureau officers, supposed to be discussing the damage done by the enemy to the railroads, etc. etc. I hope it was not a consultation upon any presumed necessity of the abandonment of the city!

We were paid to-day in $5 bills. I gave $20 for half a cord of wood, and $60 for a bushel of common white cornfield beans. Bacon is yet $8 per pound; but more is coming to the city than usual, and a decline may be looked for, I hope. The farmers above the city, who have been hoarding grain, meat, etc., will lose much by the raiders.

MARCH 3D.—Bright and frosty. Confused accounts of the raid in the morning papers.

During the day it was reported that Col. Johnson's forces had been cut up this morning by superior numbers, and that Butler was advancing up the Peninsula with 15,000 men. The tocsin was sounded in the afternoon, and the militia called out; every available man being summoned to the field for the defense of the city. The opinion prevails that the plan to liberate the prisoners and capture Richmond is not fully developed yet, nor abandoned. My only apprehension is that while our troops may be engaged in one direction, a detachment of the enemy may rush in from the opposite quarter. But the attempt must fail. There is much excitement, but no alarm. It is rather eagerness to meet the foe, and a desire that he may come.

The Department Battalion returned at 2 P.M. to attend the funeral of Capt. Ellery, and expect to be marched out again this evening toward Bottom's Bridge, where the enemy is said to be in considerable force.

Custis, though detailed to duty in the department, threw down his pen to-day, and said he *would* go out and be in the next fight. And so he left me suddenly. The Secretary, to whom I communicated this, said it was right and proper for him to go—even without orders. He goes without a blanket, preferring not to sleep, to carrying one. At night he will sit by a fire in the field.

Some of the clerks would shoot Mr. Memminger cheerfully. He will not pay them their salaries, on some trivial informality in the certificates; and while they are fighting and bleeding in his defense, their wives and children are threatened to be turned out of doors by the boarding-house keepers.

MARCH 4TH.—Bright and frosty in the morning; warm and cloudy in the afternoon. The enemy have disappeared.

On the 17th inst., Gen. Lee wrote the Secretary of War that he had received a letter from Gen. Longstreet, asking that Pickett's Division be in readiness to join him; also that a brigade of Gen. Buckner's Division, at Dalton, be sent him at once. He says the force immediately in front of him consists of the 4th, 11th, 9th, and 23d corps, besides a large body of cavalry from Middle Tennessee. Gen. Lee says the railroad from Chattanooga to Knoxville, being about completed, will enable the enemy to combine on either Johnston or Longstreet. He (Gen. Lee) says, however, that the 4th and 11th corps are small, and may have been consolidated; the 23d also is small; but he does not know the strength of the enemy. He thinks Pickett's Division should be sent as desired, and its place filled with troops from South Carolina, etc., where operations will probably soon cease. The Secretary sent this to the President. The President sent it back to day, indorsed, "How can Pickett's Division be replaced?—J. D."

Henly's Battalion returned this evening; and Custis can resume his school, unless he should be among the list doomed to the rank in the field, for which he is physically incapable, as Surgeon Garnett, the President's physician, has certified.

MARCH 5TH.—Clear and pleasant, after a slight shower in the morning.

The raid is considered at an end, and it has ended disastrously for the invaders.

Some extraordinary memoranda were captured from the raiders, showing a diabolical purpose, and creating a profound sensation here. The cabinet have been in consultation many hours in regard to it, and I have reason to believe it is the present purpose to deal summarily with the captives taken with Dahlgren, but the "sober second thought" will prevail, and they will not be executed, notwithstanding the thunders of the press. Retaliation for such outrages committed on others having been declined, the President and cabinet can hardly be expected to begin with such sanguinary punishments when *their own* lives are threatened. It would be an act liable to grave criticism. Nevertheless, Mr. Secretary Seddon has written a letter to-day to Gen. Lee, asking his views on a matter of such importance as the execution of some *ninety* men of Dahlgren's immediate followers, not, as he says, to divide the responsibility, nor to effect a purpose, which has the sanction of the President, the cabinet, and *Gen. Bragg*, but to have his *views*, and information as to what would probably be its effect on the army under his command. We shall soon know, I hope, what Gen. Lee will have to say on the subject, and I am mistaken if he does not oppose it. If these men had been put to death in the heat of passion, on the field, it would have been justified, but it is too late now. Besides, *Gen. Lee's son* is a captive in the hands of the enemy, designated for retaliation whenever we shall execute any of their prisoners in our hands. It is cruelty to Gen. Lee!

It is already rumored that Gen. Butler has been removed, and a flag of truce boat is certainly at City Point, laden with prisoners sent up for exchange.

The Commissary-General has sent in a paper saying that unless the passenger cars on the Southern Road be discontinued, he cannot supply half enough meal for Lee's army. He has abundance in Georgia and South Carolina, but cannot get transportation. He says the last barrel of flour from Lynchburg has gone to the army.

We have news from the West that Morgan and his men will be in the saddle in a few days.

After all, Mr. Lyon's house was not touched by any of the enemy's shells. But one shell struck within 300 yards of one house in Clay Street, and not even the women and children were alarmed.

The price of a turkey to-day is $60.

MARCH 6TH.—My birthday—55. Bright and frosty; subsequently warm and pleasant. No news. But some indignation in the streets at the Adjutant-General's (Cooper) order, removing the clerks and putting them in the army, just when they had, by their valor, saved the capital from flames and the throats of the President and his cabinet from the knives of the enemy. If the order be executed, the heads of the government will receive and merit execration. It won't be done.

MARCH 7TH.—Bright and frosty morning; cloudy and warm in the evening. Cannon and musketry were heard this morning some miles northwest of the city. Probably Gen. Hampton fell in with one of the lost detachments of the raiders, seeking a way of escape. This attempt to surprise Richmond was a disgraceful failure.

The Secretary of War has gone up to his farm for a few days to see the extent of injury done him by the enemy.

Mr. Benjamin and Assistant Secretary Campbell are *already* "allowing" men to pass to the United States, and even directly to

Washington. Surely the injury done us by information thus conveyed to the enemy hitherto, ought to be a sufficient warning.

Gen. Bragg has resolved to keep a body of 1500 cavalry permanently within the city and its vicinity.

MARCH 8TH.—An application of Capt. C. B. Duffield, for a lieutenant-colonelcy, recommended by Col. Preston, came back from the President to-day. It was favorably indorsed by the Secretary, but Gen. Cooper marked it adversely, saying the Assistant Adjutant-General should not execute the Conscription act, and finally, the President simply said, "The whole organization requires revision.—J. D." I hope it *will* be revised, and nine-tenths of its officers put in the army as conscripts.

Raining this morning, and alternate clouds and sunshine during the day.

One of the clerks who was in the engagement, Tuesday night, March 1st, informed me that the enemy's cavalry approached slowly up the hill, on the crest of which the battalion was lying. At the word, the boys rose and fired on their knees. He says the enemy delivered a volley before they retreated, killing two of our men and wounding several.

Reports from the Eastern Shore of Virginia indicate that Gen. Butler's rule there has been even worse than Lockwood's. It is said that the subordinate officers on that quiet peninsula are merely *his* agents, to tax and fine and plunder the unoffending people,—never in arms, and who have, with few exceptions, "taken the oath" repeatedly. One family, however (four sisters, the Misses P.), relatives of my wife, have not yielded. They allege that their father and oldest sister were persecuted to death by the orders of the general, and they *could not* swear allegiance to any government sanctioning such outrages in its agents. They were repeatedly arrested, and torn from their paternal roof at all hours of the day and night, but only uttered defiance. They are ladies of the first standing, highly accomplished, and of ample fortune, but are ready to suffer death rather than submit to the behests of a petty tyrant. Butler abandoned the attempt, but the soldiery never lose an opportunity of annoying the family.

MARCH 9TH.—A frosty morning, with dense fog; subsequently a pretty day.

This is the famine month. Prices of every commodity in the

market—up, up, up. Bacon, $10 to $15 per pound; meal, $50 per bushel. But the market-houses are deserted, the meat stalls all closed, only here and there a cart, offering turnips, cabbages, parsnips, carrots, etc., at outrageous prices. However, the superabundant paper money is beginning to flow into the Treasury, and that reflex of the financial tide may produce salutary results a few weeks hence.

MARCH 10TH.—Raining fast all day.

There was a rumor to-day that the enemy were approaching again, but the Secretary knew nothing of it.

Major Griswold is at variance with Gen. Winder, who has relieved him as Provost Marshal, and ordered him to Americus, Ga., to be second in command of the prisons, and assigned Major Carrington to duty as Provost Marshal here. Major Griswold makes a pathetic appeal to the President to be allowed to stay here in his old office.

The following, from the *Dispatch*, differs from the *Examiner's* account of the disposal of Col. Dahlgren's body:

"*Col. Dahlgren's Body.*—On Sunday afternoon last, the body of Col. Ulric Dahlgren, one of the leaders of the late Yankee raid on this city, and on whose body the paper revealing their designs, if successful, were found, was brought to this city on the York River Railroad train, and remained in the car (baggage) in which it was till yesterday afternoon, when it was transferred to some retired burial place. The object in bringing Dahlgren's body here was for identification, and was visited, among others, by Captain Dement and Mr. Mountcastle, of this city, who were recently captured and taken around by the raiders. These gentlemen readily recognized it as that of the leader of the band sent to assassinate the President and burn the city. The appearance of the corpse yesterday was decidedly more genteel than could be expected, considering the length of time he has been dead. He was laid in a plain white pine coffin, with flat top, and was dressed in a clean, coarse white cotton shirt, dark blue pants, and enveloped in a dark military blanket. In stature he was about five feet ten inches high, with a long, cadaverous face, light hair, slight beard, closely shaven, and had a small goatee, very light in color. In age we suppose he was about thirty years, and the expression of his countenance indicated that of pain."

MARCH 11TH.—Rained all night—a calm, warm rain. Calm and warm to-day, with light fog, but no rain.

It is now supposed the clerks (who saved the city) will be kept here to defend it.

MARCH 12TH.—It cleared away yesterday evening, and this morning, after the dispersion of a fog, the sun shone out in great glory, and the day was bright, calm, and pleasant. The trees begin to exhibit buds, and the grass is quite green.

My wife received a letter to-day from Mrs. Marling, Raleigh, N. C., containing some collard seed, which was immediately sown in a bed already prepared. And a friend sent us some fresh pork spare ribs and chine, and four heads of cabbage—so that we shall have subsistence for several days. My income, including Custis's, is not less, now, than $600 per month, or $7200 per annum; but we are still poor, with flour at $300 per barrel; meal, $50 per bushel; and even fresh fish at $5 per pound. A market-woman asked $5 to-day for a half pint of snap beans, to plant!

MARCH 13TH.—A lovely spring day—bright, warm, and calm.

There is nothing new, only the burning of houses, mills, etc. on the York River by the Yankees, and that is nothing new.

Subsequently the day became very windy, but not cold. The roads will be dry again, and military operations will be resumed. The campaign will be an early one in Virginia, probably. Our people are impatient to meet the foe, for they are weary of the war. Blood will flow in torrents, unless the invaders avoid great battles; and in that event our armies may assume the offensive.

It is now thought that the Department Battalion will be kept here for the defense of the city; the clerks, or most of them, retaining their offices. Those having families may possibly live on their salaries; but those who live at boarding-houses cannot, for board is now from $200 to $300 per month. Relief *must* soon come from some quarter, else many in this community will famish. But they prefer death to submission to the terms offered by the Abolitionists at Washington. The government must provide for the destitute, and array every one capable of bearing arms in the field.

MARCH 14TH.—Bright, pleasant day. The city is full of generals—Lee and his son (the one just returned from captivity), Longstreet, Whiting, Wise, Hoke, Morgan (he was ordered by

Gen. Cooper to desist from his enterprise in the West), Evans, and many others. Some fourteen attended St. Paul's (Episcopal) Church yesterday, where the President worships. Doubtless they are in consultation on the pressing needs of the country.

About noon to-day a dispatch came from Lieut.-Col. Cole, Gen. Lee's principal commissary, at Orange Court House, dated 12th inst., saying *the army was out of meat, and had but one day's rations of bread.* This I placed in the hands of the Secretary myself, and he seemed roused by it. Half an hour after, I saw Col. Northrop coming out of the department with a pale face, and triumphant, compressed lips. He had indorsed on the dispatch, before it came—it was addressed to him—that the state of things had come which he had long and often *predicted*, and to avert which he had repeatedly suggested the remedy; but the Secretary would not!

No wonder the generals are in consultation, for all the armies are in the same lamentable predicament—to the great triumph of Col. N., whose prescience is triumphantly vindicated! But Gen. Wise, when I mentioned these things to him, said *we would starve in the midst of plenty,* meaning that Col. N was incompetent to hold the position of Commissary-General.

At 2 P.M. a dispatch (which I likewise placed in the hands of the Secretary) came from Gen. Pickett, with information that thirteen of the enemy's transports passed Yorktown yesterday with troops from Norfolk, the Eastern Shore of Virginia, Washington City, etc.—such was the report of the signal corps. They also reported that Gen. Meade would order a general advance, to *check Gen. Lee.* What all this means I know not, unless it be meant to aid Gen. Kilpatrick to get back the way he came with his raiding cavalry—or else Gen. Lee's army is in motion, even while he is here. It must do something, or starve.

L. P. Walker, the first Secretary of War, is here, applying for an appointment as judge advocate of one of the military courts.

Gen. Bragg is at work. I saw by the President's papers to-day, that the Secretary's recommendation to remit the sentence to drop an officer was referred to him. He indorsed on it that the sentence was just, and ought to be executed. The President then indorsed: "Drop him.—J. D."

MARCH 15TH.—A clear, cool morning; but rained in the evening.

By the correspondence of the department, I saw to-day that 35,000 bushels of corn left North Carolina nearly a week ago for Lee's army, and about the same time 400,000 pounds of bacon was in readiness to be shipped from Augusta, Ga. At short rations, that would furnish bread and meat for the army several weeks.

We hear nothing additional from the enemy on the Peninsula. I doubt whether they mean fight.

We are buoyed again with rumors of an intention on the part of France to recognize us. So mote it be! We are preparing, however, to strike hard blows single-handed and unaided, if it must be.

MARCH 16TH.—There was ice last night. Cold all day. Gen. Maury writes that no immediate attack on Mobile need be apprehended now. He goes next to Savannah to look after the defenses of that city.

The *Examiner* to-day publishes Gen. Jos. E. Johnston's report of his operations in Mississippi last summer. He says the disaster at Vicksburg was owing to Gen. Pemberton's disobedience of orders. He was ordered to concentrate his army and give battle before the place was invested, and under no circumstances to allow himself to be besieged, which must of course result in disaster. He says, also, that he was about to manœuvre in such manner as would have probably resulted in the saving a large proportion of his men, when, to his astonishment, he learned that Gen. P. had capitulated.

Willoughby Newton reports that the enemy are building a number of light boats, to be worked with muffled oars, at Point Lookout, Md., and suggests that they may be designed to pass the obstructions in the James River, in another attempt to capture Richmond.

It is said Lieut.-Gen. E. Kirby Smith, trans-Mississippi, has been made a full general, and that Major-Gen. Sterling Price relieves Lieut.-Gen. Holmes, who is to report at Richmond. If this be so, it is very good policy.

Gen. Lee is still here, but will leave very soon.

Gen. Bragg has taken measures to insure the transportation of meat and grain from the South. Much food for Lee's army has arrived during the last two days.

MARCH 17TH.—Bright, clear, and pleasant; frosty in the morning.

Letters from Lieut.-Gen. Hood to the President, Gen Bragg, and the Secretary of War, give a cheering account of Gen. Johnston's army at Dalton. The men are well fed and well clothed. They are in high spirits, "and eager for the fray." The number is 40,000. Gen. H. urges, most eloquently, the junction of Polk's and Loring's troops with these, making some 60,000,—Grant having 50,000,—and then uniting with Longstreet's army, perhaps 30,000 more, and getting in the rear of the enemy. He says this would be *certain* to drive Grant out of Tennessee and Kentucky, and probably end the war. But if we lie still, Grant will eventually accumulate overwhelming numbers, and penetrate farther: and if he beats us, it would be difficult to rally again for another stand, so despondent would become the people.

Gen. Hood deprecates another invasion of Pennsylvania, which would be sure to result in defeat. He is decided in his conviction that the best policy is to take the initiative, and drive the enemy out of Tennessee and Kentucky, which could be accomplished to a *certainty*.

MARCH 18TH.—Bright and warmer, but windy.

Letters received at the department to-day, from Georgia, show than only one-eighth of the capacity of the railroads have been used for the subsistence of the army. The rogues among the multitude of quartermasters have made fortunes themselves, and almost ruined the country. It appears that there is abundance of grain and meat in the country, if it were only equally distributed among the consumers. It is to be hoped the rogues will now be excluded from the railroads.

The belief prevails that Gen. Lee's army is in motion. It may be a feint, to prevent reinforcements from being sent to Grant.

My daughter's cat is staggering to-day, for want of animal food. Sometimes I fancy I stagger myself. We do not average two ounces of meat daily; and some do not get any for several days together. Meal is $50 per bushel. I saw adamantine candles sell at auction to-day (box) at $10 per pound; tallow, $6.50. Bacon brought $7.75 per pound by the 100 pounds.

My good friend Dr. Powell and his family were absent from the farm near the city during the late raid. The enemy carried off several of his finest horses and mules, and consumed much of his supplies of food, etc., but utterly failed to induce any of his negroes to leave the place—and he has many. One of the female servants, when the enemy approached, ran into the house and secured all the silver, concealing it in her own house, and keeping it safely for her mistress.

MARCH 19TH.—Warmer, calm and cloudy.

I saw a large turkey to-day in market (wild), for which $100 was demanded.

I saw Dr. Powell to-day. He says the Federals asked his servants where the master and mistress had gone? and they were told that they had been called to Petersburg to see a sick daughter. They then asked where the spoons were, and were told none were in the house. They asked if there was not a watch, and the servant said her master wore it. They then demanded where the money was kept, and were told it was always kept in bank. They made the servants open drawers, press, etc.; and when they discovered some pans of milk, they took them up and drank out of them with eagerness. They took nothing from the house, destroyed nothing, and the doctor deems himself fortunate. They left him two horses and eight mules.

MARCH 20TH.—Bright and beautiful weather.

There are fires occurring now every night; and several buildings have been burned in the immediate vicinity of the War Department. These are attributed to incendiary Yankees, and the guard at the public offices has been doubled.

Mrs. Seddon, wife of the Secretary of War, resolved not to lose more wine by the visits of the Federal raiders, sent to auction last week twelve demijohns, which brought her $6000—$500 a demijohn.

MARCH 21ST.—Although cloudy, there was ice this morning, and cold all day.

Yesterday another thousand prisoners were brought up by the flag of truce boat. A large company of both sexes welcomed them in the Capitol Square, whither some baskets of food were sent by those who had some patriotism with their abundance. The President made them a comforting speech, alluding to their toils, bravery, and sufferings in captivity; and promised them, after a brief respite, that they should be in the field again.

The following conversation took place yesterday between the President and some young ladies of his acquaintance, with whom he promenaded:

Miss.—Do you think they will like to return to the field?

President.—It may seem hard; but even those boys (pointing to some youths around the monument twelve or fourteen years old) will have their trial.

Miss.—But how shall the army be fed?

President.—I don't see why rats, if fat, are not as good as squirrels. Our men *did* eat mule meat at Vicksburg; but it would be an expensive luxury now.

After this, the President fell into a grave mood, and some remark about recognition caused him to say twice—" We have no friends abroad!"

MARCH 22D.—Cloudy morning, with ice; subsequently a snow-storm all day long. No war news. But meat and grain are coming freely from the South. This gives rise to a rumor that Lee will fall back, and that the capital will be besieged; all without any foundation.

A Mrs. —— from Maryland, whose only son is in a Federal prison, writes the President (she is in this city) that she desires to go to Canada on some secret enterprise. The President favors her purpose in an indorsement. On this the Secretary indorses a purpose to facilitate her design, and suggests that she be paid $1000 in gold from the secret service fund. She is a Roman Catholic, and intimates that the bishops, priests, and nuns will aid her.

MARCH 23D.—Snow fell all night, and was eight or ten inches deep this morning; but it was a bright morning, and glorious sunshine all day,—the anniversary of the birth of Shakspeare, 300 years ago,—and the snow is melting rapidly.

The Secretary of War had a large amount of plate taken from the department to-day to his lodgings at the Spottswood Hotel. It was captured from the enemy with Dahlgren, who had pillaged it from our opulent families in the country.

MARCH 24TH.—A bright pleasant day—snow nearly gone.

Next week the clerks in the departments, between the ages of eighteen and forty-five, are to be enrolled, and perhaps the greater number will be detailed to their present employments.

Gov. Vance is here, and the President is about to appoint some of his friends brigadiers, which is conciliatory.

Gen. Longstreet has written a letter to the President, which I have not seen. The President sent it to the Secretary to-day, marked "confidential." It must relate either to subsistence or to important movements in meditation. If the latter, we shall soon know it.

MARCH 25TH.—Raining moderately.

Yesterday Mr. Miles, member of Congress from South Carolina, received a dispatch from Charleston, signed by many of the leading citizens, protesting against the removal of 52 companies of cavalry from that department to Virginia. They say so few will be left that the railroads, plantations, and even the City of Charleston will be exposed to the easy capture of the enemy; and this is "approved" and signed by T. Jordan, Chief of Staff. It was given to the Secretary of War, who sent it to Gen. Bragg, assuring him that the citizens signing it were the most *influential* in the State, etc.

Gen. Bragg sent it back with an indignant note. He says the President gave the order, and it was a proper one. These companies of cavalry have not shared the hardships of the war, and have done no fighting; more cavalry has been held by Gen. Beauregard, in proportion to the number of his army, than by any other general; that skeleton regiments, which have gone through fire and blood, ought to be allowed to relieve them; and when recruited, would be ample for the defense of the coast, etc. Gen. Bragg concluded by saying that the offense of having the military orders of the commander-in-chief, etc. exposed to civilians, to be criticised and protested against—and "approved" by the Chief of Staff—at such a time as this, and in a matter of such grave importance—ought not to be suffered to pass without a merited rebuke. And I am sure poor Beauregard will get the rebuke; for all the military and civil functionaries near the government partake of something of a dislike of him.

And yet Beauregard was wrong to make any stir about it; and the President himself only acted in accordance with Gen. Lee's suggestions, noted at the time in this Diary.

Gen. Polk writes from Dunapolis that he will have communications with Jackson restored in a few days, and that the injury to the railroads was not so great as the enemy represented.

Mr. Memminger, the Secretary of the Treasury, is in a black Dutch fury. It appears that his agent, C. C. Thayer, with $15,000,000 Treasury notes for disbursement in Texas, arrived at the mouth of the Rio Grande in December, when the enemy had possession of Brownsville, and when Matamoras was in revolution. He then conferred with Mr. Benjamin's friend (and Confederate States secret agent) Mr. Quintero, and Quartermaster Russell, who advised him to deposit the treasure with P. Milmo & Co.—a house with which our agents have had large transactions, and Mr. M. being son-in-law to Gov. Vidurri—to be shipped to Eagle Pass *via* Monterey to San Antonio, etc.

But alas! and alas! P. Milmo & Co., upon being informed that fifteen millions were in their custody, notified our agents that they would seize it all, and hold it all, until certain alleged claims they held against the Confederate States Government were paid. Mr. Quintero, who sends this precious intelligence, says he thinks the money will soon be released—and so do I, when it is ascertained that it will be of no value to any of the parties there.

Mr. Memminger, however, wants Quartermaster Russell cashiered, and court-martialed, and, moreover, decapitated!

MARCH 26TH.—Bright morning, but a cold, cloudy, windy day.

A great crowd of people have been at the Treasury building all day, funding Treasury notes. It is to be hoped that as money gets scarcer, food and raiment will get cheaper.

Mr. Benton, the dentist, escaped being conscribed last year by the ingenuity of his attorney, G. W. Randolph, formerly Secretary of War, who, after keeping his case in suspense (alleging that dentists were physicians or experts) as long as possible, finally contrived to have him appointed *hospital steward*—the present Secretary consenting. But now the enrolling officer is after him again, and it will be seen what he is to do next. The act says dentists shall serve as conscripts.

And Mr. Randolph himself was put in the category of conscripts by the late military act, but Gov. Smith has decreed his exemption as a member of the Common Council! Oh, patriotism, where are thy votaries? Some go so far as to say Gov. Smith is too free with exemptions!

MARCH 27TH —Bright morning, but windy; subsequently warmer, and wind lulled. Collards coming up. Potatoes all rotted in the ground during the recent cold weather. I shall rely on other vegetables, which I am now beginning to sow freely.

We have no war news to-day.

MARCH 28TH.—April-like day, but no rain; clouds, and sunshine, and warm.

About 2 P.M. the Secretary received a dispatch stating that the enemy had appeared in force opposite Fredericksburg, and attempted, without success, to cross. A copy of this was immediately sent to Gen. Lee.

It is said that Gen. Longstreet is marching with expedition down the Valley of the Shenandoah, to flank Meade or Grant. I doubt it. But the campaign will commence as soon as the weather will permit.

A letter from G. B. Lamar, Savannah, Ga., informs the Secretary that he (L.) has command of five steamers, and that he can easily make arrangements with the (Federal) commandant of Fort Pulaski to permit them to pass and repass. His proposition to the government is to bring in munitions of war, etc., and take out cotton, charging one-half for freight. Mr. Memminger having seen this, advises the Secretary to require the delivery of a cargo before supplying any cotton. Mr. M. has a sort of *jealousy* of Mr. Lamar.

MARCH 29TH.—A furious gale, eastern, and rain.

No news, except the appearance of a few gun-boats down the river; which no one regards as an important matter.

Great crowds are funding their Treasury notes to-day; but prices of provisions are not diminished. White beans, such as I paid $60 a bushel for early in this month, are now held at $75. What *shall* we do to subsist until the next harvest?

MARCH 30TH.—It rained all night, the wind blowing a gale from the east. This morning the wind was from the west, blowing moderately; and although cloudy, no rain.

The enemy's gun-boats down the river shelled the shore where it was suspected we had troops in ambush; and when some of their barges approached the shore, it was ascertained they were not mistaken, for a volley from our men (signal corps) killed and wounded half the crew. The remainder put back to the gun-boats.

There is great tribulation among the departmental clerks, who are to be enrolled as conscripts, and probably sent to the army. The young relatives of some of the Secretaries are being appointed commissaries, quartermasters, surgeons, etc. They keep out of danger.

Many ladies have been appointed clerks. There is a roomful of them just over the Secretary's office, and he says they distract him with their noise of moving of chairs and running about, etc.

The papers publish an account of a battle of snow-balls in our army, which indicates the spirit of the troops, when, perhaps, they are upon the eve of passing through such awful scenes of carnage as will make the world tremble at the appalling spectacle.

MARCH 31ST.—Cloudy and cold. No war news, though it is generally believed that Longstreet is really in the valley.

A speech delivered by the Hon. J. W. Wall, in New Jersey, is copied in all the Southern papers, and read with interest by our people.

CHAPTER XXXVII.

Return of Mr. Ould and Capt. Hatch from Fortress Monroe.—Quarrel between Mr. Memminger and Mr. Seddon.—Famine.—A victory in Louisiana.—Vice-President Stephens's speech.—Victory of Gen. Forrest.—Capture of Plymouth, N. C.—Gen. Lee's bill of fare.

APRIL 1ST.—Cloudy all day, with occasional light showers.

No war news; but the papers have an account of the shooting of an infant by some Yankees on account of its *name*. This shows that the war is degenerating more and more into savage barbarism.

APRIL 2D.—It rained furiously all night; wind northwest, and snowed to-day until 12 M. to a depth of several inches. It is still blowing a gale from the northwest.

To-day the clerks were paid in the new currency; but I see no abatement of prices from the scarcity of money, caused by funding. Shad are selling at $10 each, paper; or 50 cents, silver. Gold and silver are circulating—a little.

A letter from Liberty, Va., states that government bacon (tithe) is spoiling, in bulk, for want of attention.

From Washington County there are complaints that Gen. Longstreet's impressing officers are taking all, except five bushels of grain and fifty pounds of bacon for each adult—a plenty, one would think, under the circumstances.

Senator Hunter has asked and obtained a detail for Mr. Daudridge (under eighteen) as quartermaster's clerk. And Mr. Secretary Seddon has ordered the commissary to let Mrs. Michie have sugar and flour for her family, white and black.

Mr. Secretary Benjamin sent over, to-day, for passports to the Mississippi River for two "secret agents." What for?

Gen. Lee has made regulations to prevent cotton, tobacco, etc. passing his lines into the enemy's country, unless allowed by the government. But, then, several in authority *will* "allow" it without limit.

I set out sixty-eight early cabbage-plants yesterday. They are now under the snow!

APRIL 3D.—The snow has disappeared; but it is cloudy, with a cold northwest wind. The James River is very high, and all the streams are so much swollen that no military operations in the field are looked for immediately. It is generally believed that Grant, the Federal lieutenant-general, will concentrate an immense army for the capture of Richmond, and our authorities are invoked to make the necessary dispositions to resist the attempt.

The papers contain a supplemental proclamation of President Lincoln, and understand it to be merely an electioneering card to secure the Abolition vote in the convention to nominate a candidate for the Presidency. If it does not mean that, its object must be to induce us to send an army North to burn and pillage, so that the Federal authorities may have a pretext to raise new armies, and prosecute the war, not for the Union, but for conquest and power.

Custis and I received yesterday $500 in the *new* Treasury notes, but we had to pay $16 for two pounds of bacon. So no diminution of prices is yet experienced. *It is now a famine,* although I believe we are starving in the midst of plenty, if it were only equally distributed. But the government will not, it seems, require the railroads to bring provisions to the exclusion of freight for the speculators. Certain non-combating officers of the government have abundance brought them by the *Southern* Express Co., and the merchants have abundance of goods brought hither by the same company for the purposes of speculation. Well, we shall see the result! One is almost ready to believe that the government declines to fill the depots here, harboring the purpose of abandoning the city. That would be abandonment of the cause. Nearly all who own no slaves would remain citizens of the United States, if permitted, without further molestation on the part of the Federal authorities, and many Virginians in the field might abandon the Confederate States army. The State would be lost, and North Carolina and Tennessee would have an inevitable avalanche of invasion precipitated upon them. The only hope would be civil war in the North, a not improbable event. What could they do with four millions of negroes arrogating equality with the whites?

APRIL 4TH.—A cold rain all day; wind from northwest.

Mr. Ould and Capt. Hatch, agents of exchange (of prisoners), have returned from a conference with Gen. Butler, at Fortress Monroe, and it is announced that arrangements have been made for an immediate resumption of the exchange of prisoners on the old footing. Thus has the government abandoned the ground so proudly assumed—of non-intercourse with Butler, and the press is firing away at it for negotiating with the "Beast" and outlaw. But our men in captivity are in favor of a speedy exchange, no matter with whom the agreement is made.

Forrest has destroyed Paducah, Ky.

There is a little quarrel in progress between the Secretaries of War and the Treasury. Some days ago the Postmaster-General got from the President an order that his clerks should be detailed for the use of the department until further orders. The Secretary of the Treasury made an application to the Secretary of War for a similar detail, but it was refused. Mr. Memminger appealed, with some acerbity, to the President, and the President indorsed on the paper that the proper rule would be for the Secretary of War to detail as desired by heads of departments. Nevertheless, the clerks were detailed but for thirty days, to report at the Camp of Instruction, if the detail were not renewed. To-day Mr. Memminger addresses a note to Mr. Seddon, inquiring if it was his purpose to hold his clerks liable to perform military duty after the expiration of the thirty days, and declaring that the incertitude and inconvenience of constantly applying for renewal of details, deranged and obstructed the business of his department. I know not yet what answer Mr. S. made, but doubtless a breach exists through which one or both may pass out of the cabinet. The truth is, that all clerks constitutionally appointed are legally exempt, and it is the boldest tyranny to enroll them as conscripts. But Mr. Memminger has no scruples on that head. All of them desire to retain in "soft places" their own relatives and friends, feeling but little sympathy for others whose refugee families are dependent on their salaries.

On Saturday, the cavalry battalion for local defense, accepted last summer by the President, were notified on parade that 20 days would be allowed them to choose their companies in the army, and if the choice were not made, they would be assigned to companies. They protested against this as despotic, but there is no remedy.

APRIL 5TH.—Cold rain all night and all day; wind northwest.

The Quartermaster-General *now* recommends that no furloughs be given, so as to devote the railroads to the transportation of grain to Virginia.

The Commissary-General again informs the Secretary of War, to-day, that unless the passenger trains were discontinued, the army could not be subsisted, and Richmond and all Virginia might have to be abandoned, and the country might be pillaged by our own soldiers. Not a word against the Southern (Yankee) Express Company.

Our prospects are brighter than they have been for many a day, and the enemy are doomed, I think, to a speedy humiliation.

I saw a note to-day from Mr. Memminger stating his fears that the amount of Treasury notes funded will not exceed $200,000,000, leaving $600,000,000 still in circulation! It is true, some $300,000,000 might be collected in taxes, if due vigilance were observed,—but *will* it be observed? He says he can make between $2,000,000 and $3,000,000 of the new currency per day. If this be done, the redundancy will soon be as great as ever. Nothing but success in the field will prevent an explosion and repudiation of the currency, sooner or later.

April 6th.—At mid-day it cleared off; wind still northwest, and cool.

Beans (white) were held to-day at $5 per quart! and other articles of food in proportion. How we are to live is the anxious question. At auction old sheets brought $25 a piece, and there seemed to be an advance on everything, instead of a decline as was expected. The speculators and extortioners seem to act in concert, and the government appears to be no match for them. It is not the scarcity of food which causes the high prices, for wood and coal sell as high as other things, and they are no scarcer than at any former period. But it is an insatiable thirst for gain, which I fear the Almighty Justicer will rebuke in some signal manner, perhaps in the emancipation of the slaves, and then the loss will be greater than all the gains reaped from the heart's blood of our brave soldiers and the tears of the widow and orphan! And government still neglects the wives and children of the soldiers,— a fearful risk!

But, alas! how are our brave men faring in the hands of the demon fanatics in the United States? It is said *they* are dying like sheep.

April 7th.—A bright spring day.

We look for startling news from the Rappahannock in a few days. Longstreet will be there.

Gen. Lee writes that the fortifications around Richmond ought to be pushed to completion: 2000 negroes are still at work on them.

April 8th.—Bright and warm—really a fine spring day. It is the day of *fasting*, humiliation, and prayer, and all the offices are closed. May God put it into the hearts of the extortioners to relent, and abolish, for a season, the insatiable greed for gain! I paid $25 for a half cord of wood to-day, new currency. I fear a nation of extortioners are unworthy of independence, and that we must be chastened and purified before success will be vouchsafed us.

What enormous appetites we have now, and how little illness, since food has become so high in price! I cannot afford to have more than an ounce of meat daily for each member of my family of six; and to-day Custis's parrot, which has accompanied the family in all their flights, and, it seems, will *never* die, stole the cook's ounce of fat meat and gobbled it up before it could be taken from him. He is permitted to set at one corner of the table, and has lately acquired a fondness for meat. The old cat goes staggering about from debility, although Fannie often gives him her share. We see neither rats nor mice about the premises now. This is famine. Even the pigeons watch the crusts in the hands of the children, and follow them in the yard. *And, still, there are no beggars.*

The plum-tree in my neighbor's garden is in blossom to-day, and I see a few blossoms on our cherry-trees. I have set out some 130 early York cabbage-plants—very small; and to-day planted lima and snap beans. I hope we shall have no more cold weather, for garden seed, if those planted failed to come up, would cost more than the crops in ordinary times.

APRIL 9TH.—Rained all day.

Lieut. Tyler, grandson of President Tyler, is here on furlough, which expires to-morrow. His father (the major), whom he has not seen for two years, he learns, will be in the city day after to-morrow; and to-day he sought admittance to Mr. Secretary Seddon to obtain a prolongation of his furlough, so as to enable him to remain two days and see his parent. But Mr. Kean refused him admittance, and referred him to the Adjutant-General, who was sick and absent; and thus "red tape" exhibits its insensibility to the dictates of humanity, even when no advantage is gained by it. Robert Tyler subsequently addressed a note to Mr. K., the purport of which I did not inquire.

We have no war news—indeed, no newspapers to-day. The wet weather, however, may be in our favor, as it will give us time to concentrate in Virginia. Better give up all the cities South, than lose Richmond. As long as we hold Richmond and Virginia, the "head and heart" of the "rebellion," we shall not only be between the enemy (south of us) and their own country, but within reach of it.

APRIL 10TH.—Rained all night. Cloudy to-day; wind southwest.

The Secretary of War must feel his subordination to Gen. Bragg. Gen. Fitz Lee recommended strongly a Prussian officer for appointment in the cavalry, and Mr. Seddon referred it to Gen. B., suggesting that he might be appointed in the cavalry corps to be stationed near this city. Gen. B. returns the paper, saying the President intends to have an organized brigade of cavalry from the Army of Northern Virginia on duty here, and there will be no vacancy in it. From this it seems that the Secretary is not only not to be gratified by the appointment, but is really kept in ignorance of army movements in contemplation!

Major Griswold has resigned, at last. He did not find his position a bed of roses. I believe he abandons the Confederate States service altogether, and will attend to the collection of claims, and the defense of prisoners, probably arrested by Major Carrington, his successor in office.

To-day I saw two conscripts from Western Virginia conducted to the cars (going to Lee's army) *in chains*. It made a chill shoot through my breast. I doubt its policy, though they may be peculiar offenders.

The benevolent Capt. Warner, being persecuted by the Commissary-General for telling the *truth* in regard to the rations, etc., is settling his accounts as rapidly as possible, and will resign his office. He says he will resume his old business, publishing books, etc.

APRIL 11TH.—Rained all night, but clear most of the day.

There are rumors of Burnside landing troops on the Peninsula; also of preparations for movements on the Rappahannock—by which side is uncertain. It is said troops are coming from Mississippi, Lieut.-Gen. (Bishop) Polk's command.

The FAMINE is still advancing, and his gaunt proportions loom up daily, as he approaches with gigantic strides. The rich speculators, however, and the officers of influence stationed here, who have secured the favor of the Express Company, get enough to eat. Potatoes sell at $1 per quart; chickens, $35 per pair; turnip greens, $4 per peck! An ounce of meat, daily, is the allowance to each member of my family, the cat and parrot included. The pigeons of my neighbor have disappeared. Every day we have accounts of robberies, the preceding night, of cows, pigs, bacon, flour—and even the setting hens are taken from their nests!

APRIL 12TH.—Cloudy—rained in the afternoon.

This is the anniversary of the first gun of the war, fired at Fort Sumter.

It is still said and believed that Gen. Lee will take the initiative, and attack Grant. The following shows that we have had another success:

"MOBILE, April 11th, 1864.
"TO GEN. S. COOPER, A. & I. GENERAL.

"The following report was received at Baton Rouge, on the 3d inst., from the Surgeon-General of Banks's army: We met the enemy near Shreveport. Union force repulsed with great loss. How many can you accommodate in hospitals at Baton Rouge? Steamer Essex, or Benton, destroyed by torpedoes in Red River, and a transport captured by Confederates.

"Farragut reported preparing to attack Mobile. Six monitors coming to him. The garrisons of New Orleans and Baton Rouge were very much reduced for the purpose of increasing Banks's forces.

"D. H. MAURY, *Major-General Commanding.*"

APRIL 13TH.—A clear, but cool day. Again planted corn, the other having rotted.

There is an unofficial report that one of our torpedo boats struck the Federal war steamer Minnesota yesterday, near Newport News, and damaged her badly.

I learn (from an official source) to-day that Gen. Longstreet's corps is at Charlottesville, to co-operate with Lee's army, which will soon move, no doubt.

Gen. Bragg received a dispatch yesterday, requesting that commissary stores for Longstreet be sent to Charlottesville, and he ordered his military secretary to direct the Commissary-General accordingly. To this Col. Northrop, C. G. S., took exceptions, and returned the paper, calling the attention of Gen. B.'s secretary to the Rules and Regulations, involving a matter of red tape etiquette. The C. G. S. can only be *ordered* or *directed* by the Secretary of War. Gen. B. sent the paper to the Secretary, with the remark that if he is to be restricted, etc., his usefulness must be necessarily diminished. The Secretary sent for Col. N., and I suppose pacified him.

APRIL 14TH.—Bright morning—cloudy and cold the rest of the day.

No reliable war news to-day; but we are on the tip-toe of expectation of exciting news from the Rapidan. Longstreet is certainly in communication with Lee; and if the enemy be not present with overwhelming numbers, which there is no reason to anticipate, a great battle may be imminent.

Read Vice-President Stephens's speech against the suspension of the writ of *habeas corpus* to-day. He said independence without liberty was of no value to him, and if he must have a master, he cared not whether he was Northern or Southern. If we gain our independence, this speech will *ruin* Mr. S.; if we do not, it may *save* him and his friends.

APRIL 15TH.—Cloudy—slight showers. I published an article yesterday in the *Enquirer*, addressed to the President, on the subject of supplies for the army and the people (the government to take all the supplies in the country), the annihilation of speculation, and the necessary suppression of the Southern (Yankee) Express Company. This elicited the approval of Col. Northrop, the Commissary-General, who spoke to me on the subject. He told me the Express Company had attempted to *bribe* him, by offering to bring his family supplies gratis, etc. He said he had carried his point, in causing Gen. Bragg to address him according to military etiquette. He showed me another order from Bragg (through the Adjutant-General), to take possession of the toll meal at Crenshaw's mills. This he says is contrary to contract, and he was going to the Secretary to have it withdrawn. "Besides," said he, "and truly, it would do no good. The people must eat, whether they get meal from Crenshaw or not. If not, they will get it elsewhere, and what they do get will be so much diverted from the commissariat."

There are rumors of the enemy accumulating a heavy force at Suffolk.

The guard at Camp Lee are going in the morning to Lee's army; their places here to be filled by the reserve forces of boys and old men. This indicates a battle on the Rapidan.

APRIL 16TH.—Rained all night, and in fitful showers all day.

We have more accounts (unofficial) of a victory near Shreveport, La. One of the enemy's gun-boats has been blown up and sunk in Florida.

By late Northern arrivals we see that a Mr. Long, member of Congress, has spoken in favor of our recognition. A resolution of expulsion was soon after introduced.

Gen. Lee has suggested, and the Secretary of War has approved, a project for removing a portion of the population from Richmond into the country. Its object is to accumulate supplies for the army. If some 20,000 could be moved away, it would relieve the rest to some extent.

Troops are passing northward every night. The carnage and carnival of death will soon begin!

APRIL 17TH.—Rained until bedtime—then cleared off quite cold. This morning it is cold, with occasional sunshine.

Gen. Beauregard's instructions to Major-Gen. Anderson in Florida, who has but 8000 men, opposed by 15,000, were referred by the Secretary of War to Gen. Bragg, who returned them with the following snappish indorsement: "The enemy's strength seems greatly exaggerated, and the instructions too much on the defensive."

APRIL 18TH.—Cleared away in the night—frost. To-day it clouded up again!

We have an account from the West, to the effect that Forrest *stormed* Fort Pillow, putting all the garrison, but one hundred, to the sword; there being 700 in the fort—400 negroes.

APRIL 19TH.—Cloudy and cold.

We have no authentic war news, but are on the tip-toe of expectation. The city is in some commotion on a rumor that the non combating population will be required to leave, to avoid transportation of food to the city. Corn is selling at $1.25 per bushel in Georgia and Alabama; here, at $40—such is the deplorable condition of the railroads, or rather of the management of them. Col. Northrop, Commissary-General, said to-day that Gen. Lee and the Secretary of War were responsible for the precarious state of affairs, in not taking all the means of transportation for the use of the army; and that our fate was suspended by a hair.

The President returned the paper to day, relating to the matter of etiquette between Col. Northrop and Gen. Bragg's military secretary. The President says that Gen. B. certainly has the right to give orders—being assigned to duty here, and, I presume, representing the President himself; but that any one of his staff, unless directing those of inferior rank, ought to give commands "by order" of Gen. Bragg. Col. N. says that don't satisfy him; and that no general has a right to issue orders to him!

AT THE CONFEDERATE STATES CAPITAL.

The famine is becoming more terrible daily; and soon no salary will suffice to support one's family.

The 1st and 2d Auditors and their clerks (several hundred, male and female) have been ordered to proceed to Montgomery, Ala. Perhaps the government will soon remove thither entirely. This is ill-timed, as the enemy will accept it as an indication of an abandonment of the capital; and many of our people will regard it as a preliminary to the evacuation of Richmond. It is more the effect of extortion and high prices, than apprehension of the city being taken by the enemy.

APRIL 20TH.—A clear morning, but a cold, cloudy day.

The following dispatch from Gen. Forrest shows that the bloody work has commenced in earnest:

"DEMOPOLIS, ALA., April 19th.

" To GEN. S. COOPER.

" The following dispatch has just been received from Gen. Forrest, dated Jackson, Tenn., April 15th.

"L. POLK, *Lieut.-General.*

" I attacked Fort Pillow on the morning of the 12th inst., with a part of Bell's and McCulloch's brigades, numbering ——, under Brig.-Gen. J. R. Chalmers. After a short fight we drove the enemy, seven hundred strong, into the fort, under cover of their gun-boats, and demanded a surrender, which was declined by Major L. W. Booth, commanding United States forces. I stormed the fort, and after a contest of thirty minutes captured the entire garrison, killing 500 and taking 100 prisoners, and a large amount of quartermaster stores. The officers in the fort were killed, including Major Booth. I sustained a loss of 20 killed and 60 wounded. The Confederate flag now floats over the fort.

"(Signed) N. B. FORREST, *Major-General.*"

There is a rumor that Grant's army is falling back toward Centreville.

It is supposed by many that all the departments will follow the Auditor to Montgomery soon.

APRIL 21ST.—Bright sunshine all day, but cool.

Gen. Bragg received a dispatch to day from Gen. Hoke, of Plymouth, N. C., stating that he had (yesterday) *stormed* Plymouth, taking 1600 prisoners, 25 cannon, stores, etc. etc. This put the city in as good spirits as possible.

But the excitement from Hoke's victory was supplanted by an excitement of another kind. A report was circulated and believed that the President resolved yesterday to remove the government to South Carolina or Alabama; and the commotion was very great. The President's salary is insufficient to meet his housekeeping expenditures; and Mrs. D. has become, very naturally, somewhat indignant at the conduct of the extortioners, and, of course, the President himself partook of the indignation.

At 2 P.M. to-day the President's papers came in. Among them was one from the Commissary-General, stating that the present management of railroad transportation would not suffice to subsist the army. This had been referred to Gen. Bragg yesterday (who seems to *rank* the Secretary of War), and he made an elaborate indorsement thereon. He recommended that all passenger trains be discontinued, except one daily, and on this that government agents, soldiers, etc. have preference; that arrangements be made at once to hasten on the freight trains (taking military possession of the roads) without breaking bulk; and finally to reduce consumers here as much as possible by a reduction of civil officers, etc. etc. in the departments—that is, sending to other places such as can perform their duties at distant points. On this the President indorsed a reference to the Secretary of War, requiring his opinion in writing, etc. Since then, the President and cabinet have been in consultation, and we shall probably know the result to-morrow.

If the departments are sent South, it will cause a prodigious outburst from the press here, and may have a bad, blundering effect on the army in Virginia, composed mostly of Virginians; and Gen. Bragg will have to bear the brunt of it, although the government will be solely responsible.

Gov. Vance recommended the suspension of conscription in the eastern counties of North Carolina the other day. This paper was referred by the Secretary to the President, by the President to Gen. B. (who is a native of North Carolina), and, seeing what was desired, Gen. B. recommended that the conscription be proceeded with. This may cause Gov. V. to be defeated at the election, and Gen. B. will be roundly abused. He will be unpopular still.

APRIL 22D.—A bright day and warmer. Cherry-trees in blossom. We have the following war news:

"PLYMOUTH, N. C., April 20th.
"To GEN. BRAGG.
"I have stormed and captured this place, capturing 1 brigadier, 1600 men, stores, and 25 pieces of artillery.
"R. F. HOKE, *Brig.-General.*"

The President has changed his mind since the reception of the news from North Carolina, and has determined that *all* the government shall not leave Richmond until further orders. All that can be spared will go, however, at once. The War and Navy Departments will remain for the present. The news is said to have had a wonderful effect on the President's mind; and he hopes we may derive considerable supplies from Eastern North Carolina. So do I.

Gov. Watts writes to the Secretary that commissary agents, who ought to be in the ranks, are making unnecessary impressments, leaving to each negro only four ounces of bacon per day. He says the government has already some 10,000,000 pounds of bacon in Alabama; and that if the other States, east of the Mississippi, furnish a proportional amount, there will be 60,000,000 pounds—enough to feed our armies twelve months.

The Commissary-General's estimates for the next six months are for 400,000 men.

APRIL 23D.—A bright day, with southern breezes.

It is rumored and believed that Gen. Lee's army is in motion. If this be so, we shall soon hear of a "fight, or a foot race." And how can Grant run away, when Mr. Chase, the Federal Secretary of the Treasury, openly proclaims ruin to the finances unless they speedily achieve success in the field? I think he must fight; and I am sure he will be beaten, for Lee's strength is probably underestimated.

We are also looking to hear more news from North Carolina; and Newbern will probably be stormed next, since storming is now the order of the day.

APRIL 24TH.—Cloudy and windy, but warm.

We have none of the details yet of the storming of Plymouth, except the brief dispatches in the newspapers; nor any reliable accounts of subsequent movements. But a letter from Gen. Whiting indicates that all his troops had been taken northward, and we may expect something further of interest.

It is still believed that Lee's and Grant's armies are in motion on the Rappahannock; but whether going North or coming South, no one seems to know. Our people unanimously look for a victory.

I bought a black coat at auction yesterday (short swallow-tailed) for $12. It is fine cloth, not much worn—its owner going into the army, probably—but out of *fashion*. If it had been a frock-coat, it would have brought $100. It is no time for *fashion* now.

Gen. Johnston's Chief Commissary offers to send some bacon to Lee's army. A short time since, it was said, Johnston was prevented from *advancing* for want of rations.

APRIL 25TH.—A bright and beautiful day; southern breezes.

No reliable war news; but there are rumors that our victory at Shreveport was a great one. Nothing additional from North Carolina, though something further must soon occur there. It is said the enemy's killed and wounded at Plymouth amounted to only 100: ours 300; but we got 2500 prisoners.

President Lincoln has made a speech at Baltimore, threatening retaliation for the slaughter at Fort Pillow—which was *stormed*.

Lieut.-Gen. Polk telegraphs that our forces have captured and burnt one of the enemy's gun-boats at Yazoo City—first taking out her guns, eight rifled 24-pounders.

To-day Mr. Memminger, in behalf of the ladies in his department, presented a battle-flag to the Department Battalion for its gallant conduct in the repulse of Dahlgren's raid. But the ladies leave early in the morning for South Carolina.

The President still says that many of the government officers and employees must be sent away, if transportation cannot be had to feed them here as well as the armies.

APRIL 26TH.—Another truly fine spring day.

The ominous silence on the Rapidan and Rappahannock continues still. The two armies seem to be measuring each other's strength before the awful conflict begins.

It is said the enemy are landing large bodies of troops at Yorktown.

Major-Gen. Ransom has been assigned to the command of this department; and Gen. Winder's expectations of promotion are blasted. Will he resign? I think not.

The enemy's accounts of the battle on the Red River do not agree with the reports we have.

Neither do the Federal accounts of the storming of Fort Pillow agree with ours.

APRIL 27TH.—Another bright and beautiful day; and vegetation is springing with great rapidity. But nearly all my potatoes, corn, egg-plants, and tomatoes seem to have been killed by the frosts of March. I am replanting corn, lima beans, etc. The other vegetables are growing well. One of my fig-bushes was killed—that is, nearly all the branches. The roots live.

It is rumored that the armies on the Rapidan were drawn up in line.

The enemy have again evacuated Suffolk.

Gen. Beauregard is at Weldon. Perhaps Burnside may hurl his blows against North Carolina.

Food is still advancing in price; and unless relief comes from some quarter soon, this city will be in a deplorable condition. A good many fish, however, are coming in, and shad have fallen in price to $12 per pair.

The government ordered the toll of meal here (which the miller, Crenshaw, sold to the people) to be taken for the army; but Col. Northrop, Commissary-General, opposes this; and it is to be hoped, as usual, he may have his way, in spite of even the President. These papers pass through the hands of the Secretary of War.

The French ships have gone down the river, without taking much tobacco; said to have been ordered away by the United States Government.

Col. W. M. Browne (the President's English A.D.C.), it is said, goes to Georgia as commandant of conscripts for that State. It is probable he offended some one of the President's family, domestic or military. The *people* had long been offended by his presence and arrogance.

The *Enquirer*, to-day, has a communication assaulting Messrs. Toombs and Stephens, and impeaching their loyalty. The writer denounced the Vice-President severely for his opposition to the suspension of the writ of *habeas corpus*. During the day the article was sent to Mr. Secretary Seddon, with the compliments of Mr. Parker—the author, I suppose.

APRIL 28TH.—After a slight shower last night, a cool, clear morning.

The ominous silence or pause between the armies continues. Lieut.-Gen. Longstreet, it is said, is "hidden." I suppose he is working his way around the enemy's right flank. If so, we shall soon hear thunder.

It is also supposed that Lee meditates an incursion into Pennsylvania, and that Gen. Beauregard will protect his rear and cover this city. All is merely conjecture.

We are amused at the enemy's accounts of the storming of Plymouth. Their papers pretend to have not heard the result, and would lead their readers to believe that Gen. Hoke was repulsed, and that the place is "impregnable."

The following appears in the morning papers:

"GEN. LEE'S BILL OF FARE.—The Richmond correspondent of the Mobile *Advertiser* gives the following about Gen. Lee's mode of living:

"In Gen. Lee's tent meat is eaten but twice a week, the general not allowing it oftener, because he believes indulgence in meat to be criminal in the present straitened condition of the country. His ordinary dinner consists of a head of cabbage, boiled in salt water, and a pone of corn bread. In this connection rather a comic story is told. Having invited a number of gentlemen to dine with him, Gen. Lee, in a fit of extravagance, ordered a sumptuous repast of cabbage and middling. The dinner was served: and, behold, a great pile of cabbage and a bit of middling about four inches long and two inches across! The guests, with commendable politeness, unanimously declined middling, and it remained in the dish untouched. Next day Gen. Lee, remembering the delicate tit-bit which had been so providentially preserved, ordered his servant to bring 'that middling.' The man hesitated, scratched his head, and finally owned up: 'De fac is, Masse Robert, dat ar middlin' was borrid middlin'; we all did'n had nar spec; and I done paid it back to de man whar I got it from.' Gen. Lee heaved a sigh of deepest disappointment, and pitched into his cabbage."

By a correspondence between the Secretaries of the Treasury and War, I saw that Mr. Memminger has about *a million and a quarter in coin* at Macon, Ga., seized as the property of the New Orleans banks—perhaps belonging to Northern men. I believe it was taken when there was an attempt made to smuggle it North. What it is proposed to do with it *I know not*, but I think neither the President nor the Secretaries will hesitate to use it—if there be a "military necessity." Who knows but that one or more members of Mr. Lincoln's cabinet, or his generals, might be purchased with gold? Fortress Monroe would be cheap at that price!

APRIL 29TH.—A letter from Major-Gen. Hoke, dated Plymouth, April 25th, and asking the appointment of Lieut.-Col. Dearing to a brigadiership, says his promotion is desired to lead a brigade in the expedition against Newbern. The President directs the Secretary to appoint him temporarily "for the expedition." Soon we shall know the result.

By flag of truce boat, it is understood Northern papers admit a Federal defeat on the Red River, the storming of Plymouth, etc., and charge the Federal authorities at Washington with having published falsehoods to deceive the people. Gold was $1.83.

Troops are passing through Richmond now, day and night, concentrating under Lee. The *great* battle cannot be much longer postponed.

Last night was clear and cold, and we have fire to-day.

The President has decided not to call into service the reserve class unless on extraordinary occasions, but to let them remain at home and cultivate the soil.

It is now probable the Piedmont Railroad will be completed by the 1st June, as extreme necessity drives the government to some degree of energy. If it had taken up, or allowed to be taken up, the rails on the Aquia Creek Road a year ago, the Piedmont connection would have been made ere this; and then this famine would not have been upon us, and there would have been abundance of grain in the army depots of Virginia.

APRIL 30TH.—Federal papers now admit that Gen. Banks has been disastrously beaten in Louisiana. They also admit their calamity at Plymouth, N. C. Thus in Louisiana, Florida, West Tennessee, and North Carolina the enemy have sustained severe defeats: their losses amounting to some 20,000 men, 100 guns, half a dozen war steamers, etc. etc.

Gen. Burnside has left Annapolis and gone to Grant—whatever the plan was originally; and the work of concentration goes on for a *decisive* clash of arms in Virginia.

And troops are coming hither from all quarters, like streamlets flowing into the ocean. Our men are confident, and eager for the fray.

The railroad companies say they can transport 10,000 bushels corn, daily, into Virginia. That will subsist 200,000 men and 25,000 horses. And in June the Piedmont connection will be completed.

The *great* battle may not occur for weeks yet. It will probably end the war.

CHAPTER XXXVIII.

Dispatch from Gen. J. E. Johnston.—Dispatch from Gen. Lee.—Mr. Saulsbury's resolution in the U. S. Senate.—Progress of the enemy.—Rumored preparations for the flight of the President.—Wrangling of high officials.—Position of the armies.

MAY 1ST.—Cloudy and showery, but warm, and fine for vegetation. My lettuce, cabbage, beans, etc. are growing finely. But the Yankee corn and lima beans, imported by Col. Gorgas, Chief of Ordnance, have rotted in the ground.

No war news.

Yesterday a paper was sent to the President by Gen. Pickett, recommending Gen. Roger A. Pryor for a cavalry command in North Carolina. But the President sent it to the Secretary of War with the curt remark that the command had already been disposed of to Col. Dearing, on Gen. Hoke's recommendation. Thus Gen. P. is again whistled down the wind, in spite of the efforts of even Mr. Hunter, and many other leading politicians. It is possible Gen. P. may have on some occasion criticised Lee.

MAY 2D.—A cool day, sunshine and showers.

To-day Congress assembled, and the President's message was delivered, although he buried his youngest son yesterday, who lost his life by an accidental fall from the porch on Saturday.

We have abundance of good news to-day.

First, the Florida has captured one, and destroyed another of the enemy's vessels of war in the West Indies.

Second, we have authentic intelligence of the evacuation of Washington, N. C. by the enemy, pursued by our forces toward Newbern.

Third, four steamers have arrived at Wilmington laden with quartermaster and ordnance stores. Col. Gorgas, Chief of Ordnance, says we now have arms and ammunition enough.

A letter from Gen. Lee indicates the propriety of Gen. Imboden retaining his recruits (which the Secretary wanted to take from him, because they were liable to conscription) in the Shenandoah Valley. This does not look like a purpose of an advance on Lee's part. He will probably await the attack.

The President, in an indorsement, intimates to the Secretary of War that Gen. Pryor might be assigned to a brigade of the Reserve class.

About 5 o'clock this afternoon we had a tornado from the southwest which I fear has done mischief in the country. It blew off half a dozen planks from my garden fence, and I had difficulty in nailing them on again with such rusty nails as I could find. Nails are worth almost their weight in silver.

The gardeners sell tomato-plants for $10 per dozen, and cabbage-plants for 50 cts. each! But I am independent, having my own little hot-beds.

MAY 3D.—A cold, windy day, with sunshine and clouds.

It is rumored that Grant's army is in motion, and the great battle is eagerly looked for. The collision of mighty armies, upon the issue of which the fate of empire depends, is now imminent.

The following dispatch was received to-day from Gen. Johnston:

"DALTON, May 2d, 1864.

"Two scouts, who went by Outawah and Cleveland, report the enemy sending all Southern people and heavy baggage to the rear, stopping rations to the inhabitants, collecting a large supply of trains at Graysville, and bringing their cavalry from Middle Tennessee. An officer just from Columbia reports 13,000 had been collected there. All scouts report Hooker's troops in position here. J. E. JOHNSTON, *General*."

MAY 4TH.—Bright, beautiful, and warmer; but fire in the morning.

The following dispatch from Gen. Lee was received by Gen. Bragg to-day and sent to the Secretary.

"ORANGE C. H., May 4th, 1864.

"Reports from our lookouts seem to indicate that the enemy is in motion. The present direction of his column is to our right.

"Gen. Imboden reports the enemy advancing from Winchester, up the Valley, with wagons, beef cattle, etc.   R. E. LEE."

There is a rumor of fighting at Chancellorville, and this is the anniversary, I believe, of the battle there. May we be as successful this time! But the report is not authentic. Firing is heard now in the direction of York River.

MAY 5TH.—We have many rumors to-day, and nothing authentic, except that some of the enemy's transports are in the James River, and landing some troops, a puerile demonstration, perhaps. The number landed at West Point, it seems, was insignificant. It may be the armies of the United States are demoralized, and if so, if Grant be beaten, I shall look for a speedy end of the invasion. It is said some of the advanced forces of Grant were at Spottsylvania C. H. last night, and the great battle may occur any hour.

Gov. Smith is calling for more exemptions (firemen, etc.) than all the governors together.

Col. Preston asks authority to organize a company of conscripts, Reserve classes, in each congressional district, the President having assigned a general officer to each State to command these classes. The colonel wants to command something.

The Commissary-General, Col. Northrop, being called on, reports that he can feed the army until fall with the means on hand and attainable. So, troops didn't starve in thirty days several months ago!

A Mr. Pond has made a proposition which Mr. Memminger is in favor of accepting, viz.: the government to give him a bill of sale of 10,000 bales of cotton lying in the most exposed places in the West, he to take it away and to take all risks, except destruction by our troops, to ship it from New Orleans to Antwerp, and he will pay, upon receiving said bill of sale, 10 pence sterling per pound. The whole operation will be consummated by the Belgian Consul in New Orleans, and the Danish Vice-Consul in Mobile. It is probable the United States Government, or some members of it, are interested in the speculation. But it will be advantageous to us.

"A PERTINENT RESOLUTION.—The following was offered recently in the United States Senate, by Mr. Saulsbury, of Delaware:

'*Resolved*, That the Chaplain of the Senate be respectfully requested hereafter to pray and supplicate Almighty God in our behalf, and not to lecture Him, informing Him, under pretense of prayer, his, said chaplain's, opinion in reference to His duty as the Almighty; and that the said Chaplain be further requested, as aforesaid, not, under the form of prayer, to lecture the Senate in relation to questions before the body.'"

APRIL 6TH.—Bright, warm, beautiful.

We have a sensation to-day, but really no excitement. A dispatch from Gen. Lee (dated last night) says the *enemy* opened the battle yesterday, and the conflict continued until night put an end to the carnage. He says we have many prisoners, captured four guns, etc., losing two generals killed, one, Gen. J. M. Jones. But our position was maintained, and the enemy repulsed. Doubtless the battle was renewed this morning.

Some *fifty-nine* transports and several iron-clad gun-boats, monitors, etc., came up the James River yesterday and last night. A heavy force was landed at Bermuda Hundred, within a few miles of the railroad between Richmond and Petersburg.

And the enemy likewise came up the Peninsula, and there was fighting this morning on the Chickahominy.

Thus the plan of the enemy is distinctly pronounced, and the assaults were designed to be made simultaneously. Yet there is no undue excitement.

A dispatch from Gen. Pickett at Petersburg, this morning, to Gen. Bragg, asked if he (Bragg) intended to defend the railroad between Richmond and Petersburg. He said, "the enemy will attack the road to-day, marching from Bermuda Hundred, I think."

At 3 P.M. we are waiting with anxiety for news from all quarters.

Both my sons marched out in the Department Battalion. Two Tennessee regiments marched down to Drewry's Bluff yesterday, and Hunton's brigade, that left there yesterday, were ordered back again last night. It is said troops were passing south through the city all night. And I know heavy forces are on the way from North Carolina. Gen. Pickett likewise has the greater part of his division in supporting distance. So, if the enemy have not cut the road by this time, it is probably safe, and the expedition will be a failure. If Lee defeats Grant, the city will certainly be saved. All the local troops are out.

Gen. Beauregard is expected to-day, but it is reported he is sick at Weldon. On the 3d inst. the following dispatch was received from him:

"KINSTON, N. C.

"GEN. COOPER.

"Orders should be given for the immediate re-establishment of fisheries at Plymouth and Washington, also to get large supplies of pork in Hyde County and vicinity.

"G. T. BEAUREGARD, *General.*"

On this the Commissary-General indorsed that the matter had been attended to—had, indeed, been anticipated.

The best indication of the day (to me) was the smiling face of Mr. Hunter as he came from the Secretary's office. He said to me, "The ball is opening well."

The President and his aids rode over the river to-day: what direction they took I know not; but this I know, he has no idea of being taken by the enemy. And he cannot think the city will be taken, for in that event it would be difficult for him to escape.

MAY 7TH.—Bright and warm. The following is Gen. Lee's dispatch, received yesterday morning—the *italics* not his.

"HEADQUARTERS ARMY NORTHERN VIRGINIA,
"May 5th, 1864.

"HON. SECRETARY OF WAR.

"The enemy crossed the Rapidan at Ely's and Germania fords. Two corps of this army moved to oppose him—Ewell by the old turnpike, and Hill by the plank-road.

"They arrived this morning in close proximity to the enemy's line of march.

"A strong attack was made upon Ewell, who repulsed it, *capturing many prisoners and four pieces of artillery.*

"The enemy subsequently concentrated upon Gen. Hill, who. with Heth's and Wilcox's divisions, *successfully resisted repeated and desperate assaults.*

"A large force of cavalry and artillery on our right was *driven back* by Rosser's brigade.

"By the blessing of God, we maintained our position *against every effort* until night, when the contest closed.

"We have to mourn the loss of many brave officers and men. The gallant Brig.-Gen. J. M. Jones was killed, and Brig.-Gen. Stafford, I fear, mortally wounded, while leading his command with conspicuous valor.

"(Signed) R. E. LEE."

A dispatch from Gen. Lee this morning says Hill's corps was thrown into confusion yesterday by an attack of the enemy when some of the divisions were being relieved. But afterward we recovered the ground, strewn with the dead and wounded of the enemy. Then we attacked their whole line, driving them behind their breastworks. He concludes by thanks for our ability still to withstand all assaults. No doubt Grant has overwhelming numbers, and Lee is under the necessity of sparing his men as much as possible, while his adversary leads into action a succession of fresh troops. Gen. Longstreet is wounded.

Gen. Beauregard is at Petersburg, charged with the defense of this city and the railroad. Troops have been marching toward Drewry's Bluff during the day. If the attack be delayed 24 hours more, we shall be strong enough to repel even the then greatly superior numbers of the invader.

But there is more anxiety manifested to-day. Senator Hunter and Mr. Ould, the agent of exchange, have been in the office next to mine once or twice, to drink some of the good whisky kept by Mr. Chapman, the disbursing clerk of the department. Mr. H.'s face is quite red.

5 P.M. The tocsin is sounding, for the militia, I suppose, all others being in the field. It is reported that the attack on Drewry's Bluff, or rather on our forces posted there for its defense, has begun. Barton's brigade marched thither to-day. It is said

the enemy have 40,000 men on the south side of James River—we, 20,000.

There is now some excitement and trepidation among the shopkeepers and extortioners, who are compelled by State law to shoulder the musket for the defense of the city, and there is some running to and fro preliminary to the *rendezvous* in front of the City Hall. The alarm, however, I learnt at the department, is caused by reports brought in by countrymen, that the enemy is approaching the city from the *northeast,* as if from Gloucester Point. It *may* be so—a small body; but Gen. Ransom, Gen. Elzey's successor here, doubts it, for his scouts give no intelligence of the enemy in that quarter. But the 19th Militia Regiment and the Foreign Battalion will have the pleasure of sleeping in the open air to-night, and of dreaming of their past gains, etc.

May 8th.—Bright and hot.

The tocsin sounded again this morning. I learned upon inquiry that it was merely for the militia again (they were dismissed yesterday after being called together), perhaps to relieve the local battalions near the city.

The Secretary of War received a dispatch to-day from Gen. Lee, stating that there was no fighting yesterday, only slight skirmishing. Grant remained where he had been driven, in the "Wilderness," behind his breastworks, completely checked in his "On to Richmond." He may be badly hurt, and perhaps his men object to being led to the slaughter again.

There has been no fighting below, between this and Petersburg, and we breathe freer, for Beauregard, we know, has made the best use of time. It is said another of the enemy's gun-boats has been destroyed by boarding and burning. We have three iron-clads and rams here *above* the obstructions, which will probably be of no use at this trying time.

A few days more will tell the story of this combined and most formidable attempt to take Richmond; and if it be the old song of failure, we may look for a speedy termination of the war. So mote it be!

Meantime my vegetables are growing finely, except the corn and lima beans (Yankee), Col. Gorgas's importation, which have not come up.

A cow and calf now sells for $2500. My friend, Dr. Powell,

has just sold one for a great price, he would not tell me what. But I told him that the greed for gain was the worst feature in our people, and made me sometimes tremble for the cause. I fear a just retribution may entail ruin on the farmers, who seem to think more of their cattle than of their sons in the field.

MAY 19TH.—Bright and sultry.

A dispatch from Gen. Lee says the enemy is moving down toward Fredericksburg, and yesterday the advance of our army encountered his right wing at Spottsylvania Court House, and repulsed it "with great slaughter." Strong language for Lee.

A dispatch received this morning said the enemy was advancing on the railroad. Subsequently cannon could be heard in the direction of Drewry's Bluff.

The tocsin has been sounding all day, for the militia, which come slowly, after being summoned and dismissed so often. I fear, when they are sent over the river, if all the men at the defenses on the north side are sent over also, that a cavalry raid from the north may dash into the city and burn the bridges on the James; then our army would be in a "fix." I have expressed this apprehension to the Secretary, and asked him to arm the old men, for the defense of the bridges, public buildings, etc. He awaits *events*. Mr. Hunter and other public characters are looking very grave.

The following dispatch was received to-day from Weldon, via Raleigh and Greensborough, N. C.:

"May 8th.

The enemy destroyed the wire from Stony Creek to within three miles of Belfield, a distance of about fifteen miles. Our men and employees are repairing it, and we hope to have communication reopened to-morrow. W. S. HARRIS."

Col. Preston, Superintendent of Bureau of Conscription, has written another letter to the Secretary, urging the promotion of Captain C. B. Duffield, who threatens to leave him for a position with Gen. Kumper, at Lynchburg, where he can live cheaper. He says he has urged the President, to no avail.

The Secretary has roused himself. Since 3 P.M. he has issued a call "To ARMS!" All men capable of bearing arms are requested to report to Gen. Kemper, Franklin Street, to be armed and organized "temporarily" for the defense of the city. Gen. Ransom had previously issued a placard, calling on officers and men on furlough to meet in Capitol Square for temporary organization. This may involve some etiquette, or question of jurisdiction between the generals. Gen. Winder is utterly ignored.

I have just heard that the Departmental Battalion has been marched across Mayo's Bridge to the fortifications of Manchester, on the south side of the river. The militia regiment will go to the place on the north side heretofore occupied by them.

Another dispatch from Gen. Lee, received since 3 P.M. to-day, says Grant attacked him again yesterday, after the slaughter by our Gen. Anderson, and was handsomely repulsed. Grant's tactics seem to be to receive his stripes by installments.

MAY 10TH.—Bright, but windy and dusty.

There is an excitement at last; but it is sullen rather than despairing. No one seems to doubt our final success, although the enemy have now some 200,000 in Virginia, and we but little over half that number.

We have nothing from Lee to-day, but it is believed he is busy in battle.

A portion of Grant's right wing, cut off at Spottsylvania Court House, endeavored to march across the country to the Peninsula. They cut the railroad at Beaver Dam, and destroyed some of our commissary stores. But it is likely they will be captured.

The enemy beat us yesterday at Dublin Depot, wounding Gen. Jenkins.

On the other hand, Gen. McNeal (C. S.) has cut the Baltimore and Ohio Railroad, destroying millions of property. Thus the work goes on!

There was no general engagement down the river.

At 12 o'clock last night a column of infantry passed our house, going down Clay Street. Many thought it was the enemy.

I saw a letter to-day from Gen. Beauregard to Gen. Bragg, dated Weldon, April 29th, giving the names of the Federal generals commanding forces on the Southern coast, so that the arrival of any of these officers in Virginia would indicate the transfer of their troops thither. He concluded by saying that if it were desired he should operate on the north side of James River, maps ought to be prepared for him, and timbers, etc. for bridges; and that he would serve with pleasure under the immediate command of Gen. Lee, "aiding him to crush our enemies, and to achieve the independence of our country."

Gen. Bragg, May 2d, sent this to Gen. Cooper, who referred it to the Secretary of War. Gen. Bragg indorsed on it that several of the Federal generals named had arrived at Fortress Monroe.

The Secretary sent it to the President on the 7th of May.

To-day the President sent it back indorsed as follows: "Maps of the country, with such additions as may from time to time be made, should be kept on hand in the Engineer Bureau, and furnished to officers in the field. Preparations of material for bridges, etc. will continue to be made as heretofore, and with such additional effort as circumstances require.

"I did not doubt the readiness of Gen. Beauregard to serve under any general who ranks him. The right of Gen. Lee to command would be derived from his superior rank.

"JEFFERSON DAVIS.

"9th May, 1864."

MAY 11TH.—Bright and pleasant—breezy. This has been a day of excitement.

At midnight the Departmental Battalion were marched from the south side of the river back to the city, and rested the remainder of the night at Camp Lee. But at 9 A.M. they were marched hurriedly to Meadow Bridge. They came past our house. Custis and his brother Thomas ran in—remaining but a moment. Custis exclaimed: "Let me have some money, mother (I had to go to the office), or we will starve. The government don't feed us, and we are almost famished. Cook something, and get Captain Warner to bring it in his buggy—do, if possible." He got $20. They looked worn, and were black with dust, etc. My daughter said "they looked like negroes."

The Secretary issued this morning a new edition of his hand-bills, calling the people "to arms."

Mr. Mallory's usual red face turned purple. He has not yet got out the iron-clad Richmond, etc., which might have sunk Gen. Butler's transports.

Lieut.-Col. Lay was exhibiting a map of our defenses, and predicting something,—whether good or evil, I did not stay to learn. But I thought such maps ought not to be shown in the public hall of the department.

The armory was open to-day, and all who desired them were furnished with arms.

The Governor, I hear, issued a notification that the enemy would be here to day, etc. I did not see it.

All classes not in the army were gathered up and marched to the defenses.

2 P.M. Respectable men just from the vicinity report a great victory for Lee, yesterday, though we have nothing from him. The Secretary believes these concurring reports, which state that the battle, beginning near Spottsylvania Court House, ended at Fredericksburg, indicating a WATERLOO.

And a dispatch from Gen. Ransom from the south side of the river, states that Butler's army is *retreating to the transports.* This is regarded as confirmation of Lee's victory.

Several dispatches from Gen. Stuart state that the raiders have been severely beaten in several combats this morning, and are flying toward Dover Mills. They may come back, for *they* have not heard of Grant's defeat.

Mr. Memminger is said to have been frightened terribly, and arrangements were made for flight.

MAY 12TH.—Thunder, lightning, and rain all day.

The report of Gen. Lee's victory was premature, and Butler has not gone, nor the raiders vanished. On the contrary, the latter were engaged in battle with Stuart's division late in the afternoon, and recommenced it this morning at 3 o'clock, the enemy remaining on the ground, and still remain, some five miles from where I write. Major-Gen. J. E. B. Stuart was wounded last evening, through the kidney, and now lies in the city, in a dying condition ! Our best generals thus fall around us.

The battle raged furiously; every gun distinctly heard at our house until 1 P.M.—the enemy being intrenched between our middle and outer line of works. Meantime our ambulances are arriving every hour with the wounded, coming in by the Brooke Turnpike.

The battalion my sons are in lost none of its men, though shelled by the enemy early in the morning; nor do we know that our battery did any execution. Capt. Warner delivered the provisions their mother cooked for them yesterday. He saw only Custis, who gladly received the bread, and meat, and eggs; but he and Tom were both drenched with rain, as they had no shelter yesterday. But a comrade, and one of Custis's Latin pupils, whom I saw, returned on sick leave, says Thomas stands the fatigue and exposure better than Custis, who was complaining.

About 11 A.M. to-day there was very heavy reports of cannon heard in the direction of Drewry's Bluff, supposed to be our battery shelling the country below, for some purpose.

I understand one or more of our iron-clads will certainly go out this evening, or to-night; we shall know it when it occurs, for the firing will soon follow.

Worked in my garden; set out corn and (yellow) tomatoes; the former given me by my neighbor, to whom I had given lettuce and beet plants.

My wife spent a miserable day, some one having reported that the Departmental Battalion was cut to pieces in the battle. When I came in, she asked me if Custis and Thomas were alive, and was exceedingly glad to know not a man in the company had been even wounded.

I shall never forget the conformation of the clouds this morning as the storm arose. There were different strata running in various directions. They came in heaviest volume from the southeast in parallel lines, like lines of battle swooping over the city. There were at the same time shorter and fuller lines from the southwest, and others from the north. The meeting of these was followed by tremendous clashes of lightning and thunder; and between the pauses of the artillery of the elements above, the thunder of artillery on earth could be distinctly heard. Oh that the strife were ended! But Richmond is to be defended at all hazards.

It is said, however, that preparations have been made for the flight of the President, cabinet, etc. up the Danville Road, in the event of the fall of the city. Yet no one fears that the present forces environing it could take it. If Lee withstands Grant another week, all will be safe. My greatest fear is the want of provisions. My wife bought a half bushel of meal; so we have a week's supply on hand, as we were not quite out. I hope Beauregard will soon restore communication with the South.

MAY 13TH.—Cloudy and showery all day.

Last night my youngest son Thomas came in, furloughed (unsolicited) by his officers, who perceived his exhaustion.

The enemy disappeared in the night. We suffered most in the several engagements with him near the city. I suppose some sympathizer had furnished him with a copy of our photograph map of the fortifications and country in the vicinity.

But the joy of many, and chagrin of some at his escape so easily, was soon followed by the startling intelligence that a raid from Gen. Butler's army had cut the *Danville* Road! All communication with the country from which provisions are derived is now completely at an end! And if supplies are withheld that long, this community, as well as the army, must be without food in ten days! Col. Northrop told me to-day that unless the railroads were retaken and repaired, he could not feed the troops ten days longer. And he blamed Gen. Lee for the loss of over 200,000 pounds of bacon at Beaver Dam. He says Gen. Lee ordered it there, instead of keeping it at Charlottesville or Gordonsville. Could Lee make such a blunder?

Most of the members of Congress, when not in session, hang about the door and hall of the War Department, eager for news, Mr. Hunter being the most prominent, if not the most anxious among them. But the wires are cut in all directions, and we must rely on couriers.

The wildest rumors float through the air. Every successive hour gives birth to some new tidings, and one must be near the Secretary's table indeed to escape being misled by false reports.

For two days no dispatch has been received from Gen. Lee, although one hears of a dispatch just received from him at every corner of the streets. A courier arrived to-day from the *vicinity* of our army. He saw a *gentleman* who saw Gen. Lee's son *Robert* yesterday, and was informed by him that our army was five miles nearer Fredericksburg, having driven the enemy farther down the river.

Our iron-clads—Virginia, Richmond, and Fredericksburg—I understood from Lieut. Minor, this morning, will not go out until in readiness to cope successfully with the enemy's fleet of gun-boats and monitors. How long that will be he did not say. It may be to-day. And while I write ($4\frac{1}{2}$ P.M.) I can distinctly hear the roar of artillery down the river. It may be an engagement by land or by water, or by both; and it may be only the customary shelling of the woods by the enemy's gun-boats. But it is very rapid sometimes.

A courier reports the raid on the Danville Road as not formidable. They are said, however, to have blown up the coal-pits. They cannot *blow* coal *higher* than our own extortionate people have done.

I directed my wife to lay out all the money about the house in provisions. She got a bushel of meal and five pounds of bacon for about $100. If we must endure another turn of the screw of famine, it is well to provide for it as well as possible. We cannot starve now, in a month; and by that time, Gens. Lee and Beauregard may come to our relief. Few others are looked to hopefully. The functionaries here might have had a six-months' supply, by wise and energetic measures.

The President has had the Secretary of War closeted with him nearly all day. It is too late now for the evacuation of Richmond, and a *desperate* defense will be made. If the city falls, the consequences will be ruinous to the present government. And how could any of its members escape? Only in disguise. This is the time to try the nerves of the President and his counselors!

Gen. Bragg is very distasteful to many officers of the army; and the croakers and politicians would almost be willing to see the government go to pieces, to get rid of the President and his cabinet. Some of the members of Congress are anxious to get *away*, and the *Examiner* twits them for their cowardice. They will stay, probably.

MAY 14TH.—Warm, with alternate sunshine and showers.

With the dawn recommenced the heavy boom of cannon down the river. It was rumored this morning that our right wing at Drewry's Bluff had been flanked, but no official information has been received of the progress of the fight. I saw a long line of ambulances going in that direction.

To-day it is understood that the battle of Petersburg will be fought by Beauregard, if he be not withheld from attacking the enemy by orders from Richmond.

We have been beaten, or rather badly foiled here, by orders from high authority; and it is said Gen. Ransom finds himself merely an instrument in the hands of those who do not know how to use him skillfully.

The enemy is said to have made a bridge across the James River, either to come on the north side, or to enable the raiders to reach them. They are also planting torpedoes, for our iron rams. They are not yet ready.

Gen. Lee is prosecuting the defensive policy effectively. Couriers to the press, considered quite reliable, give some details of a most terrific battle in Spottsylvania County day before yesterday, 12th inst. Our men (with extra muskets) fought behind their breastworks. The host of assailants came on, stimulated by whisky rations, ten deep, and fearful was the slaughter. Their loss is estimated at 20,000; ours, 2000. The enemy were still in front. Grant says he will not recross the Rappahannock as long as he has a man left. Lee seems determined to kill his last man.

A great deal of time is said to have been consumed in cabinet council, making selections for appointments. It is a harvest for hunters after brigadier and major-generalships. The President is very busy in this business, and Secretary Seddon is sick—neuralgia.

Last night Custis came home on a furlough of twelve hours. He got a clean shirt, and washed himself—not having had his shoes or clothes off for more than a week. He has not taken cold, though sleeping in the water, and not having dry clothes on him for several days. And his appetite is excellent. He departed again for camp, four miles off, at 5½ A.M., bringing and taking out his gun, his heavy cartridge-box, and well-filled haversack (on his return).

Half-past four o'clock P.M. A tremendous cannonade is now distinctly heard down the river, the intonations resembling thunder. No doubt the monitors are engaged with the battery at Drewry's Bluff. It may be a combined attack.

Gen. Pemberton has resigned his commission; but the President has conferred on him a lieutenant-colonelcy of artillery. Thus the feelings of all the armies and most of the people are outraged; for, whether justly or not, both Pemberton and Bragg, to whom the President clings with tenacity, are especially obnoxious both to the people and the army. May Heaven shield us! Yet the President *may* be right.

MAY 15TH.—Clouds, sunshine, and showers.

The tremendous cannonading all day yesterday at Drewry's Bluff was merely an artillery duel—brought on by the heavy skirmishing of pickets. The batteries filled the air with discordant sounds, and shook the earth with grating vibration. Perhaps 100 on each side were killed and wounded—"not worth the ammunition," as a member of the government said.

Gen. Lee's dispatches to the President have been withheld from publication during the last four days. The loss of two trains of commissary stores affords the opportunity to censure Lee; but some think his popularity and power both with the people and the army have inspired the motive.

I saw to-day some of our slightly wounded men from Lee's army, who were in the fight of Thursday (12th inst.), and they confirm the reports of the heavy loss of the enemy. They say there is no suffering yet for food, and the men are still in good spirits.

Both the Central and the Fredericksburg Roads are repaired, and trains of provisions are now daily sent to Gen. Lee.

The Danville Road was not materially injured; the raiders being repulsed before they could destroy the important bridges. Supplies can come to Petersburg, and may be forwarded by wagons to the Danville Road, and thence to Lynchburg, etc.

Fresh troops are arriving from the South for Beauregard; but he is still withheld from decisive operations.

The Departmental Battalion is still out; the enemy still menacing us from the Chickahominy.

During the last four days correspondence has ceased almost entirely, and the heads of bureaus, captains, majors, lieutenant-colonels, adjutants, quartermasters, and commissaries, have nothing to do. They wander about with hanging heads, ashamed to be safely out of the field—I mean all under 50 years of age—and look like sheep-stealing dogs. Many sought their positions, and still retain them, to keep out of danger. Such cravens are found in all countries, and are perhaps fewer in this than any other. However, most of the population of the city between 17 and 50 are absent from the streets; some few shopkeeping Jews and Italians are imprisoned for refusing to aid in the defense, and some no doubt are hidden.

212   A REBEL WAR CLERK'S DIARY

Most of the able-bodied negro men, both free and slave, have been taken away—in the field as teamsters, or digging on the fortifications. Yet those that remain may sometimes be seen at the street corners looking, some wistfully, some in dread, in the direction of the enemy. There is but little fear of an insurrection, though no doubt the enemy would be welcomed by many of the negroes, both free and slave.

At 1 P.M. to-day a train arrived from Guinea's Station with 800 of our wounded, in Sunday's and Thursday's battles.

The following prices are now paid in this city: boots, $200; coats, $350; pants, $100; shoes, $125; flour, $275 per barrel; meal, $60 to $80 per bushel; bacon, $9 per pound; no beef in market; chickens, $30 per pair; shad, $20; potatoes, $25 per bushel; turnip greens, $4 per peck; white beans, $4 per quart, or $120 per bushel; butter, $15 per pound; lard, same; wood, $50 per cord. What a change a decisive victory—or defeat—would make!

MAY 16TH.—Warm—sunshine and light showers.

Memorable day—not yet decided at 2 P.M. Early this morning Gen. Beauregard attacked the enemy on the south side of the river, and by 9 A.M. he had sent over to the city Gen. Heckman and 840 prisoners, the entire 27th Massachusetts Regiment. Subsequently it is said 400 were sent over. By 12 M. the firing had receded out of hearing from the city, and messengers report that the enemy were being driven back rapidly. Hon. Geo. Davis, Attorney-General (from North Carolina), told me that Gen. Whiting was coming up from Petersburg, in the enemy's *rear*, with 13,000 men. So, at this hour, the prospects are glorious.

Gen. Pickett has been relieved—*indisposition.* Brig.-Gen. Barton has also been relieved, for some cause arising out of the failure to capture the raiders on this side the river.

Gens. Bragg and Pemberton made an inspection of the position of the enemy, down the river, yesterday, and made rather a cheerless report to the President. They are both supposed to be inimical to Gen. Beauregard, who seems to be achieving such brilliant success.

The President rode over to Beauregard's headquarters this morning. Some fear he will embarrass the general; others say he is near the field, prepared to fly, if it be lost. In truth, if we were defeated, it might be difficult for him to return to the city.

Gen. Breckenridge has defeated Sigel in the Shenandoah Valley.

Gen. Lee dispatches that he had no fighting Saturday and Sunday. To-day Grant is retiring his right wing, but advancing his left east of Spottsylvania Court House, where Lee's headquarters are still established.

MAY 17TH.—Sunshine and showers.

The battle yesterday decided nothing, that I am aware of. We captured 1000 prisoners, stormed some of their intrenchments; losing altogether probably as many as the enemy. But we drove them back to Bermuda Hundred, behind their fortifications, and near their ships.

Gen. Johnston was attacked at Dalton by 80,000 men last week; accounts, some five days old, say he repulsed the assaults of the enemy.

The Departmental Battalion is out yet; the city being still in danger. The government is almost suspended in its functions. The Secretary of the Treasury cannot get money from Columbia, S. C., whither he foolishly sent the girls that sign the notes.

Some of the idle military officers, always found about the departments, look grave, and do not hesitate to express some apprehension of the success of Grant in forcing Lee back, and spreading over all Northern and Northwestern Virginia. The Secretary of War is much secluded, and I see by a correspondence between him and the Secretary of the Treasury, relating to the *million and three-quarters* in coin, belonging to the New Orleans banks, that the Secretary of the Treasury can make no "valid objection to the proposition of the Secretary of War." I do not understand what disposition they propose to make of it.

A list is being prepared at the War Department (by Mr. Assistant Secretary Campbell) for Congress to pass, authorizing the seizure of all the railroads in the Confederacy. Also one establishing and reorganizing the Bureau of Conscription.

If Butler remains between Richmond and Petersburg, and is reinforced, and Grant is strong enough (two to Lee's one) to push on toward Richmond, our perils and trials will be greater than ever.

Vice-President Stephens has not yet arrived. I do not understand that he is ill.

MAY 18TH.—Showers and sunshine, the first preponderating.

Our killed and wounded in Beauregard's battle amount to some 1500. The enemy lost 1000 prisoners, and perhaps 1500 killed and wounded.

Railroad men report heavy firing this morning near Fredericksburg, and it is believed another battle is in progress.

From the West we have a report, derived from the enemy at Natchez, that Gen. Banks has surrendered to Lieut.-Gen. Smith.

It is rumored likewise that President Lincoln has called for 60,000 militia, *to defend Washington.*

A fortnight ago, Mr. Benjamin procured passports for one or two of his agents "to pass the 'lines at will." They may have procured information, but it did not prevent the enemy from coming.

Attended a funeral (next door to us) ceremony this afternoon at 5 P.M. over the body of Abner Stanfield, a nephew of Mrs. Smith, our next door neighbor, who fell in battle day before yesterday, near Drewry's Bluff. By the merest accident his relatives here learned of his fall (by the paper we loaned them), and Mr. S. had his body brought to his house, and decently prepared for the grave. His bloody garments were replaced by a fine suit of clothes he had kept with Mr. S.; his mother, etc. live in Northern Virginia, and his cousins, the Misses S., decorated the coffin beautifully with laurels, flowers, etc. He was a handsome young hero, six feet tall, and died bravely in his country's defense. He was slain by a shell. The ceremony was impressive, and caused many tears to flow. But his glorious death and funeral honor will inspire others with greater resolution to do and to dare, and to die, if necessary, for their country. The minister did him justice, for the hallowed cause in which he fell.

MAY 19TH.—Sunshine and showers, the former predominating.

Gen. Lee sends a dispatch saying the enemy's attack yesterday was repulsed easily—our loss very light.

It is said, however, that the enemy have Guinea's Station, 12 miles this side of Fredericksburg.

Gen. Beauregard intends shelling Butler in his fortifications to-morrow.

From the West, in Georgia, and beyond the Mississippi, all seem bright enough.

Congress has passed a resolution to adjourn on the 31st inst., in obedience to the wish of the President. He has a majority in both Houses, it seems; and even the bills they pass are generally dictated by the Executive, and written in the departments. Judge Campbell is much used for this purpose.

Gen. Bragg sent in a manuscript, derived from a deserter, stating that of Gen. Butler's two corps, one, the 10th, is from the Southern coast, no negroes in it, leaving only negroes in the Southern garrisons. We learned Butler was in command, and dismissed all apprehensions—and one day we had but 5000 opposed to his 40,000!

MAY 20TH.—Fog; then sunshine all day, but cool.

Troops have been marching through the city all day from the south side. I presume others take their places arriving from the South. Barton's brigade had but 700 out of 2000 that went into battle last Monday. Our wounded amount to 2000; perhaps the enemy's loss was not so large.

Col. Northrop is vehement in his condemnation of Beauregard; says his blunders are ruining us; that he is a charlatan, and that he never has been of any value to the Confederate States; and he censures Gen. Lee, whom he considers a general, and the only one we have, and the Secretary of War, for not providing transportation for supplies, now so fearfully scarce.

I read an indorsement to-day, in the President's writing, as follows: "Gen. Longstreet has seriously offended against good order and military discipline in rearresting an officer (Gen. Law) who had been released by the War Department, without any new offense having been alleged.—J. D."

Mr. Mallory, Secretary of the Navy, wrote a pungent letter to the Secretary of War to-day, on the failure of the latter to have the obstructions removed from the river, so that the iron-clads might go out and fight. He says the enemy has captured our lower battery of torpedoes, etc., and declares the failure to remove the obstructions "prejudicial to the interests of the country, and especially to the naval service, which has thus been prevented from rendering important service."

Gen. Bragg writes a pretty tart letter to the Secretary of War to-day, desiring that his reports of the Army of Tennessee, called for by Congress, be furnished for publication, or else that the reasons be given for withholding them.

We have no war news to-day.

Mrs. Minor, of Cumberland County, with whom my daughter Anne resides, is here, in great affliction. Her brother, Col. Rudolph, was killed in the battle with Sheridan, near Richmond; shot through the head, and buried on the field. Now she learns that another brother, a cadet, just 18 years old, was killed in the battle of Gen. Breckinridge, in the valley, shot through the head; and she resolves to set out for Staunton at once, to recover his body. Her father and sister died a few months ago, and she has just heard of her aunt's death.

A lady living next door to us had two brothers wounded on Monday, and they are both here, and will recover.

Gen. Breckinridge is now marching to reinforce Lee. It is said Butler will set sail to join Grant. If so, we can send Lee 20,000 more men, and Beauregard's victory will yield substantial fruits.

MAY 21ST.—Sun all day, but a little hazy; perhaps a battle.

There was quite a battle yesterday on the south side. The accounts in the morning's paper fall short of the whole of our success. The enemy, it is said to-day, did not regain the works from which they were driven, but are now cooped up at Bermuda Hundred. Nothing is feared from Butler.

Nothing from Lee, but troops are constantly going to him.

I saw some 10,000 rusty rifles, brought down yesterday from Lee's battle-field. Many bore marks of balls, deeply indenting or perforating the barrels. The ordnance officer says in his report that he has collected many thousands more than were dropped by our killed and wounded. This does not look like a *Federal* victory!

MAY 22D.—Clear and warm, but the atmosphere is charged with the smoke and dust of contending armies. The sun shines but dimly.

Custis was with us last night, and returned to camp at 5 A.M. to-day. He gets from government only a small loaf of corn bread and a herring a day. We send him something, however, every other morning. His appetite is voracious, and he has not taken cold. He loathes the camp life, and some of the associates he meets in his mess, but is sustained by the vicissitudes and excitements of the hour, and the conviction that the crisis must be over soon.

Last night there was furious shelling down the river, supposed to be a night attack by Butler, which, no doubt, Beauregard anticipated. Result not heard.

The enemy's cavalry were at Milford yesterday, but did no mischief, as our stores had been moved back to Chesterfield depot, and a raid on Hanover C. H. was repulsed. Lee was also attacked yesterday evening, and repulsed the enemy. It is said Ewell is now engaged in a flank movement, and the GREAT FINAL battle may be looked for immediately.

Breckinridge is at Hanover Junction, with other troops. So the war rolls on toward this capital, and yet Lee's headquarters remain in Spottsylvania. A few days more must tell the story. If he cuts Grant's communications, I should not be surprised if that desperate general attempted a bold dash on toward Richmond. I don't think he could take the city—and he would be between two fires

I saw some of the enemy's wounded this morning, brought down in the cars, dreadfully mutilated. Some had lost a leg and arm—besides sustaining other injuries. But they were cheerful, and uttered not a groan in the removal to the hospital.

Flour is selling as high as $400 per barrel, and meal at $125 per bushel. The roads have been cut in so many places, and so frequently, that no provisions have come in, except for the army. But the hoarding speculators have abundance hidden.

The Piedmont Road, from Danville, Va., to Greensborough, is completed, and now that we have two lines of communication with the South, it may be hoped that this famine will be of only short duration. They are cutting wheat in Georgia and Alabama, and new flour will be ground from the growing grain in Virginia in little more than a month. God help us, if relief come not speedily! A great victory would be the speediest way.

My garden looks well, but affords nothing yet except salad.

MAY 23D.—Fair and warm, with pleasant breezes.

Gen. Johnston, without a defeat, has fallen back to Calhoun, Ga.

Gen. Lee, without a defeat, has fallen back to Hanover Junction, his headquarters at Ashland. Grant is said to be worming his way eastward to the Peninsula, the field occupied by McClellan in 1862. Why, he might have attained that position without the loss of a man at the outset!

On Saturday night Gen. Butler made the following exploit:

"On Saturday night the enemy renewed his assault, assailing that portion of our line held principally by Wise's brigade. In some manner our men had become apprised of the intention of the enemy to make a night attack, and were fully prepared for it. The enemy were allowed to advance, our men deliberately reserving their fire until they were within 20 or 30 yards of them, when they poured into their ranks a most terrific volley, driving them back with great slaughter. The repulse is said to have been a most decided success; the enemy were thrown into great confusion and retreated rapidly.

"The enemy's loss is said to have been very severe, and is estimated at hardly less than four or five hundred *in killed alone*, while we are said to have lost none in killed, and some thirty or forty wounded."

There was an immense mail to-day, and yet with my sore eyes I had no aid from my son, still at the intrenchments. I hinted my desire to have him, but young Mr. Kean opposed it.

MAY 24TH.—Clear and warm.

No fighting yesterday besides small collisions near Hanover Junction. It is said to-day that Grant threatens the Central Railroad, on Lee's left. This is regarded as a serious matter. We want *men*.

An armed guard is now a fixture before the President's house.

Peas were in market on the 18th inst.; price $10 a half peck. Strawberries are $10 per quart. There has been no meat in market for a long time, most of the butchers' stalls being closed during the last three months. Unless government feeds the people here, some of us may starve.

MAY 25TH.—Sunshine and showers.

Custis is back again, the battalion of clerks being relieved, after three weeks' service in the field.

Yesterday there was skirmishing between the armies, near Hanover Junction—25 miles distant from the city.

Nothing of importance from the south side. But our iron-clads are certainly going down the river—they *say*.

To-day it is thought a battle comm𝑒nced between Lee and Grant. It will be, perhaps, a decisive engagement, whenever it does take place. And yet there is no trepidation in the community; no apparent fear of defeat. Still, there is some degree of feverish anxiety, as Lee retires nearer to the capital followed by the enemy. A little delay would make us stronger, as reinforcements, especially of cavalry, are daily arriving. The trains run from the city to Lee's headquarters in one hour and a half.

A letter from Senator Henry, of Tennessee, to the Secretary, suggests that Forrest's cavalry be now sent to the rear of Sherman's army in Georgia, to cut off his supplies, etc., resulting in his destruction. Perhaps this is the purpose. And Lee may have some such design. A few days will develop important events. May they put an end to this desolating war.

MAY 26TH.—Sunshine and showers.

Senator Henry's letter was referred to Gen. Bragg, who returned it to-day with the indorsement that the suggested movement had not escaped attention, and a good result might soon be looked for. And sure enough, a dispatch was received from Atlanta to-day, announcing the capture of some 250 of the enemy's wagons laden with stores!

It is to be hoped that Gen. Lee has some scheme of a similar character, to relieve Grant of his supply trains. Troops are daily coming hither, infantry and cavalry, whence in one hour and a half the former reach Lee's army. The great battle still hangs fire, but to be of greater magnitude when it does occur.

Gen. Bragg did a good thing yesterday, even while Senator Orr was denouncing him. He relieved Gen. Winder from duty here, and assigned him to Goldsborough, N. C. Now if the rogues and cut-throats he persisted in having about him be likewise dismissed, the Republic is safe! Gen. Ransom has now full charge of this department.

Mr. Secretary Seddon is sick, and Mr. Assistant Secretary Campbell is crabbed—Congress not having passed his Supreme Court bill. And if it were passed, the President would hardly appoint him judge.

It is said one of our iron-clads is out—the rest to follow immediately. Let Butler beware!

MAY 27TH.—Clouds and sunshine; cooler.

Nothing additional from the West. Several thousand Georgia mounted troops have arrived during the last 24 hours, in readiness to march to Lee. One Georgia regiment has 1200, and a South Carolina regiment that went up this morning 1000 men.

Lee's army is at Ashland—17 miles distant. The enemy are marching down the Pamunky, north side. They will doubtless cross it, and march through New Kent and Charles City Counties to the James River, opposite Butler's army. Grant probably intends crossing his army to the south side, which, if effected, might lose us Richmond, for the city cannot subsist a week with its southern communications cut. We should starve.

But Beauregard means to make another effort to dislodge Butler, immediately. It will probably be a combined movement, the iron clads co-operating. It is a necessity, and it must be done without delay, no matter what the cost may be. If Butler remains, the railroads will be cut. If the city be taken, not only will the iron-clads be lost, but a large proportion of the army may be cut off from escape. Immense munitions would certainly fall into the hands of the enemy.

The *Whig* and *Enquirer* both denounced Gen. Bragg to-day.

Senator Orr's assault in the Senate on Gen. Bragg was followed by another from Wigfall, who declared there was a want of confidence in the President. Mr. Orr said his appointment was discourtesy to the Secretary of War, whereupon the Secretary fell ill yesterday, but to-day he is well again. Nevertheless, the Senate voted Gen. B. the salary, etc. allowed a general in the field.

And Gen. Winder has been treated as cavalierly as he treated me. Retribution is sure.

The city is excited with rumors. One is that Beauregard, when about to engage the enemy last week, was ordered by Bragg to evacuate Petersburg—certainly an insane measure. Gen. Beauregard (so the story runs) telegraphed the President (who was with him, as I heard) to know if such an order had his sanction. The President replied that Gen. Bragg's orders were authorized by him. Beauregard *disregarded* the order and fought the battle, saving Petersburg. Then Beauregard tendered his resignation, which was not accepted. It is also said that the order was directed to the commandant of the garrison; but the courier was stopped by Generals Wise and Martin, who gave the paper to Beauregard.

There is another rumor that Bragg's orders caused Lee to fall back; and, of course, the credulous people here are despondent; some in despair. There may be some design against the President in all this.

MAY 28TH.—Showers and sunshine.

Grant has crossed the Pamunky, and Lee is at the Yellow Tavern—not more than *six miles* from the city. The hostile armies are only a few miles apart, and the GREAT BATTLE may occur at any time, at any hour; and we shall hear both the artillery and musketry from my dwelling.

All is quiet on the south side of the river. Nothing from Georgia, except a short address from Gen. Johnston to the army, stating that, having the enemy now where he wants him, he will lead the soldiers to battle.

War and famine develop some of the worst instincts of our nature. For five days the government has been selling meal, by the peck, for $12: and yet those who have been purchasing have endeavored to keep it a secret! And the government turns extortioner, making $45 profit per bushel out of the necessities of the people!

I saw a dispatch, to-day, from Gen. Johnston to his Chief Commissary, at Atlanta, ordering him, after reserving ten days' rations, to send the rest of the stores to Augusta!

It is said Mr. Memminger and certain members of Congress have in readiness the means of sudden flight, in the event of Grant's forcing his way into the city.

It is thought, to-day, that Bragg will resign. If he does, then the President will be humiliated; for the attacks on Bragg are meant principally for Mr. Davis. But I doubt the story; I don't think the President will permit Bragg to retire before his enemies, unless affairs become desperate by the defeat of our army in this vicinity.

MAY 29TH.—Bright and quite cold.

There was skirmishing yesterday evening on the Chickahominy.

The armies are confronting each other, but Grant is moving gradually to the right of us, as if with an intention to reach the James River; but probably it is with the view of enveloping us with his superior numbers, and the GREAT BATTLE may occur at any hour. The train of cars, laden, in Broad Street, destined a few days ago to transport provisions, etc. to Gen. Lee's army, are visited hourly by wagons from the army, now in the immediate vicinity.

This morning the Secretary's time is occupied in giving audience to citizens who have fled from the vicinity of the enemy, but whose exaggerated accounts really furnish no reliable information. Of what benefit, in such a crisis as this, is the tale of desolation in the track of Grant's army, the destruction of crops, the robbery of children of their silver cups and spoons, etc.? And yet these are the things which occupy much time.

MAY 30TH.—Fair and cool; hot at noon.

It is rumored that Mr. Memminger will resign. If he does, it will cause much rejoicing. Mr. Foote censured him severely in Congress; and moved a resolution of censure, which was *not* laid on the table—though moved, and voted on—but postponed.

Gen. Lee has been a little ill from fatigue, exposure, and change of water; but was better yesterday, and is confident.

Messrs. Cardoza and Martin, who sell a peck of meal per day to each applicant for $12, or $48 per bushel, flour at $1.60 per pound, and beans $3 per quart, are daily beset with a great crowd, white and black. I do not think they sell for the government, but they probably have facilities from it. The prices are only about half charged in the shops.

But Messrs. Dunlop and Moucine are selling meal (on their own account, I believe) at $25 per bushel, or 50 cts. per pound, allowing each white member of the family about five ounces per day; and selling them twice per month, or nine pounds per month to each. The rule is to sell to only the indigent, refugees, etc. My friend James G. Brooks, Clay Street, informed me this morning that he got half a bushel there. He is rich!

MAY 31ST.—Clear, with hot sun.

Last evening there was some fighting on Lee's right, and 125 prisoners were sent in.

This morning cannon and musketry could be distinctly heard east of my dwelling; but at 3 P.M. I have not been able to learn the extent of it or the result.

But the GREAT BATTLE is imminent. Troops have been coming over from the south side (Beauregard's) for twenty hours, and marching down Main Street toward the Williamsburg road. It is doubtless a flank movement of Beauregard, and an attack on Grant may be expected any hour; and must occur, I think, to-morrow at furthest.

I have not learned that Butler has retired from his position—and if not, our communications must be in peril. But no matter, so Grant be beaten.

All the local troops are ordered to be in readiness to march at a moment's warning, this evening or night.

CHAPTER XXXIX.

Beauregard's plan.—The battle.—Defeat near Staunton.—Fight at Petersburg.—Decision about Marylanders —Beauregard in disgrace.—Dispatch from Gen. J. E. Johnston.

JUNE 1ST.—Bright and warm.

At $7\frac{1}{2}$ A.M. cannon and musketry heard northeast of the city, which either ceased or receded out of hearing at 12 M.; or else the hum of the city drowned the sounds of battle. Up to 3 P.M. we have no particulars. Beauregard is on the right of our line; Lee's headquarters was at Yellow Tavern. He is sufficiently recovered to direct the battle.

Butler has mostly if not entirely evacuated Bermuda Hundred; doubtless gone to Grant. The President rode out this morning toward the battle-field. Every one is confident of success, since Beauregard and Lee command.

The Secretary of War granted a passport to Mr. Pollard, who wrote a castigating history of the first years of the war, to visit Europe. Pollard, however, was taken, and is now in the hands of the enemy, at New York.

Another row with the Bureau of Conscription. Brig.-Gen. Chilton, Inspector-General, has been investigating operations in Mississippi, at the instance of Gen. Polk; and Col. Preston, Superintendent of the Bureau, disdains to answer their communications.

My landlord, Mr. King, *has not* raised my rent!

JUNE 2D.—Very warm and cloudy.

There was no general engagement yesterday, but heavy skirmishing, and several assaults at different points; and a dispatch from Gen. Lee says they resulted favorably to our arms.

A dispatch from Gen. Johnston says his men are in good plight, after combats enough to make a battle, in all of which the enemy suffered most.

The local troops (Custis's battalion, etc.) were ordered out to-day. I have not understood to what point they were ordered; but it indicates the imminency of a battle. Lee has not less than 80,000 men—veterans.

I saw, to day, Gen. Beauregard's plan, dated May 14th. It was addressed to Gen. Bragg, "Commanding Confederate States Armies." He suggested the falling back on the defenses of Richmond, and detaching 15,000 to the south side to crush or drive away Butler. He would then not only return the 15,000 to the north side, but bring over 25,000 additional to crush Grant.

This scheme was rejected by Bragg on the 19th, after consultation with the President and the Secretary: the latter indorsing *his* concurrence in the rejection, the President not *committing himself in writing*. But Beauregard was ordered to attack Butler without delay, which was done, and successfully; but he was not crushed, and still threatens our railroads with a portion of his army, while the rest has been sent to reinforce Grant.

Nevertheless, Beauregard is here with some 20,000, and Lee *did* fall back to the defenses of Richmond.

Congress has passed a bill increasing the compensation of themselves 100 per cent. Perhaps they will not adjourn now, but remain and await events.

Senator Hunter and the Secretary of War promenaded the Square yesterday afternoon in a long "confabulation," supposed by some to relate to political matters.

5 O'CLOCK P.M.—Heavy and quick cannonading heard some eight or ten miles east of the city. It continued until night, when it was raining and cold; and Custis had no blanket, not anticipating such a change.

JUNE 3D.—Raining gently, and cool.

As early as 4 A.M. there was an incessant roar of artillery, the vibrations of which could be felt in the houses. It could be heard distinctly in all parts of the city. And ever and anon could be distinguished great crashes of musketry, as if whole divisions of infantry were firing at the word of command. It continued until 11 o'clock A.M., when it ceased. A dispatch from Lee stated that his line (behind breastworks, center and left) had been repeatedly assaulted, and every time the enemy was repulsed. The attack, it was supposed, was made to check a flanking movement made yesterday afternoon, by Gen. Ewell, on the enemy's left, to cut his communications with the White House, his base of supplies. No doubt the slaughter has been great!

The dispatch from Beauregard indicates that he may be still on the other side of the river. It may be a *ruse de guerre*, or it may be that the general's enemies here (in the government) are risking everything to keep him from participation in the great battles.

Mr. Hunter, being short and fat, rolls about like a pumpkin. He is everywhere, seeking tidings from the field. It is said the enemy, at last, has visited his great estates in Essex County; but he'll escape loss "by hook or by crook." He has made enormously by his crops and his mills: nevertheless, he would sacrifice all for the Presidency—and independence.

The President, yesterday, forbade details from the Department Battalion to remain in the city.

The *Southern* Express Company has bribed the quartermasters, and is at its work again, using fine horses and stout details that should be in the army. Its wagon was at the department to-day with a box of bacon for Judge Campbell.

About 800 prisoners were marched into the city this afternoon, and it is believed many more are on the way.

Cannonading was heard again in a northeast direction this evening from 6 till 8½ o'clock, when it ceased—perhaps the prelude to another scene of carnage to-morrow!

JUNE 4TH.—Showers and sunshine. It is believed Grant has lost 40,000 within the last week!

To-day there has been more or less cannonading along the line; but it is not known if any infantry were engaged.

The battalion to which Custis (my son) belongs is at Bottom's Bridge, some sixteen miles distant on the Chickahominy; and I learn that the enemy shelled it yesterday and last night, without injury, shells falling short.

It is suspected that Sherman will be ordered from Georgia to reinforce Grant! It seems Lincoln would give up his hopes of heaven, and plunge into hell, for the PRESIDENCY.

The Commissary General says Lee must beat Grant before the latter is reinforced, "or we are gone;" for their destruction of the railroads, north and northwest, will ruin us—the southern roads being insufficient to transport stores for the army.

'My nephew, Col. R. H. Musser, trans-Mississippi, I am told by Senator Clark, was complimented on the field of victory by Gen. Taylor. His brigadier-general having fallen, Col. M. commanded the brigade.

Last evening, about 6 P.M., a cloud nearly overhead assumed the shape of a section of our fortifications, the segment of a circle, with the triangle penetrating through from the north. These shapes were distinctly defined. Could the operations beneath have produced this phenomenon? was it accidental? or a portent of the future? God knows!

JUNE 5TH.—Raining.

The sudden booming of artillery, shelling our department boys, intrenching at Bottom's Bridge, was heard until bedtime. I have heard no results of yesterday's operations.

All is quiet to-day, up to 9 A.M.

Received a letter from Custis. I have not heard whether he received the food and blanket sent him yesterday; the latter, he says, was wanted badly the night before. He charges Fanny, as usual, to be regular in feeding and watering Polly, his parrot; and never to leave the door of his cage open, for fear he may fly away.

JUNE 6TH.—Clear and hot, but with a fine breeze—southwest.

All is quiet around the city. Saturday night the enemy *again* penetrated Gen. Breckinridge's line, and *again* were repulsed by the Floridians. Some of his regiments (as Mr. Mallory, Secretary of the Navy, who stopped in front of my house yesterday, told me) did not behave well.

Yesterday, I learn, both sides buried the dead, with the exception of some Federals piled up in front of Lee's breastworks. A deserter says Grant intends *to stink* Lee out of his position, if nothing else will suffice. What a war, and for what? The *Presidency* (United States), perhaps!

I learn that the Departmental Battalion, near Bottom's Bridge, has been moved back a mile, out of range of the enemy's shells and sharpshooters.

We have met with a defeat in the Valley, near Staunton, which place has probably fallen. A letter from Gen. Bragg, this morning, in reply to Mr. Secretary Seddon's inquiries, says it is too true, and he indorses copies of dispatches from Gen. Vaughn and Col. Lee to Gen. R. E. Lee, who sent them to the President, and the President to Gen. B., who sends them now to the Secretary. Gen. V. calls loudly for reinforcements to save Staunton, and says Gen. W. E. Jones, who commanded, was killed. Col. Lee says, "We have been pretty badly whipped." Gen. Bragg knows of no reinforcements that can be sent, and says Gen. R. E. Lee has command there as well as here, and was never interfered with. Gen. B. says he had tendered Gen. Lee his services, but they had not been accepted.

Small heads of early York cabbage sold in market to-day at $3, or $5 for two. At that rate, I got about $10 worth out of my garden. Mine are excellent, and so far abundant, as well as the lettuce, which we have every day. My snap beans and beets will soon come on. The little garden is a little treasure.

June 7th.—Rained in the night, clear and cool in the morning.

Gen. Breckinridge's division started toward the Valley early this morning.

All is quiet near the city; but firing has been heard in the direction of Bottom's Bridge.

A man from New Kent County, coming through the lines, reports that Gen. Grant was quite drunk yesterday, and said he would try Lee once more, and if he failed to defeat him, "the Confederacy might go to hell." It must have been some other general.

June 8th.—Clouds and sunshine—cool.

No war news except what appears in the papers.

There was a rumor yesterday that several of the companies of the Departmental Battalion were captured on Monday, but it was not confirmed by later accounts.

Our battery of 49 guns was unmasked, and opened on the enemy, who had been firing over the heads of our young men (clerks). This was replied to by as many guns from the enemy. Thus both fires were over the heads of the infantry in the low ground between, and none were hurt, although the shell sometimes burst just over them.

A pontoon train passed down the river to-day, on this side, one captured from the United States, and brought from Gordonsville. If Grant crosses, Lee will cross, still holding the "inside track."

Received a letter from Custis. He is at Gen. Custis Lee's headquarters on ordnance duty. A pretty position, if a shell were to explode among the ammunition! He says he has plenty of bread and meat, and so we need not send any more. But he considers it a horrible life, and would rather be without his rations than his daily reading, etc. So I sent him reading enough for a week—all the newspapers I had; a pamphlet on the Bible Society in the South; Report of the Judiciary Committee on the Suspension of the *habeas corpus;* and, finally, the last number of the *Surgical Magazine,* in which he will find every variety of *gunshot wounds, operations,* etc. etc. I had nothing else to send him.

JUNE 9TH.—Sunshine and clouds—warm.

No fighting yesterday. It is reported that the enemy's cavalry and a corps of infantry recrossed the Pamunky this morning, either after Breckinridge, or to guard communications with the Rappahannock.

There is a pause also in Georgia.

Yesterday the President vetoed a bill exempting the publishers of periodicals, etc. He said the time had arrived when "every man capable of bearing arms should be found in the ranks." But this does not affect the young and stalwart *Chefs du Bureaux,* or acting assistant generals, quartermasters, commissaries, etc. etc., who have safe and soft places.

My little garden now serves me well, furnishing daily in cabbage, lettuce, beets, etc. what would cost $10.

JUNE 10TH.—Clear and cool.

All quiet round the city; but Petersburg was assaulted yesterday and successfully defended.

The battalion of clerks still remains at Bottom's Bridge, on the Chickahominy. The pickets hold familiar conversation every day with the pickets of the enemy, the stream being narrow, and crossed by a log. For tobacco and the city papers our boys get sugar, coffee, etc. This intercourse is wrong. Some of the clerks were *compelled* to volunteer to retain their offices, and may desert, giving important information to the enemy.

I had snap beans to-day from my garden. I have seen none in market.

JUNE 11TH.—Sunshine and cloudy—warmer.

There is a calm in military matters, but a storm is gathering in the Valley of Virginia. Both sides are concentrating for a battle. If we should be defeated (not likely), then our communications may be cut, and Grant be under no necessity of fighting again to get possession of Richmond. Meantime it is possible Grant will retire, and come again on the south side of the James River.

Congress is debating a measure increasing the President's compensation—he cannot subsist on his present salary. Nor can any of us. Mr. Seddon has a large private income, and could well afford to set the patriotic example of working ".for nothing."

We have heard to-day that Lincoln was nominated for re-election at Baltimore on the 7th inst., and gold rose to $196. Fremont is now pledged to run also, thus dividing the Republican party, and giving an opportunity for the Democrats to elect a President. If we can only *subsist* till then, we may have peace, and must have independence at all events.

But there is discontent, in the Army of the West, with Gen. Johnston, and in the East with Bragg, and among the croakers with the President.

New potatoes sold to-day for $5 per quart, $160 per bushel!

Mr. Rhodes, Commissioner of Patents, told me to-day that Gen. Forrest, at last accounts, was at Tupelo, Miss., doing nothing,—Gen. Wheeler, his junior in years, superior in rank, to whom he is again subordinated by the potency of Gen. Cooper's red tape, having most of his men.

Robert Tyler has been with the Departmental Battalion at Bottom's Bridge, doing service as a private, though the head of a bureau.

This evening at 7 o'clock we heard artillery in the direction of Lee's army.

JUNE 12TH.—Cold and cloudy.

Some firing again this morning, supposed to be merely an artillery duel.

Heard from Custis, in pencil mark on the back of envelope;

and he has applied for and obtained a transfer from ordnance duty in the rear, back to his company in the front.

It is rumored that Sheridan has cut the road between Gordonsville and Charlottesville, and between that place and Lynchburg. If this be true, he will probably strike south for the Danville Road. Then we shall have *confusion here, and the famine intensified.* There seems to be no concert among the military commanders, and no unity of purpose among civil functionaries. They mistrust one another, and the people begin to mistrust them all. Meantime the President remains inflexible.

All has been quiet to-day. I suppose the enemy is fortifying, with an intention to move half his army to the south side of the river—distracting us by menacing the city and threatening our communications at the same time.

It is believed here by the croakers that Gen. Lee has lost much of his influence, from the moment Mr. Foote named him as Dictator in the event of one being declared.

Now, it would seem, if the plan of Beauregard, rejected by Bragg, had been adopted, our condition would have been better. It is the curse of Republics to be torn by the dissensions of rival chieftains in moments of public danger!

JUNE 13TH.—Clear and cool.

Gen. Bragg sent to the Secretary of War to-day a copy of a letter from him to the President, yesterday, proposing to send 6000 more troops to Western Virginia, as Breckinridge has only 9000 and the enemy 18,000.

Lieut.-Gen Holmes sends from Raleigh, N. C., a letter from Hon. T. Bragg, revealing the existence of a secret organization in communication with the enemy, styled the "H. O. A.;" and asking authority to arrest certain men supposed to be implicated.

A letter was received from G. W. Lay, his son-in-law, by the Assistant Secretary of War, Judge Campbell, dated near Petersburg, stating that the Southern Express Company would bring articles from Charleston for him. That company seems to be more potential than ever.

Cannonading was heard far down the Chickahominy this morning. And yet Lieut.-Gen. Ewell marched his corps to-day out the Brooke Road, just in the opposite direction! It is rumored

that he is marching away for Washington! If he had transportation, and could march in that direction, no doubt it would be the
speediest way of relieving Richmond. Gen. Lee, however, knows
best.

At the conclave of dignitaries, Hunter, Wigfall, and Secretary
Seddon, yesterday, it is reported that when Mr. Seddon explained
Grant's zigzag fortifications, Senator Hunter exclaimed he was
afraid we could never beat him; when Senator Wigfall said
nothing was easier—the President would put the old folks and
children to *praying* at 6 o'clock A.M. Now if any one were to
tell these things to the President, he would not believe him.

JUNE 14TH.—Clear and cool.

Gen. Grant has changed his base—disappearing from the front
of Lee in the night. He is supposed to be endeavoring to get his
army below the city, and in communication with Butler on the
south side.

A dispatch from Gen. Lee says Gen. Hampton has defeated
Sheridan.

Forrest has gained a victory in the West.

Lincoln has been nominated—Andrew Johnson, of Tennessee,
for Vice-President.

Gen. Whiting writes that supplies from abroad are coming in
abundantly at Wilmington, N. C.

If we can only preserve our communications with the South, I
regard the campaign, if not the war, pretty nearly at an end, and
Richmond safe! Grant has failed, after doing his utmost to take
Richmond. He has shattered a great army to no purpose; while
Lee's army is as strong as ever. This is true generalship in Lee.
But Grant can get more men.

JUNE 15TH.—Clear and cool; warm late in the day.

It is rumored now that the enemy got to Westtown yesterday,
some ten miles below the point on this side occupied by Butler;
and to-day he is leaving, either crossing to the south side (probably to cut the railroad), or embarking in his transports for no one
knows whither. So, this attempt to take Richmond is as bad a
failure as any. Grant has *used up* nearly a hundred thousand
men—to what purpose? We are not injured, after withstanding
this blow of the concentrated power of the enemy. It is true some
bridges are burned, some railroads have been cut, and the crops

in the line of the enemy's march have been ruined; but our army is intact: Lee's losses altogether, in killed and wounded, not exceeding a few thousand.

A report of an officer states that the James River is not fordable anywhere above for forty miles.

There is a rumor on the street that the head of Ewell's corps (commanded by Gen. Early) crossed the Rappahannock, yesterday, at United States Ford. If this be so, there must be consternation in Washington; and the government there will issue embarrassing orders to Grant.

The spirits of the people here are buoyant with the Western news, as well as with the result of Lee's campaign.

The death of Gen. Polk, however, is lamented by a good many.

The operations of Forrest and Morgan are inspiring.

JUNE 16TH.—Clear and pleasant weather, but dusty.

The Departmental Battalion marched away, last night, from the Chickahominy (guarding a ford when no enemy was on the other side!) for Chaffin's Farm, on the James River. They were halted after marching an hour or so, and permitted to rest (sleep) while the rest of the brigade passed on. When Custis awoke he was alone, the battalion having left him; and he was ill, and knew not the road. So he set out for the city, with the intention of going down the river road this morning. But he grew worse after reaching home. Still, he resolved to go; and at 8 A.M., having marched all night nearly, he set out again, and met his sergeant—who had likewise diverged as far as the city—who said if he was really too ill to march, he would deliver the captain a surgeon's certificate to that effect, which would be a sufficient explanation of his absence. So, Surgeon C. Bell Gibson, upon an examination, pronounced him *sick*, and certified to the captain that he could not be fit for service for a week or ten days. At 3 P.M. he is in bed with a raging fever.

There was a fight at Malvern Hill yesterday, the enemy being repulsed.

There was also another assault on Petersburg, repulsed three times; but the fourth time our forces, *two regiments*, were forced back by overwhelming numbers from the outer line of defenses.

To-day it is reported that they are fighting again at Petersburg, and great masses of troops are in motion. The war will be determined, perhaps, by the operations of a day or two; and much anxiety is felt by all.

A letter from Hon. G. A. Henry, on the Danville Railroad, saying only 1000 men were there to defend it, with but two cannon without appropiate ammunition!

Soon after a dispatch came from Col. Withers, at Danville, stating it was reported 10,000 of the enemy were approaching the road, and only thirty-two miles distant. He called for reinforcements, but stated his belief that the number of the enemy was exaggerated.

I delivered these to the Secretary myself, finding him engaged writing a long letter to Gen. Kirby Smith, beyond the Mississippi!

In this moment of *doubt* and *apprehension*, I saw Mr. Randolph, formerly Secretary of War, and Mr. G. A. Myers, his law colleague, at the telegraph office eagerly in quest of news.

To-day the President decided that Marylanders here are "residents," or "alien enemies;" if the former, they must fight—if the latter, be expelled. A righteous judgment.

Last night, as Custis staggered (with debility) upon the pickets at the fortifications of the city, not having a passport, he was refused permission to proceed. He then lay down to rest, when one of the pickets remarked to him that he was not "smart, or he would flank them." Custis sprang up and thanked him for the *hint*, and proceeded to put it in practice.

The *Examiner* to-day says that Col. Dahlgren, a month before his death, was in Richmond, under an assumed name, with a passport signed by Gen. Winder, to go whithersoever he would. I think this probable.

At 3 P.M. the wires cease to work between here and Petersburg, and there are many rumors. But from the direction of the wind, we cannot hear any firing.

JUNE 17TH.—Clear and pleasant.

A dispatch from Beauregard states that two assaults of the enemy yesterday, at Petersburg, were repulsed with loss; and it is reported that he recovered all lost ground to-day. Yet Beauregard has an enemy in his rear as well as in his front.

When the battles were fought on the south side of the river in May, it appears that one of Gen. B.'s brigadiers (Colston) stopped some battalions on the way to Richmond, in an emergency, and this has certainly given umbrage to the President, as the following indorsement, which I found on a paper to-day, will show :

"No officer has a right to stop troops moving under the orders of superior authority. If he assumes such power, he does it at his hazard, and must be justified by subsequent events rather than by good intentions.

"Gen. Beauregard has, in this case, by approving and continuing the order (Gen. Colston's) assumed the responsibility of the act. —J. D. June 16th, 1864."

JUNE 18TH.—Clear and cool.

To-day, heavy firing is heard on the south side of the river. It is believed a general engagement is in progress. It is the anniversary of the battle of WATERLOO. If we gain the day, it will end the war.

It is now said Gen. Early (with Ewell's corps) has reached Lynchburg, where a battle must occur.

Gen. Ewell has been assigned to the command of this department, Gen. Ransom going West.

We have advices (4 P.M.) of a terrific battle at Petersburg last evening, which raged until 11 o'clock at night. The slaughter of the enemy is reported as unprecedented. Our troops repulsed the assailants at all points but one, and that, which was carried by the enemy, was soon recovered.

At 11 P.M. Lee's reinforcements came up, and it is supposed, from the sounds of cannon, that the battle was recommenced at dawn to-day, and continued all day. The result has not transpired. This tremendous conflict *must* be followed by decisive results. If Lee and Beauregard gain the day, peace must follow speedily, I think. If they are beaten, Richmond's fall can hardly be averted. Our shattered army could hardly get back across the Appomattox, with Butler's army interposed between—if he still has his army at Bermuda Hundred.

JUNE 19TH, SUNDAY.—Hazy and cool.

We have no details this morning of the fighting yesterday, and some doubt if a battle was fought. I presume assaults were made on our intrenchments in diverse places, and repulsed.

Beauregard's battle, Friday night, is still in smoke, but it is rumored the enemy lost 9000 killed and wounded.

Firing is heard to-day. There may be good policy in keeping back accounts from the field, until it is all over and something decisive accomplished. We have not met with serious disaster at all events, else there would be consternation in the city, for bad news flies fast, and cannot be kept back.

There was fighting yesterday at Lynchburg,—no result known yet.

Every Sunday I see how shabby my clothes have become, as every one else, almost, has a good suit in reserve. During the week all are shabby, and hence it is not noticeable. The wonder is that we are not naked, after wearing the same garments three or four years. But we have been in houses, engaged in light employments. The rascals who make money by the war fare sumptuously, and "have their good things in this world."

The weather is dry and dusty; the hazy atmosphere produced perhaps by the smoke of battle and the movements of mighty armies.

Eight P.M. The city is still in utter ignorance of the details and result of the battle yesterday—if there was one. If the government is in possession of information, it is, for some purpose, studiously kept from the public, and why, I cannot imagine, unless there has been a disaster, or Beauregard has done something not approved.

I do not think the people here appreciate the importance of the contest on the south side of the river. If Lee's army were broken, I doubt whether it would even attempt to regain the fortifications of Richmond, for then it might share the fate of Pemberton's army at Vicksburg. And the fall of Richmond would involve the fall of the State, and Virginia would immediately become a free State.

JUNE 20TH.—A fog; subsequently dry and dusty, but the sun in a haze, like Indian summer.

As I feared; there is trouble with Beauregard. He drew off his troops from in front of Bermuda Hundred to reinforce the fewer regiments at Petersburg, and *saved* that city, and Gen. Lee had to drive the enemy off again from the abandoned line. It is said Beauregard acted contrary to orders, and has been suspended from command by order of the President. At all events, Lee is at Petersburg.

Sheridan's raiders are near the city again, followed and preceded by Wade Hampton and Fitz Lee. Their cannon has been heard all the morning.

Mr. Secretary Memminger has resigned.

JUNE 21ST.—Clear and warmer.

Gen. Beauregard has not been removed from his command,—it would be too great a shock to popular sentiment.

The iron-clads went out this morning and proceeded down the river, supported by Custis Lee's brigade of local troops, including the Departmental Battalion, marching a dozen miles in the sun and dust. More will be on the sick list.

JUNE 22D.—Dry and pleasant.

The city full of idle rumors—that the whole brigade of local troops were captured yesterday—that Gen. Fitz Lee has again been made prisoner, and that another raiding party is threatening the Danville Road, the canal, etc. There is no foundation for any of them, so far as I can learn.

JUNE 23D.—Clear and warm.

The news of the capture of 1600 Federals, 4 guns, etc., yesterday at Petersburg, has put the people here in better humor, which has been bad enough, made so by reported rapes perpetrated by negro soldiers on young ladies in Westmoreland County. There has been talk of vengeance, and no doubt such atrocities cause many more to perish than otherwise would die.

A Mr. Sale, in the West, sends on an extract from a letter from Col. ——, proposing to the government to sell cotton on the Mississippi River for sterling exchange in London, and indicating that in this manner he has large sums to his own credit there, besides $100,000 worth of cotton in this country. Col. —— is a commissary, against whom grave charges have been made frequently, of speculation, etc., but was defended by the Commissary-General.

Mr. Harvey, president Danville Railroad, telegraphs to Gen. Bragg to send troops without delay, or the road will be ruined by the raiders. Bragg sends the paper to the Secretary of War, saying there are no troops but those in the army of Gen. Lee, and the reserves, the latter now being called out. Ten days ago, Mr. Secretary Seddon had fair warning about this road.

JUNE 24TH.—Hot and hazy; dry.

The news (in the papers) of the cutting of our railroad communications with the South creates fresh apprehension among the croakers.

But at 12 m. we had news of the recovery of the Weldon Road last evening, and the capture of 500 more prisoners.

We have nothing from the south side raiders since their work of destruction at Burkesville, cutting the Danville Road.

Mr. Hunter sheds tears over his losses in Essex, the burning of his mill, etc. But he had been a large gainer by the war.

There is a rumor of fighting at Petersburg to-day.

June 25th.—Hot and dry.

Twelve hundred Federal prisoners passed our door to-day, taken at Petersburg—about half the number captured there during the last two days.

The news of the cutting of the Danville Railroad still produces despondency with many. But the people are now harvesting a fair crop of wheat, and the authorities do not apprehend any serious consequences from the interruption of communication with the South—which is, indeed, deemed but temporary, as sufficient precaution is taken by the government to defend the roads and bridges, and there seems to be discussions between the generals as to authority and responsibility. There are *too many* authorities. Gen. Lee will remedy all this.

The clerks are still kept out, on the north side of the James River, while the enemy is on the south side—the government, meantime, being almost in a state of paralysis. Such injustice, and such obtuseness, would seem to be inexcusable.

The Secretary has sanctioned the organization of a force in the Northern Neck, to capture and slay without mercy such of the enemy as may be found lurking there, committing outrages, etc.

The President still devotes much time to the merits of applicants for appointments on military courts, brigadier-generals, etc.

It is reported that Grant has announced to his army that the fighting is over, and that the siege of Richmond now begins. A fallacy! Even if we were unable to repair the railroads, the fine crop of wheat just matured would suffice for the subsistence of the army—an army which has just withstood the military power of the North. It is believed that nearly 300,000 men have invaded Virginia this year, and yet, so far from striking down the army of Lee with superior numbers, we see, at this moment, the enemy intrenching himself at every new position occupied by him. This manifests an apprehension of sudden destruction himself!

But the country north and east and west of Richmond is now free of Yankees, and the railroads will be repaired in a few weeks at furthest. Gen. Hunter, we learn to-day, has escaped with loss out of the State to the Ohio River, blowing up his own ordnance train, and abandoning his cannon and stores. So we shall have ammunition and salt, even if the communication with Wilmington should be interrupted. No, the war must end, and is now near its end; and the Confederacy will achieve its independence. This of itself would suffice, but there may be a diversion in our favor in the North—a revolution there—a thing highly probable during the excitement of an embittered Presidential campaign. Besides, there may at any moment be foreign intervention. The United States can hardly escape a quarrel with France or England. It may occur with both.

JUNE 26TH.—Hot and dry, but breezy.

A dispatch from Gen. Lee, 9 P.M. last evening, says nothing of moment occurred along the lines yesterday. Our loss in the unsuccessful attempt of Gen. Haygood to storm a portion of the enemy's works, on Friday, was 97 killed and wounded, and 200 missing.

Gen. Hampton dispatches Gen. Lee that he attacked the enemy's cavalry in Charles City County, Friday, and drove them out of their intrenchments, pursuing them eight miles, nearly to Charles City Court House. The enemy left their killed and wounded on the ground, and strewn along the route. Gen. Lee says Gen. H. deserves much credit. The enemy (a portion of Sheridan's force) are still prevented from forming a junction with Grant.

Flour fell yesterday from $500 to $300 per barrel.

An official report shows that we lost no arms or ordnance stores of consequence at Staunton. Communications will be restored in that direction soon. The Valley and Western Virginia, being clear of the enemy, the fine crop of wheat can be gathered.

Beauregard *is* in disgrace, I am informed on pretty good authority; but while his humiliation is so qualified as not to be generally known, for fear of the resentment of his numerous friends, at the same time he is reticent, from patriotic motives, fearing to injure the cause.

It is stigmatized as an act of perfidy, that the Federal Government have brought here and caused to be slaughtered, some 1600 out of 1900 volunteers from the District of Columbia, who were to serve only 30 days in defense of the Federal city. At the same time our government is keeping in the service, at hard labor on the fortifications, Custis Lee's brigade of clerks, who were assured, when volunteering, that they never would be called out except to defend the fortifications of the city, built by negroes!

JUNE 27TH.—Bright and hot—afterward light showers.

By the papers we learn that President Lincoln has been on a visit to Grant's army. If Grant does not accomplish some great wonder in a few days, his campaign will be noted a failure, even in the North.

We learn to-day that gold is now at $2.15 in the North.

The raiders are beginning to pay the penalty of their temerity; besides Hampton's fight with them, on this side the James River, we learn that W. H. F. Lee has struck them a blow on the south side.

JUNE 28TH.—Bright and cool—a little rain last night.

The Departmental Battalion is still kept out. They have built a line of fortifications four miles long—to Deep Bottom from near Chaffin's Farm. The Secretary of War intimates that these clerks are kept out by Gen. R. E. Lee.

The superintendent of the Central Railroad informed the Secretary of War to-day that the road would be reopened to Staunton on Thursday (day after to-morrow), such is the slight damage done by the enemy. He asks that the bridge near Hanover Junction be defended, that being the only part of the road that can be much injured by a small raiding party. And he don't want the papers to say anything about the reopening of the road.

The news from the North, that Congress has refused to repeal the $300 clause in their military bill—allowing drafted men to buy out at $300 each—and the rise of gold to $2.30 for $1—together with the apparent or real *inertia* of Grant, seem to inspire great confidence in our people to-day. They think the worst is really over, and so do I.

My little garden, during the month of June, has saved me $150. A single cabbage head to-day in market was sold for $10. Although the joint salaries of Custis and myself amount now to $8000 per annum, we have the greatest difficulty to subsist. I hope we shall speedily have better times, and I think, unless some terrible misfortune happens to our arms, the invader will surely be soon hurled from our soil. What President Lincoln came to Grant for is merely conjecture—unquestionably *he* could not suggest any military enterprise more to our detriment than would occur to his generals.

JUNE 29TH.—Clear and cool—afterward hazy.

"MARIETTA, June 27th.

"GENERAL BRAXTON BRAGG.

"The enemy advanced on our whole line to-day. They assaulted French, Cheatham, Cleburn, Stevenson, and Quarles, by whom they were repulsed.

"On the rest of the line the skirmishing was severe.

"Their loss is supposed to be great. Ours is known to be small. "J. E. JOHNSTON, *General.*"

The dispatch from Gen. Johnston gives an encouraging account of the fight in Georgia. But a dispatch from the West states that reinforcements (20,000) for Sherman's army are marching from La Grange. It is reported and believed that Gen. Early, at the head of 25,000 men, marched out of Staunton on Monday *toward the North.* I hope it may not prove a recruiting measure for Lincoln !

A good deal of firing (cannon) was heard down the river this morning.

Judge Campbell is again "allowing" many persons to pass into the United States.

JUNE 30TH.—Clear and cool—afterward warm and cloudy.

Our people are made wild with joy to-day, upon hearing of the capture of a whole brigade of the raiders on the south side, the same that have been tearing up the Danville Road. The details, with Gen. Lee's dispatch, will be in the paper to-morrow. It is said we have the general commanding the raid, etc.

Judge Reagan said to me to-day, when I told him the news, his dark eye flashing, that sooner or later, but inevitably, these raiders must be *killed,* and not captured. And Mr. Seddon says he was always in favor of fighting under the black flag ; but, I believe, he never proposed it.

CHAPTER XL.

Gen. Lee's dispatch announcing Gen. Hampton's victory.—Cost of a cup of coffee.—From Gens. Johnston and S. D. Lee.—Gen. Early in Maryland. Rumored capture of Baltimore.—Letter from Gen. Lee.—Dispatch from Gen. Hood.—Status of the local troops.

JULY 1ST.—Clear, hot, and dry; my snap beans, corn, etc. burning up.

The papers this morning fail to confirm the capture of as many prisoners, near Petersburg, as were reported yesterday. But the dispatch (subjoined) of Gen. Lee renders it certain that the enemy was routed. There is a suspicion that our exasperated men *refused quarter* to some hundreds of the raiders, on the plea that they ravish, murder, burn, pillage, etc. It may be so.

"HEADQUARTERS ARMY NORTHERN VIRGINIA,
"June 29th, 1864—8·30 P.M.

"HON. SECRETARY OF WAR.

"SIR:—Gen. Hampton reports that he attacked the enemy's cavalry yesterday afternoon, on their return from Staunton River bridge, this side of Sappony Church, and drove them beyond that point.

"The fight continued during the night, and at daylight this morning he turned their left and routed them.

"When they reached Ream's Station, they were confronted by a portion of Mahone's division, who attacked them in front, while their left flank was turned by Gen. Fitz Lee's cavalry.

"The enemy was completely routed, and several pieces of artillery, with a number of prisoners, wagons, ambulances, etc., captured. The cavalry are in pursuit.

"R. E. LEE, *General*."

Gen. Early, with perhaps 10,000 men, is believed to be in Winchester to-day. He will probably be soon playing havoc with the enemy's railroads, stores, etc., and perhaps may threaten Washington or Harrisburg, or both; and so have Grant called off from his "siege of Richmond."

We were paid our salaries yesterday, and Custis, after his campaign and his sickness, resolved on a little indulgence. So he had a couple of small saucers of ice-cream—one for his mother, costing $6; quarter pound of coffee and two pounds of sugar, $25; and to-day a rice pudding, two pounds of rice, $5; one pound of sugar, $10; two quarts of milk, $5; total, $51!

Col. Shields, Commandant of Conscripts, etc., informed me to-day that he received only yesterday the order to proceed to the enrollment of Maryland and foreign residents. Thus the express orders of the President are delayed in the execution, and in such an exigency as this! I know Judge Campbell, Assistant Secretary of War, more than a year ago, attempted to interpose grave constitutional obstacles; but surely he can hardly have had the temerity to thwart the President's wishes, so plainly expressed. Nevertheless, the delay has been caused by some one; and Col. S. has apprehensions that some wheel within a wheel will even now embarrass or defeat the effective execution of the order.

Brig.-Gen. Gardner, successor of Brig.-Gen. Winder, has not yet assumed supervision of the passport business, and it remains in the hands of Judge Campbell and Provost Marshal Carrington. Very many persons are going to the United States via the Potomac.

JULY 2D.—Hot and dry.

A dispatch from Gen. Lee (will be published on Monday) says Gen. Beauregard reports the number of prisoners taken from Wilson's south side raiding party about 1000, besides the killed and wounded, and several hundred negroes recaptured, 13 guns, many small arms, wagons, etc. It is said the killed and wounded amount to 1500, of whom there are not exceeding 300 of the latter, *leaving* 1200 *killed*.

Gen. Morgan has got back to Western Virginia with 1800 men, having lost but 200. He did not fight a battle with Gen. Burbridge at all; hence the Federal account of Morgan's defeat was without foundation. Morgan will probably soon be in Maryland and Pennsylvania, attending to the enemy's railroads, bridges, mills, etc.

The President said (so reported) to Dr. Garnett, yesterday, he hoped to hear of no more raids, since the last fared so badly.

I drank two cups of coffee this morning, which seem to have had an extraordinary effect upon my strength, activity, and spirits; and indeed the belief that the discontinuance of the use of this beverage, about two years ago, may have caused the diminution of all. I am, and have long been, as poor as a church mouse. But the coffee (having in it sugar and cream) cost about a dollar each cup, and cannot be indulged in hereafter more than once a week. We had also boiled beans to-day, followed by fritters, the cherries from our garden, with sugar-sauce. This the family consider a sumptuous dinner—with no meat!

JULY 3D.—Clear and dry; pleasant temperature.

I learn that Petersburg has not been much injured by the enemy's batteries, and that Gen. Lee has ordered the casting of mortars for use immediately.

To-morrow being the anniversary of the surrender of Vicksburg to Grant, I should not be surprised if that general let off some fire-works, not only in commemoration of that event, but in pursuance of some desperate enterprise against Richmond. I don't see how he can feel any veneration for the day of Independence for the "rebels" of 1776, without sympathy for the "rebels" of 1864, struggling also for independence.

After the failure of the enemy's next move, I think the tempest of war will rapidly abate. Nearly every movement in this (I think final) effort to capture Richmond has failed. Sheridan failed to destroy the Central, Hunter the South Side, and Wilson the Danville Railroad—each losing about half his men and horses. Grant himself, so far, has but "swung round" a wall of steel, losing 100,000 men, and only gaining a position on the James River which he might have occupied without any loss. On the other hand, Lee wields a larger army than he began with, and better armed, clothed, and fed.

This *ought* to end the vain attempt at subjugation. But if not, the Confederate States, under the new policy (defensive), might maintain the contest against a half million of invaders. Our crop of wheat is abundant, and the harvest *over;* our communications will be all re-established in a few days, and the people being armed and drilled everywhere, the enemy's raiders will soon be checked in *any* locality they may select as the scene of operations. All the bridges will be defended with fortifications. Besides, Lee is gathering rapidly an army on the Potomac, and may not only menace the enemy's capital, but *take* it. Early and Breckinridge, Imboden and Morgan, may be at this moment inflicting more serious injury on the enemy's railroads and canals than we have sustained in Virginia. And it is certain the stores of•the Federal army in Georgia have been captured or destroyed to a very serious extent.

Still, in this hour of destitution and suffering among certain classes of the people, we see *no beggars* in the streets.

Likewise, notwithstanding the raiding parties penetrate far in the rear of our armies, there has been no instance of an attempt on the part of the slaves to rise in insurrection.

JULY 4TH.—Cloudy, but still hot and dry.

From the clouds of dust seen rising between Petersburg and the James River, it is conjectured that Grant's army is in motion.

The Federal Congress has authorized the drafting of 200,000 more men, after 60 days' fruitless attempt to raise volunteers. So it will be September before the draft, and January before the men will be soldiers.

JULY 5TH.—Cool and dry, everything suffering for rain.

All quiet about Petersburg, but later in the day a rumor sprung up that fighting had recommenced there. I doubt it, because by *Northern* accounts I see Gen. Early is destroying railroads beyond the Potomac, and will undoubtedly threaten Washington itself. If Grant fails to send troops there, Early may even throw shell into the Federal city.

Peter V. Daniel sends the Secretary of War a letter from Mr. Westmoreland, Wilmington, complaining that he is not allowed by government agents to transport cotton to that port, where his steamers are, *in redemption of Confederate States bonds*, while private persons, for speculative purposes, are, through the favor (probably for a consideration) of government officials, enabled to ship thousands of bales, and he submits a copy of a correspondence with Col. Sims, Assistant Quartermaster-General, and Lieut.-Col. Bayne, who is charged with the control of the exporting and importing business. Mr. Daniel thinks there is some "bribery and corruption" even in the South. But Mr. Seddon is incredulous sometimes.

The express company has an arrangement with Col. Sims, the Assistant Quartermaster-General, by which much freight is transported.

New potatoes are selling at $4 per quart in the market.

JULY 6TH.—Hot and dry.

We have no news to-day, but there are rumors that Grant is preparing to abandon his position. He cannot remain where he is, inactive. There is a scarcity of water, and the location is unhealthy.

We had corn bread and gravy for dinner, with a tremendous dessert, the suggestion of Custis, consisting of whortleberry flitters, with butter and sugar sauce, costing about $16.

JULY 7th.—Hot and dry, but a light shower at 2 P.M., laying the dust.

A letter from Gen. Gilmer states that the Danville Railroad will not be fully repaired before the last of this month. But there is a good wagon road, and the army can be supplied by wagons when the cars cannot run, some 25 miles.

There is an idle rumor that Wilmington has been taken by the enemy. This, indeed, would hurt us. But we get neither letters nor dispatches from beyond Petersburg.

Last week, when the local forces were recalled, one of the clerks in the Treasury Department, upon being dismissed, fell upon his lieutenant, who had insulted him while in the military service, and as a civilian, gave him a beating. To-day the officer, after consulting his lieutenant-colonel commanding, and, it is said, the Secretary of War, sent a subaltern to the department to arrest the clerk, who resisted. The subaltern said he acted by authority of the lieutenant-colonel and the Secretary of War, and would arrest him and throw him in prison, if he had to come with force enough to pull down the building. To all this the Secretary of the Treasury demurred, and made a formal complaint to the President, who most indignantly indorsed on the paper that the conduct of the officer was "very reprehensible," that if when the offense was committed, the battalion had been dismissed, the military authority of the officers ceased, and as civil officers, all were on the same footing. He ordered the Secretary to make this known to the officers, etc. None believe now that the President ever threatened to turn the clerks out of office, as represented, nor wished them put in the army, as hinted.

JULY 8TH.—Clear; hot and dusty.

The news of the falling back of Gen. Johnston on Atlanta, Ga., causes no uneasiness, for the destruction of Sherman's army is deemed the more certain the farther he penetrates.

There is nothing of interest from Petersburg, but there are rumors of demoralization and disaffection in Grant's army. His men suffer for water.

Still we get no letters from the South, beyond the point on the Danville Railroad reached by the raiders, who tore up 18 miles of the track.

We have nothing definite from Early's column yet, but no doubt there is alarm enough in Pennsylvania and in Washington City by this time.

JULY 9TH.—Dry and pleasant.

We have a rumor to-day of the success of a desperate expedition from Wilmington, N. C., to Point Lookout, Md., to liberate the prisoners of war (20,000) confined there and to arm them. If this be confirmed, the prisoners will probably march upon Washington City, and co-operate with Gen. Early, who has taken Martinsburg (with a large supply of stores), and at last accounts had driven Sigel back to Washington, and on the 6th inst. was (by Northern accounts) at Hagerstown, Md. Much excitement prevails there. Lincoln has called for the militia of the surrounding States, etc.

We have British accounts of the sinking of the ALABAMA, near Cherbourg, by the United States steamer Kearsarge, but Semmes was not taken, and his treasure, etc. had been deposited in France.

JULY 10TH —The drought continues; vegetation wilting and drying up. There is no war news, save some shelling by the enemy at Petersburg.

The raiders have caused many who were hiding and hoarding their meat and grain to bring them to market, for fear of losing them. This has mitigated the famine, and even produced a slight reduction of prices.

But the gardens are nearly ruined, and are only kept alive by watering freely. Mine has repaid me. The tomatoes are growing apace, and seem to endure the drought pretty well; also the lima beans. We are now eating the last of the cherries. We began to pull them about one month ago.

Some of the members of the Tredegar Battalion have been detected endeavoring to pass over to the enemy. It is said (maliciously) Jos. R. Anderson's works (the Tredegar) would not be destroyed if the enemy were to capture the city, nor Crenshaw's nor Haxall's mills, all having an understanding that the party in *power* shall enjoy the benefits of them. The fall of Richmond would exhibit strange developments among men of wealth. The poor could not get away, and would have no alternative but submission. But Richmond will not be *taken*.

JULY 11TH.—Hot and dry, and the famine continues.

The Secretary of War intimated on Saturday that if the clerks of the bureaus would raise a fund and send an agent South to buy provisions, he would insure them transportation, etc. To-day he denies that he made the promise, and refuses to aid them.

The government now proposes to increase its schedule of prices from 300 to 500 per cent., thus depreciating its own credit. *Before* harvest the impressing agents allowed about $40 per barrel for flour; now, that we have a good harvest, about $130 will be paid, thus raising the price everywhere. The transportation is the expensive item.

A dispatch from Gen. Johnston, at Atlanta, says the enemy having flanked him with his cavalry, he has fallen back across the Chattahoochee.

Dispatches from Gen. S. D. Lee, Tupelo, state that a column of the enemy, 20,000 strong, is about marching from New Orleans against Mobile, and he fears he cannot spare men to resist them. *The reserve class is not ready.* Also that 15,000 of the enemy are marching from Lagrange, and he will have to dismount some of Forrest's cavalry. Gen. E. K. Smith will not cross the Mississippi to assist in repelling the foe without orders. Orders have been sent from the Secretary of War—I fear too late!

Northern papers of the 8th inst. indicate a state of high excitement. Some there believe we have an army of 60,000 pouring into Pennsylvania. Gold was $2.65 for one.

There is some commotion in Grant's army, and it is believed by some that he is about to retire down the river.

It is rumored that the prisoners heretofore confined at Point Lookout have been removed by the Federal Government.

At 7 P.M. we had a gentle shower, lasting more than an hour.

JULY 12TH.—Clear and warm—the earth refreshed.

Gen. Johnston telegraphs to Gen. Bragg to have the United States prisoners at Andersonville " distributed immediately." He does not allege a reason for the necessity. It may be danger of an outbreak—or that the yellow fever has broken out among them.

I think Grant is about to have a race with Lee for Washington. The news from the Northern frontier is interesting.

A slight shower in the evening—heavy a few miles distant.

JULY 13TH.—Bright and pleasant.

The city is in great excitement and joy. Gen. Early has gained a victory in Maryland, near Frederick, defeating Gen. Wallace, capturing Gen. Tyler and Col. Seward (son of the Secretary), besides many prisoners. The slaughter was great, and the pursuit of the routed army was toward BALTIMORE.

Grant is certainly sending away troops.

Gen. Lee writes a particular letter to the Secretary (dated 9th inst.), desiring most specially that the papers be requested to say nothing of his movements for some time to come, and that the department will not publish any communication from him, which might indicate from its date his *distance* from Richmond. This is mysterious. He may be going to Maryland.

Gen. Johnston telegraphs from near Atlanta that the enemy holds several fords above, and a portion of his forces have crossed, and are intrenched. Some cannonading is going on—ineffective—aimed at the railroad depot. Some think Lee is going thither. Others that he is going to flank what remains of the Federal army in front of Petersburg.

JULY 14TH.—The drought continues here; but at some other places there has fallen heavy rain.

The excitement on the news of our successes in Maryland is intense, and a belief prevails that great results will grow out of this invasion of the country held by the enemy. Twice before but little if any benefit resulted from crossing the Potomac.

It is rumored to-day that Longstreet's corps has marched to Maryland, and that Lee is with it.

JULY 15TH.—Clear and cool; subsequently cloudy.

The *Washington Chronicle* of the 12th, received yesterday, indicates that Washington or Baltimore, or both, were in danger of falling into our possession.

Lieut.-Col. G. W. Lay said, this morning, in my office, that Grant would not leave—that he held a most important position—that he would not fail in his campaign; that our operations beyond the Potomac were not of sufficient magnitude to produce important results; and, finally, that Germany and Ireland would replenish the armies of the United States, while our last reserves were now in the field. The colonel had come into my office more than a month ago and said Grant had outgeneraled Pemberton, and would capture Vicksburg. I reminded him of this to-day, and asked his opinion on the present aspect of affairs. He has been recently on Gen. Beauregard's staff, and is irritated at the supposed hard treatment which that general receives from the President. He is a little bitter against the President, and is no special admirer of Lee, who, he thinks, committed a blunder in not fighting Grant at Hanover Junction. And he thinks, if Gen. Johnston forbears to fight Sherman, in pursuance of orders from Richmond, disaster will ensue. But neither he nor any one is capable of sounding the profound plans of Lee. Grant's forces are now far away from Washington.

2½ o'clock P.M. An officer just from Petersburg, arrived at the War Department with the intelligence that a Washington paper of the 13th inst. had been received at headquarters, announcing the capture of BALTIMORE by our troops! The inhabitants within, or a large proportion of them, co-operated with our army! Our people are in ecstasies! This is the realization of the grand conception of a great general, and Lee is immortalized—if it only be true.

JUNE 16TH.—Bright and cool—the canopy assuming a *brassy* aspect from the drought.

Alack! all the rejoicings are checked, and the public seems to have been hoaxed by the officer who reported that a Washington paper of the 13th inst. contained an account of the surrender of Baltimore to the Confederate States forces! The paper of that date, it appears, contains nothing of the kind, or else the account has been suppressed, to subserve some military purpose. But our people bear the disappointment well, not doubting but success will ultimately come.

There is a rumor that we sank two of the enemy's transports to-day in James River.

An immense mass of letters, etc.—175 bags—has just come in; the first mail matter that has arrived from beyond the breaks in the Danville Railroad, perpetrated by Wilson's raiders.

JULY 17TH.—Dry—the sky bright and brassy—the gardens almost ruined.

Last evening definite news came in the *Washington Chronicle* of the 14th. Gen. Early was recrossing the Potomac with an immense amount of stores levied in the enemy's country, including thousands of horses, etc. This, the *Chronicle* thinks, will be beneficial to the United States, as recruiting will be stimulated, to punish us for making prize of provisions, etc. in the enemy's country, after the enemy had despoiled us of everything in their power!

Troops are still going up toward Washington from our army, as well as from the enemy's before Petersburg; and Early, after bestowing his prizes in a place of safety, may return to Maryland and Pennsylvania for another supply. That may be the best policy to get the enemy off our soil. His cutting off communications with the South will not signify much, if we can derive supplies from the North.

JULY 18TH.—Clear and dry.

It is believed that a battery sent down opposite to Harrison's Bar in the James River sank two of the enemy's transports, Saturday, and drove back five others to Grant.

It is rumored that Gen. Johnston has been relieved at Atlanta, and Lieut.-Gen. Hood placed in command. I doubt.

It is said Mr. Trenholm, firm of Fraser, Trenholm & Co., bankers, Charleston, has been appointed Secretary of the Treasury. Mr. Seddon holds on to the office he occupies.

A letter from Gen. Lee ("Headquarters Army Northern Virginia") says Gen. Early has recrossed the Potomac, and is at Leesburg, safe,—I hope with his captured supplies.

The following is a synopsis of Gen. Kirby Smith's brilliant campaign of 1864; official report. Enemy's losses.

In Louisiana, 5000 killed and wounded, 4000 prisoners, 21 pieces artillery, 200 wagons, 1 gun-boat, 3 transports.

In Arkansas, 1400 killed, 2000 wounded, 1500 prisoners, 13 pieces of artillery, 900 wagons,

Confederate losses, 3000 killed, wounded, and missing.
Enemy's losses, 14,000.
Confederate strength, 15,000.
Enemy's strength, 47,000.
In Georgia, 35,000. In Arkansas, 12,000.

JULY 19TH.—A steady, gentle rain from 8 A.M. till 4 P.M.

A dispatch from Gen. Hood, who relieves Gen. Johnston, was received to-day. It was in cipher, and I did not learn the contents.

I strove in vain to-day to buy a few cabbage seed!

The following is a copy of a letter received from Gen. Lee, his *locality* not indicated, but from the date, he must be near the city:

"HEADQUARTERS, ARMY NORTHERN VIRGINIA,
"17th July, 1864.

"HON. SECRETARY OF WAR, RICHMOND.

"SIR:—I have received a dispatch from Gen. Early, dated at Leesburg on the 15th inst. On the 8th he crossed South Mountain, leaving Sigel at Maryland Heights. On the 9th he reached Frederick, and in the afternoon attacked and routed the enemy, ten thousand strong, under Wallace, at Monocacy Junction. The next day he moved on Washington, and arrived in front of the fortifications around that city on the 11th. The defenses were found very strong, and were not attacked. After a reconnoissance on the night of the 12th, he withdrew, and crossed the Potomac at White's Ford on the 14th, bringing off everything safely and in good order. He reports the Baltimore and Ohio Railroad to have been cut in several places, and severely damaged. The bridges over Gunpowder River, Northern Central and Philadelphia Railroads were burned, and the connection between Washington and Baltimore cut by Johnson's cavalry. The 6th corps (Federal) had arrived at Washington, and it was reported that other parts of Grant's army had reached there, but of the latter he was not certain. Hunter had passed Williamsport, and was moving toward Frederick. Gen. Early states that his loss was light.

"I am, with great respect,
"Your obed't servant."

(Not signed.)

Custis walked with Lieut. Bell last evening a mile from Hanover Junction to the battle-field of last month (just a month ago), and beheld some of the enemy still unburied! They fell very near our breastworks.

JULY 20TH.—Cloudy and warm, but no rain up to 5 P.M. There is no news of importance; but a battle is momentarily expected in Georgia. The *Examiner* says the President bears malice against Johnston, and embraces an occasion to ruin him at the risk of destroying the country. That he was not allowed the aid of detachments necessary to success, and hence he could not fight; but all aids will he give his successor, Hood, who will be successful. And that this game was played on Johnston in 1862 in Virginia, and when Lee took command, every facility was afforded by the government. In short, Gen. Johnston cannot be vindicated unless our army be destroyed; and if Hood wins a victory, he is ruined. This is an unpleasant predicament for a general.

Planted some cabbage-seeds given me; no plants are for sale.

JULY 21ST.—Clear and warm. Bought fifty cabbage-plants and set them out before breakfast.

Gen. Early met Gen. Hunter at Snicker's Gap, and whipped him.

All quiet at Petersburg. Grant must be dead, sure enough.

Gen. Bragg left the city some days ago. The following is a verbatim dispatch received from him yesterday:

"MONTGOMERY, ALA., July 19th, 1864.

"COL. J. B. SALE:—The enemy still hold West Point Railroad. Forces are moving forward to dislodge them. Gen. S. D. Lee informs me 5000 (13th Army Corps) passed Vicksburg on the 16th, supposed to be going to White River. Reported Memphis, 19th Army Corps, Franklin left New Orleans on the 4th for Fort Monroe, 13,000 strong. Ought not Taylor's forces to cross the Mississippi?

"I hear nothing from Johnston.

"Telegraph me to Columbus, Ga.

"B. BRAGG, *General*."

JULY 22D.—Bright and dry again. Gen. Johnston has been relieved. It would seem that Gen. Hood has made a successful debut as a fighting general in command of the army, since Gen. Johnston's removal.

A dispatch from Gen. Bragg, dated yesterday, states that the enemy is withdrawing from Arkansas, either to operate in Mississippi, or to reinforce Sherman.

Gen. Lee is opposed to retaliating on innocent prisoners the cruelties committed by the guilty in executing our men falling into their hands.

JULY 23D.—Clear, but a smoky atmosphere, like Indian summer. A dispatch was received to-day at M. from Gen. Hood, dated last night at 10 o'clock, stating that Gen. Hardee had made a night march, driving the enemy from his works, and capturing 16 guns and several colors, while Gen. Cheatham captured 6 guns. We took 2000 prisoners. Also that Gen. Wheeler had routed the enemy's cavalry at Decatur, capturing his camp. Our Major-Gen. Walker was killed and three brigadiers were wounded. Whether the battle was resumed to-day is not yet ascertained. All are now anxious to get further news from Atlanta.

And the local forces here are ordered to be in readiness; perhaps Lee meditates, likewise, a night march, and an attack on Grant.

The Danville and the Weldon Railroads are now in active operation, and I hope supplies will soon come in abundance.

Our government blundered in sanctioning the schedule of prices fixed by the commissioners on impressments for the next two months. The prices are five times those hitherto paid. The whole country cries shame, and a revision is demanded, else the country will be ruined.

JULY 24TH.—Cloudy and cool, but dry.

Yesterday and last night both Grant and Lee, or Beauregard, were moving pretty heavy forces from the south side to the north side of the river. I am not advised which initiated this manœuvre, but it indicates renewed activity of the armies in this vicinity.

I hope the roads will not be cut again, or we shall starve!

JULY 25TH.—It rained all night! Cloudy and windy to-day.

Gen. Hood corrects his dispatch of Saturday; we captured only 13 guns; but we captured some 18 stand of colors.

"HEADQUARTERS, ATLANTA,
"July 23d, 1864.

"HON. JAMES A. SEDDON, SECRETARY OF WAR.

"The enemy shifted his position on Peach Tree Creek last night, and Gen. Stewart's and Cheatham's corps formed line of battle around the city.

"Gen. Hardee's corps made a night march, and attacked the enemy's extreme left to-day. About 1 o'clock he drove him from his works, capturing artillery and colors. Gen. Cheatham attacked the enemy, capturing six pieces of artillery.

"During the engagement we captured about 2000 prisoners.

"Gen. Wheeler's cavalry routed the enemy in the neighborhood of Decatur, to-day, capturing his camp.

"Our loss is not yet fully ascertained.

"Major-Gen. Walker was killed. Brig.-Gens. Smith, Gist, and Mercer were wounded.

"Prisoners report that Gen. McPherson was killed.

"Our troops fought with great gallantry.

"J. B. HOOD, *General.*"

It is certain that a considerable force of the enemy has crossed to the north side of James River; for what purpose is not yet clear.

A detachment of our forces has been defeated near Winchester, by superior numbers, losing 4 guns.

The *Dispatch* of this morning says:

"All accounts received of the engagement at Snicker's represent that the Yankees were badly whipped on that occasion. It is stated that some fifteen hundred of the enemy fell to rise no more, and only six were made prisoners. It is probable that a considerable number were drowned in their attempt to recross the Shenandoah."

Gen. Beauregard wrote to the department a few days ago that the country in the rear of the enemy was filled with their deserters, and suggested that by proclamation or otherwise, desertion should be encouraged. They ought to be welcomed and subsisted, and transported to any point near their own country designated by them. On this the Secretary of War indorsed rather a cold negative. But he went too far—the country *must* be saved—and the

President, while agreeing that no proclamation should be issued, indorsed an emphatic approval of any other means to encourage desertion from the enemy.

My cabbages and turnips (fall) are coming up already.

We had but 13,500 men and 44 pieces artillery in the recent march into Maryland. The enemy say we had 40,000!

Letters are pouring in, denouncing the new schedule of prices, sanctioned by the Secretary, and demanding a prompt modification. The President wrote the Secretary to-day that immediate action is necessary.

JULY 26TH.—Clear and pleasant; later cloudy.

Yesterday, Mr. Peck, our agent, started South to buy provisions for the civil officers of the department. He had $100 from each, and it is to be hoped he will be back soon with supplies at comparatively low prices. He obtained transportation from the Quartermaster-General, with the sanction of the Secretary, although that —— —— had refused to order it himself.

Gen. Lee advises that all government stores be taken from Wilmington, as a London newspaper correspondent has given a glowing account (republished in the *New York Herald*) of the commerce of that place, and the vast amount of government property there. Gen. Lee advises that the stores be deposited along the line of railroad between Columbia and Danville, and be in readiness to move either way, as the roads are "liable to be cut at any moment." Will the government act in time to save them?

Gen. Cooper went to the President to-day in high dudgeon, because papers were referred to him from the Quartermaster-General's and Ordnance offices signed by subordinates, instead of the heads of the bureaus. The President wrote an elaborate decision in favor of the general, and ordered the Secretary to "make a note of it." Thus, important affairs wait upon "red tape."

I saw Secretaries Benjamin and Mallory, and some lesser lights, riding down the river in an ambulance-wagon, supposed to be going a fishing. They were both excessively fat and red.

JULY 27TH.—Cloudy and warm; light shower at 3. P.M.

Gen. Lee's dispatch, giving an account of a victory last Sunday, near Winchester, has diffused hope and satisfaction anew in the city.

The following dispatch was received from Gen. Bragg:

"ATLANTA, July 26th, 1864.

"Leave to-morrow to confer with Major-Gen. Maury at Montgomery, and urge matters beyond. Lieut.-Gen. Lee arrived. Tone of the army fine, and strength increasing daily, etc. All is quiet to-day.

"B. BRAGG, *General.*
"COL. J. B. SALE, *Mil. Sec.*"

Nevertheless, the clerks are ordered out this afternoon at five, to march to Chaffin's Farm.

I met Mr. Benjamin as I was passing to the office of the Secretary of War with Gen. Bragg's dispatch, and showed it him. After reading it carefully, he said, "That's very good."

Gen. Lee may be on the eve of attacking Grant, or Grant him, or we may be reinforcing Early, as the solution of the marching of the clerks. No doubt one of Grant's corps is on this side of the river, but I think that is to guard the river against our batteries.

During my conversation with Mr. Benjamin, I hoped that in two months the Federal armies would be called to Washington for the defense of the capital. He did not express any such belief. He was at the department procuring passports from Judge Campbell, for a young Jew to pass the lines into the United States.

JULY 28TH.—Cloudy, but no rain.

Nothimg new from Georgia or Petersburg. But a dispatch from Gen. Ewell, received to-day at half past two P.M., orders the local troops (they did not march yesterday) or other disposable forces to occupy the Darby Town, New Bridge, and Williamsburg roads, for the enemy's cavalry were working round to our left. This was dated "27" when, no doubt, it should be 28th. The Secretary was over at the President's office, whither I sent the dispatch. I suppose the troops were ordered out, provided there was a mistake in the *date.* All dispatches should have the *day* written out in full as well as the day of the month, for the salvation of a city might depend on it.

JULY 29TH.—Clear and warm.

The local troops did not march until this morning, and no one supposes Richmond is seriously menaced by Grant. I believe the object of the demonstration on the part of the enemy is to draw our forces away from the vicinity of Washington.

The Chief of the Signal Corps reports, on information supposed by him to be reliable, that Gen. Early's captures in Maryland were worth $12,000,000—consisting of some 10,000 horses, 10,000 cattle, 7000 hogs, 4000 sheep, 200,000 barrels of flour, and a large amount of bacon, etc. Also, that he got between 2000 and 3000 recruits. All this doubtful.

Mr. G. W. Lamar, Augusta, Ga., writes the Secretary of War that he knows, personally, over one hundred men who have *bought* exemptions, and that they are bought and sold every day at a certain price. Now will the Secretary order an investigation? Mr. L. has, or had, nine sons in the army, and he says he could have bought exemptions for all, as he is rich. And yet a poor ensigncy is refused one of his sons.

JULY 30TH.—Clear and hot.

Dispatches from Bragg, at Montgomery, of yesterday, give no accounts of more fighting, although the press dispatches, etc. did mention four of our generals who have been wounded.

There is a revival of murmurs against the President. He will *persist* in keeping Bragg in command, that is "of the armies in the field," though he does not lead any of them, and Gen. *Pemberton* really has command of all the batteries defending Richmond. The raiders are cutting the Georgia and Alabama Road since Bragg went South, and we have lost four pieces of artillery near this city a few days ago. ILL LUCK is indefensible!

To-day the enemy sprung a mine at Petersburg, but were repulsed in the attempt to rush in. This is all we know of it yet. Again it is rumored that the major parts of both armies are on *this* side of the river. This I believe, and I think that unless there be a battle immediately, Grant's intention is to abandon the "siege" of Richmond at the earliest practicable moment.

The local troops are back again. The President *directed* the Secretary of War to inform Gen. Ewell that he misapprehended the character of these troops. They were only for special and temporary service, having also civil duties to perform, and desired them to be sent back in twenty-four, or at at most, forty-eight hours. Gen. E. writes that he will employ them exclusively hereafter in the city fortifications, and only in times of extreme peril. And he says there *was* peril on Thursday, the enemy's cavalry being *between our infantry and the city*, and it will not do to rely always on his want of enterprise.

JULY 31ST.—Clear, dry, and *hot*.

A dispatch from Gen. Lee (I have not seen it yet) says, in the repulse of the enemy's assault on the breach made by their mine, we captured over 800 prisoners—a general and his staff among them—some 12 stands of colors, and killed some 500. Our loss very light.

The enemy has mostly countermarched from this side of the river, followed, of course, by our army at double-quick, and rumor says there are little or no forces of either party on the north side of the James this morning.

This was probably Grant's grand stratagem for our destruction, and it has failed disastrously for him. What will he do next? No matter what, Lee is the master of the situation.

My daughter's large pet cat died last night under the cherry-tree, and was buried this morning under a rose-bush. I sympathize with Fannie in the grief natural on such an occasion; but really, the death of the cat in such times as these is a great relief to me, as he was maintained at the cost of not less than $200 per annum. His death was probably occasioned by a surfeit of meat which his mistress obtained unexpectedly, seeing it fall in the street, and sending a servant for it.

This morning a large fat chicken was found in my yard, picked and prepared for cooking, brought hither by a cat which had stolen it from some kitchen. A portion of the breast only had been eaten, and our cook seized upon the remains for her own benefit. To such straits are we reduced by this cruel war!

CHAPTER XLI.

From the Northern papers.—Letter from J. Thompson, Canada.—From Mr. McRae, our foreign agent.—Dispatch from Major-Gen. Maury.—"General Order No. 65."—Battle of Reams's Station.

AUGUST 1ST.—Hot and clear; but it rained yesterday three-quarters of an hour in the afternoon.

Our loss in the affair at Petersburg is about 800, the enemy's 3500. We captured 2000 small arms.

We have nothing yet from Atlanta, but no doubt there has been another battle. I hope no disaster has befallen us there. No doubt the wires have been cut by the raiders, and roads also. It is a critical time in Georgia. But if Virginia triumphs over the assaults of Grant, all will go well.

August 2d.—Bright and hot. At 4 p.m. a cloud rising. Fear my wife, and daughter Fannie, and Custis (who has a days' furlough), who went this morning per Fredericksburg Railroad into Hanover County to gather blackberries, will be caught in a rain. Nevertheless, the rain is wanted.

Assistant Secretary Campbell is again "allowing" doubtful characters to pass out of the Confederate States to the United States; among these is Dr. McClure, "the embalmer," who, too, carried others out for bribes.

The Signal Bureau gives information to-day of Grant's purpose to spring the mine already sprung, also of a raid, that was abandoned, north and west of Richmond. They say Grant has now but 70,000 men, there being only a few men left at Washington. Can the agents paid by the Signal Bureau be relied on?

Gen. Bragg telegraphs from Columbus, Ga., that Gen. Roddy has been ordered to reassemble his forces in North Alabama, to cut Sherman's communications.

The news from Georgia is more cheering.

The commissioners (of prices) have reduced the schedule: it was denounced universally. It is said by the *Examiner* that the extravagant rates, $30 per bushel for wheat, and $50 for bacon, were suggested by a farmer in office.

Gen. Lee writes that he had directed Morgan to co-operate with Early, but he was sick.

The enemy's account of our loss in the battle before Atlanta is exaggerated greatly. Sherman's army is *doomed*, I think.

Seven p.m. No rain here, but my family were drenched in a hard shower at Hanover Junction, and what was worse, they got no blackberries, the hot sun having dried the sap in the bushes.

August 3d.—Cloudy, but no rain.

The press dispatches last night assert that still another raiding party, besides Stoneman's, was dispersed or captured.

It is rumored to-day that Beauregard has sprung a mine under Grant's fortifications. This may be so. *Later.* It was *not* so.

AUGUST 4TH.—Clear and hot.

All quiet at Petersburg. President Lincoln was at Fortress Monroe on Sunday last, after the explosion and its failure.

The Northern papers acknowledge that Grant sustained a terrible disaster at Petersburg, losing in killed, wounded, and missing 5000. They say the negro troops caused the failure, by running back and breaking the lines of the whites. The blacks were pushed forward in front, and suffered most.

From the same source we learn that our troops have penetrated Pennsylvania, and laid the city of Chambersburg in ashes. This may be so, as they have burned some half dozen of our towns, and are now daily throwing shell into Charleston, Atlanta, and Petersburg.

A letter to the Secretary from J. Thompson, in Canada (per Capt. Hines), was received to-day. He says the *work* will not probably begin before the middle of August. I know not what sort of work. But he says *much caution is necessary*. I suppose it to be the destruction of the Federal army depots, etc. in the United States.

Public meetings and the public press continue to denounce in unmeasured terms the high schedule of prices recently sanctioned by the Commissary and Quartermaster's bureaus. And, although the schedule has been modified, much odium will attach to all concerned in it. A large farmer, at the rates fixed for his products, would realize, perhaps, $200,000 per annum.

AUGUST 5TH.—Hot and dry. I hope there will be a rain-cloud this evening.

No war news, except a letter from Gen. Lee, indicating that Gen. Morgan is probably on a raid in Northwest Virginia and in Pennsylvania. Morgan proposed going into Georgia (rear of Sherman), but the Secretary indorsed that perhaps the matter had as well be left to Gen. Lee. The President quietly indorsed that he "concurred in the conclusion that all the movements of troops in Virginia had best be left to the discretion of Gen Lee."

Gen. Hood telegraphs that no important change has occurred in front of Atlanta. There was some skirmishing yesterday, and shell thrown into Atlanta.

My daughter Anne, after ten months' residence in the country, returned to-day (with Miss Randolph, of Loudon Co.) in perfect health. She brought apples, eggs, a watermelon, cucumbers, etc.

Mr. Davies sold my reel (German silver) to-day for $75, or about $3.20 in gold—enough to buy a cord of wood. I parted with it reluctantly, as I hope to catch fish yet.

AUGUST 6TH.—Hot and dry.

The booming of cannon heard yesterday evening was from one of our batteries below Drewry's Bluff. The enemy answered from their batteries, the existence of which we had no knowledge of before. No one was hurt.

About the same time Gen. Beauregard sprung a mine *under* the enemy's mine, and blew it up, no doubt destroying many lives. This was succeeded by heavy, but, perhaps, harmless shelling along the lines.

Another raiding party has been defeated and dispersed at Madison, Ga.

But we have been unfortunate in a naval engagement in the lower bay, at Mobile. We have lost Admiral Buchanan's ram "Tennessee," and several other steamers. One of the enemy's monitors was sunk. They had five vessels to our one.

Battles are momentarily expected at Atlanta and Winchester. We have nothing additional from the North.

AUGUST 7TH.—Hot and dry; but heavy rains in other parts of the State.

The 1st Army Corps moved through the city last night, via the Central and Fredericksburg Railroads, and this morning Fitzhugh Lee's cavalry corps is passing in the same direction—9 A.M.

All this indicates a transferrence of the scene of operations nearer the enemy's country—the relief of Richmond—the failure of Grant's MAD BULL campaign, prompted by President Lincoln, who is no general.

Honor to Lee!—the savior of his country! and the noble band of heroes whom he has led to victory!—but first to God.

AUGUST 8TH.—Hot and dry.

There are rumors of battles near Winchester and in Georgia.

Mr. Benjamin writes the Secretary of War for a passport for ———, who is going to New York, "for our service."

In the assault on the fortifications near Petersburg last week, it is said Hancock's (enemy's) corps lost half its men.

Watermelons have sold at $20 each; corn, $10 per dozen ears; and everything else in the markets in proportion.

My yellow tomatoes are just maturing. The dry weather has ruined nearly everything else in the garden.

AUGUST 9TH.—Very hot; very dry; very dusty.

The President has directed the late Gen. (now Lieut.-Col.) Pemberton to organize a mortar and cavalry force to dislodge the enemy from Deep Bottom, on this side of the river, and to select three or four batteries to render the navigation of the James River difficult and dangerous. Col. P. says he must have some 1500 cavalry, etc.

Letters from Mr. McRae, our agent abroad, show that our finances and credit are improving wonderfully, and that the government will soon have a great many fine steamers running the blockade. Mr. McR. has contracted for eight *steel*-clad steamers with a single firm, Frazer, Trenholm & Co.—*the latter now our Secretary of the Treasury.*

The President indorsed a cutting rebuke to both the Secretary of War and a Mr. (now Lieut.-Col.) Melton, A. A. General's office, to day. It was on an order for a quartermaster at Atlanta to report here and settle his accounts. Mr. M. had written on the order that it was issued "by order of the President." The President said he was responsible for all orders issued by the War Department, but it was a great presumption of any officer in that department to assume to indorse on any paper that it was by his special order, and that, too, "by command of the Secretary of War," the usual form.

AUGUST 10TH.—Hot and dry until 4 P.M. Gust, and 15 minutes' rain. Good for turnips.

Forts Gaines and Powell are lost—the latter blown up. Gen. Maury telegraphs for infantry, has some 4000 men for the defense of Mobile, etc.

Our raiders, under McCausland and Bradley Johnson, it is said were surprised and defeated last Sunday, with loss of 400 men, 500 horses, and 4 pieces of artillery. A rumor prevails that Early has gained another victory near Winchester.

No news yet from our agent sent to North Carolina to purchase supplies, but we learn flour and bacon are not held one quarter as high there as here. I do sincerely hope Grant's raiders will keep quiet until *I* can get something to eat!

AUGUST 11TH.—Hot and dry.

Dispatches from secret agents at Washington state that Grant and his staff have arrived, that half his army preceded him, and the remainder will soon follow. The campaign is considered a disastrous failure, and it is anticipated that henceforth the scene of operations is to be transferred from Richmond to Washington. They say President Lincoln's face expresses "great terror," and affairs there are in a critical condition.

A dispatch from Gen. Lee states that Gen. Bradley Johnson's brigade of cavalry was surprised and routed on the 7th inst. by Averill. He has directed that Gen. J. be relieved.

A dispatch from Gen. Hood (Atlanta, Ga.) says no important change in affair has occurred since yesterday, except that Major-Gen..Bates is wounded. There are 5000 militia in the trenches.

AUGUST 12TH.—Hot and dry. At 3 P.M. rained about three minutes. We are burning up.

There is no war news. A rumor in the street says Atlanta has fallen. I don't believe it. Yesterday Gen. Hood said no important change had occurred, etc.

I saw a soldier to-day from Gen. Early's army near Martinsburg, and the indications were that it was on the eve of crossing the Potomac. He left it day before yesterday, 10th inst. He says Kershaw's division was at Culpepper C. H., 50 miles from Early.

Detachments of troops are daily passing through the city, northward. All is quiet below on the James River. Grant's campaign against Richmond is confessedly a failure.

AUGUST 13TH —Hot and dry. Large green worms have attacked my tomatoes, and from the leaves are proceeding to the fruit. But not many of them will escape! I am warring on them.

No war news, except the continuation of the movement of troops *northward*. Hampton's division of cavalry, at least three brigades, passed this morning.

From Mobile and Atlanta we have nothing of interest.

Flour is falling: it is now $200 per barrel—$500 a few weeks ago; and bacon is falling in price also, from $11 to $6 per pound. A commission merchant said to me, yesterday, that there was at least eighteen months' supply (for the people) of breadstuffs and meats in the city; and pointing to the upper windows at the corner of Thirteenth and Cary Streets, he revealed the ends of many barrels piled above the windows. He said that flour had been there two years, held for "still higher prices." Such is the avarice of man. Such is war. And such the greed of extortioners, even in the midst of famine—and famine in the midst of plenty!

AUGUST 14TH.—Hot and dry.

Rumors of a fight down the river yesterday, driving the enemy from Deep Bottom, and grounding of the Richmond. Guns were heard, and I suppose we made a demonstration both by land and water.

Cavalry (Hampton's) still pass northward. They ride as if they grew to the horses. As they trot past, they can be seen cutting and dividing large round watermelons, and none are permitted to fall. Occasionally a staring negro in the street is astonished by the crushing of a rind on his head.

I never saw melons and other fruit so abundant; but they are held so high I cannot indulge.

Mr. Seddon draws 75 pounds rice per month, his family being fifty; and gets 12 pads cotton yarn from the State distribution. I shall get $10\frac{1}{2}$ pounds rice, at 50 cents—retail price, $2; and perhaps 1 pad—5 pounds—yarn for $45; my family being seven.

AUGUST 15TH.—Cloudy, damp, and pleasant. A rain fell last night, wetting the earth to a considerable depth; and the wind being southeast, we look for copious showers—a fine season for turnips, etc.

Cannon was distinctly heard from my garden yesterday evening, and considerable fighting has been going on down the river for several days; the result (if the end is yet) has not been officially stated. It is rumored that Pemberton lost more batteries; but it is only rumor, so far. Nor have we anything definite from Early or Hood.

Bacon has fallen to $5 and $6 per pound, flour to $175 per barrel. I hope we shall get some provisions from the South this week.

Sowed turnip-seed in every available spot of my garden to-day. My tomatoes are beginning to mature—better late than never.

The following official dispatch was received on Saturday:

"MOBILE, August 11th.—Nothing later from Fort Morgan. The wires are broken. Gen. Forrest drove the enemy's advance out of Oxford last night.

"All the particulars of the Fort Gaines surrender known, are that the commanding officer communicated with the enemy, and made terms, without authority. His fort was in good condition, the garrison having suffered little.

"He made no reply to repeated orders and signals from Gen. Page to hold his fort, and surrendered upon conditions not known here. D. H. MAURY, *Major-General.*"

Gen. Taylor will cross the Mississippi with 4000 on the 18th of this month. Sherman must get Atlanta quickly, or not at all.

AUGUST 16TH.—Warm and cloudy.

There are movements of interest of the armies below, from the fact that we have as yet no authentic account of the fighting during the last few days. I fear we have not been so successful as usual.

The enemy is reported to be in force on this side (north) of the river, and marching toward this city. The local (clerks) troops have been called out to man the fortifications. But the blow (if one really be meditated) may fall on the other (south) side of the river.

Col. Moseby has taken 200 of the enemy near Berryville, burning 75 wagons, and capturing 600 horses and mules. His loss trifling.

AUGUST 17TH.—Cloudy, and slight showers. In the afternoon dark clouds going round.

We have nothing from below but vague rumors, except that we repulsed the enemy yesterday, slaughtering the negro troops thrust in front.

From Atlanta, it is said the enemy have measurably ceased artillery firing, and it is inferred that their ammunition is low, and perhaps their communications cut.

The President and Secretary of War were in council all the morning, it is said, on *appointments* and *promotions* in the army.

The President rode out toward the battle-field at $2\frac{1}{2}$ P.M. There have been no guns heard to-day.

AUGUST 18TH.—Cloudy and pleasant.

Still we have no authentic account of the details of the fights on the north side of the James River. We know we lost two brigadier-generals, and that we captured some 600 prisoners. Of the number killed and wounded on either side is all conjecture, although a semi-official statement makes our loss but "light."

Nevertheless, I happen to know that the President rode out yesterday, and remained until late in the night: for Mr. Craddock, his special detective (and formerly his messenger), whom he sent for to accompany him, assures me while on the field there was a flag of truce to bury the dead, and that the slaughter had been large. Our cavalry had suffered; but he thinks the enemy's infantry lost many more men than all our slain together. He says, moreover, that only one negro prisoner reached the city. The rest, thrust forward, being killed on the field in action, I suppose.

At 2 P.M. a rumor began to be expanded that a terrific and probably a decisive battle was going on at Petersburg. One report says the enemy assaulted our lines, the operations on this side of the river having been more a feint to draw our forces away; another that Gen. Beauregard attacked the enemy, finding their troops in large force had crossed over to this side, and this in the absence of Gen. Lee, he taking the responsibility. Be this as it may, some stir was in the cabinet: and the Secretary of War was with the President from 11 A.M. till 3 P.M. This might be on "appointments and promotions," and it might be on Beauregard.

About 5 P.M. brisk artillery firing was heard in a southeast direction, which increased in rapidity, and apparently became nearer the city, until musketry could be distinctly heard from all parts of the city. My daughter Anne and her younger brother, Thomas, had walked out to Hollywood Cemetery, where they could not only hear the firing, but could see the lines of smoke below the city, on the left or north bank. Between 6 and 7 P.M. the sound seemed to recede, indicating that the assault had been repulsed; and finally all was silent again. It is probable the battle raged likewise on the south side of the river, and it may be hoped the assault on Petersburg was similarly repulsed. We shall know to-morrow.

AUGUST 19TH.—Damp and cloudy.

There was no serious battle. The wind was in a quarter which brought the sounds to us, even from the skirmishers, ten miles distant. But our gun-boats shelled the enemy out of their position on Signal Hill, and there was heavy cannonading along the line on the south side of the river. And, as appears by the papers, there was severe fighting at different points of the line.

We have now some further details of the battle of Tuesday. Our loss was 1000; the enemy's, it is said, 5000 to 8000.

It is now, 5 P.M., raining gently, thank Heaven!

To-day we had a distribution of meats, etc. brought from North Carolina by our agent. Custis and I invested $200: we have received 26 pounds bacon and 24 smoked herrings—worth here about $200. Half the money remains in the agent's hands, for which we expect to get 300 pounds of flour—if the enemy will let the railroads alone.

It is believed another raid has crossed the Weldon Road, and is sweeping in the direction of the Lynchburg and Danville Road. The speculators are on the *qui vive* already, and no flour can be had. I fear *our* flour will be intercepted, delayed, and perhaps lost! The meat we got to-day will supply but two ounces for each member of my family daily for two months. This is war, terrible war! But if Grant is not rapidly reinforced, at the present rate of his losses his army will be consumed in two months. There is some consolation in that prospect!

August 20th.—Rained hard all night, and a good deal to-day. Between 10 and 11 P.M. last evening, as we were retiring, a musket was fired somewhere in the rear of the building, and fragments of lime and brick were heard rattling against the window-shutters. This morning I perceived where the ball struck, a few inches below the window-sill of the chamber on the second floor, where Custis and Tom were lying. Some one, I suppose, had heedlessly fired his gun, after returning from the fortifications.

Well, the papers to-day fall below the official announcement of the work of yesterday afternoon. Gen. Lee's dispatch says we captured 2700 prisoners near Petersburg on the Weldon Road. No other particulars are given, and the affair is still in mystery, for some purpose, perhaps.

It is rumored that Gen. Hampton captured 4000 men last night or this morning; but I doubt. Without that, the week's work is good—Grant losing from 10,000 to 15,000 men. A few more weeks, at that rate, will consume his army, and then—peace?

Gen. Bragg complains, in a letter to the Secretary of War, that the orders of the department, and of the Adjutant-General, are not furnished him, which must diminish, if persisted in, his usefulness in the important position to which the President has called him. They are all inimical to Bragg—all but the President, who is bound in honor to sustain him.

The price of flour has fallen again; Lee's victory frightening the dealers.

Robert Hill, commission merchant, Bank Street, gave me two pounds of coffee to-day when I told him of Lee's dispatch. It was accepted, of course, and is worth some $20 per pound.

Guns are heard down the river again this evening, and all are wondering what Lee is doing now.

AUGUST 21ST.—Cloudy and pleasant; no rain last night, but the earth is saturated. No additional news from the army. It is said Gen. Bragg prevents news, good or bad, from expanding—believing that any intelligence whatever in the newspapers affords information to the enemy; and he is right. All the mysteries will be solved in a few days, and we shall have all the news, good, bad, and indifferent. I heard cannon last evening; also this morning. Our casualties could not have been large, else the ambulance train would have been in motion. That is certain. It may be that Grant's army is *crumbling*,—I hope so; and it may possibly be that *negotiations* are in progress. There *must* be an end of this; for the people of both sections are tired of it.

So far Grant has unquestionably failed in his enterprises against Richmond, and his present reduced strength certainly renders it unlikely that he can prevail against us hereafter. His new levies, if he gets any, will not be fit for the field this year; and all his veterans will soon be gone,—killed, or home,—never to return. Thank God, the prospect of peace is "bright and brightening," and a dark cloud is above the horizon in the North. Lincoln and his party are now environed with dangers rushing upon them from every direction.

No doubt Lee's army is weakened by detachments sent to Early; but then the local troops have been sent home, which is at least a favorable augury. The following order is published:

"GENERAL ORDER No. 65.

"It having been represented to the War Department that there are numbers of foreigners entrapped by artifice and fraud into the military and naval service of the United States, who would gladly withdraw from further participation in the inhuman warfare waged against a people who have never given them a pretext for hostility; and that there are many inhabitants of the United States now retained in that service against their will, who are averse to aiding in the unjust war now being prosecuted against the Confederate States; and it being also known that these men are prevented from abandoning such compulsory service by the difficulty they experience in escaping therefrom, it is ordered that all such persons coming within the lines of the Confederate armies shall be received, protected, and supplied with means of subsistence, until such of them as desire it can be forwarded to the most convenient points on the border, where all facilities will be afforded them to return to their homes.

"By order,
 "(Signed) S. COOPER,
  A. and I. General."

My turnips have not come up yet, and I fear the hot sun has destroyed the vitality of the seed. It is said the enemy still hold the Weldon Road; if so, then I fear our flour will be delayed, if not lost.

What if Grant now had the 140,000 more—lost in this campaign? Or if Lincoln should succeed in getting into the field the 500,000 men now called for?

The next two months will be the most interesting period of the war; everything depends upon the result of the Presidential election in the United States. We rely some little upon the success of the peace party.

The order from the Adjutant-General's office was first suggested by Gen. Beauregard, discountenanced by Mr. Secretary Seddon, approved by the President, and slightly modified by Gen. Lee. It remains to be seen what will be its effect. Deserters are certainly coming over in large numbers; so much so, that it is proposed to establish a depot for them in Georgia. Gen. Winder writes that it is not his province to be charged with them as well as with the prisoners. He is miserable; his rogues and cut-throats have mostly remained behind, preferring a city residence; and the Bureau of Conscription *will not*, it seems, conscribe Marylanders, most of whom have grown rich here. Will the President and the Secretary of War yield to Assistant Secretary Campbell, and the "Bureau," and Judge Halliburton,—or will they execute the act of Congress, enrolling all "residents" for the common defense? *Nous verrons.*

One meets no beggars yet, although we have been suffering a famine for more than a year.

The State Government is now selling a little rice—one and a half pounds per month to each member of a family—at 50 cents per pound, the ordinary price being about $2. And the City Council has employed a butcher to sell fresh meat at about $3.50 per pound. The State will also distribute cotton cloth and yarn, at something less than the usual prices. There would be quite enough of everything necessary, if it were equally distributed.

August 22d.—Sunshine and clouds, cool and pleasant.

There was heavy fighting on the Weldon Road yesterday evening, still held by the enemy; but no official account of the result—if it has yet reached a result—has been received. The city is full of extravagant rumors, and I incline to the belief that we gained no advantage yesterday. We took some 300 prisoners, certainly; but I fear Haygood's Brigade of South Carolinians ventured too far, when they were enveloped by greatly superior numbers—and —we shall know all to-morrow.

The news from Hood, Wheeler, Forrest, etc. in the Southwest promises well.

August 23d.—Clear and pleasant.

The enemy still occupy the Weldon Road, beyond Petersburg, in great force. Our loss in killed, wounded, and captured is estimated (in Sunday's fight) at 1000; under the mark, perhaps.

I hear of no raid yet against the Danville Road; but the flour speculators have put up the price again. Gen. Kemper told me this morning that he had 3000 of the reserves defending the Danville Road, the number Gen. Lee asked for.

Gen. Hood is so strong at Atlanta, that he has promised to send, in an emergency, a brigade to Mobile.

Interesting events will crowd each other rapidly, now.

August 24th.—Clear and pleasant.

Operations now must be initiated by the enemy. Gen. Lee writes that he is too weak to attempt to dislodge the Yankees from the Weldon Railroad. He cannot afford the loss of men necessary to accomplish it. He says the enemy, however, was "worsted" in the two conflicts, that of Friday and Sunday. And if he were to drive him away, the road would still be subject to interruption. He thinks we can still get supplies, by wagons, round the enemy's position, as well as by the Danville Road. He also suggests that corn be imported at Wilmington, and that every effort be made to accumulate supplies here; and he thinks we can hold out until corn matures some six weeks hence, so that the moral effect will be good, when it is apparent the efforts of the enemy to cut off our supplies are thwarted. He thinks the enemy has relinquished the idea of forcing our fortifications. But he says that Grant intended to force his way into Richmond last week.

I wrote a letter to the President to-day, urging the necessity of preventing the transportation of any supplies on the railroads except for distribution at cost, and thus exterminating the speculators. The poor must be fed and protected, if they be relied upon to defend the country. The rich bribe the conscription officers, and keep out of the ranks, invest their Confederate money and bonds in real estate, and would be the first to submit to the United States Government; and the poor, whom they oppress, are in danger of demoralization from suffering and disgust, and might also embrace reunion rather than a prolongation of such miseries as they have so long experienced. The patriotism of 1861 must be revived, or independence cannot be achieved. If a Peace Democrat be elected, no doubt terms of peace will be tendered, on the basis of *reunion;* and if they be rejected, perhaps the war may be continued. Or Lincoln may modify his conditions of peace; and the rich, always seeking repose and security, may embrace them. The surest plan is to break up speculation, and put the rich as well as the poor in the army. We must *deserve* independence, else we shall not get it. There must be no partiality, and especially in favor of the rich. I wrote plainly, intimating the danger of Reconstruction, without the greatest care, and a scrupulous performance of duty.

AUGUST 25TH.—Clear and warm.

No war news, except reports that Gen. Wheeler has destroyed much of the railroad in Sherman's rear, and that Early has forced Sheridan back across the Potomac.

Gen. Lee writes that he already notices the good effect of the order published by our government, encouraging desertions from the enemy's armies. He suggests that it be translated into the German, and circulated extensively in the enemy's country.

My turnips seem to be coming up at last; have sown them everywhere, so that when other crops come off, the ground will still be producing something.

Bought a bushel of red peas to-day for $30—the last for sale—the rest being taken for *horses*. Such is the food that my family is forced to subsist on.

Mr. Haxall, a millionaire, of conscript age, has just been appointed assessor of tax-in-kind. The salary is a pitiful sum, but the rich man is kept out of the army while the poor man is forced to fight in defense of his property.

The President is indefatigable in his labors. Every day the papers he sends to the department bear evidence of his attention to the minutest subject, even to the small appointments; he frequently rejects the Secretary's recommendations.

Gen. Bragg recommends that publication be made here, in the United States, and in Europe, encouraging enlistments of foreigners in our army.

AUGUST 26TH.—Clear; but rained copiously last night.

A letter from Gen. Lee indicates that the "Bureau of Conscription" fails to replenish the army. The rich men and slaveowners are but too successful in getting out, and in keeping out of the service. The Governor, who commissions magistrates, is exempting some fifty daily, and these, in many instances, are not only young men, but speculators. And nearly every landed proprietor has given bonds to furnish meal, etc. to obtain exemption. Thus *corruption* is eating to the heart of the cause, and I fear the result of the contest between speculation and patriotism. Mr. Seddon says he has striven to make the conscription officers do their duty, and was not aware that so many farmers had gotten exemption. He promises to do all in his power to obtain recruits, and will so use the strictly *local* troops as to render the Reserves more active. What that means we shall soon see.

A dispatch from Mobile says Fort Morgan is in the possession of the enemy! *Per contra*, a dispatch from the same place says Memphis is in the possession of Forrest.

August 27th.—Bright morning, and fine shower last night.

The people are smiling to-day from our success of Thursday, announced in the following dispatch from Gen. Lee:

"Headquarters Army Northern Virginia,
"August 26th, 1864.

"Hon. J. A. Seddon, Secretary of War.

"General A. P. Hill attacked the enemy in his intrenchments at Reams's Station yesterday evening, and at the second assault carried his entire line.

"Cook's and McRae's North Carolina brigades, under Gen. Heth, and Lane's North Carolina brigade, of Wilcox's division, under Gen. Connor, with Pegram's artillery, composed the assaulting party.

"One line of breastworks was carried by the cavalry under Gen. Hampton with great gallantry, who contributed largely to the success of the day.

"Seven stands of colors, two thousand prisoners, and nine pieces of artillery are in our possession.

"The loss of the enemy in killed and wounded is reported to be heavy—ours relatively small.

"Our profound gratitude is due to the Giver of all victory, and our thanks to the brave men and officers engaged.

"R. E. Lee."

It is said to-day that our captures will amount to 2500, and a brigadier-general is among the prisoners.

The President intimated to-day to the Secretary that when he respites a prisoner condemned to death, he does not desire the case brought to him again to approve the execution.

August 28th.—A bright, pleasant day.

No news. Walked, as usual, to the department to see if any important letters had come, and then hastened back that the family might go to church in time.

Oh what a lovely day in such an unlovely time! The recent rains have washed the dust from the still dark-green leaves of the trees and vegetation in my little yard and garden, and they rustle in a genial sunlight that startles a memory of a similar scene, forty or more years ago! It is a holy Sabbath day upon the earth,—but how unholy the men who inhabit the earth! Even the tall garish sun-flowers, cherished for very memories of childhood's days by my wife, and for amusement by my little daughter, have a gladdening influence on my spirits, until some object of scanty food or tattered garment forces upon the mind a realization of the reign of discord and destruction without. God grant there may be a speedy end of the war! And the words Armistice and Peace are found in the Northern papers and upon every one's tongue here.

My tomato vines are looking well and are bearing well, now. My turnips are coming up everywhere. The egg-plants I nurtured so carefully have borne no fruit yet, but are going to blossom. The okras have recovered under the influence of recent showers, and have new blossoms.

Our agent in North Carolina has been delayed by illness, and has bought us no flour yet, but we still have hope. We trust that the enemy will not cut our communications with the South, since he has met with so many heavy mishaps in attempting it. Grant has attempted everything in his power to get Richmond, and was foiled in all. I hope he will withdraw soon. Why stay, with no prospect of success? A few days more may solve his purposes and plans, or Lee may have more enterprises against him.

It is a cloudless, silent, solemn Sabbath day, and I thank God for it!

AUGUST 29TH.—Bright and pleasant morning; another fine shower last night.

No important intelligence from the armies.

AUGUST 30TH.—Bright and pleasant.

Gen. Hood telegraphs Gen Bragg that the enemy has shifted his line somewhat, drawing back his left and extending his right wing. Also that dispatches from Wheeler (August 19th) informs him that Dalton was captured, as stated, with 200 prisoners, 200 mules, a large amount of stores; several train supplies destroyed, as well as twenty-five miles of railroad in Sherman's rear. If that don't disturb the equanimity of Sherman, he must be an extraordinary general indeed.

Gen. Lee says the Bureau of Conscription has ceased to send forward recruits, and suggests that the conscript officers and their tens of thousands of details be now ordered into the ranks themselves. The Secretary does not agree to this, and the Assistant Secretary's son-in-law is one of "the Bureau."

Nine-tenths of the President's time and labor consist of discriminating between applicants for office and for promotion. They are all politicians still! And the Secretaries of State, Navy, and the Postmaster-General are getting to be as fat as bears, while some of the subordinates I wot of are becoming mere shadows from scarcity of food.

AUGUST 31ST.—Bright and pleasant.

The only news to-day was a dispatch from Gen. Hood, stating that the enemy had left Holly Springs, Miss., for the Mississippi River, supposed to reinforce Sherman, whose communications are certainly cut. It seems to me that Sherman must be doomed. Forces are gathering from every quarter around him, and it is over 200 miles to Mobile, if he has any idea to force his way thitherward.

Attended an auction to-day. Prices of furniture, clothing, etc. still mounting higher.

Common salt herrings are at $16 per dozen; salt shad, $8 a piece. Our agent was heard from to-day. He has no flour yet, but we still have hopes of getting some.

CHAPTER XLII.

The Federal Presidency.—The Chicago Convention.—Fall of Atlanta.—Bureau of Conscription.—From Gen. Hood.—Vice-President Stephens on the situation.—Letter from Mrs. Mendenhall.—Dispatch from Gen. Lee.—Defeat of Gen. Early.—From Gov. Vance.—From Gov. Brown, of Georgia.—Gen. Lee's indorsement of Col. Moseby.—Hon. Mr. Foote.—Attack on Fort Gilmer.—Indiscriminate arrest of civilians.

SEPTEMBER 1ST.—Clear, bright, and cool.

The intelligence from the North indicates that Gen. McClellan will be nominated for the Presidency. Judge Campbell, Assistant Secretary of War, shakes his head, and says he is not the right man. Our people take a lively interest in the proceedings of the Chicago Convention, hoping for a speedy termination of the war.

Senator Johnson, of Missouri, has a project of taxation for the extinguishment of the public debt—a sweeping taxation, amounting to one-half the value of the real and personal estate of the Confederate States. He got me to commit his ideas to writing, which I did, and they will be published.

Gen. Kemper told me to-day that there were 40,000 able-bodied men in Virginia now detailed.

There is a project on the tapis of introducing lady clerks into this bureau—all of them otherwise able to subsist themselves—while the poor refugees, who have suffered most, are denied places. Even the President named one to-day, Mrs. Ford, who, of course, will be appointed.

SEPTEMBER 2D.—Bright, and cool, and dry.

It is reported that a battle has occurred at Atlanta; but I have seen no official confirmation of it.

It is rumored that Gen. McClellan has been nominated by the Chicago Convention for President, and Fernando Wood for Vice-President. There is some interest felt by our people in the proceedings of this convention, and there is a hope that peace candidates may be nominated and elected.

Senator Johnson (Missouri) told me to-day that he had seen Mrs. Vaughan (wife of our Gen. V.), just from the United States, where she had been two months; and she declares it as her belief that Gen. McClellan will be elected, if nominated, and that he is decidedly for peace. She says the peace party would take up arms to put an end to Lincoln's sanguinary career, but that it is thought peace can be soonest restored by the ballot-box.

The President to-day arrested the rush of staff appointments.

To-day an old gentleman, after an interview with Mr. Secretary ——, said he might be a good man, an honest man; but he certainly had a "most villainous face."

SEPTEMBER 3D.—Slight rain in the morning.

There is an ugly rumor on the streets to-day—disaster to Gen. Hood, and the fall of Atlanta. I cannot trace it to an authentic source; and, if true, the telegraph operatives must have divulged it.

A dispatch from Petersburg states that there is much cheering in Grant's army for McClellan, the nominee of the Chicago Convention for the Presidency.

I think the resolutions of the convention amount to a defiance of President Lincoln, and that their ratification meetings will inaugurate civil war.

AT THE CONFEDERATE STATES CAPITAL. 277

The President has called upon the Governor of Alabama for the entire militia of the State, to be mustered into the service for the defense of the States. It is dated September 1st, and will include all exempted by the Conscription Bureau as *farmers*. Every farm has its exempted or detailed man under bonds to supply meat, etc.

I incline to the belief that Hood has met with disaster at Atlanta. If so, every able-bodied man in that State will be hunted up for its defense, unless, indeed, the Union party should be revived there.

There will be a new clamor against the President, for removing Johnston, and for *not* putting Beauregard in his place.

But we may get aid from the North, from their civil dissensions. If Lincoln could precipitate 500,000 additional men upon us now, we should be compelled to give back at all points. But this he cannot do. And the convention at Chicago did not adjourn *sine die*, and may be called again at any time to exercise *other* functions than the mere nomination of candidates, etc.

SEPTEMBER 4TH.—Showery.

Atlanta has fallen, and our army has retreated some thirty miles; such is Hood's dispatch, received last night.

The cheering in Grant's camp yesterday was over that event. We have not had sufficient generalship and enterprise to destroy Sherman's communications.

Some 40,000 landowners, and the owners of slaves, are at their comfortable homes, or in comfortable offices, while the poor and ignorant are relied upon to achieve independence! and these, very naturally, disappoint the President's expectations on momentous occasions.

SEPTEMBER 5TH.—Clear and warm.

Gen. Lee has called for 2000 negroes (to be impressed) to work on the Petersburg fortifications. Gen. Lee has been here two days, giving his advice, which I hope may be taken. He addresses Gen. Bragg as "commanding armies C. S." This *ought* to be an example for others to follow.

The loss of Atlanta is a stunning blow.

I am sick to-day—having been swollen by beans, or rather cowpeas.

SEPTEMBER 6TH.—Raining moderately, and cool.

Gen. Bragg has taken the Bureau of Conscription in hand, since Col. August, "acting superintendent," wrote him a "disrespectful and insubordinate" note. He required a report of the officers in the bureau, from Lieut.-Col. Lay, "Acting Superintendent,"—there have been three "acting superintendents" during the last three days,—and Col. Lay furnished it. On this Gen. B. remarks that one young and able-bodied colonel (August) was here while his regiment was in the field, and recommended that he be permitted to have an opportunity to see some "service" before the war is ended, and military experience, which will teach him to be more respectful to seniors, etc.; and that the able-bodied lieutenant-colonel (Lay), from whom he can get no report of inspections, and who remains here idle most of his time, could render more efficient service in the field.

And he thought Lieut. Goldthwait, relative of the Assistant Secretary of War, in the bureau, was performing functions that would better pertain to an older and more experienced man. In short, the whole organization required modification.

These papers, with this indorsement, being sent to the President, that functionary sends them to the Secretary of War, with an indorsement intimating that such remarks from Gen. Bragg required *action*. Here's a row! Perhaps the Secretary himself may *flare up*, and charge Gen. B. with interference, etc.;—but no, he must see that Gen. B. is acting with the concurrence of the President.

But the Assistant Secretary, Col. August, Lieut.-Col. Lay, etc. will be like so many hornets stirred up with a pole, and no doubt they are rich enough to defy the emoluments of office.

SEPTEMBER 7TH.—Clear and cool; rained in the night.

Gen. J. H. Morgan is dead,—surprised and killed in Tennessee,—and his staff captured.

Gen. Hood telegraphs that the enemy is still *retreating*—toward Atlanta, I suppose.

The cruiser Tallahassee having run into Wilmington, that port is now pretty effectually closed by an accumulation of blockaders.

It is said Gen. Forrest has blown up Tunnel Hill; if so, Sherman must be embarrassed in getting supplies of ordnance stores.

Sir Wm. Armstrong has sent from England one or two splendid guns (a present) to our government, with equipments, etc.

And the manufacturers have presented us with a battery of Whitworth guns, six in number, but they have not arrived yet.

SEPTEMBER 8TH.—Bright and cool; subsequently cloudy and warm.

Dispatches from Gen. Hood (Sept. 7th) state—1st dispatch: that Sherman still holds his works one and a half miles from Jonesborough. 2d dispatch, same date: "Sherman continues his retreat!" He says, in a 3d dispatch, that Sherman visited the hospitals, and said he would rest awhile at Atlanta, and then march away to Andersonville, where we keep the Federal prisoners. Although Hood attaches no importance to declarations from such a source, yet he deems it a matter of first importance to remove the prisoners, which suggestion Gen. Bragg refers to the Secretary of War without remark. Gen. Hood also urges the reinforcing of his army from the trans-Mississippi Department. He is sending a brigade to Opelika, to await a raid.

Gen. Forrest has been ordered, the President approving, to Middle Tennessee; but, contrary to his desire, he is not allowed to proclaim amnesty to the thousands of deserters expected to join him, so firmly do the President and Gen. Bragg adhere to Gen. Lee's advice never to proclaim pardon in advance to deserters, even at this critical epoch in our affairs.

All of us have been made sick by eating red peas, or rather *over*eating.

Our cause is in danger of being lost for want of horses and mules, and yet I discovered to-day that the government has been *lending* horses to men who have but recently suffered some of the calamities of war! I discovered it in a letter from the Hon. *R. M. T. Hunter*, of Essex County, asking in behalf of himself and neighbors to be permitted to retain the borrowed horses beyond the time specified—Oct. 1st. Mr. Hunter borrowed two horses and four mules. He is worth millions, and only suffered (having a mill burned) his first loss by the enemy a few weeks ago! Better, far better, would it be for the Secretary to borrow or impress one hundred thousand horses, and mount our infantry to cut the communications of the enemy, and hover on his flanks like the Cossacks in Russia.

SEPTEMBER 9TH.—Rained last night; clear to-day.

We hear of great rejoicing in the United States over the fall of

Atlanta, and this may be premature. President Lincoln has issued a proclamation for thanksgiving in the churches, etc.

Mr. Benjamin informs the Secretary of War that the President has agreed to facilitate the emigration of Polish exiles and a few hundred Scotchmen, to come through Mexico, etc. The former will enter our service.

The "Hope" has arrived at Wilmington with Sir Wm. Armstrong's present of a fine 12-pounder, all its equipments, ammunition, etc. Also (for sale) two 150-pounder rifled guns, with equipments, etc.

SEPTEMBER 10TH.—Slight showers, and warm.

Gen. J. H. Morgan was betrayed by a woman, a Mrs. Williamson, who was entertaining him.

Custis made an estimate of the white male population in seven States this side of the Mississippi, leaving out Tennessee, between the ages of fifteen and fifty, for Gen. Kemper, for Gen. Lee, which is 800,000, subject to deduction of those between fifteen and seventeen, disabled, 250,000, leaving 550,000—enough for defense for several years yet, if the Bureau of Conscription were abolished and a better system adopted.

It is said the draft is postponed or abandoned in the United States. I hope so.

Two 32-pounder guns passed down the river to-day on this side. We shall probably hear from them soon, and then, perhaps—lose them.

SEPTEMBER 11TH.—Showery.

No war news, though important events are looked for speedily. It is time. If our coat-tails were off, we should, in nine cases out of ten, be voted a nation of *sans cullottes*. We are already meager and emaciated. Yet I believe there is abundance of clothing and food, held by the extortioners. The government should wage war upon the speculators—enemies as mischievous as the Yankees.

SEPTEMBER 12TH.—Clear, and quite cold.

Gen. Hood has agreed to a short armistice with Sherman, ten days, proposed by the latter. Our people don't know what to think of this, and the government is acquiescent.

But there is a mournful gloom upon the brows of many, since Gen. Grant holds the Weldon Road, and is daily receiving reinforcements, while we get but few under the Conscription system and the present organization of the bureau.

There is a rumor of an intention to abandon Petersburg, and that 20,000 old men and boys, etc. must be put in the trenches on our side immediately to save Richmond and the cause.

Over 100,000 landed proprietors, and most of the slaveowners, are now out of the ranks, and soon, I fear, we shall have an army that will not fight, having nothing to fight for. And this is the result of the pernicious policy of partiality and exclusiveness, disintegrating society in such a crisis, and recognizing distinction of ranks,— the *higher* class staying home and making money, the *lower* class thrust into the trenches. And then the infamous schedule, to make the fortunes of the farmers of certain counties.

I bought 30 yards of brown cotton to-day, at $2.50 per yard, from a man who had just returned from North Carolina. The price here is $5. I sold my dear old silver reel some time ago (angling) for $75, the sum paid for this cotton.

Already the *Dispatch* is publishing paragraphs in praise of the "Bureau of Conscription," never dreaming that it strikes both Gen. Bragg and the President. These articles are written probably by Lieut.-Col. Lay or Col. August. And the *Examiner* is opening all its batteries again on the President and Gen. Bragg. The conscription men seem to have the odds; but the President, with a single eye, can discern his enemies, and when fully aroused is apt to pounce upon them like a relentless lion. The times are critical, however, and the Secretary of War is very reserved, even when under positive orders to act.

SEPTEMBER 13TH.—A bright, cool morning.

Dispatches from Lieut.-Gen. R. Taylor indicate that Federal troops are passing up the Mississippi River, and that the attack on Mobile has been delayed or abandoned.

Gen. Lee writes urgently for *more men*, and asks the Secretary to direct an inquiry into alleged charges that the bureaus are getting able-bodied details that should be in the army. And he complains that rich young men are elected magistrates, etc., just to avoid service in the field.

Gen. McClellan's letter accepting the nomination pledges a restoration of the Union "at all hazards." This casts a deeper gloom over our croakers.

"Everybody" is now abusing the President for removing Gen. Johnston, and demand his restoration, etc.

Our agent has returned, without wheat or flour. He says he has bought some wheat, and some molasses, and they will be on soon. I hope Gen. Grant will remain quiet, and not cut our only remaining railroad (south), until we get a month's supply of provisions! I hear of speculators getting everything they want, to oppress us with extortionate prices, while *we* can get nothing through on the railroads for our famishing families, even when we have an order of the government for transportation. The companies are bribed by speculators, while the government pays more moderate rates. And the quartermasters on the roads are bribed, and, although the Quartermaster-General is apprised of these corruptions, nothing is done to correct them.

And Mr. Seward has promised, for President Lincoln, that slavery will not be disturbed in any State that returns to the Union; and McClellan pledges States rights, and all the constitutional guarantees, when the Union is re-established. A few more disasters, and many of our croakers would listen to these promises. The rich are looking for security, and their victims, the poor and oppressed, murmur at the Confederate States Government for its failure to protect them.

In this hour of dullness, many are reflecting on the repose and abundance they enjoyed once in the Union. But there are more acts in this drama! And the bell may ring any moment for the curtain to rise again.

Dr. Powell brought us some apples to-day, which were fried for dinner—a scanty repast.

SEPTEMBER 14TH.—Bright and cold.

Gen. Lee is in the city, looking after recruits, details, etc.

Mr. Secretary Seddon appears to be in very high spirits to-day, and says our affairs are by no means so desperate as they seem on the surface. I hope the good coming will come soon.

Gen. Beauregard has been sent to North Carolina on a tour of inspection.

No news of our wheat and molasses yet; and we have hardly money enough to live until the next pay-day. We have no coal yet.

Four o'clock P.M. A brisk cannonade down the river is distinctly heard. It is not supposed to be a serious matter,—perhaps we are shelling Gen. Butler's observatory, erected within his lines to overlook ours.

SEPTEMBER 15TH.—Bright and pleasant.

The firing was from our gun-boats and two batteries, on Gen. Butler's canal to turn the channel of the river.

Our fondly-cherished visions of peace have vanished like a mirage of the desert; and there is general despondency among the croakers.

Mr. Burt, of South Carolina (late member of Congress), writes from Abbeville that Vice-President A. H Stephens crossed the Savannah River, when Sherman's raiders were galloping through the country, in great alarm. To the people near him he spoke freely on public affairs, and criticised the President's policy severely, and the conduct of the war generally. He said the enemy might now go where he pleased, our strength and resources were exhausted, and that we ought to make *peace.* That we could elect any one we might choose President of the United States, and intimated that this would enable us to secure terms, etc., which was understood to mean reconstruction of the Union.

A dispatch from Gen. Hood, dated yesterday, says Wheeler has been forced, by superior numbers, south of the Tennessee River; and he now proposes that he (W.) shall retreat south along the railroad, which he is to destroy. This is the very route and the very work I and others have been hoping would engage Wheeler's attention, for weeks. For one, I am rejoiced that the enemy "forced" him there, else, it seems, Sherman's communications never would have been seriously interrupted. And he proposes sending Forrest to operate with Wheeler. Forrest is in Mobile!

Gen. Morgan's remains are looked for this evening, and will have a great funeral. And yet I saw a communication to the President to-day, from a friend of his in high position, a Kentuckian, saying Morgan did not die too soon; and his reputation and character were saved by his timely death! The charges, of course, will be dropped. His command is reduced to 280 men; he was required to raise all his recruits in Kentucky.

SEPTEMBER 16TH.—Bright and pleasant—the weather.

Gen. Hood telegraphs that his army is so much mortified at the feeble resistance it made to Sherman, that he is certain it will fight better the next time.

Mr. Benjamin asks a passport and transportation for Mrs. Jane L. Brant, who goes to Europe in the employment of the government.

Gen. Morgan's funeral took place to-day. None were allowed to see him; for the coffin was not opened. On the way to Hollywood Cemetery, Gen. Ewell received a dispatch that our pickets were driven in at Chaffin's Farm. This demonstration of the enemy compelled him to withdraw the military portion of the procession, and they were hurried off to the battle-field.

The local troops (clerks, etc.) are ordered to assemble at 5 P.M. to-day. What does Grant mean? He chooses a good time, if he means anything serious; for our people, and many of the troops, are a little despondent. They are censuring the President again, whose popularity ebbs and flows.

SEPTEMBER 17TH.—Bright and dry.

The demonstration of the enemy yesterday, on both sides of the river, was merely reconnoissances. Our pickets were driven in, but were soon re-established in their former positions.

The Secretary of War is now reaping plaudits from his friends, who are permitted to bring flour enough from the Valley to subsist their families twelve months. The poor men in the army (the rich are not in it) can get nothing for their families, and there is a prospect of their starving.

Gen. Hood is a prophet. I saw a letter from him, to-day, to the President, opposing Gen. Morgan's last raid into Kentucky: predicting that if he returned at all, it would be with a demoralized handful of men—which turned out to be the case. He said if Morgan had been with Gen. Jones in the Valley, we might not have been compelled to confess a defeat, and lament the loss of a fine officer.

They do not take Confederate notes in the Valley, but sell flour for $8 per barrel in gold, which is equal to $200 in paper; and it costs nearly $100 to bring it here. Chickens are selling in market for $7 each, paper, or $37\frac{1}{2}$ cents, specie.

SEPTEMBER 18TH.—Cool and cloudy; symptoms of the equinoctial gale.

We have intelligence of another brilliant feat of Gen. Wade Hampton. Day before yesterday he got in the rear of the enemy, and drove off 2500 beeves and 400 prisoners. This will furnish fresh meat rations for Lee's army during a portion of the fall campaign. I shall get some shanks, perhaps; and the prisoners of war will have meat rations.

Our people generally regard McClellan's letter of acceptance as a war speech, and they are indifferent which succeeds, he or Lincoln, at the coming election; but they incline to the belief that McClellan will be beaten, because he did not announce himself in favor of peace, unconditionally, and our independence. My own opinion is that McClellan did what was best for him to do to secure his election, and that he will be elected. Then, if we maintain a strong front in the field, we shall have peace and independence. Yet his letter convinces me the peace party in the United States is not so strong as we supposed. If it shall appear that subjugation is not practicable, by future success on our part, the peace party will grow to commanding proportions.

Our currency was, yesterday, selling $25 for $1 in gold; and all of us who live on salaries live very badly: for food and everything else is governed by the specie value. Our $8000 per annum really is no more than $320 in gold. The rent of our house is the only item of expense not proportionably enlarged. It is $500, or $20 in gold. Gas is put up to $30 per 1000 feet.

Four P.M. We hear the deep booming of cannon again down the river. I hope the enemy will not get back the beeves we captured, and that my barrel of flour from North Carolina will not be intercepted!

J. J. Pollard's contract to bring supplies through the lines, on the Mississippi, receiving cotton therefor, has been revoked, it being alleged by many in that region that the benefits reaped are by no means mutual.

And Mr. De Bow's office of Cotton Loan Agent has been taken away from him for alleged irregularities, the nature of which is not clearly stated by the new Secretary of the Treasury, who announces his removal to the Secretary of War.

The President has had the porch of his house, from which his son fell, pulled down.

A "private" letter from Vice-President Stephens was received by Mr. Secretary Seddon to-day.

The cannonading ceased at sundown. The papers, to-morrow, will inform us what it was all about. Sunday is not respected in war, and I know not what is. Such terrible wars as this will probably make those who survive appreciate the blessings of peace.

SEPTEMBER 19TH.—Clear and pleasant.

We have nothing yet explanatory of the shelling yesterday.

To-day we have news of an expedition of the enemy crossing Rapidan Bridge on the way toward Gordonsville, Charlottesville, etc. Gen. Anderson's division, from Early's army, is said to be marching after them. We shall learn more of this business very soon.

Mrs. D. E. Mendenhall, Quaker, Jamestown, N. C., has written a "strictly confidential" letter to Mr. J. B. Crenshaw, of this city (which has gone on the files of the department), begging him to use his influence with Mr. Secretary Seddon (which is great) to get permission for her to send fourteen negroes, emancipated by her late husband's will, to Ohio. She says there is but one able to bear arms, and he is crazy; that since the enemy uses negro soldiers, she will withhold the able-bodied ones; that she has fed our soldiers, absolutely starving some of her stock to death, that she might have food for our poor men and their families, etc. etc.

No news from our flour.

I saw Nat Tyler to-day, and told him to call upon the farmers, in the *Enquirer*, to send their provisions to the city immediately, or they may lose their crops, and their horses too. He said he would.

The only news of interest is contained in the following official dispatch from Gen. Lee:

"HEADQUARTERS ARMY NORTHERN VIRGINIA,
"September 17th, 1864.

"HON. J. A. SEDDON, SECRETARY OF WAR.

"At daylight yesterday the enemy's skirmish line west of the Jerusalem Plank Road was driven back upon his intrenchments along their whole extent. Ninety prisoners were taken by us in the operation.

"At the same hour Gen. Hampton attacked the enemy's position north of the Norfolk Railroad, near Sycamore Church, and captured about three hundred prisoners, some arms and wagons, a large number of horses, and twenty-five hundred cattle.

"Gen. Gregg attacked Gen. Hampton, on his return in the afternoon, at Belches' mill, on the Jerusalem Plank Road, but was repulsed and driven back. Everything was brought off safely.

"Our entire loss does not exceed fifty men.   R. E. LEE."

Gen. Preston, Superintendent Bureau of Conscription, has made a labored defense (written by Colonels Lay and August) of the bureau against the allegations of Gen. Bragg. This was sent to the President by the Secretary of War, "for his information." The President sent it back, to-day, indorsed, "the subject is under general consideration."

The "Bureau," by advertisement, to-day, calls upon everybody between the ages of sixteen and fifty to report at certain places named, and be registered, and state the reasons why they are not now in the army and in the field. What nonsense! How many do they expect to come forward, voluntarily, candidates for gunpowder and exposure in the trenches?

SEPTEMBER 20TH.—Bright and pleasant.

An order has been given to impress *all* the supplies (wheat and meat) in the State, and Gen. Kemper has been instructed to lend military aid if necessary. This is right, so that speculation may be suppressed. But, then, Commissary-General Northrop says it is *all* for the army, and the *people*—non-producers—may starve, for what he cares. If this unfeeling and despotic policy be adopted by the government, it will strangle the Confederacy—strangle it with red-tape.

I learned, to-day, that Gen. Preston, Superintendent of the Bureau of Conscription, resigned upon seeing Gen. Bragg's and the President's indorsements on the bureau papers; but the Secretary and the President persuaded him to recall the resignation. He is very rich.

A practical railroad man has sent to the Secretary a simple plan, by which twenty-five men with crowbars can keep Sherman's communications cut.

There is a rumor that Sherman has invited Vice-President Stephens, Senator H. V. Johnson, and Gov. Brown to a meeting with him, to confer on terms of peace—*i.e.* the return of Georgia to the Union. The government has called for a list of all the Georgians who have sailed from our ports this summer.

A letter from Hon. R. W. Barnwell shows that he is opposed

to any conference with the enemy on terms of peace, except unconditional independence. He thinks Hood hardly competent to command the army, but approves the removal of Johnston. He thinks Sherman will go on to Augusta, etc.

The raid toward Gordonsville is now represented as a small affair, and to have returned as it came, after burning some mills, bridges, etc.

I saw a letter, to-day, written to the President by L. P. Walker, first Secretary of War, full of praise. It was dated in August, before the fall of Atlanta, and warmly congratulated him upon the removal of Gen. Johnston.

Gov. Bonham sent a telegram to the Secretary of War, to-day, from Columbia, asking if the President would not soon pass through that city; if such were his intentions, he would remain there, being very anxious to see him.

Beauregard is at Wilmington, while the whole country is calling for his appointment to the command of the army in Georgia. Unless some great success crowns our arms before Congress reassembles, the President will be assailed with great bitterness, and the consequences may be fatal.

SEPTEMBER 21ST.—Cloudy and somber.

We have authentic intelligence of the defeat of our forces under Gen. Early, near Winchester. Two generals, Rhodes and Godwin, were killed. We lost some guns, and heavily in killed and wounded. The enemy have Winchester, and Early has retreated, bringing off his trains, however. This has caused the croakers to raise a new howl against the President, for they know not what.

Mr. Clapman, our disbursing clerk (appointed under Secretary Randolph), proposed, to-day, to several in his office—jestingly, they supposed—revolution, and installing Gen. Lee as Dictator. It may be a jest to some, but others mean it in earnest.

I look for other and more disastrous defeats, unless the speculators are demolished, and the wealthy class put in the ranks. Many of the privates in our armies are fast becoming what is termed machine soldiers, and will ere long cease to fight well— having nothing to fight for. Alas, the chivalry have fallen! The lagging land proprietors and slaveowners (as the Yankees shrewdly predicted) want to be captains, etc. or speculators. The poor will not long fight for their oppressors, the money-changers, extortioners, etc., whose bribes keep them out of the service.

Mr. Foote openly advocates a convention; and says the other States will have one certainly: and if Virginia declines to unite in it, she will be "left out in the cold." This is said of him; I have not heard him say it. But I believe a convention in any State or States, if our disasters continue, will lead to reconstruction, if McClellan be elected. If emancipation, confiscation, etc. be insisted on, the war will never terminate but in final separation.

SEPTEMBER 22D.—Cloudy; rained much last night.

The following is all we know yet of Early's defeat:

"HEADQUARTERS ARMY OF NORTHERN VIRGINIA,
"September 20th, 1864.
"HON. JAMES A. SEDDON.

"Gen. Early reports that, on the morning of the 19th, the enemy advanced on Winchester, near which place he met his attack, which was resisted from early in the day till near night, when he was compelled to retire. After night he fell back to Newtown, and this morning to Fisher's Hill.

"Our loss reported to be severe.

"Major-Gen. Rhodes and Brig.-Gen. Godwin were killed, nobly doing their duty.

"Three pieces of artillery of King's battalion were lost.

"The trains and supplies were brought off safely.

"(Signed) R. E. LEE."

The profound chagrin produced by this event is fast becoming a sort of reckless unconcern. Many would fight and die in the last ditch, rather than give up Richmond; and many others are somewhat indifferent as to the result, disgusted with the management of affairs.

The President left the city on Monday, ignorant of the defeat of Early, for Georgia. It is said Beauregard is with him; but this is not certain. His private secretary, Mr. Burton Harrison, says he will be absent at least a month, perhaps until Christmas. Congress meets early in November; and before that day we may have terrible events—events determining the fate of the war.

We have heard heavy firing down the river all day; but it may not be a serious matter, though a general battle is looked for soon on the south side.

Gen. Lee will soon be reinforced materially. The President has adopted a suggestion I made to Gen. Bragg, and a general order is published to-day virtually abolishing the Bureau of Conscription. The business is mostly turned over to the commanders of the Reserves; and conscription is to be executed by Reserve men unfit for duty in the field. All the former conscript officers, guards, details, clerks, etc. fit to bear arms, are to go into the ranks.

"When the cat's away, the mice will play," is an old saying, and a true one. I saw a note of invitation to-day from Secretary Mallory to Secretary Seddon, inviting him to his house at 5 P.M. to partake of "pea-soup" with Secretary Trenholm. His "pea-soup" will be oysters and champagne, and every other delicacy relished by epicures. Mr. Mallory's red face, and his plethoric body, indicate the highest living; and his party will enjoy the dinner while so many of our brave men are languishing with wounds, or pining in a cruel captivity. Nay, they may feast, possibly, while the very pillars of the government are crumbling under the blows of the enemy.

It is said the President has gone to Georgia to prevent Governor Brown, Stephens, H. V. Johnson, Toombs, etc. from making peace (for Georgia) with Sherman.

A splenetic letter from Gov. Vance indicates trouble in that quarter. He says the Confederate States Government threw every possible impediment in his way when he bought a steamer and imported machinery to manufacture clothing for the North Carolina troops, and now the Confederate States Quartermaster-General is interfering with these factories, because, he says, he, the Governor, is supplying the troops at less expense than the Quartermaster-General would do. He demands details for the factories, and says if the Confederate States Government is determined to come in collision with him, he will meet it. He says he will not submit to any interference. Gov. Vance was splenetic once before, but became amiable enough about the time of the election. Since his election for another term, he shows his teeth again.

SEPTEMBER 23D.—Raining.

Our loss, killed, wounded, and taken in the battle near Winchester, is estimated by our people at 2500. The enemy say they got 2500 prisoners. The enemy's loss in killed and wounded amounted probably to as much as ours.

Gen. Lee writes that, in his opinion, the time has come for the army to have the benefit of a certain per cent. of the negroes, free and slave, as teamsters, laborers, etc.; and he suggests that there should be a corps of them permanently attached to the army. He says if we do not make use of them in the war, the enemy will use them against us. He contemplates staying where he is during the winter, and proposes building a railroad from his rear to the oak woods, as the pines do not answer a good purpose.

Gen. Hood telegraphs (dated yesterday) his intention to get in the enemy's rear, and intercept supplies from Dalton. Sherman must either attempt to drive him from that position (north bank of the Chattahoochee), or advance farther south with his supplies cut off and our army assaulting his rear.

Mr. Roy (clerk), cousin of Mr. Seddon, said to-day that he regarded the Confederacy near its end, and that the Union would be reconstructed.

Our good friend Dr. Powell brought us a gallon of sorghum molasses to-day.

SEPTEMBER 24TH.—Raining alternate hours and warm. Had a chill this morning, and afterward several spells of blindness, from rushes of blood to the head. Came home and bathed my feet and recovered.

Another disaster! but no great loss of men. Gen. Early was compelled to retreat again on Thursday, 22d inst., the enemy flanking him, and getting in his rear. He lost 12 more guns. This intensifies the chagrin and doubts prevalent in a certain class of the community. However, Lee commands in Virginia, and there may be better luck next time, which will cause everybody's spirits to rise.

Gen. Lee writes a long letter to the Secretary of War, deprecating the usage of the port of Wilmington by the Tallahassee and other cruisers, that go out and ravage the enemy's commerce, such as the destruction of fishing smacks, etc. Already the presence of the Tallahassee and the Edith at Wilmington has caused the loss of one of our blockade-runners, worth more than all the vessels destroyed by the Tallahassee, and the port is now guarded by such an additional number of blockaders that it is with difficulty our steamers can get in with supplies. Gen. L. suggests that Charleston or some other port be used by our cruisers; and that

Wilmington be used exclusively for the importation of supplies—quartermaster's, commissary's ordnance, etc. Gen. L. advises that supplies enough for two or three years be brought in, so that we shall not be under apprehension of being destitute hereafter. Such were his ideas. Lieut. Wood, who commads the Tallahassie, is the President's nephew, and gains eclat by his chivalric deeds on the ocean; but we cannot afford to lose our chances of independence to glorify the President's nephew. Gen. Lee but reiterates what has been written on the same subject by Gen. Whiting at Wilmington.

SEPTEMBER 25TH.—Clear and cool. Pains in my head, etc.

Hon. Mr. Foote told G. Fitzhugh early this morning that he had learned Gen. Early's army was scattered to the winds; that the enemy had the Central Railroad (where?) and would soon have all the roads. This is not credited, though it may be so.

There is a mysterious fascination in scenes of death and carnage. As I crossed Franklin Street, going down to the department this morning, I heard on my right the cry of "halt!" and saw a large man in citizen's clothes running toward me pursued by a soldier—coming from the direction of Gen. Ewell's headquarters. The man (perhaps a deserter) ran on, and the soldier took deliberate aim with his rifle, and burst a cap. I stood and watched the man, being riveted to the spot by a strange fascination, although I was nearly in a line with the pursuit. An irresistible curiosity seized me to see the immediate effects of the shot. The man turned up Ninth Street, the soldier fixing another cap as he ran, and, taking deliberate aim, the cap failed to explode the charge again. I saw several persons crossing the street beyond the flying man, who would have been greatly endangered if the rifle had been discharged. In war the destruction of human life excites no more pity than the slaughter of beeves in peace!

SEPTEMBER 26TH.—Bright and cool.

Gen. Early is still falling back; on Saturday he was at Port Republic, but he will soon be reinforced, and may turn the tide on Sheridan.

A long letter was received at the department to-day from Gov. Brown, absolutely *refusing* to respond to the President's call for the militia of that State. He says he will *not* encourage the President's ambitious projects by placing in his hands, and under his unconditional control, all that remains to preserve the reserved rights of his State. He bitterly and offensively criticises the President's management of military affairs—sending Morgan into Kentucky, Wheeler into East, and Forrest into West Tennessee, instead of combining all upon Sherman's rear and cutting his communications. He says Georgia has fifty regiments in Virginia, and if the President won't send reinforcements, then he *demands* the return of Georgia troops, and he will endeavor to defend the State without his aid, etc.

SEPTEMBER 27TH.—Bright and pleasant.

We have rumors of heavy fighting yesterday near Staunton, but no authentic accounts.

A dispatch from Gen. R. Taylor says Gen. Forrest had gained a victory at Athens, Ala., capturing some 1500 prisoners, 500 horses, etc. etc.

We still hear the thunder of artillery down the river—the two armies shelling each other, I suppose, as yet at a safe distance. A few more days and the curtain will rise again—Lee and Grant the principal actors in the tragedy!

The President is making patriotic speeches in Alabama and Georgia.

Mr. Hudson, of Alabama, proposes to deliver to the government 5,000,000 pounds of bacon for the same number of pounds cotton, delivered at the same place.

Our cotton agent in Mississippi is authorized by the government here to sell cotton in exposed situations to the enemy's agents for *specie*, and to buy for Confederate notes.

The funeral expenses of Gen. Morgan the other day amounted to $1500; the Quartermaster-General objects to paying it, and sends the bill to the Secretary for instructions.

The following is a copy of Gen. Lee's indorsement on Lieut.-Col. Moseby's report of his operations from the 1st of March to the 11th of September, 1864:

"HEADQUARTERS, ARMY NORTHERN VIRGINIA,
"September 19th, 1864.

"Respectfully forwarded to the Adjutant and Inspector-General for the information of the department. Attention is invited to the activity and skill of Col. Moseby, and the intelligence and courage of the officers and men of his command, as displayed in this report.

"With the loss of little more than 20 men, he has killed, wounded, and captured, during the period embraced in this report, about 1200 of the enemy, and taken more than 1600 horses and mules, 230 beef cattle, and 85 wagons and ambulances, without counting many smaller operations. The services rendered by Col. Moseby and his command in watching and reporting the enemy's movements have also been of great value. His operations have been highly creditable to himself and his command.

"(Signed)   R. E. LEE, *General.*
"Official: JOHN BLAIR HOGE,
"*Major and Assistant Adjutant-General.*"

SEPTEMBER 28TH.—Bright; subsequently cloudy and warm rain.

Staunton was entered by the enemy's cavalry on Monday afternoon.

We have no news whatever to-day from any quarter. But the deep booming of cannon is still heard down the river, foreboding an awful conflict soon.

I saw three 10-inch Columbiads at the Petersburg depot to-day; they are going to move them toward Petersburg, I believe.

Gold is thirty for one to-day, and still rising, Forrest's exploit having done nothing to revive confidence in Treasury notes here.

SEPTEMBER 29TH.—Bright and beautiful.

As I walked down to the department, heavy and brisk cannonading below assailed the ear. It was different from the ordinary daily shelling, and to my familiar senses, it could only be a BATTLE. The sounds continued, and even at my desk in the department the vibrations were very perceptible.

About 10 o'clock, when walking down Main Street (the cannon still heard), I met Robert Tyler and Mr. Foote, member of Congress, the latter in some excitement, denouncing the management of affairs by the Executive. He said if Richmond were lost, he should move that the people take matters in their own hands, and proclaim a DICTATOR. Mr. Tyler, commanding his temper, banteringly told him that he ran some risk of being arrested, tried by drum-head court-martial, and shot—before night. Mr. Foote whirled away, repeating his desperate purpose; and Tyler repeating, more gravely, that he might be arrested for treasonable language—and ought to be.

Mr. Tyler then invited me to join him at breakfast at a neighboring restaurant, where we had each a loaf of bread, a cup of coffee with milk (but brown sugar), and three eggs. The bill was sixteen dollars!

When I returned to the department, information came that the enemy had captured Fort Harrison (Signal Hill), near Chaffin's Bluff, and were advancing toward the city. From that moment much excitement sprung up (the greatest I have ever known here), and all the local organizations were immediately ordered out. Not only this, but squads of guards were sent into the streets everywhere with orders to arrest every able-bodied man they met, regardless of papers; and this produced a consternation among the civilians. The offices and government shops were closed, and the tocsin sounded for hours, by order of the Governor, frightening some of the women.

At 2 P.M. the fight was nearer, and it was reported that the enemy were at the intermediate fortifications—three miles distant.

From the observatory on the War Department we could see the puffs of white smoke from our guns; but these were at the intermediate line, several miles distant, and the enemy were, of course, beyond. We could see our cannon firing from right to left at least a mile in length; and the enemy had evidently made much progress toward the city. The firing then ceased, however, at 3 P.M., indicating that the enemy had withdrawn from that point; but the booming of artillery was still heard farther to the right on or near the river. And this continued until the present writing, 5 P.M. We have no particulars; but it is reported that the enemy were handsomely repulsed. Clouds of dust can be seen with the telescope in that direction, which appears to the naked eye to be smoke. It arises no doubt from the march of troops, sent by Gen. Lee. We must soon have something definite from the scene of action.

Half-past five P.M. Gen. Ewell dispatches that the enemy's attack on Fort Gilmer (five miles below the same we saw) was handsomely repulsed.

A dispatch from Gen. Pemberton, on Williamsburg Road, says there is no immediate danger there.

Another dispatch from Georgia says Forrest has captured 800 more men somewhere in Alabama, on the railroad.

At night, distant cannon heard. Gen. Ewell said in his last dispatch that as soon as certain reinforcements came up he would take the offensive, attacking the enemy. The conflict recedes, and I presume he is driving the enemy back.

Mr. Foote intimates that the President will not return to Richmond, and did not intend to return.

SEPTEMBER 30TH.—Cloudy, and occasional showers.

None of the papers except the *Whig* were published this morning, the printers, etc. being called out to defend the city. Every device of the military authorities has been employed to put the people here in the ranks. Guards everywhere, on horseback and on foot, in the city and at the suburbs, are arresting pedestrians, who, if they have not passes from Gen. Kemper, are hurried to some of the depots or to the City Square (iron palings), and confined until marched to the field or released. Two of the clerks of the War Department, who went down to the Spottswood Hotel to hear the news, although having the Secretary's own details, were hustled off to a prison on Cary Street to report to Lieut. Bates, who alone could release them. But when they arrived, no Lieut. Bates was there, and they found themselves incarcerated with some five hundred others of all classes and conditions. Here they remained cooped up for an hour, when they espied an officer who knew them, and who had them released.

To-day the guards arrested Judges Reagan and Davis, Postmaster-General and Attorney-General, both members of the cabinet, because neither of them were over fifty years old. Judge Reagan grew angry and stormed a little; but both were released immediately.

Gen. Lee dispatched Gen. Bragg, at 9 P.M. last night, that all the assaults of the enemy on Fort Gilmer had been repulsed, the enemy losing many in killed, and wounded, and prisoners, while our loss was small.

And we have driven the Yankees from Staunton, and have them in full retreat again as far as Harrisonburg.

To-day at 2 P.M. another battle occurred at or near Fort Harrison or Signal Hill, supposed to be an attempt on our part to retake the post. I never heard more furious shelling, and fear our loss was frightful, provided it was our assault on the enemy's lines. We could see the white smoke, from the observatory, floating along the horizon over the woods and down the river. The melee of sounds was terrific: heavy siege guns (from our steam-rams, probably) mingled with the incessant roar of field artillery. At 3 P.M. all was comparatively quiet, and we await intelligence of the result.

CHAPTER XLIII.

Attempt to retake Fort Harrison.—A false alarm.—Dispatches from Gen. Lee.—Impressments.—Gen. Butler's generosity.—Matters in and about the city.—Beverly Tucker's contract with a New York firm for supplies.

OCTOBER 1ST.—Raining and cold. Horrible for the troops in the trenches!

The battle, yesterday (on this side of the river), was an attempt of Gen. Lee to retake Fort Harrison, near Chaffin's Bluff, which *failed*, after two essays. Gen. Lee deemed its recapture important, and exposed himself very much in the assault: so much so as to cause a thrill of alarm throughout the field. But it all would not do; the enterprise of the enemy had in a few hours rendered the place almost impregnable. Judge Lyons, who came in to-day (from a visit to the field), estimates our killed and wounded at from 700 to 1000.

But we have better news from other quarters. Generals Hampton and Heath attacked the enemy on the south side of the river, yesterday, and captured 900 men.

Gen. Early sends word that the whole force of the enemy (Sheridan's army) is in full retreat, and he is in pursuit.

Gen. Echols, West Virginia and East Tennessee, reports several successes to our arms in that region.

This has been a terrible day; a storm of wind and driving rain. Heavy guns are heard at intervals down the river.

At 4 P.M., while writing the last line, a furious cannonade has sprung up on the southeast of the city, and seemingly very near to it. It may be a raid. The firing increases in rapidity, mingled, I think, with the roar of small arms. We can hear distinctly the whistle of shot and shell, and the detonations shake the windows. It may be that the atmosphere (dampness) and the wind from the east cause some deception as to the distance; but really it would seem that from the apparent proximity of the enemy's guns, some of the shells must reach the eastern parts of the city. After thirty minutes' quick firing, it ceases in a great measure. At 5 P.M. it was resumed, and continued until dark. Some think it but a raid, others report 40,000 men engaged. If this be so, to-morrow will probably be fought the great battle for Richmond. Doubtless, Grant is eager to hold some position from which he can shell the city.

OCTOBER 2D.—Cloudy and calm.

All quiet. It was a false alarm yesterday evening. Nothing but some of the enemy's cavalry scouts were seen from the intermediate batteries, and it was merely a waste of ammunition on our part, and destruction of timber where the enemy were partially sheltered. Not a gun, so far as I can learn, was fired against our fortifications. Gen. Pemberton must have known that none of the enemy's infantry and artillery had marched in this direction through the storm, and in the mud, or else our scouts are worthless.

But we have news of the capture of 500 more prisoners near Petersburg, yesterday. The particulars of the fight have not yet been received.

Every male between seventeen and fifty-five is now required to have a pass, from Gen. Kemper or Gen. Barton, to walk the streets, even to church. The militia are all out, except those hidden in the back rooms of their shops—extortioners; and the city is very quiet. No wonder the women and children were thrown into a panic yesterday.

The shelling did some good in the Saturday evening market, as most of the people were eager to get home. A boy sold me apples at 75 cents per quart, instead of $1.

The physicians have had a meeting, and agree to charge $30 per visit.

The bombardment is still in progress at Charleston, and there has never been any intermission. The enemy's batteries now reach over two-thirds of that devoted city.

I see by a Northern paper that Gen. Grant is having his children educated at Burlington, N. J.; perhaps at the same institutions where mine were educated; and I perceive that our next door neighbor, Mrs. Kinsey, has been waving the "glorious Stars and Stripes" over Gen. G.'s head, from her ample porch. Well, I would not injure that flag; and I think it would never be assailed by the Southern people, if it were only kept at home, away from our soil. We have a flag of our own we prefer.

OCTOBER 3D.—Misty and damp, but warm.

Guns heard down the river. On Friday, it seems, the enemy penetrated and held a portion of our works below Petersburg; and although we captured many prisoners, it does not appear that we regained the works or retook the cannon.

So far, although the enemy's loss in men may have been greater in the operations of the last few days, it would seem that we have *lost ground;* that our forts, etc. have been captured and *held,* up to this moment; and that both the right and left wings of Grant have been *advanced,* and established in the positions taken. All this, too, under the eye of Gen. Lee. It is enough to make one tremble for Richmond. They do not heed his calls for *men.*

In the North, the Presidential campaign is growing *warm.* McClellan's friends have been denounced as "traitors" in Ohio, and one of their meetings broken up by the soldiers. This fire may spread, and relieve us.

It is now said a corps of the enemy's infantry was really peeping from the groves and lanes west of the city, on Saturday, when the furious shelling took place.

Rumors—we have nothing but rumors—of fighting, said to be in progress on the south side of the river. It is said the enemy, that were a few days ago menacing Richmond, are recrossing to the Petersburg side.

OCTOBER 4TH.—Foggy; then bright; then very warm.

Gen. Lee is at Chaffin's Bluff. A dispatch from him this morning states that the enemy's infantry are near Harrisonburg, in the Valley, and that his cavalry is retiring.

9 A.M. Another dispatch from Gen. Lee. The raiders' cavalry, only 250 strong, are at Brandy Station, a body of their infantry at Bealton Central Railroad.

9½ A.M. Gen. Lee says Gen. Breckinridge repulsed the enemy's attack on Saltville, on Sunday, 2d inst.; it was a "bloody" repulse, and Gen. B. is *pursuing.*

Gen. Beauregard has been appointed to the supervisory command of the army in Georgia, etc.; in response to the universal calls of the people.

The enemy threw up earthworks yesterday, toward the city, from Fort Harrison, one mile in length. He is now within five miles of the city, and if his progress is not checked, he will soon be throwing shells at us.

But Lee is there, digging also.

Flour rose yesterday to $425 per barrel, meal to $72 per bushel, and bacon $10 per pound. Fortunately, I got 100 pounds of flour from North Carolina a few days ago at $1.20 per pound. And Thomas, my son, detailed as clerk for Gen. Kemper, will draw 30 pounds of flour and 10 pounds bacon per month.

OCTOBER 5TH.—Bright, and very warm.

There is a report that Gen. Hood's army is at Marietta, in Sherman's rear, and it may be so.

One of the clerks (Mr. Bechtel) was killed yesterday by one of the enemy's sharpshooters at Chaffin's Farm. He was standing on the parapet, looking in the direction of the enemy's pickets. He had been warned to no purpose. He leaves a wife and nine children. A subscription is handed round, and several thousand dollars will be raised. Gen. R. E. Lee was standing near when he fell.

All is quiet to-day. But they are impressing the negro men found in the streets to-day to work on the fortifications. It is again rumored that Petersburg is to be given up. I don't believe it.

OCTOBER 6TH.—Bright, and very warm.

The President returned this morning, hastened hither by the perils environing the capital.

An order is published this morning revoking all details for the army of persons between the ages of eighteen and forty-five years of age. If this be rigidly enforced, it will add many thousands to the army. It is said there are 8000 details in the military bureaus of this State.

A dispatch from Gen. Hood, near Lost Mountain (in Georgia, Sherman's rear), dated yesterday, says Sherman is marching out of

Atlanta to attack him. He says Gen. Stewart's corps struck the railroad at Big Shanty, capturing 350 prisoners, and destroying ten miles of the road. Gen. Forrest is marching against Altoona. We shall soon have stirring news.

All is quiet near Petersburg and Richmond to-day. Eight of the local companies (clerks) have been ordered to guard the prisoners to Salisbury, N. C.

I saw a New York *Tribune* to-day, of the 17th inst., and find the Peterson's are advertising new editions of several of my books.

OCTOBER 7TH.—Bright and beautiful.

The government, after giving the news from Georgia, position of Hood, to the press, suppressed it. It is well, perhaps, not to permit Grant, who sees our papers daily, to know what we are doing there.

There are rumors of fighting to-day near Chaffin's Bluff, but we hear no cannon, except an occasional shell at long intervals.

Gen. Bragg is now in hot water with the Quartermaster-General, for ordering the trial of Lieut.-Col. Cone and Major Maynard, Quartermasters, in the city, for alleged violation of law and orders.

Gen. Preston is away again or sick, and Col. August and Lieut.-Col. Lay are again signing papers at "the Bureau," as "acting superintendents." Bragg may aim another bomb at the refractory concern.

OCTOBER 8TH.—Cloudy, windy, and cold.

The fighting yesterday was more serious than I supposed. It was supposed the conflict would be resumed to-day, but we have no information of any fighting up to this hour—5 P.M.

From Gen. Hood we have a dispatch, saying Major-Gen. French attacked Altoona day before yesterday. He carried all the outworks, but failed at the inner one, and learning a body of the enemy were approaching his rear, Gen. F. withdrew to the main body of the army. He says nothing of the loss, etc. on either side.

At the Tredegar Works, and in the government workshops, the detailed soldier, if a *mechanic*, is paid in money and in rations (at the current prices) about $16 per day, or nearly $6000 per annum. A member of Congress receives $5500, a clerk $4000.

OCTOBER 9TH, SUNDAY.—Cloudy, windy, and very cold.

I hear of no operations yesterday, although, as usual, some cannonnading was audible yesterday evening.

It is said Gen. Pemberton was in great perturbation during the several advances of the enemy last week. Like Boabdil, the Unlucky of Grenada, he lost some of his cannon, and every one anticipated disaster under his command. This will furnish fresh material for assaults in Congress on the President, if that body should meet again next month, for placing this officer in so responsible a command, whatever may be his skill, when the soldiers and the people have no faith in him. It is characteristic of the President to adhere to what he deems just and proper, regardless of anticipated consequences. This was the habit of Cæsar—but he fell.

An effort is again being made to replenish Lee's army with able-bodied details employed in the various departments, but I fear it will only result, as heretofore, in sending to the ranks the weak and diseased who are poor and friendless.

OCTOBER 10TH.—*A white frost;* first frost of the season. All quiet below.

Gen. W. M. Gardner (in Gen. Winder's place) reports that of the exempts and citizens taken from the streets to the front, last week, *a majority have deserted* This proves that even a despotic military act cannot be committed with impunity.

Gen. Beauregard telegraphs from Opeleka, Ala., that he has arranged matters satisfactorily between Gov. Brown of Georgia and Gen. Cobb, regarding exempts and State militia.

The President directs the Secretary to ascertain if this has been done in accordance with law and the interests of the service.

Gen. R. Taylor telegraphs that Gen. E. K. Smith has proclaimed pardon to deserters, from trans-Mississippi Department, after he had arrested most of them and sent them to their regiments, and now he recommends that no more troops be brought over the river or they will be sure to desert. The President directs the Secretary to correspond with Gen. Smith on the subject. Gen. Taylor is the President's kinsman—by his first marriage.

Gen. Beauregard left Opeleka on the 7th inst. for Hood's army, so in a few days we may expect a battle.

OCTOBER 11TH.—Bright and pleasant. All is quiet below.

From Georgia we have many rumors. It is reported that a

battle has been fought (second time) at Altoona, which we captured, with 4000 prisoners; that Rome has been taken, with 3000 negro prisoners; and, finally, that we have Atlanta again. I have seen no such dispatches. But the gentleman who assured me it was all true, has a son a clerk at the President's office, and a relative in the telegraph office. Dispatches may have come to the President; and, if so, it may be our policy to forbid their publication for the present, as the enemy would derive the first intelligence of their disaster from our newspapers.

Well, Gen. Gardner reports, officially, that of the number of exempts, and of the mixed class of citizens arrested in the streets, and summarily marched to the "front," "a majority have deserted!" Men, with exemptions in their pockets, going to or returning from market, have been seized by the Adjutant-General's orders, and despotically hurried off without being permitted even to send a message to their families. Thousands were entrapped, by being directed to call at Gen. Barton's headquarters, an immense warehouse, and receive passes; but no Gen. Barton was there—or if there, not visible; and all the anxious seekers found themselves in prison, only to be liberated as they were incorporated into companies, and marched "to the front." From the age of fifteen to fifty-five, all were seized by that order—no matter what papers they bore, or what the condition of their families—and hurried to the field, where there was no battle. No wonder there are many deserters—no wonder men become indifferent as to which side shall prevail, nor that the administration is falling into disrepute at the capital.

OCTOBER 12TH.—Bright and beautiful. All quiet below, save an occasional booming from the fleet.

Nothing from Georgia in the papers, save the conjectures of the Northern press. No doubt we have gained advantages there, which it is good policy to conceal as long as possible from the enemy.

Squads of able-bodied *detailed* men are arriving *at last*, from the interior. Lee's army, in this way, will get efficient reinforcements.

The Secretary of the Treasury sends a note over to the Secretary of War to-day, saying the Commissary-General, in his estimates, allows but $31,000,000 for tax in kind—whereas the tax collectors show an actual amount, credited to farmers and planters, of $145,000,000. He says this will no doubt attract the notice of Congress.

Mr. Peck, our agent to purchase supplies in North Carolina, has delivered no wheat yet. He bought supplies for his family; 400 bushels of wheat for 200 clerks, and 100 for Assistant Secretary of War, Judge Campbell, and Mr. Kean, the young Chief of the Bureau. This he says he bought with private funds; but he brought it at the government's expense. The clerks are resolved not to submit to his action.

I hear of more desertions. Mr. Seddon and Mr. Stanton at Washington are engaged in a singular game of chance. The harsh orders of both cause mutual abandonments, and now we have the spectacle of men deserting our regiments, and quite as many coming over from the enemy's regiments near the city.

Meantime Gen. Bragg is striving to get the able-bodied men out of the bureaus and to place them in the field.

The despotic order, arresting every man in the streets, and hurrying them to "the front," without delay, and regardless of the condition of their families—some were taken off when getting medicine for their sick wives—is still the theme of execration, even among men who have been the most ultra and uncompromising secessionists. The terror caused many to hide themselves, and doubtless turned them against the government. They say now such a despotism is quite as bad as a Stanton despotism, and there is not a toss-up between the rule of the United States and the Confederate States. Such are some of the effects of bad measures in such critical times as these. Mr. Seddon has no physique to sustain him. He has intellect, and has read much; but, nevertheless, such great men are sometimes more likely to imitate some predecessor at a critical moment, or to adopt some bold yet inefficient suggestion from another, than to originate an adequate one themselves. He is a scholar, an invalid, refined and philosophical—but effeminate.

OCTOBER 13TH.—Rained all night; clear and cool this morning.

The government publishes nothing from Georgia yet; but it is supposed there is intelligence of an important character in the city, which it would be impolitic to communicate to the enemy.

All still remains quiet below the city. But the curtain is expected to rise on the next act of the tragedy every moment. Gen. Grant probably furloughed many of his men to vote in Pennsylvania and Ohio, on Tuesday last—elections preliminary to the Presidential election—and they have had time to return to their regiments.

If this pause should continue a week or two longer, Gen. Lee would be much strengthened. Every day the farmers, whose details have been revoked, are coming in from the counties; and many of these were in the war in '61 and '62—being experienced veterans. Whereas Grant's recruits, though greater in number, are raw and unskilled.

The Medical Boards have been instructed to put in all men that come before them, capable of bearing arms *ten days*. One died in the trenches, on the eleventh day, of consumption!

There is a rumor of a fight on our extreme left. It is said Field's division (C. S.) repulsed three assaults of the enemy. If the battle be still continued (4 P.M—the wind from the west prevents us from hearing guns), no doubt it is the beginning of a general engagement—decisive, perhaps, of the fate of Richmond.

We have many accounts of evasions of military service, occasioned by the alleged bad faith of the government, and the despotic orders from the Adjutant-General's office.

And yet Gov. Smith's certificates for exemption of rich young Justices of the Peace, Commissioners of the (county) Revenue, Deputy Sheriffs, clerks, constables, officers and clerks of banks, still come in daily; and they are "allowed" by the Assistant Secretary of War. Will the poor and friendless fight their battles, and win their independence for them? It may be so; but let not rulers in future wars follow the example! Nothing but the conviction that they are fighting for their families, their sacred altars, and their little property induces thousands of brave Southerners to remain in arms against such fearful odds as are now arrayed against them.

Mr. Kean, the young Chief of the Bureau of War, has come in from "the front," with a boil on his thigh. He missed the sport of the battle to-day.

Mr. Peck, the agent to purchase supplies for his starving fellow-clerks, confesses that he bought 10 barrels of flour and 400 pounds of bacon for himself; 4 barrels of flour for Judge Campbell, Assistant Secretary of War; 4 barrels for Mr. Kean, 1 for Mr. Cohen, and 1 for Mr. Shepherd. This has produced great indignation among the 200 clerks who sent him, and who got but 73½ pounds each, and they got 13 pounds of bacon each; while Mr. P. bought for himself 400 pounds.

OCTOBER 14TH.—The following dispatch from Gen. Lee cheered the city this morning. None of the particulars of the battle have yet transpired, and all are looking hourly for a renewal of the contest.

"HEADQUARTERS ARMY OF NORTHERN VIRGINIA,
"October 13th, 1864.

"HON. JAMES A. SEDDON, SECRETARY OF WAR.

"At seven o'clock this morning the enemy endeavored to advance between the Darbytown and Charles City Roads, but was repulsed in every attempt. The most strenuous effort was made about four P.M., after which he withdrew, leaving many dead. Our loss very slight.

"Gen. Breckinridge reports that a force of the enemy came to Greenville on the 12th, and was defeated by Gen. Vaughan. Some prisoners, two stands of colors, many horses and arms were captured. The enemy lost many killed and wounded. Our loss slight.

"R. E. LEE, *General.*"

It is now 2 P.M., and yet we hear no cannon. If Grant does not renew the strife immediately, it will be natural to suppose he failed in his purpose yesterday, or that some unforeseen occurrence within his lines has happened. Be it either, it is a grateful respite to us.

On the 8th inst., Judge Campbell, Assistant Secretary of War, wrote the President a letter in vindication of P. Hamilton's loyalty. Mr. H. is commissioner under suspension of the writ of *habeas corpus* to look into the loyalty of others, and was appointed on Judge C.'s recommendation. Some private individual in Mobile wrote the President, impeaching the patriotism of Mr. H., and also hinted something in relation to the loyalty of Judge C. This matter was shown to Mr. Seddon by the President, and Mr. S. spoke to Judge C. about it in his own manner, which produced the letter of Judge C. to the President. The President sends back the letter to-day, to the "Secretary of War," indorsed in substance as follows: "He was surprised to receive such a letter, when he had intimated no purpose to have the matter investigated." Judge C. had procured indorsements of Mr. H. from Alabama, which *let the matter out;* and it would have been *appropriate*—the President uses this word rather than *improper*, as he cannot dispense with either the Secretary or his assistant just now—to have consulted him before taking any steps whatever in the business. He seems vexed, even at Mr. S.

OCTOBER 15TH.—A bright and glorious day—above.

All was quiet yesterday below, indicating that the enemy suffered severely in the last assault on our lines.

But we have nothing from Georgia. From the Valley, our cavalry had the misfortune to lose eleven guns by indiscreetly venturing too far in pursuit.

And the news from the United States indicates that Pennsylvania, Ohio, and Indiana have gone for the Republican candidates. This foreshadows Lincoln's re-election, and admonishes us to prepare for other campaigns, though languishing for peace.

The farmers are now pouring in to replenish the armies, under the recent order revoking the details of agriculturists; and these are fine-looking men, and there will soon be successes in the field. Lately the indulgence of details to an immoderate extent, and corruption in the business of conscription, had depleted the armies extensively of men of substance and standing, and this may account for our disasters. Men, to fight well, must have something to fight for.

Gen. Price, at the head of 20,000 men, is in Missouri. To expel him, many troops will be required; and this may relieve us a little in the East.

My wife lost her purse in market this morning, before making any purchases; it contained $22 and her eye-glasses. I don't think there are any pickpockets except the extortioners.

OCTOBER 16TH, SUNDAY.—A pleasant sunny Sabbath morn.

The quiet below continues. Not a gun has been heard for three days; the longest intermission we have had for many months. What can it mean? Sheridan has spread desolation in the Shenandoah Valley, perhaps to prevent Early from penetrating Pennsylvania, etc., intending to come with all expedition to Grant.

Troops, or rather detailed men, and late exempts, are beginning to arrive from North Carolina. I saw 250 this morning. Some of them were farmers who had complied with the terms prescribed, and a week ago thought themselves safe from the toils and dangers of war. They murmur, but there is no escape. They say the Governor has called out the militia officers, and magistrates also.

Desertion is the order of the day, on both sides. Would that the *men* would take matters in their own hands, and end the war, establishing our independence. Let every man in both armies desert and go home!

Some one has sent a "Circular" of the "Bureau of Conscription" to the President, dated some few weeks ago, and authorizing enrolling officers everywhere to furlough farmers and others for sixty days, to make out their claims for exemption. This the President says in his indorsement defeats his efforts to put the whole able-bodied male population in the field; and no doubt has been the source of the many abuses charged against the "bureau." The Secretary sends the paper to the "bureau" for report, stating that he felt great surprise at the terms of the "Circular," and had no recollection of having seen or sanctioned such a document. The Superintendent reports that it was issued by the authority of the Secretary of War, and was warranted by law—looking to the interests of agriculture, etc. The truth is that the Circular was prepared by a subordinate in the Bureau of Conscription, and signed by Col. August, "Acting Superintendent." It was approved by Judge Campbell, Assistant Secretary of War, "by order of the Secretary of War" who never saw it. Mr. Seddon has left all the business of conscription in the hands of Judge Campbell; and poor Gen. Preston—indolent and ill—has been compelled to sign, sanction, and defend documents he knew nothing about; and Mr. Seddon is in a similar predicament.

The Secretary of War has written a long letter to Gen. Lee, suggesting that he assemble a council of officers to decide what measure shall be adopted in regard to the treatment of prisoners in the hands of the enemy. It appears that Gen. Butler has notified Gen. Lee that he is now retaliating fearfully—making them work in his canal—on certain Confederates for some alleged harsh treatment of *negro* prisoners in our hands—sending slaves back to their masters. Mr. Seddon, without assuming any responsibility himself, yet intimates the idea that this government is prepared to sanction the most sanguinary remedy; and I understand several members of the cabinet to have always been in favor of fighting—that is, having others fight—under the black flag. If the government had only listened to Gen. Lee's suggestions, we should have had abundance of men in the field to beat the enemy out of Virginia. I hope the present recruiting excitement comes not too late. And I trust he will interpose so far in behalf of the country as to wrest the railroads from the hands of the speculators and the dishonest quartermasters.

Not a gun has been heard by me to-day, and the mysterious silence defies my powers of penetration. I only hope it may continue *sine die.*

OCTOBER 17TH.—Bright and beautiful.

Still all quiet below, and reinforcements (details revoked) are not arriving—1000 per day.

The Northern news makes some doubt as to the result of the election in Pennsylvania.

From the Valley we have rumors of victory, etc.

A thrill of horror has been produced by a report that Gen. Butler has, for some time past, kept a number of his prisoners (Confederates) at work in his canal down the river, and supposing they were Federals, our batteries and gun-boats have been shelling our own men!

OCTOBER 18TH.—Cloudy and cool.

Quiet below, but it is rumored that the enemy has erected one or two sand batteries, mounted with 400-pounders, bearing on our fleet of gun-boats.

The following dispatch was received from Gen. Hood to-day:

"9 MILES SOUTH OF LAFAYETTE, GA.,
"Oct. 15th, via SELMA, Oct. 17th, 1864.

"GEN. BRAGG.

"This army struck the communications of the enemy about a mile above Resaca on the 12th inst., completely destroying the railroad, including block-houses, from that point to within a short distance of Tunnel Hill, and about four miles of the Cleaveland Railroad, capturing Dalton and all intermediate garrisons, with their stores, arms, and equipments, and about 1000 prisoners.

"The main body of Sherman's army seems to be moving toward Dalton.   J. B. HOOD, *General.*"

The following was received from Gen. Lee yesterday:

"HEADQUARTERS ARMY NORTHERN VIRGINIA,
"Oct. 16th, 1864.

"HON JAMES A. SEDDON, SECRETARY OF WAR.

"On the 14th instant, Col. Moseby struck the Baltimore and Ohio Railroad at Duffield, and destroyed a United States mail train, consisting of a locomotive and ten cars, and securing twenty prisoners and fifteen horses.

"Among the prisoners are two paymasters, with one hundred and sixty-eight thousand dollars in government funds.

"R. E. LEE."

It is reported also that Gen. Early has gained some advantage in a battle; not authentic.

Gen. Bragg is going away, probably to Wilmington. The combination against him was too strong.

But "the Bureau of Conscription" is pretty nearly demolished under his blows. Order 81 directs the generals of Reserves to appoint inspecting officers for all the Congressional Districts, to revise all exemptions, details, etc., with plenary powers, without reference to "the Bureau"

The passport checks on travel Northward are now the merest farce, and valuable information is daily conveyed to the enemy.

OCTOBER 19TH.—Bright and beautiful.

Still all quiet below, the occasional bombarding near Petersburg being beyond our hearing.

Yesterday, Gen. Preston, a millionaire, who can stalk stiffly anywhere, had an interview with the President, who admitted that he had dictated the General Orders—"76," "77," "78,"—rushing almost everybody into the army, but that it was not his meaning to take the whole business of conscription from "the Bureau." Yet Gen. P., the superintendent, thinks the *reading* of the orders will admit of that construction, and he has written to the President asking another order, defining his position, etc., else his occupation is gone. The President cannot afford to lose Gen. P.

From Gen. Early's army we learn that the detailed men and reserves are joining in great numbers, and the general asks 1000 muskets. Col. Gorgas, Chief of Ordnance, says he has but 300 available, his shops being closed, the workmen in the trenches, etc.

All the ordnance, quartermaster, and commissary stores of Hood's army were ordered to Columbus, Ga. We expect stirring news from Georgia daily, and the opinion prevails that Sherman will "come to grief."

The militia, furloughed by Gov. Brown so inopportunely, are returning to the front, the time having expired.

A Mr. B. is making Lincoln speeches in New York. It seems to me he had a passport from Mr. Benjamin, Secretary of State.

Gen. Lee writes to-day that negroes taken from the enemy, penitentiary convicts, and recaptured deserters ought not to be sent by the Secretary to work on the fortifications.

OCTOBER 20TH.—Cloudy. There is a street rumor of a battle below, and on the Petersburg line. The wind is from the west, and yet we hear no guns.

The Secretary of the Treasury sent to the Secretary of War to-day an argument showing that, without a violation of the Constitution, clerks appointed to places created by Congress cannot be removed. We shall see what the Secretary says to that.

OCTOBER 21ST.—Bright.

Fort Harrison (Federal) opened its batteries on our lines at Chaffin's Farm yesterday evening, without effect. An officer tells me that heavy and quick firing was also heard on the Petersburg lines, indicating, he thought, a battle. We have nothing of this in the papers, or in any dispatch I have seen.

Assistant Secretary Campbell is writing a portion of Mr. Secretary Seddon's report for him. Mr. C.'s son was promoted to a majority yesterday.

At 2 P.M. we have a rumor that Gen. Early has been defeated, losing all his guns but one.

A letter from the Secretary of the Treasury recommends the detail or exemption of the bank officers of South Carolina. The poor country clod-hoppers have no friends, and must do the fighting.

The following order, dictated by the President, has been published:

"ADJUTANT AND INSPECTOR-GENERAL'S OFFICE,
"RICHMOND, October 20th, 1864.

"GENERAL ORDERS No. 82.

"I. The Chief of the Bureau of Ordnance will, without delay, take measures to place in the field one-fifth of all the men employed in his department (including contractors and their employees) of the classes specified in General Order No. 77, A. and I. G. Office (current series). To this end he will direct the several officers in charge of arsenals, workshops, depots, etc. to turn over to the nearest enrolling officers, by lists showing their ages, occupations, and residences, such proportion of their employees (including contractors and employees under them) of the classes above referred to as will constitute in the aggregate one-fifth of the whole number in the said classes, according to returns in his office of Sept. 30th, 1864. Duplicates of such lists will be sent to the Generals of Reserves of the States, and triplicates to the Chief of Ordnance. Three days are allowed for the execution of this Order after its reception at any post or station of the Ordnance Department.

"II. The Chief of the Niter and Mining Bureau will, in like manner, turn over, on similar lists, one-fifth of all men of the classes specified in General Order No. 77, employed in iron, lead, copper, and coal mines, and all service appertaining thereto, whether directly under officers of his Bureau or by contractors. Duplicate and triplicate lists to be furnished as above directed in the Ordnance Bureau, and will in the same manner turn over one-fifth of all such men now employed in the Niter service.

"The period of three days, under the same conditions as above mentioned, is allowed for the execution of this order.

"III. The list of persons directed in the foregoing sections to be turned over to the enrolling officers will be prepared at once on the reception of this Order, and will be furnished to the said officers within three days, as above prescribed, by the various officers of each of the above Bureaus, having men under their charge, and every assistance will be rendered by the latter to the enrolling officer to carry out the intention of this order.

"IV. So much of General Order No. 77 as relates to men employed in the two Bureaus named above is hereby suspended, and the foregoing Orders will stand in lieu of all requirements under the former.

"By order. S. COOPER,
"*A. and I. General.*"

OCTOBER 22D.—Cloudy; rained last night. 2 P.M.—Cold, and prospects of snow.

The news of Early's disaster, and loss of artillery at Strasburg, is confirmed, and casts a new vexation over the country.

Mr. M. Byrd, Selma, Ala., is addressing some bold letters to the President on the blunders of the administration.

Gen. Longstreet has resumed command of the first army corps.

G. W. Custis Lee (son of the general) has been made a major-general.

There was no fighting below yesterday, that I have heard of.

Gold, which was $1 for $30 in Confederate States notes, commands $35 for $1 to-day, under the news from the Valley. Yet our sagacious statesmen regard the re-election of Lincoln (likely to follow our reverses) as favorable to independence, though it may prolong the war. It is thought there will certainly be revolution or civil war in the North, if the Democrats be beaten; and that will relieve us of the vast armies precipitated on our soil. Many of the faint-hearted croakers are anxious for peace and reconstruction.

Gen. Butler, called "the Beast" by the press, has certainly performed a generous action. Messrs. McRae and Henley, two government clerks in the local battalion, wandered into the enemy's lines, and were put to work in the canal by Gen. Butler, who had been informed that we made some prisoners taken from him work on the fortifications. This was done but a short time, when they were relieved; and Mr. McRae was permitted to return to the city, to learn whether the Federal prisoners were really required to perform the labor named. No restrictions were imposed on him, no parole required. He came with Gen. B.'s passport, but felt in honor bound to communicate no intelligence, and voluntarily returned to captivity. We *had* Federal prisoners at work, but they were remanded to prison.

SUNDAY, OCTOBER 23D.—Bright and frosty.

From the United States papers we learn that a great victory is claimed over Gen. Early, with the capture of forty-three guns!

It is also stated that a party of "Copperheads" (Democrats), who had taken refuge in Canada, have made a raid into Vermont, and robbed some of the banks of their specie.

The fact that Mr. McRae, who, with Mr. Henley (local forces), fell into the hands of the enemy a few miles below the city, was permitted to return within our own lines with a passport (without restrictions, etc.) from Gen. Butler, has not been mentioned by any of the newspapers, gives rise to many conjectures. Some say that "somebody" prohibited the publication; others, that the press has long been misrepresenting the conduct of the enemy; there being policy in keeping alive the animosities of the army and the people.

The poor clerks in the trenches are in a demoralized condition. It is announced that the Secretary of War has resolved to send them all to Camp Lee, for medical examination: those that have proved their ability to bear arms (in defense of the city) *are to be removed from office*, and put in the army. One-half of them will desert to the enemy, and injure the cause. About one hundred of them were appointed before the enactment of the act of Conscription, under the express guarantee of the Constitution that they should not be molested during life. If the President removes these, mostly refugees with families dependent upon their salaries, it will be a plain violation of the Constitution; and the victims cannot be relied on for their loyalty to the government. If the government wastes precious time in such small matters, while events of magnitude demand attention, the cause is fast reaching a hopeless condition. The able-bodied money-changer, speculator, and extortioner is still seen in the street; and their number is legion.

The generals in the field are sending back the poor, sickly recruits ordered out by the Medical Board: the able-bodied rich men escape by bribery and corruption; and the hearty *officers*—acting adjutant-generals, quartermasters, and commissaries—ride their sleek horses through the city every afternoon. This, while the cause is perishing for want of men and horses!

OCTOBER 24TH.—Clouds and sunshine. Nothing new of importance from the army.

Gov. Smith has been writing letters to Gen. Lee, asking that Gen. Early be superseded in the Valley. Pity it had not been done! Gen. Lee replied, expressing confidence in Early; and the President (since the disaster!) coincides with Lee.

The President administers a sharp rebuke to Gen. Whiting, for irregularly corresponding with Generals Lee and Beauregard on the subject of Lieut. Taylor Wood's naval expedition, fitting out at Wilmington.

The President and cabinet are still at work on the one hundred clerks in the departments whom they wish to displace.

I append the result of my gardening this year. The dry weather in May and June injured the crop, or the amount would have been much larger. Total valuation, at market prices, $347.

OCTOBER 25TH.—Bright and beautiful morning.

All quiet below. Mr. McRae has been permitted by Gen. Butler to return again to the city to await his exchange, pledged not to bear arms, etc. Many more of the government employees, forced into the trenches, would be happy to be in the same predicament. A great many are deserting under a deliberate conviction that their rights have been despotically invaded by the government; and that this government is, and is likely to be, as tyrannous as Lincoln's. No doubt many give valuable information to the enemy.

The Superintendent of the Bureau of Conscription is at open war with the General of Reserves in Virginia, and confusion is likely to be worse confounded.

Gen. Cooper, A. and I. General (Pennsylvanian), suggests to the President the appointment of Gen. Lovell to the command of all the prisons containing Federal captives. Gen. Lovell, too, is a Northern man.

OCTOBER 26TH.—Clear and frosty. Quiet below.

Gen. W. M. Gardner (in Gen. Winder's place here) has just got from Judge Campbell passports for his cousin, Mary E. Gardner, and for his brother-in-law F. M. White, to go to Memphis, Tenn., where they mean to reside.

Mr. Benjamin publishes a copy of a dispatch to Mr. Mason, in London, for publication there, showing that if the United States continue the war, she will be unable to pay her debts abroad, and therefore foreigners ought not to lend her any more money, or they may be ruined. This from a Secretary of State! It may be an electioneering card in the United States, and it may reconcile some of our members of Congress to the incumbency of Mr. B. in a sinecure position.

A friend of Mr. Seddon, near Vicksburg, writes for permission to sell thirty bales of cotton—$20,000 worth—to the enemy. He says Mr. Seddon's estate, on the Sunflower, has not been destroyed by the enemy. That's fortunate, for other places have been utterly ruined.

Investigations going on in the courts show that during Gen. Winder's "Reign of Terror," passports sold for $2000. Some outside party negotiated the business and procured the passport.

Gen. Early has issued an address to his army, reproaching it for having victory wrested out of its hands by a criminal indulgence in the plunder found in the camps captured from the enemy. He hopes they will retrieve everything in the next battle.

Governor Smith's exemptions of magistrates, deputy sheriffs, clerks, and constables, to-day, 56.

OCTOBER 27TH.—Slightly hazy and sunshine.

Quiet, save aimless and bootless shelling and picket firing along the lines on the south side of the river.

Hon. Geo. Davis, Attorney-General, to whom was referred the question of the constitutionality of the purposed removal from office of clerks appointed to fill places specifically created by act of Congress previous to the enactment of the Conscript law, without there being alleged against them any misconduct, inefficiency, dishonesty, etc., has reported that as several subsequent acts of Congress already indicate an intention to put all capable of bearing arms in the army, it is the duty of the President and the Secretary of War *to carry out the intentions of Congress*, leaving the constitutional question to the decision of the courts! The Constitution they swore upon the holy, etc. to support! Thus, a refugee must either starve his wife and children by relinquishing office, or be disgraced by appealing to the courts!

It is reported that 30,000 of the enemy crossed to this side of the river last night, and that fighting has began at 10 A.M.; but I hear nothing save an occasional report of cannon.

It is said brisk skirmishing is now (12 M.) going on along the lines.

Gen. Cooper and Mr. Secretary Seddon wants Brig.-Gen. R. (Charleston) relieved, for insulting a lady in one of his fits of drunkenness. The President is reluctant to consent.

We have intelligence to-day of gun-boats and transports ascending the Rappahannock River. Another squall from that quarter!

Three P.M. The cannonading has grown quick and terrific along the lines, below the city (north side), with occasional discharges nearer, and farther to the left (north), as if the enemy were attempting to flank our army.

The sounds are very distinctly heard, the weather being damp and the wind from the southeast. We can distinguish the bursting of the shell quickly after the discharge of the cannon.

The firing ceased at dark. It rains hard and steadily, now. What a life! what suffering, in mud and water, without tents (in the trenches), burdened with wet blankets, and perhaps without food! To-morrow, in all probability, a battle will be fought.

Gen. Lee, for several weeks, as if aware of the impending operations in this vicinity, has been on this side of the river, superintending in person the fortifications multiplied everywhere for the defense of the city, while reinforcements have been pouring in by thousands. It must be a fearful struggle, if Gen. Grant really intends to make another effort to capture Richmond by assault! Our works, mostly made by the negroes, under the direction of skillful engineers, must be nearly impregnable, and the attempt to take them will involve a prodigious expenditure of blood.

OCTOBER 28TH.—Rained all night, but bright this morning.

We have no clear account yet of the fighting yesterday; but we know the enemy was repulsed on this side of the river. It is thought that the operations on the south side were of greater magnitude, where we lost a brigadier-general (Dearing) of cavalry. We shall know all in a few days. The fighting was not resumed this morning.

It is rumored that Mr. Seddon will resign, and be succeeded by Gen. Kemper. I am incredulous.

The "dog-catchers," as the guards are called, are out again, arresting able-bodied men (and sometimes others) in the streets, and locking them up until they can be sent to the front. There must be extraordinary danger anticipated by the authorities to induce a resort to so extreme a measure.

TWO P.M. No news from the field—no cannon heard to-day.

Large amounts of cloth from Europe for the army have recently arrived at Wilmington, N. C.; but the speculators occupy so much space in the cars, that transportation cannot be had for it. The poor soldiers are likely to suffer in consequence of this neglect of duty on the part of the government.

OCTOBER 29TH.—Clear and pleasant.

We are beginning to get authentic accounts of the operations on Thursday; and yet, from the newspaper publications, we see that the government has withheld one of Gen. Lee's dispatches from publication. Altogether, it must be regarded as a decisive failure on the part of the enemy to obtain any lodgment nearer to the objective point; while his loss was perhaps two to our one.

A letter from Gen. Howell Cobb, Macon, Ga., in reply to one from the Secretary by the President's direction, states that Gen. Beauregard, in arranging difficulties with Gov. Brown, did not compromise the dignity or interests of the Confederate States Government, or violate any law.

It is now said Sheridan is retreating toward the Potomac, followed by Early. Some 500 more recruits for Early left Richmond yesterday. This would indicate that Gen. Lee has men enough here.

The President suggests that confidential inspectors be sent to ascertain whether Gen. Early's army has lost confidence in him. Both Gen. Lee and the President are satisfied that the charges of drunkenness against Gen. E. merit no attention. The Secretary had indorsed on a paper (referred by him to the President) that he shared the belief in the "want of confidence," etc.—and no doubt would have him removed.

SUNDAY, OCTOBER 30TH.—Bright and beautiful.

Some firing was heard early this morning on the Darbytown road, or in that direction; but it soon ceased, and no fighting of moment is anticipated to-day, for Gen. Longstreet is in the city.

My son Thomas drew a month's rations yesterday, being detailed for clerical service with Gen. Kemper. He got 35 pounds of flour (market value $70), 31 pounds of beef ($100.75), 3 pounds of rice ($6), one sixth of a cord of wood ($13.33), salt ($2), tobacco ($5), vinegar ($3)—making $200 per month; clothing furnished by government, $500 per annum; cash, $18 per month; $4 per day extra, and $40 per month for quarters; or $5000 per annum. Custis and I get $4000 each—making in all $13,000! Yet we cannot subsist and clothe the family; for, alas, the paper money is $30 for one in specie!

The steamers have brought into Wilmington immense amounts of quartermaster stores, and perhaps our armies are the best clad in the world. If the spirit of speculation be laid, and all the men and resources of the country be devoted to defense (as seems now to be the intention), the United States could never find men and material sufficient for our subjugation. We could maintain the war for an indefinite period, unless, indeed, fatal dissensions should spring up among ourselves.

OCTOBER 31ST.—Bright. Tom's rations came in—worth $200—for a month.

Gen. Lee writes that it is necessary for the gun-boats to guard the river as far below Chaffin's Bluffs as possible, to prevent the enemy from throwing a force to the south bank in the rear of Gen. Pickett's lines; for then Gen. P. must withdraw his forces, and the abandonment of Petersburg will follow, "with its railroad connections, throwing the whole army back to the defense of Richmond. I should regard this as a great disaster, and as seriously endangering the safety of the city. We should not only lose a large section of country from which our position enables us to draw supplies, but the enemy would be brought nearer to the only remaining railway communication between Richmond and the South. It would make the tenure of the city depend upon our ability to hold this long line of communication against the largely superior force of the enemy, and I think would greatly diminish the prospects of successful defense." He suggests that more men and small boats be put in the river to prevent the enemy from placing torpedoes in the rear of the iron-clads, when on duty down the river at night.

J. H. Reagan, Postmaster-General, has written a furious letter to the Secretary, complaining of incivility on the part of Mr. Wilson, Commissary Agent to issue beef in Richmond. Judge R. went there to draw the beef ration for Col. Lubbock, one of the President's aid-de-camps (late Governor of Texas). He says he is able-bodied and ought to be in the army. Mr. Wilson sends in certificates of two men who were present, contradicting the judge's statement of the language used by Mr. W. The Secretary has not yet acted in the case.

Beverly Tucker is in Canada, and has made a contract for the Confederate States Government with —— & Co., of New York, to deliver bacon for cotton, pound for pound. It was made by authority of the Secretary of War, certified to by Hon. C. C. Clay and J. Thompson, both in Canada. The Secretary of the Treasury don't like it.

It is reported that after the success reported by Gen. Lee, Early was *again* defeated.

CHAPTER XLIV.

Proclamation for a day of public worship.—Gov. Allen, of Louisiana.—Letter from Gen. Beauregard.—Departure for Europe.—Congress assembles.—Quarrel between Gens. Kemper and Preston.—Gen. Forrest doing wonders.—Tennessee.—Gen. Johnston on his Georgia campaign.—John Mitchel and Senator Foote.—Progress of Sherman.—From Gov. Brown, of Georgia.—Capture of Gen. Pryor.

NOVEMBER 1ST.—Bright and frosty morning.

All quiet. No confirmation of Early's defeat; and the night-feat of Mahone puts the people in better hope.

One-third of all our lead comes from the mines near Wytheville, Virginia.

I got 128 pounds of flour from the investment in supplies in North Carolina, and one-fourth of that amount is still behind. We got 26 pounds of bacon, worth $260; the flour received, and to be received, 160 pounds, $320; and we expect to get 6 gallons molasses, $30 per gallon, $180 : total, $760; and only $200 invested. This shows the profits of the speculators!

Gov. Yates, of Illinois, has declared Richmond will be in the hands of the Federals before the 8th of November. This is the 1st. It may be so; but I doubt it. It cannot be so without the effusion of an ocean of blood!

I learned to-day that every tree on Gov. Wise's farm of any size has been felled by the enemy. What harm have the poor trees done the enemy? I love trees, anywhere.

The President attends to many little matters, such as solicitations for passports to leave the country, details or exemptions of husbands and sons; and generally the ladies who address him, knowing his religious bias, frame their phraseology accordingly, and often with effect.

The following is his last proclamation:

Proclamation appointing a Day for Public Worship.

"It is meet that the people of the Confederate States should, from time to time, assemble to acknowledge their dependence on Almighty God, to render devout thanks for his manifold blessings, to worship his holy name, to bend in prayer at his footstool, and to accept, with reverent submission, the chastening of his all-wise and all-merciful Providence.

"Let us, then, in temples and in fields, unite our voices in recognizing, with adoring gratitude, the manifestations of his protecting care in the many signal victories with which our arms have been crowned; in the fruitfulness with which our land has been blessed, and in the unimpaired energy and fortitude with which he has inspired our hearts and strengthened our arms in resistance to the iniquitous designs of our enemies.

"And let us not forget that, while graciously vouchsafing to us his protection, our sins have merited and received grievous chastisement; that many of our best and bravest have fallen in battle; that many others are still held in foreign prisons; that large districts of our country have been devastated with savage ferocity, the peaceful homes destroyed, and helpless women and children driven away in destitution; and that with fiendish malignity the passions of a servile race have been excited by our foes into the commission of atrocities from which death is a welcome escape.

"Now, therefore, I, Jefferson Davis, President of the Confederate States of America, do issue this my proclamation, setting apart Wednesday, the sixteenth day of November next, as a day to be specially devoted to the worship of Almighty God; and I do invite and invoke all the people of these Confederate States to assemble on the day aforesaid, in their respective places of public worship, there to unite in prayer to our heavenly Father, that he bestow his favor upon us; that he extend over us the protection of his Almighty arm; that he sanctify his chastisement to our improvement, so that we may turn away from evil paths and walk righteously in his sight; that he restore peace to our beloved country, healing its bleeding wounds, and securing to us the continued enjoyment of our right of self-government and independence;

and that he graciously hearken to us, while we ascribe to him the power and glory of our deliverance.

"Given under my hand and the seal of the Confederate States, at Richmond, this 26th day of October, in the year of our Lord one thousand eight hundred and sixty-four.

"JEFFERSON DAVIS.
"By the President:
"J. P. BENJAMIN, *Secretary of State.*"

The President gets but few letters from members of Congress.
NOVEMBER 2D.—Dark and dismal.

The Governor continues his exemptions, now amounting to thousands. S. Basset French (State agent to buy and sell supplies to the people), with one or more clerks, and such laborers, etc. as may be necessary, I find among his last exemptions. A smart and corrupt agent could make a fortune out of these exemptions. Of course, the *Governor's* A. D. C. will do no such thing.

No news from below.

Rev. John Clark writes from Stafford County that the conscripts there have hid themselves in White Oak Swamp, because the Secretary of War has exempted an able-bodied man to work for Mrs. ——, his —— widow.

Gen. Winder, with the prisoners in the South, is in hot water again. He wants to make Cashmyer suttler (like ancient Pistol), and Major ——, the Secretary's agent, opposes it, on the ground that he is a "Plug Ugly rogue and cut-throat."

Mr. George Davis, Attorney-General Confederate States, has given it as his opinion that although certain civil officers of the government were exempted from military service by the Constitution, yet a recent act of Congress, decreeing that all residents between the ages of 17 and 50 are in the military service, must be executed. In other words, the cabinet ministers must "see that the laws be faithfully executed," even should they be clearly and expressly unconstitutional. Is not the Constitution the law? Have they not sworn to support it, etc.? It seems to me that this is a weak opinion.

It makes the President ABSOLUTE. I fear this government in future times will be denounced as a Cabal of bandits and outlaws, making and executing the most despotic decrees. This decision will look bad in history, and will do no good at present. How *could* the President "approve" such a law?

The desertions from the Tredegar Battalion and other workshops—local defense—amount to between one and two hundred since the 1st of September.

NOVEMBER 3D.—Cold rain; rained all night.

Gen. Lee, urging that his regiments from Texas, Louisiana, Mississippi, Georgia, etc. etc. be recruited from their respective States, concludes a recent letter thus: "I hope immediate action will be taken upon this subject, as I think our success depends much upon a speedy increase of our armies in every possible way."

This dismal weather casts a deeper gloom upon the spirits of the croakers. They fear Richmond cannot be long defended.

Plymouth, N. C., has been retaken by the enemy.

During this damp weather the deep and sullen sounds of cannon can be heard at all hours, day and night. The firing is mostly from our iron-clads.

The market was well supplied this morning with abundance of good meat, vegetables, fruit, etc.; and I was glad to see but few making purchases. The reason may have been that the extortionate prices repelled the people; or it may have been the rain. I passed on.

NOVEMBER 4TH.—Rained all night; glimpses of the sun between the running clouds this morning. Windy, and likely to be cold.

Our iron-clad "Albemarle" was blown up by a handful of the enemy at Plymouth—surprising the water pickets (all asleep). The *manner* of the loss of the town, and of the counties east of it, is not known yet; but everything was foretold by Mr. Burgyson to the cabinet then devoting their attention to the problem how to violate the Constitution, and put into the trenches some fifty delicate clerks, that their places might be filled by some of their own special favorites. Mr. George Davis, Attorney-General, the instrument selected to rend the Constitution, or rather to remove the obstacles out of the way, is from North Carolina; and this blow has fallen upon his own State!

We learn that gold is rising rapidly in the North, which may be significant of President Lincoln's re-election next week.

We get no news from our armies except through the Northern papers—not reliable just now.

Gov. Allen, of Louisiana, writes a furious letter to the Secretary of War, who ordered the disbandment of the State Battalion. He says the order is a personal offense to him and an insult to his State (he is a native Virginian), and he will resent it and resist it to the last extremity. He gives notice that the 3d battalion has been ordered back from the east side of the Mississippi River. The battalion disbanded numbered but 150 men! A little business—like losing one-fourth of North Carolina, to put out of office fifty clerks, whose tenure, by the Constitution, is for life!

NOVEMBER 5TH.—Clear and cold.

Grant has attempted nothing this week, and it is probably too late for any demonstration to affect the election. I infer that the government is convinced President Lincoln will be re-elected, else some desperate effort would have been made in his behalf by his generals. Will he float on a sea of blood another four years? I doubt it. One side or the other must, I think, give up the contest. *He* can afford to break with the Abolitionists now. We *cannot* submit without the loss of everything.

It is thought Grant will continue to "swing to the left," making a winter campaign on the coasts of North and South Carolina—mean time leaving Butler's army here, always menacing Richmond.

Gen. Beauregard writes from Gadsden, Ala., October 24th, that his headquarters will be at Tuscumbia, Ala.; will get supplies from Corinth to Tuscumbia. Forrest has been ordered to report to Gen. Hood, in Middle Tennessee. The railroad iron between Corinth and Memphis will be taken to supply wants elsewhere. Gen. Dick Taylor is to guard communications, etc., has directed Gen. Cheatham to issue an address to the people of Tennessee, saying his and Gen. Forrest's command have entered the State for its redemption, etc., and calling upon the people to aid in destroying the *enemy's communications,* while the main army is between Atlanta and Chattanooga, when the purpose is to precipitate the *whole army* upon it, etc. Gen. B. doubts not he will soon be able to announce good tidings, etc. etc. This letter to Gen. Cooper is "submitted to the Secretary of War," by whom it is "submitted for the information of the President," and sent back by him—" Read and returned, 4th Nov. '64.—J. D."

Gen. B. was to leave that day to join Gen. Hood, in vicinity of

Guntersville, on Tennessee River. Sherman's army was between Dalton and Gadsden, 15 miles from Gadsden.

SUNDAY, NOVEMBER 6TH.—Bright and frosty.

All quiet below. Another day, and if it remains quiet, we may know that Lincoln will be re-elected.

It is said news came from the North last night, that gold sold for $260, and that Governor Seymour had ordered the militia of New York to be in readiness for the protection of the polls on Tuesday next.

G. W. Randolph, late Secretary of War, has sailed for Europe, taking his family with him. Other quondam Confederate States functionaries have gone, or are going. Many have realized fortunes, who were poor, and this country has ceased to be the one to *enjoy* them in.

A parting letter was written by Mr. Randolph to his friend, R. G. H. Kean, Chief of the Bureau of War—appointed by Mr. R., and from whom I derived the information of the sailing of his patron. Such departures, at a crisis like this, spread additional doubts in the community. Mr. R. was not liable to conscription, if averse to fighting more in our cause, being exempted by Governor Smith as a member of the Common Council.

To-morrow is the day fixed for the reassembling of our Congress, but doubts are entertained whether there will be a quorum.

We shall soon have lively news from Beauregard. If I understand his letter of the 24th ult., he is determined to march the army without delay into Middle Tennessee, leaving Sherman on his right flank and rear. It is a desperate conception, and will probably be a brilliant success—or a sad disaster. Napoleon liked such games. If Beauregard really has great genius, he has now the field on which to display it. If the Tennesseeans and Kentuckians rise, momentous events may follow; if not, it is probably the last opportunity they will have. They have their choice—*but blood is the price of independence.*

NOVEMBER 7TH.—Dark and raining. Cannon heard down the river.

To-day our Congress assembles. Senator Johnson, of Missouri (who relinquished six years in United States Senate and $200,000 for the cause), called to see me. He is hopeful of success in the West.

By the Northern papers we see that Mr. Seward has discovered a "conspiracy" to burn all the Northern cities on election day. It may be so—by Northern incendiaries.

Our citizens are still asking permits to bring flour and meal to the city (free from liability to impressment) for "family use." The speculators divide and subdivide their lots, and get them in, to sell at extortionate prices.

Rumors of fighting toward Petersburg—nothing reliable.

Gen. Lee writes that he sent in the Tredegar Battalion to the foundry a few days ago (desertions being frequent from it); and now he learns it is ordered out to report to Lieut.-Col. Pemberton. He requests that it be ordered back to the foundry, where it is absolutely necessary for the supply of munitions, etc.

NOVEMBER 8TH.—Wet and warm; all quiet below, and much mud there.

Congress assembled yesterday, and the President's message was read. He recommends the employment of 40,000 slaves in the army, not as soldiers, unless in the last extremity; and *after* the war he proposes their *emancipation*. This is supposed to be the idea of Mr. Benjamin, for foreign effect. It is denounced by the *Examiner*. The message also recommends the abolition of all class exemptions, such as editors, etc. The *Examiner* denounces this as a blow at the freedom of the press.

The message is cheerful and full of hope, showing that the operations of the year, in the field, have resulted in no disadvantage to us.

By the Northern papers we find that a fleet of four or five cruisers is devastating their commerce. They sailed recently from Wilmington, in spite of Gen. Whiting.

No attack was made on Richmond during the last few days. I have no doubt it was deemed unnecessary by the enemy to secure Mr. Lincoln's re-election. To-day, no doubt, the election in the United States will result in a new lease of presidential life for Mr. Lincoln. If this result should really have been his *motive* in the conduct of the war, perhaps there may soon be some relaxation of its rigors—and possibly peace, for it is obvious that subjugation is not possible. President Lincoln may afford to break with the Abolition party now, and, as has been often done before, kick down the ladder by which he ascended to power. This is merely speculation, however; he may resolve to wield the whole military strength and resources of the United States with more fury than ever. But there will henceforth be a dangerous party against him in the rear. The defeated Democrats will throw every obstruction in his path—and they may *chock* his wheels—or even give him employment for the bayonet at home.

Dispatches from Beauregard and Hood, November 4th, at Tuscumbia, say that Sherman is concentrating at Huntsville and Decatur. Part of our army is at Florence. Gen. B. says his advance has been retarded by bad weather and want of supplies, but that he will march into Tennessee immediately. Gen. Forrest is throwing difficulties in the way of Sherman. The armies are equidistant from Nashville, and if Sherman's supplies fail, his condition becomes desperate.

Captain Manico (acting lieutenant-colonel Departmental Regiment) informs me that the enemy will certainly open batteries in a day or two on our troops at Chaffin's Bluff, and will be replied to vigorously, which he thinks will bring on a battle. We shall hear more thunder, as the distance is only seven or eight miles.

It seems to be clearing up, and there may be news before night. When election news arrives per telegraph from the North—if favorable—it is supposed the enemy will celebrate it by *shotted* salutes, and thus recommence the slaughter.

NOVEMBER 9TH.—Rained last night; clear this morning, and warm. All quiet below, except the occasional bombs thrown at the canal by our iron-clads.

The press is mostly opposed to the President's *project* of employing 40,000 slaves in the army, under promise of emancipation. Some indicate the belief that the President thinks the alternatives are subjugation or abolition, and is preparing the way for the latter.

The *Enquirer* is averse to conscribing editors between the ages of eighteen and forty-five. The editor says it would be a violation of the Constitution, etc.

We all believe Lincoln has been easily re-elected.

It is supposed Grant will soon receive large accessions from Sheridan's army, and make another attempt to take Richmond.

It will be the most formidable attempt, and will be the most formidably resisted.

A row between Gen. Kemper and Gen. Preston: latter refers papers directly to Col. Shields, Gen. K.'s subordinate. Gen. K. asks to be relieved: Secretary Seddon agrees to it, taking sides with the Bureau of Conscription. But the President does not (yet) agree to it, asks investigation of Gen. K.'s complaints, etc.; and so it rests at the present. The Assistant Secretary of War, his son-in-law Lieut.-Col. Lay, etc. etc. are all on the side of the Bureau of Conscription; but I suspect the President is on the *other* side. My opinion is that unless the Bureau of Conscription be abolished or renovated, our cause will fare badly. The President states his suspicions of "malpractice" in his indorsement.

Much cheering has been heard this morning in the enemy's lines —over election news, probably: whether McClellan's or Lincoln's success, no one here knows; but no doubt the latter.

NOVEMBER 10TH.—Warm; rain and wind (south) all night.

Quiet below. One of the enemy's pickets said to one of ours, last night, that Warren's corps had voted unanimously for McClellan, and that New York City has given a majority of 40,000 for him. This is hardly reliable.

Mr. Foote offered a resolution, yesterday, condemning the President's suggestion that *editors* be put in the ranks as well as other classes. Now I think the President's suggestion will be adopted, as Mr. Foote is unfortunate in his resolutions. Mr. Barksdale (President's friend) had it easily referred to the Committee on Military Affairs.

Hon. J. A. Gilmer, North Carolina, is applying for many passports through the lines for people in his district. He applies to Judge Campbell.

Coal is selling at $90 per load, twenty-five bushels.

The vote referring Foote's resolution (on the exemption of editors) was passed unanimously, which is regarded as favoring the President's recommendation. Mr. Foote had denounced the President as a despot.

Bought two excellent knit undershirts, to-day, of a woman who gets her supplies from passing soldiers. Being washed, etc., they bore no evidences of having been worn, *except two small round holes in the body.* Such are the straits to which we are reduced.

I paid $15 each; the price for new ones, of inferior quality, is $50 a piece.

NOVEMBER 11TH.—Clear and pleasant. All quiet. No doubt, from the indications, Lincoln has been re-elected.

Now preparations must be made for the further "conflict of opposing forces." All our physical power must be exerted, else all is lost.

Mr. Sparrow, Louisiana, chairman of the Committee on Military Affairs, introduced a measure, yesterday, in the Senate, which, if consummated, might put all our able-bodied men in the field. It would equalize prices of the necessaries of life, and produce a panic among the speculators. I append it. But, probably, the press will have to be suppressed, "as a war measure," too, to pass it:

"*A bill to extend the assessment of prices for the army to all citizens of the Confederate States:*

"*Whereas,* the depreciation of our currency is, in a great measure, produced by the extortion of those who sell the necessaries of life; and whereas, such depreciation is ruinous to our Confederacy and to the means of prosecuting the war; therefore

"*The Congress of the Confederate States of America do enact, as a necessary war measure,* That the prices assessed for the army by the commissioners of assessment shall be the prices established for all citizens of the Confederate States; and that any person who shall charge any price beyond such assessment shall be deemed guilty of a criminal offense, and be subject to a fine not exceeding five thousand dollars and to imprisonment not exceeding one year."

We are now tending rapidly, under fearful exigencies, to the absolutism which, in a republic, alone can summon the full forces into the field. Power must be concentrated, and wielded with promptitude and precision, else we shall fail to achieve our independence. All obstructions in the way of necessary war measures must be speedily removed, or the finances, and the war itself, will speedily come to an ignominious end.

The Secretary recommends, and the President orders, that Gen. Bragg be assigned to the command of North Carolina. The President yields; Bragg is "given up."

The Richmond *Enquirer* is out, to-day, in an article advocating the employment of 250,000 negroes in our army.

NOVEMBER 12TH.—Bright and pleasant.

The rumor is revived that Mr. Seddon will resign. If he really does resign, I shall regard it as a *bad* sign. He must despair of the Republic; but, then, his successor may be a man of greater energy and knowledge of war.

We are destitute of news, with an awful silence between the armies. We believe this cannot last long, and we know Grant has a great superiority of numbers. And he knows our weakness; for the government will persist in keeping "at the front" local defense troops, smarting under a sense of wrong, some of whom are continually deserting.

The money-changers and speculators, who have lavished their bribes, are all in their places, preying upon the helpless women and children; while the clerks—the permanence of whose tenure of office was guaranteed by the Constitution—are still kept in the trenches, and their families, many of them refugees, are suffering in destitution. But Mr. Seddon says they *volunteered*. This is not candid. They were told by Mr. Memminger and others that, unless they *volunteered*, the President had decided their dismissal —when conscription into the army followed, of course!

NOVEMBER 13TH.—Bright and cold; ice on the porch. All quiet below, save the booming of bombs every night from our iron-clads, thrown at the workmen in the canal.

There is a dispatch from the West, relating to Gen. Forrest's operations in Tennessee, understood to be good news. I did not wait to see, knowing the papers will have it to-morrow.

Mr. Hunter was with Mr. Secretary Seddon, as usual, this Sunday morning, begging him not to resign. This is flattery to Mr. Seddon.

NOVEMBER 14TH.—Clear and cold.

Lincoln is re-elected, and has called for a *million* of men! This makes many of our croaking people despondent; others think it only a game of brag.

I saw the President to-day in earnest conversation with several members of Congress, standing in the street. It is not often he descends from his office to this mode of conference.

Some one of the family intimating that stains of blood were on my undershirts (second hand), I was amused to see Mrs. J. lifting them with the *tongs*. They have been thoroughly washed, and prove to be a first-rate article. I am proud of them, for they are truly comfortable garments.

Gen. Forrest is doing wonders in Tennessee, as the appended dispatch from Gen. Beauregard shows:

"Tuscumbia, Ala., Nov. 8th, 1864.
" Gen. S. Cooper, A. and I. General.

" Gen. Forrest reports on the 5th instant that he was then engaged fighting the enemy at Johnsonville, having already destroyed four gun-boats, of eight guns each, fourteen steamers, and twenty barges, with a large quantity of quartermaster and commissary stores, on the landing and in warehouses, estimated at between seventy-five and one hundred thousand tons. Six gun-boats were then approaching, which he hoped to capture or destroy.

"G. T. Beauregard."

November 15th.—Fair and cold; ice. Quiet below; rumors of further successes in the Southwest, but not official.

Congress did nothing of interest yesterday in open session, but spent most of its time in secret session. There will probably be stringent martial law, for the strong hand of unlimited power will be required to correct abuses, repress discontent, and bring into the field the whole military strength of the Confederacy. The large majorities for Lincoln in the United States clearly indicate a purpose to make renewed efforts to accomplish our destruction.

It is now contradicted that Lincoln has called for 1,000,000 men.

Three P.M. Cloudy, and threatening snow.

An attack upon the city seems to be apprehended. All men must now have passes from Mr. Carrington, Provost Marshal, or be liable to arrest in the street. Such are the changes, indicating *panic* on the part of official dignitaries.

November 16th.—Bright and frosty.

This is the day designated by the President for worship, etc., and the offices and places of business are all closed. It is like Sunday, with an occasional report of cannon down the river.

I doubt whether the clerks in the trenches will pray for the President. Compelled to *volunteer* under a threat of removal, they were assured that they would only be called out in times of great urgency, and then be returned to their offices in a few days. They have now been in the front trenches several months; while the different secretaries are quietly having their kinsmen and favorites detailed back to their civil positions, the poor and friendless are still "left out in the cold." Many of these have refugee families dependent on them, while those brought in are mostly rich, having sought office merely to avoid service in the field. The battalion, numbering 700, has less than 200 now in the trenches. Hundreds of the local forces, under a sense of wrong, have deserted to the enemy.

Gen. Breckinridge has beaten the enemy at Bull's Gap, Tenn., taking several hundred prisoners, 6 guns, etc.

Mr. Hunter was at the department early this morning in quest of news.

Gave $75 for a load of coal.

Messrs. Evans & Cogswell, Columbia, S. C., have sent me some of their recent publications: "A Manual of Military Surgery, by I. Julian Chisolm, M.D., 3d edition;" "Digest of the Military and Naval Laws," by Lester & Bromwell; "Duties of a Judge Advocate, etc." by Capt. R. C. Gilchrist; and "A Map of East Virginia and North Carolina;" all beautifully printed and bound.

NOVEMBER 17TH.—Dark and dismal—threatening rain or snow. Quiet below; but we have no papers to-day, yesterday being holiday.

It is rumored that Gen. Sheridan (Federal) is sailing from Washington to reinforce Grant, and that Gen. Early is marching hitherward from the Valley. There may be renewed operations against Richmond, or Grant may penetrate North Carolina. No one knows what will happen a month or a week hence.

Mr. Hunter was again with Mr. Seddon this morning.

Governor Smith's exemption mill is yet grinding out exemptions, sometimes fifty per day. Constables, department clerks, and sheriffs, commonwealth's attorneys, commissioners of the revenue, etc. etc., who win his favor, get his certificate of exemption, as necessary for the State administration.

A dispatch from Gen. Wheeler, Jonesborough, November 14th, says Sherman has three corps at *Atlanta*, and is destroying railroads between him and Marietta, probably intending to move forward—farther South.

Another dispatch from Gen. W., dated 14th inst., Lovejoy's, Georgia, says scouts from enemy's rear report that Sherman left Atlanta yesterday morning, with 15th, 17th, and 21st corps, in two columns, one on the Jonesborough, and one on the McDonough Roads—cavalry on his flanks. Many houses have been burned in Rome, Marietta, and Atlanta, and the railroad bridge over Chattanooga River (in his rear)! Enemy advancing this morning. To Gen. Bragg.

Twelve M. Still another dispatch from Gen. Wheeler to Gen. Bragg, dated Jonesborough, 3 P.M., 15th inst. "Enemy advanced early this morning with infantry, cavalry, artillery, and wagons—have driven our cavalry back upon this place—strength not yet ascertained, etc."

Still another dispatch:

"GRIFFIN, GA., November 16th, 1864.
"To GEN. BRAGG.

"Enemy checked this evening near Bear Creek—enemy evidently marching to Macon.

"JOS. WHEELER, *Major-General.*"

The dispatches from Gen. Weeler have produced no little commotion in the War Office.

Gen. J. E. Johnston's report of his Georgia campaign concludes by asserting that he *did* intend to defend Atlanta; that he retreated before overwhelming numbers; that the President did not favor him with any directions; that Lee retreated before Grant, and everybody praised him for it; that Gen. Hood professed to be his friend, when seeking his removal, or cognizant of the purpose to remove him; and that the vituperation heaped upon him in certain papers seemed to have Executive authorization at Richmond.

The President indorses this growlingly; that it all differs with his understanding of the facts at the time, etc.

NOVEMBER 18TH.—Bright, calm, and pleasant.

All quiet below, save our bombardment of Dutch Gap Canal.

The Senate passed a resolution yesterday, calling on the President for a statement of the number of exemptions granted by the Governors. This will, perhaps, startle Governor Smith, of Virginia, who has already kept out of the army at least a thousand.

Perhaps it will hit Governor Brown, of Georgia, also; but Sherman will hit him hardest. He must call out all his fighting people now, or see his State ravaged with impunity.

Both Houses of Congress sit most of the time in secret session, no doubt concocting strong measures under the influence of the existing crisis. Good news only can throw open the doors, and restore the hilarity of the members. When not in session, they usually denounce the President; in session, they are wholly subservient to him.

Hon. R. L. Montague has written to the Secretary of War, on behalf of the entire Virginia delegation, requesting a suspension of the impressment of slaves until further legislation by Congress; what that legislation will be, the President might tell, if he would.

A dispatch from Gen. Wheeler, dated to-day, 12 miles from Forsyth, states that Sherman advances by the most direct route toward Macon, Ga.

My wife presented me to-day an excellent pocket-handkerchief, my old ones being honey-combed and unfit for another washing. Upon inquiry (since the cost of a single handkerchief is now $20), I ascertained it to be a portion of one of my linen shirts bought in London in 1846.

We have now 200 pounds of flour in the house; 1 bushel meal; 1 bushel sweet potatoes; 1 bushel Irish potatoes; 3 half pecks white beans; 4 pumpkins; 10 pounds beef; 2 pounds butter, and 3 pounds sugar, with salt, etc. This seems like moderate stores for a family of seven, but it is a larger supply than we ever had before, and will suffice for a month. At the market price, they would cost $620. Add to this $1\frac{1}{3}$ loads coal and a quarter cord of wood—the first at $75, the last at $80—the total is $762.50. This sum in ordinary times, and in specie, would subsist my family twelve months.

NOVEMBER 19TH.—Rained all night, and still rains. All quiet below, save the occasional bomb thrown by our iron-clads.

Gen. and Hon. R. K. Wright, of Georgia, is said to have gone to Washington to negotiate a peace for Georgia.

A dispatch from Gen. Wheeler, dated yesterday, 12 miles from Forsyth, says: "I think definite orders should be sent to officers in command here, as to the line of policy to be pursued—particularly as to defending Macon, Augusta, or Columbus. If not to be defended, government stores should be removed, on enemy's approach, if possible. An officer should be sent to command everything, who knows the views, wishes, and plans of the government." I think so too!

The papers think that Grant is about to try again to force his way into Richmond, as soon as the weather will permit.

We had a delicious treat of persimmons to-night—a quart bought for a dollar. They were delicious, and we enjoyed them hugely. Also a quart of apples, for which we paid a dollar.

NOVEMBER 20TH, SUNDAY.—Rained all night—raining this morning. A dispatch from Gen. Wheeler, 18th, at Forsyth, Ga., says: "The enemy rapidly advancing."

It is said Gov. Brown has called out the men *en masse*. I think Sherman is in danger.

Mr. Foote made what is called "a compromise speech" in Congress yesterday. But although there is vacillation in the government, no compromise measures will be tolerated yet—if ever. Everything still depends upon events in the field. I think the government at Washington and the people of the United States are very weary of the war, and that peace of some sort must ensue. We shall be recognized by European powers upon the first symptoms of exhaustion in the United States; and there soon will be such symptoms, if we can only keep up a determined resistance.

Besides, the seizure of our cruiser Florida in a neutral port (Brazil) will furnish a pretext for a quarrel with the United States by the maritime powers.

I am amused by our fireside conversations at night. They relate mostly to the savory dishes we once enjoyed, and hope to enjoy again.

Gen. Butler's speech in New York, suggesting that the rebels be allowed a last chance for submission, and failing to embrace it, that their lands be divided among the Northern soldiers, has a maddening effect upon our people.

NOVEMBER 21ST.—Wet, dark, and dismal. Quiet below.

In Congress, Mr. Staples, of Virginia, unfortunately exhibited a statement obtained from the Bureau of Conscription, to the effect that while 1400 State officers, etc. were exempted in Virginia, there were 14,000 in North Carolina. This produced acrimonious debate, which is not the end of it, I fear. I don't believe the statement. Gov. Smith, of Virginia, is exempting a full share of constables, etc. etc. The Bureau of Conscription strikes, perhaps, at Gen. Bragg, a North Carolinian. It is not the end.

An anonymous letter to Gov. Bonham states that Capt. Hugener and all his officers at Fort Sumter are drunkards or gamblers, and that the place is in great danger. Gov. B. sends the letter to the President, who directs the Secretary of War to make inquiry, etc. Perhaps it will be done in time—since the fall of Plymouth.

Gold, to-day, brings $40 for $1.

Oak wood sells to-day at $100 per cord.

A large amount of apple-brandy has been made this year. A lady, whose husband is a prisoner in the North, writes to the Secretary, asking the release of her apple-brandy (in Virginia) from the clutches of the impressing officer. She and her daughters had distilled 500 gallons, upon which they depended to procure other supplies, etc. Brandy is selling at $75 per gallon—$37,500. Pretty well for the old woman and her three daughters! Apples are worth $100 per barrel; but the currency (Confederate) is nearly worthless.

NOVEMBER 22D.—Rained in torrents last night; cold this morning and cloudy.

All quiet below. But there was an alarm, night before last, growing out of a stampede of some 50 of the enemy's beeves. They charged upon our line, regardless of the fire of cannon and musketry, and were all captured after penetrating our works. Brave cattle!

Gov. Vance writes that if Wilmington be attacked by a large force in the rear of Fort Fisher, its fall is inevitable, unless two brigades of veteran troops be sent from Gen. Lee's army. He says the defense of Wilmington is as important as that of Richmond. The President directs the Secretary of War to communicate with Gen. Lee on the subject.

We learn that Gen. Grant is on a visit to his family at Burlington, N. J.; and yet the departmental troops (clerks) are still kept in the trenches. It is said the *President's family* keep them there by the most imploring appeals to Gen. Lee, and that the President himself does not feel altogether safe while the Federal army is so near him. His house is on the side of the city most exposed, if a sudden attack were made, of which, however, there seems to be no danger at present. Several brigades of Gen. Early's troops have arrived from the Valley.

Gold sells to-day at $42 for $1. And it rises in the United States. This produces trepidation in the cabinet.

Snowed a few few minutes to-day, 4 P.M. The clouds are breaking—cold.

What appetites we have! Shin-soup and bean-soup alternately are relished with shark-like appetites.

NOVEMBER 23D.—Snowed last night three inches. Clear and cold this morning; ground frozen.

Had a dream last night—that meeting a few men in my *wood and coal-house*, I nominated R. Tyler for the Presidency, and it was well received. I must tell this to Mr. T.

I narrated my dream to Mr. T. Before I left, he said a clerkship *was at the disposal of my son Thomas;* but Thomas is clerk in the conscription service, getting rations, etc. etc., better than the $4000 per annum. But still that dream may be realized. He is the son of President Tyler, deceased.

John Mitchel is now editor of the *Examiner*, and challenged *Mr. Foote yesterday*—the note was borne by Mr. Swan, of Tennessee, Mr. Foote's colleague. Mr. Foote would not receive it; and Mr. S. took offense and assaulted Mr. F. in his own house, when Mrs. F. interposed and beat Mr. S. away.

Gen. Winder has been appointed, by *Gen. Cooper*, commander of all prisons east of the Mississippi.

Gen. Winder has been made Commissary-General of all prisons and prisoners of war. The Bureau of Conscription is yet sustained in power. All this is done by Gen. Cooper,—unwise, probably *fatal* measures!

NOVEMBER 24TH.—Clear and frosty. Ice half an inch thick this morning. All quiet below.

Col. St. John, Niter and Mining Bureau, required 13,000 men to furnish ammunition, etc.

Col. Northrop, Commissary-General, reports only 15 days' bread rations in Richmond for 100,000 men, and that we must rely upon supplies hereafter from the Carolinas and Virginia alone. The difficulty is want of adequate transportation, of course. The speculators and railroad companies being in partnership, very naturally exclude the government from the track. The only remedy, the only salvation, in my opinion, is for the government to take exclusive control of the railroads, abate speculation, and change most of the quartermasters and commissaries.

Hon. J. B. Clarke proposed a resolution of inquiry in the House of Representatives, which was adopted, calling for the number and name of employees in the departments, and the State they were appointed from. Virginia has more than half of them.

Gen. Cooper, the Adjutant-General, Northern by birth, turned out twenty of his eighty clerks yesterday, to replace them with ladies.

It is said and believed that Sherman's cavalry has reached Milledgeville, and destroyed the public buildings, etc.

We have nothing from Wheeler since the 18th inst.

NOVEMBER 25TH.—Bright and frosty.

A report from the Bureau of Conscription shows after all that only some 3000 men have been sent to the army during the last two months, under General Order 77, revoking details, etc. I don't wonder, for there has been the natural confusion consequent upon a conflict of authority between Gen. Kemper and the Bureau of Conscription. About as many details have been made by the one authority as have been enrolled by the other.

NOVEMBER 26TH.—Clear and frosty.

The following dispatch was received to-day from Gen. Bragg:

"AUGUSTA, Nov. 25th, 1864.

"Arrived late last night, and take command this morning. We learn from Gen. Wagner, who holds the Oconee Railroad bridge, that the enemy has not crossed the river in any force. He has concentrated in Milledgeville, and seems to be tending South. Our cavalry, under Wheeler, is in his front, and has been ordered to destroy every vestige of subsistence and forage as it retires; to hang upon his flanks, and retard his progress by every possible means. I am informed the brigades from Southwest Virginia have joined Wheeler. President's dispatch of 23d just received.

"BRAXTON BRAGG, *General.*"

When I carried this dispatch to the Secretary I found him sitting in close conference with Mr. Hunter, both with rather lugubrious faces.

Another dispatch from Bragg:

"AUGUSTA, Nov. 25th, 8 P.M.

"The enemy has crossed the Oconee; was met this morning, in force, at Buffalo Creek, near Sandersville. His movements from that point will determine whether he designs attacking here or on Savannah."

Hon. I. T. Leach from North Carolina, yesterday introduced *submission* resolutions in the House of Representatives, which were voted down, of course,—Messrs. Logan and Turner, of North Carolina, however, voting *for* them. A party of that sort is forming, and may necessitate harsh measures.

The President orders detail of fifty men for *express company. I feared so!*

NOVEMBER 27TH.—Cloudy and warmer; slight rain. Nothing from Bragg this morning. Nothing from below the city.

When I entered the Secretary's room this morning, I found him as grave as usual. L. Q. Washington, son of Peter Washington, once a clerk under President Tyler (and he still remains in the United States), and grandson of Lund Washington, who, we learn by one of the published letters of Gen. Washington, was his overseer, with no traceable relationship to his family, was seated with him. He is chief clerk to Mr. Benjamin, a sinecure position in the State Department. He was placed there by Mr. Hunter, after writing a series of communications for the *Examiner*, as Mr. Pollard informed me, denunciatory of Mr. Stephens, Vice-President Confederate States. Mr. Kean and Mr. Shepherd, the clean chief clerk, were also present, enjoying the Hon. Secretary's confidence. They are all comparatively *young men*, whom the Secretary has *not* assigned to positions in the field, although *men* are alone wanted to achieve independence. They were discussing a resolution of Congress, calling for the names, ages, etc. of the civil and military officers employed by the Secretary in Richmond, or it might have been the subject of the removal of the government, or the chances of success, etc., or the President's appointment of Gen. Bragg to command the army in Georgia, or Mr. Hunter's prospects for the Presidency. No matter what.

It is a dismal day, and a settled vexation is on the faces of many of the officials. But if the time should come for flight, etc., I predict many will have abundance of funds in Europe. The quartermasters, commissaries, etc. will take care of themselves by submission. The railroad companies have already taken care of themselves by their partnership with the speculators. The express company bribes all branches of the government, and I fear it has *obliged* some of the members of the President's military or domestic family.

By a report from the Niter and Mining Bureau, it appears that thirteen furnaces of the thirty odd in Virginia have ceased operations. Several have been destroyed by the enemy; the ore and fuel of others have become exhausted; and those in blast threaten to cease work for want of hands, the men being put in the army.

NOVEMBER 28TH.—Calm and warm; clouds and sunshine, without wind.

All quiet below. It is reported that one of our picket boats in the James River deserted last night. It is said the crew overpowered the officers and put them ashore, and then the boat rowed down to the enemy.

I am informed by Capt. Warner that there are 12,000 graves of Federal prisoners at Andersonville, Ga. That climate is fatal to them; but the government cannot feed them here, and the enemy won't exchange.

A dispatch from Gen. Bragg:

"AUGUSTA, November 27th, 1864.—We have lost communication with the front. A small cavalry raid cut the Savannah Railroad and telegraph, this morning, at Brier Creek, twenty-six miles from here. Gen. Wheeler was, yesterday, confronting the enemy's infantry at Sandersville. An officer, who left Macon on the 23d, states that one corps of the enemy was still confronting us there; our force not exceeding 5000, nearly all militia. The force here, including all available reserves, does not exceed 6000 effectives: only one battery. I am not yet advised from Charleston and Savannah, but know the means are small. Neither point could long resist the enemy's whole force; hence my remarks about concentration. Gen. Hardee has gone to Savannah. Wheeler will continue to confront and harass the enemy. I have not learned the strength of his command. He estimates the enemy's force at about 30,000."

Gen. Beauregard has published a short proclamation, saying

he will soon arrive to the rescue in Georgia. Here, then, will be war between the two B.'s—Bragg and Beauregard; and the President will be as busy as a bee. Meantime, Sherman may possess the land at pleasure.

A long letter (twenty-five pages) from Gov. Brown, Georgia, came to hand to-day, combating, in replication, one from the Secretary relating to calling out all the militia of Georagia, etc. *State rights* and the Constitution are discussed *in extenso*, and many a hard blow is aimed at the President. The Governor regards the Secretary as merely the instrument or head clerk of the President, whom he sneers at occasionally. But he denounces as *vile* the President himself, *and refuses to obey the call*. What he will do with the militia must soon be known, for Sherman is *there*.

A great stir among the *officers* on bureau and department duty in Richmond! Congress has called on the President for a list of all commissioned officers here, their ages, etc., and how many of them are fit for duty in the field. This will be dodged, of course, if possible.

NOVEMBER 29TH.—Clear, and warm as summer almost.

Another dispatch from Bragg:

"AUGUSTA, November 28th, 1864.—On the 26th instant, the enemy started a heavy cavalry force in this direction, from his main body near Sandersville; Gen. Wheeler promptly following, leaving a portion of his force to confront Sherman. Kilpatrick reached vicinity of Waynesborough yesterday, where Wheeler overtook and attacked him. A running fight has continued to this time; the advantage with us. We are driving them toward Millen. Young's command has just arrived, and will go forward to Wheeler, who will, I hope, be able to mount most of them from his captures. Devastation marks the enemy's route. Hear nothing from the movements of the enemy's infantry, since Wheeler left their front. I fear they may cross the Savannah, and make for Beaufort. It is perfectly practicable."

The number of deserters, under General Order 65, received here and sent to Abingdon, Va., is 1224 men.

Senator Waldo P. Johnson, Missouri, told me he would move, to-day, to allow the civil officers, etc. to buy rations and clothes of government, at schedule prices. This would be better than an increase of salary.

No movements below, to-day, that I hear of.

Gen. Jos. E. Johnston was at the department to-day, and was warmly greeted by his friends. If Sherman's campaign should be a success, Johnston will be a hero; if the reverse, he will sink to rise no more. A sad condition, for one's greatness to depend upon calamity to his country!

NOVEMBER 30TH.—Clear, and warm as summer. No fires.

It is reported that Gen. Hood is still marching North, and is near Nashville.

The following telegrams were received this morning:

"AUGUSTA, November 29th, 1864.—It is reported, *via* Savannah, the enemy, with infantry and artillery, entered Millen yesterday. Wheeler is rapidly pursuing Kilpatrick, who retreats in that direction from Waynesborough.—B. B."

"AUGUSTA, November 29th, 1864.—$6\frac{1}{2}$ P.M.—Gen. Jones telegraphs from Charleston: 'Ten (10) gun-boats with transports landing troops at Boykins on Broad River. Four gun-boats with transports and barges are, by this time, at Mackay's Point, junction of Pocotaligo with Broad River. I am sending all assistance from here, and think we must make the struggle near the coast.' As this movement relieves Wilmington, might not some of the North Carolina reserves be sent to Gen. Jones?—B. BRAGG."

The following items were in the papers this morning:

"NEGRO PICKETS.—Monday morning negro pickets were placed in front of Gen. Pickett's division. Our men, taking it as an insult, yesterday fired upon them, causing a stampede among them. Their places have been supplied with white Yankees, and the lines have resumed the usual quiet.

"Two negroes, captured by Gen. Hunter in the Valley last summer, and forced into the Yankee army, deserted yesterday and came into Gen. Pickett's lines, and were brought over to this city."

"CAPTURE OF GEN. PRYOR.—The *Express* gives the following account of the capture of the Hon. Roger A. Pryor, on Monday morning:

"While riding along the lines on our right, he stopped at one of our vidette posts, and left his horse and private arms with one or two other articles in charge of the pickets, stated that he intended, as was often his custom, to go forward and exchange papers with the enemy's videttes. He advanced in the direction of the Yankee lines, flourishing a paper in his hand, in token of his object, and after proceeding some distance was met by a Yankee officer. An exchange of papers was effected, and Gen. Pryor had turned to retrace his steps, when he was suddenly seized by two or three armed men, who were lying in ambush, and hurried away. The whole transaction, we understand, was witnessed by some of our men, but at too great a distance to render any assistance. Gen. Pryor had frequently exchanged papers with the enemy, and his name and character had, no doubt, been reported to them. They resolved to have him, by fair means or foul, and descended to the basest treachery to accomplish their purpose.

"We trust that some notice may be taken of the matter by our military authorities, and every effort used to secure his early return. During the last few months the general has been acting as an independent scout, in which capacity he has rendered valuable service."

CHAPTER XLV.

Desertions.—Bragg and Kilpatrick.—Rents.—Gen. Winder's management of prisoners.—Rumored disasters in Tennessee.—Prices.—Progress of Sherman.—Around Richmond.—Capture of Fort McAlister.—Rumored death of the President.—Yankee line of spies.—From Wilmington and Charleston.—Evacuation of Savannah.

DECEMBER 1ST.—Bright and warm.

It is said there is a movement of the enemy menacing our works on the north side of the river. There was shelling down the river yesterday and day before, officially announced by Gen. Lee—two of the enemy's monitors retired.

Gen. Longstreet says "over 100 of Gen. Pickett's men are in the guard-house for desertion, and that the cause of it may be attributed to the numerous reprieves, no one being executed for two months." Gen. Lee indorses on the paper: "Desertion is increasing in the army, notwithstanding all my efforts to stop it. I think a rigid execution of the law is mercy in the end. The great want in our army is firm discipline." The Secretary of War sent it to the President "for his information." The President sent it back with the following biting indorsement: "When deserters are arrested they should be tried, and if the sentences are reviewed and remitted, that is not a proper subject for the criticism of a military commander.—JEFF. DAVIS. November 29th, 1864."

Another dispatch from Gen. Bragg:

"AUGUSTA, November 30th, 1864.—Following just received from Major-Gen. Wheeler: '*Four Miles West Buckhead Church*, November 29th, 9 P.M.—We fought Gen. Kilpatrick all night and all day, charging him at every opportunity. Enemy fought stubbornly, and left a considerable number of their killed. He stampeded, and came near capturing Kilpatrick twice; but having a fleet horse, he escaped, bareheaded, leaving his hat in our hands. Our own loss about 70, including the gallant Gen. Robertson, severely wounded. Our troops all acted handsomely.'

"Gen. Robertson has arrived here. His left arm is badly broken at the elbow, but he is doing well.—B. B."

Another dispatch of the same date: "To establish our communications west, I have ordered the immediate repair of the Georgia Railroad to Atlanta. With the exception of bridges, the damage is reported as slight. We should also have a line of telegraph on that route.—B. B."

I succeeded to-day in buying of Government Quartermaster (Major Ferguson) four yards of dark-gray cloth, at $12 per yard, for a full suit. The merchants ask $125 per yard—a saving of $450. I hope to have it cut and made by one of the government tailors, for about $50, trimmings included. A citizen tailor asks $350!

The Senate passed a bill, yesterday, increasing my salary and Custis's $500, which we don't thank them for unless we can buy rations, etc. at schedule prices. The money is worthless when we go into the open market.

My landlord, Mr. King, has gone into the grocery business; and, although he did not raise the rent for the present year, still asked more upon my offer to pay the amount of the first quarter to-day—$500, six months ago, were really worth more than $1000 to-day. At that time I acknowledged the house would bring more than $500. To-day it would rent for more than $1000. He left it to me to do what was right. I think it right to pay $800 or $1000, and will do so.

This evening our servant stepped into the yard just in time to save some clothes drying on the line. A thief was in the act of stealing them, and made his escape, springing over the fence into the alley.

DECEMBER 2D.—Warm, and raining moderately.

My landlord gets $400 of the $500 increase of my salary.

Dispatches from Gen. Bragg:

"AUGUSTA, December 1st, 1864. — Following received from Lieut.-Gen. R. Taylor, Savannah, Ga.: 'Gen. Hardee is at Grahamville. No fighting there since yesterday evening, when the enemy was driven five miles, leaving their dead upon the field.— B. B.'"

Another:

"AUGUSTA, December 1st, 1864, 12 M.—The (enemy's) cavalry having been driven in, the enemy's main force was yesterday found near Louisville, with strong outposts in this direction. They have secured large supplies in the country; but our cavalry is now all up, and it is hoped they will be prevented to a great extent in the future. The report from Savannah, of the enemy's entrance into Millen, on the 27th, was premature. Telegraphic communication was reopened to Savannah by that route yesterday. The enemy is just now reported as at Station 9, on Central Railroad, advancing.—B. B."

During the last month, 100 passports were given to leave the Confederate States by Provost Marshal Carrington and War Department.

Mr. G. B. Lamar, Savannah, Ga., tenders his services to go to New York and purchase supplies for our prisoners in the hands of the enemy, and to negotiate the sale of 1000 bales of cotton, etc.

Twelve M. Heavy and pretty rapid shelling is heard down the river.

Col. Chandler, Inspecting Officer, makes an ugly report of Gen. Winder's management of the prisons in Georgia. Brig.-Gen. Chilton appends a rebuking indorsement on Gen. W.'s conduct. The inspector characterizes Gen. W.'s treatment of the prisoners as barbarous, and their condition as a "hell on earth." And Gen. W. says his statements are "false."

DECEMBER 3D.—Very warm—clouds and sunshine, like April.

Roger A. Pryor, who resigned his brigadiership, and has been acting as a *scout* (private), fell into the hands of the enemy the other day while exchanging newspapers with their pickets. They have him at Washington, and the United States newspapers say he makes revelations of a sad state of affairs in Georgia, etc. This is doubtless erroneous.

A "peace resolution" has been introduced in the North Carolina Legislature.

Hon. Mr. Foote yesterday introduced a resolution in Congress, calling for a convention of the States—or appointment of commissioners from the States. Voted down by a large majority.

Gen. Rosser (two brigades) made a descent, a few days ago, on the Baltimore and Ohio Railroad, capturing some nine guns altogether, including four siege, which he spiked. The others he brought off, with 800 prisoners. He destroyed 200 wagons and a large amount of quartermaster and ordnance stores.

Per contra. Grant has pounced upon one of our depots at Stony Creek, Weldon Railroad, getting some 80 prisoners, and destroying a few stores. It is said he still holds the position—of some importance.

Gen. Ewell still thinks the aspect here is "threatening."

Brig.-Gen. Chilton, Inspector-General, has ordered investigations of the fortunes of bonded officers, who have become rich during the war.

A strong effort has been made to have Gen. Ripley removed from Charleston. He is a Northern man, and said to be dissipated. Senator Orr opposes the change; the Secretary recommends his retention, and the President indorses: "I prefer that Gen. Ripley should remain.—J. D."

SUNDAY, DECEMBER 4TH.—Bright, clear, and warm.

A dispatch from Gen. Bragg. "AUGUSTA, December 3d, 6 P.M.— A strong force of the enemy's cavalry and infantry advanced from Louisville and encamped last night six miles from Waynesborough. They turned off this morning toward Savannah. Our cavalry is pressing in the rear, and all available means is being thrown to their front by rail. There is time yet for any assistance which can be spared, to be sent by way of Charleston.—B. B."

The Northern papers say our army under Hood in Tennessee

has met with a great disaster. We are still incredulous—although it may be true. If so, the President will suffer, and Johnston and Beauregard will escape censure—both being supplanted in the command by a subordinate.

Brig.-Gen. Preston is still directing orders to Col. Shields, who is under the command of Major-Gen. Kemper, and the conflict of conscription authorities goes on, while the country perishes. Preston is a South Carolina politician—Kemper a Virginian. Mr. Secretary Seddon leans to the former.

The law allowing exemptions to owners of a certain number of slaves is creating an antislavery party. The non-slaveholders will not long fight for the benefit of such a "privileged class." There is madness in our counsels!

We are still favored by Providence in our family. We have, at the market prices, some $800 worth of provisions, fuel, etc., at the beginning of winter, and my son Thomas is well clad and has his order for a month's rations of beef, etc., which we get as we want it at the government shop near at hand in Broad Street. His pay and allowances are worth some $4500 per annum.

Major Ferguson having got permission of the Quartermaster-General to sell me a suit of cloth—there being a piece too dark for the army, I got four yards, enough for coat, pants, and vest, at $12 per yard—the price in the stores is $125; and I have the promise of the government tailor to make it up for some $30 or $40, the ordinary price being $350; the trimmings my family will furnish—if bought, they would cost $100. Tom has bought a new black coat, made before the war, for $175, the peace price $15, in specie, equivalent to $600. And my daughter Anne has made three fine bonnets (for her mother, sister, and herself), from the debris of old ones; the price of these would be $700. So I fear not but we shall be fed and clad by the providence of God.

December 5th.—Bright and beautiful.

Anne Samuels and many other ladies, Harrisonburg, Virginia, have petitioned the government for authority to organize themselves into a regiment for local defense.

Great excitement was produced in the House of Representatives (Congress) this morning by the entrance of a lady who proceeded vigorously to cowhide the Hon. Mr. V——, from Missouri.

Congress has passed a resolution declaring that it was not meant, in calling for the ages of the clerks in the departments, to include the ladies.

Vice-President Stephens has arrived in the city.

Our people think, in the Federal accounts of a victory over Gen. Hood, at Franklin, Tenn., they perceive a Confederate victory. It is understood that the enemy fell back upon Nashville after the battle, pursued by Hood.

We are also hopeful of the defeat of Sherman—a little delay on his part will render it pretty certain. If it should occur, will it give us peace?

The *Tribune* says President Lincoln is more determined than ever to restore the Union. But disaster will surely dishearten either side—that is, the people.

The following dispatch has been received from Gen. Bragg:

"AUGUSTA, December 4th, 1864.—The column is moving on what is known as Eastern Road, to Savannah. There are several ferries from the mouth of ―― Creek to Charleston and Savannah Railroad bridge—none below that. Gen. Hardee reports he is patrolling the river with a gun-boat. I have had all ferry boats destroyed, and ordered all roads to and from the river to be broken up and blockaded by felling heavy timber. The roads are all passed by causeways to the river on both sides over dense swamps. None of enemy's forces remain near Macon; and from best information I can obtain, it is thought all of ours have left there for Savannah. The Georgia militia, who were on Central Railroad, moved back toward Savannah, and at last accounts were at Station 4½; our cavalry, however, far in advance of them.—B. B."

At night—mended broken china and glassware again with white lead, very successfully. Such ware can hardly be bought at all—except by the rich.

DECEMBER 6TH.—Bright and beautiful. Indian summer apparently.

All quiet below—but it is anticipated by some that a battle will occur to-day, or in a day or so.

The enemy's negro troops have been brought to this side of the river, and are in full view on picket duty.

The Signal Bureau reports a large number of transports descending the Potomac a few days ago; probably Sheridan's army, to reinforce Grant.

And yet our conscription superintendents, under orders, are busily engaged furloughing and detailing the rich slaveowners! It is developing a rapidly growing *Emancipation party*, for it is the establishment of a privileged class, and may speedily prove fatal to our cause. Our leaders are *mad*, and will be destroyed, if they persist in this policy.

DECEMBER 7TH.—Raining, and warm.

It is said several hundred of the prisoners taken by Rosser in the Valley escaped, on the way to Richmond. A relaxation of vigilance always follows success. How long can this war last?

Hon. Mr. Staples procured four and two months' details yesterday for two rich farmers, Messrs. McGehee and Heard, both rosy-faced, robust men, and yet found for "light duty" by a medical board. Thus we go. The poor and weakly are kept in the trenches, to desert the first opportunity.

It is said a dispatch came from Bragg yesterday (I saw it not) stating that Wheeler and some infantry had a sharp battle with Sherman's advance, near Millen, in which the latter suffered greatly. But reinforcements coming up, our forces fell back in order, disputing the way.

Tea is held at $100 per pound! Wood still $100 per cord.

I saw Gen. Rains to-day. He says he has over 2000 shell torpedoes planted along our lines around Richmond and Petersburg.

Col. Bayne reports the importation of 6400 packages salted meats, fish, coffee, preserved vegetables, from Nassau, Bermuda, and Halifax, *since October 1st*, 1864, in fourteen different steamers.

DECEMBER 8TH.—Rained hard in the night; clear and pleasant in the morning.

A letter from John T. Bourne, St. Georges, Bermuda, says he has some 1800 barrels government gunpowder under his care, of which he desires to be relieved.

Gen. Lee sent to the Secretary the following dispatch this morning: "2d and 5th corps, Gregg's division of [enemy's] cavalry, are moving South, on Jerusalem Plank Road. Cavalry reached Sussex Court House at 7 P.M. yesterday. Hill and

Hampton [Confederate States generals] are following. Appearances indicate they are moving against Weldon, where I am concentrating all the depot guards I can.

"R. E. LEE, *General.*

"PETERSBURG, Dec. 8th, 1864."

There are rumors of the enemy having effected a lodgment on the south side of the river, between Howell and Drewry's Bluff. This may be serious. I do not learn (yet) that the Dutch Gap Canal is finished; but the enemy landed from barges in the fog. Gen. Lee, some weeks ago, designated such a movement and lodgment as important and embarrassing, probably involving the holding of Petersburg.

Nothing from Bragg.

One of Gen. Early's divisions is passing through the city toward Petersburg.

DECEMBER 9TH.—Cold and cloudy; surface of the ground frozen.

Cannon heard below. More of Gen. Early's corps arriving. The papers contradict the report that Howlett's Battery has been taken. The opinion prevails that a battle will occur to-day.

It appears that but few of the enemy's forces were engaged in the demonstration on the south side, below Drewry's Bluff, and no uneasiness is felt on account of it.

We have nothing so far to-day from the enemy's column marching toward Weldon.

Gov. Smith, in his message to the Legislature now in session, recommends the employment of negro troops, even if it results in their emancipation. He also suggests an act, putting into the army civil officers of the State under forty-five years of age. At the same time he is exempting officers (State) *under forty-five,* and there is no compulsion on him.

A dispatch from Gen. Lee last night states that from the great number of wagons taken by the enemy on the Weldon Road, the movement is formidable, and indicates a purpose of prolonged operations.

At night—and snowing—a terrible night for the poor soldiers in the field!

DECEMBER 10TH.—Snowed two inches last night. Cloudy and damp this morning.

Guns were heard down the river last night at a late hour. Perhaps it was nothing more than shelling the enemy's canal.

We have nothing yet authentic from Georgia; but many rumors of much fighting.

It is said Gen. Hampton has got in front of the enemy's column at the Weldon Railroad, and is driving them back. Gen. Hill, it is presumed, is *this* side of them.

It is also reported that Gen. Longstreet is now (12 M.) attacking the enemy on *this* side of the river, and driving them. Distant guns can be heard southeast of us, and it may be true.

Major Cummings, Confederate States, Georgia, dispatches that the railroad between Atlanta and Chattanooga should be repaired immediately, to bring off supplies from Middle Tennessee. Gen. Bragg concurs.

The following was received from Gen. Bragg to-day, 11 A.M.:

"AUGUSTA, December 10th, 1864.—The following dispatch is just received from Gen. Wheeler, twenty-seven miles from Savannah, 10 P.M., 8th December. Enemy are still moving toward Savannah, obstructing the road in the rear, and resisting warmly this morning. I cannot learn that any have crossed the Savannah River. I hear artillery firing, far in my front; do not know what it means: 14th corps and Kilpatrick's cavalry on the river road; 15th on middle ground road; and 17th, and probably 20th, on Central Railroad.

"I think the force on the right bank of Ogeechee must be small."

DECEMBER 11TH, SUNDAY.—Cloudy and melting—snow vanishing rapidly. The thousand and one rumors of great achievements of Gen. Longstreet on the north side of the river seem to have been premature. Nothing official of any advantage gained over the enemy near the city has been received so far as I can learn. Gen. Lee, no doubt, directed Longstreet to make demonstrations on the enemy's lines near the city, to ascertain their strength, and to prevent more reinforcements being sent on the south side, where the struggle will occur, if it has not already occurred.

There is no doubt that the enemy's column sent toward Weldon has been checked, and great things are reported of Gen. Hampton's cavalry.

A battle must certainly occur near Savannah, Ga. Sherman *must* assail our lines, or perish between two fires.

President Lincoln's message to the Congress of the United States, republished in our papers, produces no marked effect. His adherence to a purpose of emancipation of the slaves, and his employment of them in his armies, will suffice for an indefinite prolongation of the war, and perhaps result in the employment of hundreds of thousands of slaves in our armies. The intimation, however, that all applications for "pardon," etc. have been and are still favorably entertained, will certainly cause many of our croakers who fall into the lines of the United States forces to submit. Others, though so disposed, have not an opportunity to signify their submission. But everything depends upon events in the field.

DECEMBER 12TH.—Clear and cold. Ice half an inch thick.

Gen. Longstreet is again in the old lines on this side of the river. The reconnoissance, however, is said to have been successful. Only a few were killed and wounded on either side.

And Grant's column was turned back from Meherrin bridge. Results of the movement unimportant, and the supposition is that both armies will now go into winter quarters, after a taste of this rigorous weather.

It is rumored and believed (though I have seen no dispatch to that effect) that Sherman has beaten and out-manœuvred our generals, and got into communication with the Federal fleet.

I read President Lincoln's message carefully last night. By its commissions and omissions on Mexican affairs, I think he means to menace Louis Napoleon, who may *speak out* January 1st, 1865. Lincoln says:

"Mexico continues to be a theater of civil war. While our political relations with that country have undergone no change, we have at the same time strictly maintained neutrality between the belligerents."

And his reference to England is so equivocal, and his grouping of the Central and South American *Republics* so prominent, and the boastful allusion to the "inexhaustible" resources of the United States, may be considered as a premeditated threat to Great Britain.

A "confidential" letter came in to-day from Mr. Benjamin to the Secretary of War.

Dr. Powell has sent us a dozen ruta baga turnips, and a couple of quarts of excellent persimmons, which the family enjoys most thankfully.

Dispatches from Lee:

"HEADQUARTERS ARMY NORTHERN VIRGINIA,
"December 10th, 1864.

"HON. JAMES A. SEDDON, SECRETARY OF WAR.

"Gen. Hampton, after driving the enemy's cavalry upon his infantry, on the afternoon of the 8th, recrossed the Nottoway and reached Bellfield at daylight yesterday.

"In the afternoon the enemy attacked the position, but were successfully resisted. This morning the enemy is reported retiring and Hampton following.

"The bridge over the Meherrin was saved. Our loss, as far as known, was small. The garrison, under Garnett, and the reserves, behaved well. R. E. LEE."

"HEADQUARTERS ARMY NORTHERN VIRGINIA,
"December 10th, 1864.

"HON. JAMES A. SEDDON, SECRETARY OF WAR.

"About noon yesterday the first division of the Second Corps of the enemy, supporting their cavalry, forced back our cavalry pickets on the Vaughan Road, south of the Appomattox, and advanced toward Dinwiddie Court House.

"To-day our cavalry, reinforced by infantry, drove them back across Hatcher's Run, capturing a few prisoners and re-establishing our lines. R. E. LEE."

DECEMBER 13TH.—Cloudy and cold, but wind southeast.

The sullen sound of cannon heard this morning as usual down the river. I hear of no active operations there, although the ground is sufficiently frozen to bear horses and artillery.

Rumors of successes on the part of Sherman near Savannah are still in circulation.

The rich men are generally indignant at the President and Gov. Smith for proposing to bring a portion of the negroes into the army. They have not yet awakened to a consciousness that there is danger of losing *all*, and of their being made to fight against us. They do not even remove them beyond the reach of the enemy, and hundreds are daily lost, but still they slumber on. They abuse the government for its impressments, and yet repose in fancied security, holding the President responsible for the defense of the country, without sufficient men and adequate means.

The following dispatch from Gen. Bragg was received to-day at 10 P.M.:

"AUGUSTA, Dec. 12th.

"The telegraph having been cut, we get nothing from Savannah. A dispatch from Wheeler gives a copy of enemy's order for the line of investment around Savannah. It is about eight miles from the city, and was to have been reached on the 9th.

"B. BRAGG."

I have at length succeeded in getting a suit of clothes; it was made at the government shop for $50, the trimmings having been found (in the house) by my wife. The suit, if bought of a merchant and made by the city tailors, would cost some $1000. A Yankee prisoner (deserter) made the coat at a low price. The government means to employ them, if they desire it, in this manner. I am very thankful for my good fortune.

DECEMBER 14TH.—Cloudy, and thawing rapidly. All quiet below.

The bill to employ 40,000 negroes, as recommended by the President, for army purposes, though not *avowedly* to fight, has passed one House of Congress. So the President is *master* yet. There ought to be 100,000 now in the field.

An effort will be made by the government to put into the field the able-bodied staff and other officers on duty in the bureaus here. It will fail, probably, since all efforts have failed to put in their able-bodied clerks. If Bragg were here, and allowed his way, he would move them to the front.

The following dispatch was received from Gen. Bragg to-day:

"AUGUSTA, GA., Dec. 13th, 1864.—I go to Charleston to-morrow to see Gen. Beauregard, at his request. He has assigned me to duty.—B. B."

I got to-day from Major Cross, A. Q. M. Gen., an order to buy a pair of government shoes (British) for $10. They are most excellent in quality, heavy, with iron heels, etc., and would cost, if made here, $150. This good fortune is worthy of being thankful for.

The military officers in the bureaus, responsive to a resolution of the House of Representatives, are reporting their ages, and most of them admit they are able-bodied and fit for service in the field. They have no fear of being transferred to the front, supposing themselves indispensable as bureau officers.

DECEMBER 15TH.—Cloudy and cool.

A dispatch from the West states that the enemy have made a heavy raid from Bean's Station, Ky., cutting the railroad between Abingdon and Bristol, destroying government stores, engines, etc. Breckinridge and Vaughan, I suppose, have been ordered away. Dr. Morris, Telegraph Superintendent, wants to know of the Secretary if this news shall be allowed to go to the press.

The President is ill, some say very ill, but I saw indorsements with his own hand on the 13th (day before yesterday).

Our affairs seem in a bad train. But many have unlimited confidence in Gen. Beauregard, who commands in South Carolina and Georgia, and all repose implicit trust in Lee.

A writer in the *Sentinel* suggests that if we should be hard pressed, the States ought to repeal the old Declaration of Independence, and voluntarily revert to their original proprietors— England, France, and Spain, and by them be protected from the North, etc. Ill-timed and injurious publication!

A letter from G. N. Sanders, Montreal, Canada E., asks copies of orders (to be certified by Secretary of War) commanding the raid into Vermont, the burning, pillaging, etc., *to save Lieut. Young's life.* I doubt if such written orders are in existence—but no matter.

It is said the enemy have captured Fort McAlister, Savannah Harbor.

Mr. Hunter is very solicitous about the President's health—said to be an affection of the head; but the Vice-President has taken his seat in the Senate.

It was rumored yesterday that the President would surely die,— an idle rumor, perhaps. I hope it is not a disease of the brain, and incurable.

DECEMBER 16TH.—Clear and pleasant; subsequently cloudy and chilly.

All quiet below, save the occasional booming of our guns from the iron-clads.

The capture of Fort McAlister, Savannah, has caused a painful sensation. It is believed we have as many men on the Georgia coast as the enemy; but they are not the men of *property*—men of 1861-62; and those *without* property (many of them) are reluctant to fight for the benefit of the wealthy class, remaining at home.

The following dispatch from Gen. Bragg was received this morning:

"CHARLESTON, December 15th, 1864.—My services not being longer needed in this department, I shall leave this evening for Wilmington, and resume my command.

"Sherman has opened communication with his new base, by the Ogeechee. The means to meet him do not exceed one-half the estimate in yours of the 7th instant. BRAXTON BRAGG."

So ends Gen. Bragg's campaign against Sherman!

I have not heard about the President's health to-day. But no papers have come in from his office.

Lieut.-Col. Ruffin, Commissary Department, certifies (or Col. Northrop for him) that he is "not fit for duty in the field."

DECEMBER 17TH.—Warm and cloudy.

Quiet below.

The President was reported better, yesterday, to my wife, who called.

It is said Gen. Cooper, R. Ould, etc. etc. have never taken their compensation in Confederate States Treasury notes, hoping at a future day (which may not come) to draw specie or its equivalent!

It was reported on the streets, to-day, that the President was dead. He is much better; and will probably be at his office to-day.

The following telegram was sent over by the President this morning:

"SAVANNAH, GA., December 16th, 1864.—Sherman has secured a water base, and Foster, who is already nearly on my communications, can be safely and expeditiously reinforced. Unless assured that force sufficient to keep open my communications can be sent me, I shall be compelled to evacuate Savannah.—W. J. HARDEE, Lieut.-Gen."

Alas for President Davis's government! It is now in a painful strait. If reinforcements be sent from here, both Savannah and

Richmond may fall. Gen. Bragg will be crucified by the enemies of the President, for staying at Augusta while Sherman made his triumphant march through Georgia; and the President's party will make Beauregard the scape-goat, for staying at Charleston—for sending Hood North—which I am inclined to think he did not do, but the government itself.

Capt. Weiniger (government clothing warehouse) employs about 4000 females on soldiers' clothes.

Some people still believe the President is dead, and that it is attempted to conceal his death by saying he is better, etc. I saw his indorsements on papers, to-day, dated the 15th, day before yesterday, and it was a bold hand. I am inclined almost to believe he has not been sick at all! His death would excite sympathy: and now his enemies are assailing him bitterly, attributing all our misfortunes to his incompetence, etc. etc.

SUNDAY, DECEMBER 18TH.—Raining.

The old dull sound of bombs down the river. Nothing further from Savannah. It is now believed that the raiders in Western Virginia did not attack Saltville, and that the works are safe. For two days the speculators have been buying salt, and have put up the price to $1.50 per pound. I hope they will be losers. The State distributes salt to-morrow : ten pounds to each member of a family, at 20 cents per pound.

The President's malady is said to be neuralgia in the head—an evanescent affliction, and by no means considered dangerous. At least such is the experience in my family.

It was amusing, however, to observe the change of manner of the Secretaries and of heads of bureaus toward Vice-President Stephens, when it was feared the President was in *extremis*. Mr. Hunter, fat as he is, flew about right briskly.

If Savannah falls, our currency will experience another depreciation, and the croaking reconstructionists will be bolder.

The members of the Virginia Assembly propose paying themselves $50 per day!

Congress has not yet passed the act increasing the compensation of members.

DECEMBER 19TH.—The darkest and most dismal day that ever dawned upon the earth, except one. There was no light when the usual hour came round, and later the sun refused to shine. There was fog, and afterward rain.

Northern papers say Hood has been utterly routed, losing all his guns!

A letter from Mr. ——— to ———, dated Richmond, December 17th, 1864, says: "I have the honor to report my success as most remarkable and satisfactory. I have ascertained the *whole Yankee mail line, from the gun-boats to your city, with all the agents* save one. You will be *surprised* when informed, from the lowest to the highest class. The agent in your city, and most likely in your department, has yet to be discovered. This is as certain as what we have learned (his arrest, I mean), for the party in whose hands the mail is put coming from your city is known to us; and we have only to learn who gives him the mail, which can be done upon arrest, if *not sooner*, to know everything. What shall be done with the parties (spies, of course) when we are ready to act? If you ever intimate that *trials are tedious*, etc., the enemy seize citizens from some neighborhood as hostages, when their emissaries are disturbed. *I will dispatch*, if it be authorized, and that will end the matter. The lady I spoke to you of is the fountain-head. What to do with females troubles me, for I dislike to be identified with their arrest.

"I request that a good boat, with three torpedoes, and a man who understands working them, be sent to Milford to report to me at Edge Hill. Let the man be *mum* on all questions. I would meet him at Milford, if I knew the day (distance is twenty-five miles), with a wagon, to take him, torpedoes, and boat to the point required. I must be sure of the day.

"Have the following advertisement published in Monday's papers:

"'YANKEES ESCAPED! $1000 REWARD!—A Yankee officer and three privates escaped from prison on Thursday night, with important matter upon their persons. The above reward will be given for their detection.'

"Let me hear from you through Cawood's Line, upon receipt of this. Respectfully, etc. ———."

We have the spectacle now of three full generals—Johnston, Beauregard, and Bragg—without armies to command; and the armies in the field apparently melting away under the lead of subordinate, if not incompetent leaders. So much for the administration of the Adjutant-General's office.

Governor Smith is still exempting deputy sheriffs, constables, etc.—all able-bodied.

It is rumored on the street that we intend evacuating Savannah. How did that get out—if, indeed, such is the determination? There *are* traitors in high places—or near them.

It is also rumored that the Danville Railroad has been cut. I don't believe it—yet.

There is deep vexation in the city—a general apprehension that our affairs are rapidly approaching a crisis such as has not been experienced before. There is also much denunciation of the President for the removal of Gen. Johnston from the command of the Army of Tennessee.

Hon. Mr. Foote declared, Saturday, that he would resign his seat if the bill to suspend the writ of *habeas corpus*, now pending, became a law. There is much consternation—but it is of a sullen character, without excitement.

The United States Congress has ordered that notice be given Great Britain of an intention on the part of the Federal Government to increase the naval force on the lakes; also a proposition has been introduced to terminate the Reciprocity Treaty. And Gen. Dix orders his military subordinates to pursue any rebel raiders even *into* Canada and bring them over. So, light may come from *that* quarter. A war with England would be our peace.

At 2 P.M. it was rumored that Charleston is taken and Beauregard a prisoner. Also that Gen. Jos. E. Johnston (in the city) says Richmond will be evacuated in ten days. I do not learn what gold sells at to-day! I suspect some *coup d'état* is meditated.

DECEMBER 20TH.—A brighter morning, cool and clear.

The *President* was at work yesterday. He and the Secretary and Gen. Cooper put their heads together to make up a *regiment* for Col. Miller in Mississippi, and designate the two field officers to be under him—from two battalions and two unattached companies.

If the Northern (purporting to be official) accounts be true, Gen. Hood has sustained an irretrievable disaster, which may involve the loss of Tennessee, Georgia, etc.

Hon. Mr. Foote declared last night his purpose to leave the city in a few days, never to resume his seat in Congress, if martial law should be allowed. He said he had information that when

Charleston *fell*, South Carolina would conclude a treaty of peace (submission?) with the United States; and that North Carolina was prepared to follow the example! I have observed that these two States do not often incline to go together.

The *great* disaster would be the loss of Richmond and retreat of Lee's army southward. This would probably be followed by the downfall of slavery in Virginia.

The Secretary of War has sent an agent to the Governor of North Carolina, to ask for special aid in supplying Lee's army with meat—which is deficient here—or else it cannot be maintained in the field in Virginia! Very bad, and perhaps worse coming.

There is a rumor that Gen. Breckinridge has beaten Gen. Burbridge in Tennessee or Western Virginia.

Gen. R. E. Lee is in town, looking robust, though weather-worn. He complains that the department is depleting his army by details, often for private and speculative purposes, to the benefit of private individuals—speculators.

I drew my (State) salt to-day, 70 pounds, for 7 in family—20 cents per pound. It retails at a $1 per pound!

Mr. Secretary —— has sent (per Lieut.-Col. Bayne) some gold to Wilmington, to buy (in Nassau) loaf sugar for his family, to be brought in government steamers.

My son Thomas could get no beef ration to-day—too scarce.

DECEMBER 21ST.—Raining; rained all night.

The following dispatch was received this morning:

"WILMINGTON, December 20th, 1864, 10 A.M.—The head of the enemy's fleet arrived off this port during last night. Over thirty steamers are now assembling, and more are following.—BRAXTON BRAGG."

It may be hoped that Gen. Bragg will do something more than chronicle the successes of the enemy this time. He is nearer to him than when he remained at Augusta; and yet the press could be made reticent on arrivals, etc.

Lieut.-Col. Sims, Assistant Quartermaster General, has contracted with the *Southern Express Company* to transport all the funds of the Quartermaster's Department—hundreds of millions!

Mr. Hunter was with the Secretary this morning, when I laid before the latter Bragg's dispatch. I doubt not it failed to contribute to a mollification of their painful forebodings.

By Northern papers I see President Lincoln disapproves Gen. Dix's order to troops to cross the Canada line in pursuit of raiders.

Gold is $45 for one to-day.

The army has no meat this day, the commissaries, etc. have it all, and are speculating with it—it is said. So many high officials are *interested*, there is no remedy. We are at the mercy of the quartermasters, commissaries, railroad companies, and the *Southern* Express Company. The President and Secretary either cannot or will not break our shackles.

An official account states the number of houses burnt by the enemy in Atlanta to be 5000!

There is a rumor of another and a formidable raid on Gordonsville. The railroad is now exclusively occupied with the transportation of troops—perhaps for Wilmington. The raid may be a ruse to prevent reinforcements being sent thither.

The Andersonville Report belongs to the Adjutant-General's Office, and therefore has not come back to me.

December 22d.—Clear and cold. We have nothing from below. From Wilmington, we learn there is much commotion to resist the armada launched against that port. Gen. Lee is sending troops *via* the Danville Road in that direction.

The wire has been cut between this and Gordonsville, by the scouts of the raiders launched in that direction. We breakfast, dine, and sup on horrors now, and digest them all quite sullenly.

I am invited to a turkey dinner to-day (at Mr. Waterhouse's), and have some hesitation in accepting it at a time like this. Ought I to go? He is a skilled artisan and has made money, and no doubt the turkey is destined to be eaten by somebody.

At an auction this morning, a Jew bid off an old set of tablespoons, weighing twelve ounces and much worn, at $575. He will next *buy* his way out of the Confederacy. Mr. Benjamin and Judge Campbell have much to answer for in allowing such men to deplete the South of its specie, plate, etc. There were some commissaries and quartermasters present, who are supposed to have stolen much from the government, and desire to exchange the currency they have ruined for imperishable wealth. They, too, will run away the first opportunity.

The sun shines brightly this beautiful cold day; but all is dark in Congress. The Tennessee members say Hood's army is destroyed, that he will not get 1000 men out of the State, for the Tennesseeans, Kentuckians, etc. refuse to retire farther south, but straggle and scatter to their homes, where they will remain.

I am told we have but a thin curtain of pickets on the north side of the James River, between us and 15,000 negro troops.

The President is at work at his residence, not having yet come down to his office; and I learn it is difficult to get his attention to any business just now but *appointments;* had to get him to sign a bill passed by Congress to pay the civil officers of the government. No doubt he is anxious and very unhappy.

Hon. Mr. Foote's wife has just got a passport to return home to Nashville, Tennessee!

DECEMBER 23D —Bright and very cold.

A storm has driven off a portion of the enemy's fleet before Wilmington.

The raid toward Gordonsville and Charlottesville is not progressing rapidly. We shall have a force to meet it.

Besides the demonstration against Savannah (from which place we have no recent tidings), it appears that an attempt on Mobile is in progress. Too many attempts—some of them must fail, I hope.

From the last accounts, I doubted whether Hood's army has been so badly shattered as was apprehended yesterday.

Gen. Price (trans-Mississippi) has brought out a large number of recruits from Missouri.

I dined out yesterday, and sumptuously; the first time for two years.

Congress has done but little, so far. They are at work on the Currency bill!

Mr. Enders, broker, and exempted as one of the Ambulance Committee, I am informed paid some $8000 yesterday to Mitchell & Tyler for a few articles of jewelry for his daughter. And R. Hill, who has a provision shop near the President's office, I understand expended some $30,000 on the wedding of his daughter. He was poor, I believe, before the war.

I got an order from Lieut. Parker, Confederate States Navy, for a load of coal to-day. Good! I hope it will be received before the last on hand is gone.

The enemy's raiders camped within seven miles of Gordonsville, last night; and it will be ten o'clock to-day before our reinforcements can reach there. I hope our stores (commissary) will not be lost—as usual.

Mr. S. Norris, Signal Bureau, has just (1 P.M.) sent the following: "I am just informed that Mr. Smithers, telegraph operator at Gordonsville, is again in his office. He says fighting is going oh in sight—that troops from Richmond have arrived, and arriving —and it is expected that Gen. Lomax will be able to drive the enemy back."

Just before 3 P.M. to-day a dispatch came from Mr. Smithers, telegraph operator at Gordonsville, dated 1 o'clock, saying the enemy have been repulsed and severely punished, and are retreating the way they came, toward Sperryville. He adds that many of the enemy's dead now lie in sight of the town. So much for this gleam of good fortune, for I believe the military authorities here were meditating an evacuation of the city.

Gen. Custis Lee was at the department to-day, after the clerks detailed from his command. All, all are to be dragged out in this bitter cold weather for defense, except the speculators, the extortioners, the land and slave owners, who really have something tangible to defend, and these have exemptions or "soft places."

December 24th.—Christmas eve! Clear and cold.

A dispatch from Hon. J. L. Orr and H. V. Johnson (on their way home) informs the Secretary that from the delay in the transportation of troops over the Piedmont Railroad, there must be either criminal neglect or treachery concerned in it.

Again it is rumored that Savannah has been evacuated. There is something in the air that causes agitation in official circles. Mr. Secretary Seddon's room was locked nearly all day yesterday.

If troops cannot be transported expeditiously over the Piedmont Road, fears may be entertained for Wilmington, when, the gale subsiding, the enemy's fleet has reappeared.

There is a rumor on the street that the government is to be removed to Lynchburg.

Gen. Lee has induced the President and Secretary of War to call for the clerks (detailed ones) to repair to the trenches again— this weather. The emergency must be great, as these soldiers get, as clerks, $4000 per annum, and rations, etc.

A dispatch from Gen. Bragg.

"WILMINGTON, N. C., December 23d, 1864.—The fleet, which drew off in the rough weather, is again assembled; seventy vessels now in sight on the coast. The advance of the troops (C. S.) only reached here to-night.—B. B."

The clerks are drawing lots; one-half being ordered to the trenches. Of two drawn in this bureau (out of five) one is peremptorily ordered by the Secretary to remain, being sickly, and the other has an order to go before a medical board "to determine whether he is fit for service in the trenches for a few days." Great commotion naturally prevails in the departments, and it is whispered that Gen. Lee was governed in the matter by the family of the President, fearing a Christmas visit from the negro troops on this side the river.

The following note was received to-day from the Vice-President:

"RICHMOND, VA , December 23d, 1864.—Hon. Jas. A. Seddon, Secretary of War: Will you please send me, through the post-office, a passport to leave the city? I wish to depart in a few days. Yours respectfully,
"ALEX. H. STEPHENS."

The President is hard at work making majors, etc.

SUNDAY, DECEMBER 25TH. CHRISTMAS!—Clear and pleasant—white frost.

All quiet below. But it is believed on the street that Savannah has been evacuated, some days ago. I have not yet seen any official admission of the fact.

We have quite a merry Christmas in the family; and a compact that no unpleasant word shall be uttered, and no *scramble* for anything. The family were baking cakes and pies until late last night, and to-day we shall have *full* rations. I have found enough celery in the little garden for dinner.

Last night and this morning the boys have been firing Christmas guns incessantly—no doubt pilfering from their fathers' cartridge-boxes. There is much jollity and some drunkenness in the streets, notwithstanding the enemy's pickets are within an hour's march of the city.

A large number of the croaking inhabitants censure the President for our many misfortunes, and openly declare in favor of Lee as Dictator. Another month, and he may be unfortunate or unpopular. His son, Gen. Custis Lee, has mortally offended the clerks by putting them in the trenches yesterday, and some of them may desert.

Many members of Congress have gone home. But it is still said they invested the President with extraordinary powers, in secret session. I am not quite sure this is so.

I append the following dispatches:

"HEADQUARTERS ARMY OF NORTHERN VIRGINIA,
"December 23d, 1864.

"HON. JAMES A. SEDDON, SECRETARY OF WAR.

"On the 20th, Gen. Early reported one division of the enemy's cavalry, under Gen. Custer, coming up the valley, and two divisions, under Gen. Torbert, moving through Chester Gap, with four pieces of artillery and thirty wagons.

"On the 22d, Rosser attacked Custer's division, nine miles from Harrisonburg, and drove it back, capturing forty prisoners.

"This morning, Torbert attacked Lomax near Gordonsville, and was repulsed and severely punished. He is retreating, and Lomax preparing to follow. "R. E. LEE."

"DUBLIN, December 20th, 1864.

"A dispatch from Gen. Breckinridge to-day, dated at Mount Airy, sixteen miles west of Wytheville, says he had fought the enemy for two days, successfully, near Marion. The enemy had retired from his front; but whether they were retreating to East Tennessee or not, he had not ascertained."

"CHARLESTON, December 22d, 1864.

"To GEN. S. COOPER.

"On the 16th inst., the enemy, 800 strong, occupied Pollard. After burning the government and railroad buildings, they retired in the direction they came.

"They were pursued thirty miles, losing a portion of their transportation, baggage, and supplies, and leaving many dead negro troops on the road.

"Our force, commanded by Gen. Liddell, acted with spirit and gallantry. G. T. BEAUREGARD, *General.*"

"OUR INDIAN TROOPS.—Gen. Stand Watie, commanding our Indian troops in the trans-Mississippi Department, has fully clothed and armed all his men, and is in the vicinity of Fort Smith, attacking and destroying Yankee wagon trains."

DECEMBER 26TH —Raining—rained all night. The dark and dismal weather, together with our sad reverses, have made the countenances of croakers in the streets and in the offices more gloomy and somber than ever, foreboding evil in the future. No one doubts the evacuation of Savannah, and I suppose it must be so. Hardee had but 8000 reliable men. The Georgians in Lee's army are more or less demoralized, and a reward of a sixty days' furlough is given for shooting any deserter from our ranks.

An old black chest, containing mostly scraps and odds and ends of housekeeping, yet brought on by my family from Burlington, has remained four years unopened, the key being lost. We have felt an irrepressible anxiety to see its contents, for even rubbish is now valuable. I got a locksmith to send a man to pick the lock, last week, but he failed to find the house, and subsequently was sent to the trenches. I borrowed twenty-five keys, and none of them would fit. I got wire, and tried to pick the lock, but failed. Yesterday, however, when all were at church, I made another effort, prizing at the same time with the poker, when the screws of the hasp came out and the top flew up, revealing only "odds and ends" so far as I could see. I closed it, replaced the striped cover, and put the cage with the parrot on it, where it usually remains. The day, and the expressed objection of my wife to have the lock broken or injured, have, until to-day, restrained me from revealing to the family what I had done. But now I shall assemble them, and by a sort of Christmas story, endeavor to mollify my wife's anticipated displeasure. The examination of the contents will be a delightful diversion for the children, old and young.

My impromptu Christmas tale of the old Black Chest interested the family, and my wife was not angry. Immediately after its conclusion, the old chest was surrounded and opened, and among an infinite variety of rubbish were some articles of value, viz., of chemises (greatly needed), several pairs of stockings, 1 Marseilles petticoat, lace collars, several pretty baskets, 4 pair ladies' slippers (nearly new), and several books—one from my library, an octavo volume on Midwifery, 500 pages, placed there to prevent the children from seeing the illustrations, given me by the publisher for a notice in my paper, *The Madisonian*, more than twenty years ago. There were also many toys and keepsakes presented Mrs. J. when she was an infant, forty years ago, and many given our children when they were infants, besides various articles of infants' clothing, etc. etc., both of intrinsic value, and prized as reminiscences. The available articles, though once considered rubbish, would sell, and could not be bought here for less than $500.

This examination occupied the family the remainder of the day and night—all content with this Christmas diversion—and oblivious of the calamities which have befallen the country. It was a providential distraction.

DECEMBER 27TH.—A night of rain—morning of fog and gloom. At last we have an account of the evacuation of Savannah. Also of the beginning of the assault on Fort Fisher and Caswell below Wilmington, with painful apprehensions of the result; for the enemy have landed troops above the former fort, and found no adequate force to meet them, thanks to the *policy* of the government in allowing the *property holders* to escape the toils and dangers of the field, while the poor, who have nothing tangible to fight for, are thrust to the front, where many desert. Our condition is also largely attributable to the management of the Bureau of Conscription—really the Bureau of *Exemption*.

I saw to-day a letter from Gen. Beauregard to Gen. Cooper, wherein it was indicated that Gen. Hood's plan of penetrating Tennessee was adopted before he (Gen. B.) was ordered to that section.

The enemy *did* occupy Saltville last week, and damaged the works. No doubt salt will "go up" now. The enemy, however, have retired from the place, and the works can be repaired. Luckily I drew 70 pounds last week, and have six months' supply. I have two months' supply of coal and wood—long enough, perhaps, for our residence in Richmond, unless the property owners be required to defend their property. I almost despair of a change of policy.

It is reported that Sherman is marching south of Savannah, on some new enterprise; probably a detachment merely to destroy the railroad.

An expedition is attacking, or about to attack, Mobile.

All our possessions on the coast seem to be the special objects of attack this winter. If Wilmington falls, "Richmond next," is the prevalent supposition.

The brokers are offering $50 Confederate States notes for $1 of gold.

Men are silent, and some dejected. It is unquestionably the darkest period we have yet experienced. Intervention on the part of European powers is the only hope of many. Failing that, no doubt a negro army will be organized—and it might be too late!

And yet, with such a preponderance of numbers and material against us, the wonder is that we have not lost all the sea-board before this. I long since supposed the country would be penetrated and overrun in most of its ports, during the second or third year of the war. If the government would foster a spirit of patriotism, the country would always rise again, after these invasions, like the water of the sea plowed by ships of war. But the government must not crush the spirit of the people relied upon for defense, and the rich must fight side by side with the poor, or the poor will abandon the rich, and that will be an abandonment of the cause.

It is said Gen. Lee is to be invested with dictatorial powers, so far as our armies are concerned. This will inspire new confidence. He is represented as being in favor of employing negro troops.

A dispatch from Lieut.-Gen. Hardee (to the President), December 24th, 1864, at Charleston, S. C., says he may have to take the field any moment (against Sherman), and asks a chief quartermaster and chief commissary. The President invokes the special scrupulosity of the Secretary in the names of these staff officers.

DECEMBER 28TH.—Rained all night; warm.

A large stable burned down within sixty yards of our dwelling, last night, and not one of the family heard the uproar attending it.

Gen. Bragg telegraphs the President that the enemy failed to reduce Fort Fisher, and that the troops landed above the fort have re-embarked. But he says the enemy's designs are not yet developed; and he is such an unlucky general.

We found a caricature in the old black chest, of 1844, in which I am engaged in fight with the elder Blair. Calhoun, Buchanan, etc. are in the picture.

It is still believed that Gen. Lee is to be generalissimo, and most people rejoice at it. It is said the President and Gen. Jos. E. Johnston have become friends again.

DECEMBER 29TH.—Rained all night; spitting snow this morning. Although Gen. Bragg announces that the enemy's fleet has disappeared off Wilmington, still the despondency which has seized the croakers remains. It has probably sailed against Charleston, to co-operate with Sherman. Sherman says officially that he got, with Savannah, about 1000 prisoners, 150 heavy guns, nearly 200 cars and several locomotives, 35,000 bales of cotton, etc. etc. And Gen. Foster says the inhabitants (20,000) were "quiet, and well disposed." Most people believe Charleston will fall next, to be followed by a sweep of the entire sea-board; and grave men fear that the impetus thus given the invader cannot be checked or resisted.

The great want is *fighting men*, and they are mostly exempted or detailed under that portion of the "War Department" which is quietly worked by Judge Campbell, who is, of course, governed by his own great legal judgment. Well, the President has been informed of this, and yet waits for Mr. Secretary Seddon to suggest a remedy. I have often thought, and still think, that either the Bureau of Conscription must be abolished or the government must fail. The best generals will not avail without sufficient men to fight.

Gen. Beauregard telegraphs from Charleston, December 26th, that there is a conflict of authority at Mobile as to which branch of the service, navy or army, shall command the torpedo boat. The two Secretaries are referring it to commanders, and I fear that, by the time the question is settled, some calamity will befall the boat, and the city, and the country.

Grant is said to be moving troops to the north side of the river again, fearing an attack from us, or intending one himself.

DECEMBER 30TH.—A clear night and frosty morning.

We have no news except that gleaned from Northern papers. Gen. Hood is unable to cross the Tennessee River (now swollen), and would soon be attacked again by superior numbers.

Congress was in secret session yesterday, probably perfecting the bill for the suspension of the privilege of *habeas corpus*.

Gen. Bragg is credited with the repulse of the enemy at Wilmington.

During the late raid a close-fisted farmer lost heavily: several hundred barrels of flour and corn, one hundred barrels of apples, a large amount of bacon and sorghum, which he was hoarding, and thus contributing to produce famine in the midst of plenty. His neighbors (those few not following his example) express no sympathy for him. The enemy did not burn Liberty Mills—once in their possession, in which is stored a large amount of grain—for some unexplained reason.

The enemy's papers show that they have regular and expeditious intercourse with parties here, and are kept correctly advised of everything that transpires. This is a continuance of Mr. Benjamin's policy by Mr. Seddon. It may be lucrative to those immediately interested; but if not abated, will be the death of the Confederate States Government—as I have told them all repeatedly.

And the "Bureau of Conscription" still exists, and seems destined to "be in at the death."

I paid Lieut. Parker just $30.75 for a load of coal; selling at $75.

I saw selling at auction, to-day, second-hand shirts at $40 each, and blankets at $75. A bedstead, such as I have bought for $10, brought $700. But $50 in Confederate States paper are really worth only $1 in specie.

Jos. R. Anderson & Co. writes that unless their hands are sent in from the trenches, they cannot fill orders for ordnance stores; and Gen. Gorgas (he has been promoted) approves it, saying it is known that a number of these hands intend to desert the first opportunity.

The last call for the clerks to return to the trenches was responded to by not a man of Capt. Manico's company, War Department proper.

DECEMBER 31ST.—The last day of the year. Snowing and wet.

Gen. H. Cobb writes that the existing Conscription Bureau is a failure so far as Georgia, Alabama, etc. are concerned, and can never put the men in the field.

Wm. Johnston, president of the Charlotte (N. C.) and South Carolina Railroad, suggests the construction, immediately, of a railroad from Columbia, S. C., to Augusta, Ga., which might be easily accomplished by April or May. It would take that length of time for the government to "consider of it." It will lose two railroads before it will order the building of one.

There is supposed to be a conspiracy on foot to transfer some of the powers of the Executive to Gen. Lee. It can only be done by revolution, and the overthrow of the Constitution. Nevertheless, it is believed many executive officers, some high in position, favor the scheme.

To-morrow Gen. Lee's army is to be feasted with turkeys, etc. contributed by the country, if the enemy will permit them to dine without molestation. The enemy are kept fully informed of everything transpiring here, thanks to the vigilance of the Provost Marshal, detectives, etc. etc.

Gen. Cobb writes that he is arresting the men who remained in Atlanta during its occupation by Sherman, and subjecting themselves to suspicion, etc. Better march the men we have against Sherman now, who is still in Georgia!

Gen. Lee writes that Grant is concentrating (probably for an attack on Richmond), bringing another corps from the Valley; and if the local troops are brought in, he does not know how to replace them. His army diminishes, rather than increases, under the manipulations of the Bureau of Conscription. It is a dark and dreary hour, when Lee is so despondent!

Senator Henry writes that any delay in impressing the railroad from Danville to Greensborough will be fatal.

CHAPTER XLVI.

Waning confidence in the President.—Blockade running.—From the South.—Beauregard on Sherman.—The expeditions against Wilmington.—Return of Mr. Pollard.—The Blairs in Richmond.—Arrest of Hon. H. S. Foote.—Fall of Fort Fisher.—Views of Gen. Cobb.—Dismal.—Casualties of the War.—Peace commissioners for Washington.

SUNDAY, JANUARY 1ST, 1865.—Snowed a few inches in depth during the night—clear and cool morning. The new year begins with the new rumor that Gen. Hood has turned upon Gen. Thomas and beaten him. This is believed by many. Hood's army was *not* destroyed, and he retreated from before Nashville with some 20,000 men. Doubtless he lost many cannon; but the

Federal accounts of his disaster were probably much exaggerated.

The cabinet still remains.

The President is considered really a man of ability, and eminently qualified to preside over the Confederate States, if independence were attained and we had peace. But he is probably not equal to the rôle he is now called upon to play. He has not the broad intellect requisite for the gigantic measures needed in such a crisis, nor the health and physique for the labors devolving on him. Besides he is too much of a politician still to discard his old prejudices, and persists in keeping aloof from him, and from commanding positions, all the great statesmen and patriots who contributed most in the work of preparing the minds of the people for resistance to Northern domination. And the consequence is that many of these influential men are laboring to break down his administration, or else preparing the people for a return to the old Union. The disaffection is intense and wide-spread among the politicians of 1860, and consternation and despair are expanding among the people. Nearly all desire to see Gen. Lee at the head of affairs; and the President is resolved to yield the position to no man during his term of service. Nor would Gen. Lee take it.

The proposition to organize an army of negroes gains friends; because the owners of the slaves are no longer willing to fight themselves, at least they are not as "eager for the fray" as they were in 1861; and the armies *must* be replenished, or else the slaves will certainly be lost.

Thus we begin the new year—Heaven only knows how we shall end it! I trust we may be in a better condition then. Of one thing I am certain, the PEOPLE are capable of achieving independence, if they only had capable men in all departments of the government.

The President was at St. Paul's to-day, with a knit woolen cap on his head. Dr. Minnegerode preached a sermon against the croakers. His son has been appointed a midshipman by the President.

JANUARY 2D.—Cold, and indications of snow.

Offered the owner of our servant $400 per annum. He wants $150 and clothing for her. Clothing would cost perhaps $1000. It remains in abeyance.

Saw Gen. Wise dancing attendance in the Secretary's room. He looks seasoned and well, and may be destined to play a leading part "in human affairs" yet, notwithstanding his hands have been so long bound by those who contrive "to get possession." It is this very thing of keeping our great men in the "background" which is often the cause of calamities, and if persisted in, may bring irretrievable ruin upon the cause.

The government has forbidden the transportation of freight, etc. (private) from Georgia to Virginia, and perhaps from the intermediate States.

On Saturday the government entered the market to sell gold, and brought down the price some 33 per cent. A spasmodic effort, the currency is gone beyond redemption.

It is said Gen. Hood has collected a large amount of supplies of meat, etc. He is in North Alabama, and probably Gen. Thomas will march toward Virginia.

The Secretary had his head between his knees before the fire when I first went in this morning. Affairs are gloomy enough—and the question is how Richmond and Virginia shall be saved. Gen. Lee is despondent.

From the Northern papers we learn that Gen. Butler's expedition against Wilmington, N. C., was a failure. Gen. Bragg is applauded here for this successful defense.

The salaries of the clergymen have been raised by their congregations to $10,000 and $12,000. I hear that Dr. Woodbridge received a Christmas gift from his people of upwards of $4000, besides seven barrels of flour, etc. *He owns his own house, his own servants*, stocks, etc. Most of these fortunate ministers are natives of the North, but true to the Southern cause, so far as we know. God knows I am glad to hear of any one, and especially a minister, being made comfortable.

JANUARY 3D.—Calm and quiet; indications of snow.

By a communication sent to Congress, by the President, it is ascertained that 500,000 pairs shoes, 8,000,000 pounds bacon, 2,000,000 pounds saltpeter, 50 cannon, etc. etc., have been imported since Octoberr 1st, 1864.

When the enemy's fleet threatened Wilmington, the brokers here (who have bribed the conscript officers) bought up all the coffee and sugar in the city. They raised the price of the former from $15 to $45 per pound, and the latter to $15, from $10. An application has been made to Mr. Secretary Seddon to order the impressment of it all, at schedule prices, which he will be sure not to do.

Congress paid their respects to the President yesterday, by waiting upon him in a body.

There is a rumor of some fighting (12 M.) below, but I have not learned on which side of the river. It arises from brisk cannonading, heard in the city, I suppose.

I bought an ax (of Starke) for $15, mine having been stolen. I was asked from $25 to $35 for no better. Mr. Starke has no garden seeds yet.

The following article in the *Dispatch* to-day, seemingly well authenticated, would seem to indicate that our armies are in no danger of immediately becoming destitute of supplies; but, alas! the publication itself may cause the immediate fall of Wilmington.

"BLOCKADE-RUNNING.—Notwithstanding the alleged ceaseless vigilance of the Yankee navy in watching blockade-runners on the Atlantic and Gulf Coast of the Confederate States, their close attention has amounted to comparatively little. Setting aside all that has been imported on State and individual account, the proceeds of the blockade have been very great. The restrictions imposed upon foreign commerce by the act of Congress of last session prohibiting, absolutely, during the pending war, the importation of any articles not necessary for the defense of the country—namely: wines, spirits, jewelry, cigars, and all the finer fabrics of cotton, flax, wool, or silk, as well as all other merchandise serving only for the indulgence of luxurious habits,—has not had the effect to reduce the number of vessels engaged in blockade-running; but, on the contrary, the number has steadily increased within the last year, and many are understood to be now on the way to engage in the business.

"The President, in a communication to Congress on the subject, says that the number of vessels arriving at two ports only from the 1st of November to the 6th of December was *forty-three*, and but a very small proportion of those outward bound were captured. Out of 11,796 bales of cotton shipped since the 1st of July last, but 1272 were lost—not quite 11 per cent.

"The special report of the Secretary of the Treasury in relation to the matter shows that there have been imported into the Confederacy at the ports of Wilmington and Charleston since October 26th, 1864, 8,632,000 pounds of meat, 1,507,000 pounds of lead, 1,933,000 pounds of saltpeter, 546,000 pairs of shoes, 316,000 pairs of blankets, 520,000 pounds of coffee, 69,000 rifles, 97 packages of revolvers, 2639 packages of medicine, 43 cannon, with a large quantity of other articles of which we need make no mention. Besides these, many valuable stores and supplies are brought, by way of the Northern lines, into Florida; by the port of Galveston and through Mexico, across the Rio Grande.

"The shipments of cotton made on government account since March 1st, 1864, amount to $5,296,000 in specie. Of this, cotton, to the value of $1,500,000, has been shipped since the 1st of July and up to the 1st of December.

"It is a matter of absolute impossibility for the Federals to stop our blockade-running at the port of Wilmington. If the wind blows off the coast, the blockading fleet is driven off. If the wind blows landward, they are compelled to haul off to a great distance to escape the terrible sea which dashes on a rocky coast without a harbor within three days' sail. The shoals on the North Carolina Coast are from five to twenty miles wide; and they are, moreover, composed of the most treacherous and bottomless quicksands. The whole coast is scarcely equaled in the world for danger and fearful appearance, particularly when a strong easterly wind meets the ebb tide.

"It is an easy matter for a good pilot to run a vessel directly out to sea or into port; but in the stormy months, from October to April, no blockading vessel can lie at anchor in safety off the Carolina Coast. Therefore supplies will be brought in despite the keenest vigilance."

JANUARY 4TH.—Bright, but several inches of snow fell last night.

The President wrote a long letter to the Secretary yesterday concerning the *assignment of conscripts in Western North Carolina*, at most only a few hundred, and the appointment of officers, etc. A small subject.

Congress has passed a resolution calling on the Secretary of War for information concerning certain youths, alleged to have received passports to Europe, etc. Also one relating to the Commissary-General's traffic in Eastern North Carolina, within the enemy's lines. Also one relating to instructions to Gen. Smith, trans-Mississippi Department, who assumes control of matters pertaining to the Treasury Department.

General J. S. Preston, Superintendent Bureau of Conscription, writes a long letter from South Carolina indorsing an act of the Legislature authorizing the impressment of one-fifth of the slaves between eighteen and fifty, for work on the fortifications within the State, but also providing for impressment of an additional number by the Confederate States Government. This, Gen. P. considers a treasonable move, indicating that South Carolina, North Carolina, Alabama, Mississippi, etc. have a purpose to disintegrate Confederate authority, and that they will not contribute another man, black or white, to the Confederate service, to be commanded by Confederate States authority. And he has several thrusts at Gen. Bragg and Gen. Kemper, and, indirectly, at the President, for interfering with *his* bureau. I see nothing in the act to warrant his interpretations, and I have no faith in his predictions.

W. F. D. Saussure and others, Columbia, S. C., petition the government to send a corps of Lee's army to save their State and Georgia from devastation, as there are no adequate forces in them for defense. They confess that Richmond is important to hold, but insist that Georgia and South Carolina must be defended to hold it, etc. They are frightened evidently.

Gen. Withers, Alabama, denounces the inefficiency of the conscript system.

Lieut. Beverly Kermon writes from the Rappahannock that "thus far (to Jan. 1st) our movements (in connection with Capt. T. N. Conrad) are perfectly secret." The next day he was to go to the Potomac. What has the Secretary sent him *there* for?

J. R. Bledsoe presents a design for a "*new flag*," red, white, and blue cross, which Gen. Lee thinks both original and beautiful.

Judge Campbell has a box of clothing, sent from London by J. B. Bloodgood.

JANUARY 5TH.—Clear and cold.

It is understood now that Gen. Hood has crossed to the south side of the Tennessee River with the debris of his army.

Gen. Butler has returned to Virginia from his fruitless North Carolina expedition. It is supposed we shall have active operations again before this city as soon as the weather and roads will permit.

But it really does seem that the States respectively mean to take control of all their men not now in the Confederate States armies, and I apprehend we shall soon have "confusion worse confounded."

The President sends, "for his information," to the Secretary of War, a letter from Gen. Beauregard, dated at Augusta, Ga., Dec. 6th, 1864, in relation to Gen. Sherman's movement eastward, and Gen. Hood's Middle Tennessee campaign. It appears from Gen. B.'s letter to the President that he (Gen. B.) had control of everything. He says he did not countermand Gen. Hood's campaign, because Sherman had 275 miles the start, and the roads were impracticable in Northern Georgia and Alabama. But he telegraphed the Governors of Alabama, Georgia, etc., to concentrate troops rapidly in Sherman's front, ordered a brigade of cavalry from Hood to Wheeler, etc., and supposed some 30,000 men could be collected to oppose Sherman's march, and destroy him. He computed Sherman's strength at 36,000 of all arms. The result shows how much he was mistaken. He will be held accountable for all the disasters. Alas for Beauregard! Bragg only played the part of chronicler of the sad events from Augusta. Yet the President cannot publish this letter of Beauregard's, and the country will still fix upon him the responsibility and the odium. Gen. Beauregard is still in front of Sherman, with inadequate forces, and may again be responsible for additional calamities.

Old Mr. F. P. Blair and his son Montgomery Blair are on their way here, with authority to confer on peace and submission, etc.

Mr. Lewis, Disbursing Clerk of the Post-Office Department, on behalf of lady clerks has laid a complaint before the President that Mr. Peck, a clerk in the department, to whom was intrusted money to buy supplies in North Carolina, has failed to make return of provisions or money, retaining the latter for several months, while some of his friends have received returns, besides 10 barrels flour bought for himself, and transported at government expense. Some of the clerks think the money has been retained for speculative purposes. It remains to be seen whether the President will do anything in the premises.

The grand New Year's dinner to the soldiers, as I supposed, has produced discontent in the army, from unequal distribution, etc.

No doubt the speculators got control of it, and made money, at least provided for their families, etc.

Hon. J. R. Baylor proposes recruiting in New Mexico and Lower California. The Secretary of War opposes it, saying we shall probably require all the trans-Mississippi troops on this side the river. The President differs with the Secretary, and writes a long indorsement, showing the importance of Baylor's project, etc. Of course the Secretary will "stint and say ay." The President thinks Col. B. can enlist the Indian tribes on our side also.

There is a rumor that Mr. Foote, M. C., has gone into the enemy's lines. He considered the difference between Davis and Lincoln as "between tweedledum and tweedledee."

The prisoners of war (foreigners) that took the oath of allegiance and enlisted in the Confederate States service, are deserting *back* to the Federal service, under Gen. Sherman's promise of amnesty.

JANUARY 6TH.—Cloudy and thawing.

No war news,—but it is known Sherman's army is not quiet, and must soon be heard from in spite of the interdict of the government.

It is said Mr. Trenholm, Secretary of the Treasury, is in the market buying gold, and that the fall has already been from $50 to $30 for one.

Corn-meal has risen from $50 up to $75 per bushel. Flour to $500 per barrel.

Vice-President Stephens has not left the city, but presides in the Senate.

Messrs. B. Woolley, Hart & Co., Nassau, N. P., write most pressing letters for the liquidation of their claims against the Confederate States Government. Perhaps they are becoming alarmed after making prodigious profits, etc.

Conner's brigade and other troops are en route for South Carolina from Lee's army.

Judge Campbell, Assistant Secretary of War, was *smoked* out of his room to-day, and came into mine.

The judge, however, does but little more just now than grant passports into the enemy's lines; permission to speculators to bring into the city supplies for sale, often under pretense of being intended for their own use; exemptions, details, etc. If he were disposed, he could realize a million of dollars.

It is said the Hon. A. R. Wright went North to get his son paroled, who is in prison there.

Judge Campbell talks of resigning.

JANUARY 7TH.—Rained yesterday and last night. Clear and windy to-day.

It is said the Blairs (who have been looked for on some sort of mission) turned back after arriving in the camp of Gen. Grant. Of course they could not treat with this government, under existing circumstances. The President and his cabinet could not be expected to listen to such proposals as they might be authorized to tender.

Butler's canal is said to be completed, and probably operations will soon be recommenced in this vicinity.

Congress seems to be doing little or nothing; but before it adjourns it is supposed it will, as usual, pass the measures dictated by the President. How insignificant a legislative body becomes when it is not independent. The Confederate States Congress will not live in history, for it never really existed at all, but has always been merely a body of subservient men, registering the decrees of the Executive. Even Mr. Miles, of South Carolina, before introducing a bill, sends it to this department for approval or rejection.

Detailed soldiers here are restricted in their rations this month to 31 pounds of meal, 21 pounds of salt beef, etc. The commissary agent, Mr. Wilson, thinks no more "beef shanks" can be sold. I have been living on them!

An order has been issued that all detailed men in the bureaus (able-bodied) must go into Gen. Lee's army; and the local defense troops will not be called out again except in the last necessity, and then only during the emergency. I have not seen it, but believe Gen. Lee has some such understanding with the President.

Mayor Arnold, and other rich citizens of Savannah, have held a meeting (Union), and called upon Gov. Brown to assemble a State Convention, etc.

Mr. Hunter followed Judge Campbell into his office this morning (a second visit), as if there were "any more news." The judge gravely beckoned him into the office. I was out; so there must be news, when Mr. H. (so fat) is on the *qui vive.*

Gen. Beauregard has been ordered to the West to take command of Hood's army.

The Secretary of War has ordered Col. Bayne to have as much cotton as possible *east* of Branchville, S. C.

The farmers down the river report that Grant is sending off large bodies of troops—so the Secretary says in a letter to *Gen. Lee.*

JANUARY 8TH.—Bright and cold. Snowed yesterday, and windy.

Gen. Whiting writes that he had only 400 men in Fort Fisher, and it was a miracle that it was not taken. He looked for it, and a determined effort would have carried it. He says there is no reason to suppose the attempt has been abandoned, and it must fall if a sufficient force be not sent thither.

If the enemy are apprised of the weak condition of the fort, it is probable Grant has been sending another and a stronger expedition there, and it may be apprehended that before many days Wilmington will cease to be of value to us as a blockade-running port of entry.

I saw the Hon. Mr. Montague to-day, who told me there was a strong party in Congress (which he opposed) in favor of making Gen. Lee generalissimo without the previous concurrence of the President. He says some of the Georgia members declare that their State will re-enter the Union unless Lee be speedily put at the head of military affairs in the field—he being the only man possessing the unlimited confidence of the people. I agreed with him that the President ought to be approached in a proper manner, and freely consulted, before any action such as he indicated ; and I told him that a letter from Gen. Beauregard, dated 6th of December, to the President, if ever published, would exculpate the latter from all blame for the march (unopposed) of Sherman through Georgia.

Col. Baylor, whom the President designated the other day as the proper man to raise troops in New Mexico, Arizona, Lower California and in Mexico, is the same man who invited the Indians to a council in 1861, to receive presents, whisky, etc., and then ordered them, men, women, and children, to be *slaughtered.* Even Mr. Randolph revolted at such conduct. But now the government must employ him.

The rotund Mr. Hunter is rolling about actively to-day, hunting for more news. His cheeks, though fat, are flat and emaciated—

for he sees affairs in a desperate condition, and he has much to lose.

JANUARY 9TH.—Bright, clear, and cold.

It is said the government depot at Charlotte, N. C., has been burned (accidentally), consuming a large amount of corn.

We have nothing further of the movement of Grant's troops.

We have Hood's acknowledgment of defeat, and loss of 50 guns before Nashville.

The papers contain the proceedings of a meeting in Savannah, over which the Mayor presided, embracing the terms of submission offered in President Lincoln's message. They have sent North for provisions—indicating that the city was in a famishing condition. Our government is to blame for this! The proceedings will be used as a "form," probably, by other cities—thanks to the press!

The *Examiner* is out this morning for a convention of all the (Confederate) States, and denouncing the President. I presume the object is to put Lee at the head of military affairs.

The rumor of the death of Gen. Price is not confirmed.

Gen. Pemberton has been relieved *here* and sent *elsewhere*.

The Piedmont Railroad has been impressed. A *secret* act of Congress authorizes it.

Miers W. Fisher writes that if the cabinet indorses the newspaper suggestions of giving up slavery and going under true monarchies, it is an invitation to refugees like himself to return to their homes, and probably some of the States will elect to return to the Union for the sake of being under a republican government, etc. He says it is understood that the Assistant Secretary often answers letters unseen by the Secretary; and if so, he can expect no answer from Mr. S., but will put the proper construction on his silence, etc.

Flour is $700 per barrel to-day; meal, $80 per bushel; coal and wood, $100 per load. Does the government (alone to blame) mean to allow the rich speculators, the quartermasters, etc. to starve honest men into the Union?

JANUARY 10TH.—Rained hard all night. House leaking badly!

We have nothing new in the papers this morning. It is said with more confidence, however, that Butler's canal is not yet a success. Daily and nightly our cannon play upon the works, and the deep sounds in this moist weather are distinctly heard in the city.

The amount of requisition for the War Department for 1865 is $670,000,000, and a deficiency of $400,000,000!

Mr. Hunter had his accustomed interview with Judge Campbell this morning in quest of news, and relating to his horoscope. His face is not plump and round yet.

A Mr. Lehman, a burly Jew, about thirty-five years old, got a passport to-day on the recommendation of the Secretary of the Treasury, to arrange (as agent, no doubt) for the shipment of several thousand bales of cotton, for which sterling funds are to be paid. No doubt it is important to keep the government cotton out of the hands of the enemy; and this operation seems to indicate that some fear of its loss exists.

Some 40,000 bushels of corn, etc. were consumed at Charlotte, N.C., the other day. A heavy loss! Both the army and the people will feel it. There seems already to exist the preliminary symptoms of panic and anarchy in the government. All the dignitaries wear gloomy faces; and this is a gloomy day—raining incessantly. A blue day—a miserable day!

The city council put up the price of gas yesterday to $50 per 1000 feet.

JANUARY 11TH.—Clear and pleasant. Cannon heard down the river.

Mr. E. A. Pollard, taken by the Federals in an attempt to run the blockade last spring, has returned, and reports that Gen. Butler has been relieved of his command—probably for his failure to capture Wilmington. Mr. Pollard says that during his captivity he was permitted, on parole, to visit the Northern cities, and he thinks the Northern conscription will ruin the war party.

But, alas! the lax policy inaugurated by Mr. Benjamin, and continued by every succeeding Secretary of War, enables the enemy to obtain information of all our troubles and all our vulnerable points. The United States can get recruits under the conviction that there will be little or no more fighting.

Some $40,000 worth of provisions, belonging to speculators, but marked for a naval bureau and the Mining and Niter Bureau, have been seized at Danville. This is well—if it be not too late.

A letter from Mr. Trenholm, Secretary of the Treasury, to Mr. Wagner, Charleston, S. C. (sent over for approval), appoints him agent to proceed to Augusta, etc., with authority to buy all the cotton for the government, at $1 to $1.25 per pound; and then sell it for sterling bills of exchange to certain parties, giving them permission *to remove it within the enemy's lines;* or." better still," to have it shipped abroad on government account by *reliable* parties. This indicates a purpose to die "full-handed," if the government *must* die, and to defeat the plans of the enemy to get the cotton. Is the Federal *Government* a party to this arrangement? Gold was $60 for one yesterday. I suppose there is no change to-day.

Judge Campbell, Assistant Secretary, returned to his room to-day, mine not suiting him.

Col. Sale, Gen. Bragg's military secretary, told me to-day that the general would probably return from Wilmington soon. His plan for filling the ranks by renovating the whole conscription system, will, he fears, slumber until it is too late, when ruin will overtake us! If the President would only put Bragg at the head of the conscription business—*and in time*—we might be saved.

JANUARY 12TH.—Bright and frosty. Gold at $66 for one yesterday, at auction.

Major R. J. Echols, Quartermaster, Charlotte, N. C., says the fire there destroyed 70,000 bushels of grain, a large amount of sugar, molasses, clothing, blankets, etc. He knows not whether it was the result of design or accident. All his papers were consumed. A part of Conner's brigade on the way to South Carolina, 500 men, under Lieut.-Col. Wallace, refused to aid in saving property, but plundered it! This proves that the soldiers were all poor men, the rich having bought exemptions or details!

Gen. Lee writes on the 8th instant, that the troops sailing out of James River are, he thinks, destined for another attack on Wilmington. But none have left the lines in front of him, etc.

Gen. Lee also writes on the 9th instant, that the commissary agents have established "a large traffic through our lines, in North Carolina, for supplies;" and he desires the press to say nothing on the subject.

Mr. Ould, to whom it appears the Secretary has written for his opinion (he was editor once, and fought a duel with Jennings Wise, Mr. Seddon being his second), gives a very bad one on the condition of affairs. He says the people have confidence in Mr. *Seddon*, but not in President *Davis*, and a strong reconstruction party will spring up in Virginia rather than adopt the President's ideas about the slaves, etc.

The Chief of the Treasury Note Bureau, at Columbia, S. C., asks where he shall fly to if the enemy approaches. It is understood one of our generals, when appealed to by the Secretary, exclaimed: "To the devil!"

Mr. Miles introduced a resolution yesterday (in Congress) affirming that for any State to negotiate peace is *revolutionary. Ill timed, because self-evident.*

Gen. Bradley T. Johnson writes from Salisbury, N. C., that because the travel hither has been suspended by the government, the Central Railroad Company of that State *refuse* to send the full amount of trains for the transportation of soldiers. It must be impressed too.

I am assured by one of the President's special detectives that Francis P. Blair, Sr. is truly in this city. What for? A rumor spreads that Richmond is to be evacuated.

Gen. Lee writes for the Secretary's sanction to send officers everywhere in Virginia and North Carolina, to collect provisions and to control railroads, etc. The Secretary is sending orders to different commanders, and says *he* would rather have the odium than that it should fall on Lee! The Commissary General approves Lee's measure.

Gen. Lee's dispatch was dated last night. He says he has not *two days'* rations for his army!

Commissary-General Northrop writes to the Secretary that the hour of emergency is upon us, and that Gen. Lee's name may "save the cause," if he proclaims the necessity of indiscriminate impressment, etc.

JANUARY 13TH.—Clear and pleasant—but little frost. Beef (what little there is in market) sells to-day at $6 per pound; meal, $80 per bushel; white beans, $5 per quart, or $160 per bushel. And yet Congress is fiddling over stupid abstractions!

The government will awake speedily, however; and after Congress hurries through its business (when roused), the adjournment of that body will speedily ensue. But will the President dismiss his cabinet in time to save Richmond, Virginia, and the cause? That is the question. He can easily manage Congress, by a few letters from Gen. Lee. But will the potency of his cabinet feed Lee's army?

A great panic still prevails in the city, arising from rumors of contemplated evacuation. If it should be evacuated, the greater portion of the inhabitants will remain, besides many of the employees of government and others liable to military service, unless they be forced away. But how can they be fed? The government cannot feed, sufficiently, the men already in the field.

Everybody is conjecturing what Mr. Blair has proposed; but no one expects relief from his mission, if indeed he be clothed with diplomatic powers—which I doubt.

The President, I believe, is calm, relying upon the loyalty of his cabinet. But he is aware of the crisis; and I think his great reliance is on Gen. Lee, and herein he agrees with the people. What will be the issue of the present exigency, God only knows!

I believe there is a project on foot to borrow flour, etc. from citizens for Gen. Lee's army. Many officers and men from the army are in the city to-day, confirming the reports of suffering for food in the field.

There is a rumor that Goldsborough has been taken.

Mr. Secretary Seddon is appointing men in the various districts of the city to hunt up speculators and flour; appointing such men as W. H. McFarland and others, who aspire to office by the suffrages of the people. *They* will not offend the speculators and hoarders by taking much flour from them. No—domiciliary visits with *bayonets* alone will suffice.

Of thirty Federal deserters sent to work on the fortifications of Lynchburg, all but four ran away.

It is understood that the President announced to Congress to-day the arrest of the Hon. H. S. Foote, member of that body, near Fredericksburg, while attempting to pass into the enemy's lines. This, then, may have been Capt. Norton's secret mission; and I believe the government had traps set for him at other places of egress. Meantime the enemy *came in* at Savannah. This is considered the President's foible—a triumph over a political or personal enemy will occupy his attention and afford more delight than an ordinary victory over the common enemy. Most men will say Mr. Foote should have been permitted to go—if he desired it.

JANUARY 14TH.—Cloudy and cool. The news that Goldsborough, N. C., had been taken is not confirmed. Nor have we intelligence of the renewal of the assault on Fort Fisher—but no one doubts it.

The government sent pork, butchered and salted a few weeks ago, to the army. An order has been issued to borrow, buy, or impress flour, wherever found; but our *political* functionaries will see that it be not executed. The rich hoarders may control votes hereafter, when they may be candidates, etc. If domiciliary visits were made, many thousands of barrels of flour would be found. The speculators have not only escaped hitherto, but they have been exempted besides.

The Assembly of Virginia passed a resolution yesterday, calling upon the President to have revoked any orders placing restrictions upon the transportation of provisions to Richmond and Petersburg. The President sends this to the Secretary, asking a copy of any orders *preventing carts from coming to market.*

Flour is $1000 per barrel to-day!

F. P. Blair, Sr., has been here several days, the guest of Mr. Ould, agent of exchange. He left this morning for Grant's lines below the city. I saw him in an open carriage with Mr. Ould, going down Main Street. He looks no *older* than he did twenty years ago. Many consider Ould a fortunate man, though he is represented as a loser in the war. Blair seemed struck by the great number of able-bodied men in the streets.

Major Maynard, Quartermaster, says he will be able next week to bring 120 cords of wood to the city daily.

If Richmond be relinquished, it ought to be by convention and capitulation, getting the best possible terms for the citizens; and not by evacuation, leaving them at the mercy of the invaders. Will our authorities think of this? Doubtful.

One of the President's pages told me to-day that Mr. Blair had several interviews with the President at the latter's residence. Nothing relating to *propositions* has transpired.

The clerks are again sending out agents to purchase supplies. The President has decided that such agents have no right to expend any money but that contributed. This hits the Assistant Secretary of War, and Mr. Kean, Chief of Bureau, and our agent, Mr. Peck, for whom so many barrels of flour were purchased by the latter as agent, leaving the greater part of the contribution unexpended; nay, more, the money has not *yet* been refunded, although contributed five months ago!

Some 700 barrels of flour were realized yesterday for the army.

JANUARY 15TH.—Clear and frosty. Guns heard down the river. Dispatches came last night for ammunition—to Wilmington, I believe. We have nothing yet decisive from Fort Fisher, but I fear it will fall.

Mr. Hunter was in the Secretary's office this morning before the Secretary came. I could give him no news from Wilmington. He is much distressed; but if the enemy prevails, I have no doubt he will stipulate saving terms for Virginia. He cannot contemplate the ruin of his fortune; political ruin is quite as much as he can bear. Always at the elbow of the Secretary, he will have timely notice of any fatal disaster. He is too fat to run, too heavy to swim, and therefore must provide some other means of escape.

Last night and early this morning the Jews and others were busy, with hand-carts and wheelbarrows, removing barrels of flour from the center to the outskirts of the city, fearful of impressment. They need not fear.

I have enough flour, meal, and beans (black) to subsist my family two weeks. After that, I look to the kind Providence which has hitherto always fed us.

It is now rumored that Mr. Blair came to negotiate terms for the capitulation of Richmond, and that none were listened to. Better that, if it must fall, than be given up to pillage and the flames. If burning our cities had been the order in 1862, it might have been well; it is too late now!

JANUARY 16TH.—Clear and frosty.

We learn vaguely that the attack on the defenses of Wilmington has been progressing since Friday, and that the enemy's land forces have effected a lodgment between Fort Fisher and the town.

Another "peace" visitor has arrived—Hon. Mr. Singleton, of the United States Congress. It is *said* that the President (Confederate States) has pledged himself to appoint commissioners to fix terms of peace. This is but a forlorn-hope. No terms of peace are contemplated by any of these visitors but on the basis of reconstruction; and their utmost liberality could reach no further than a permission for the Southern States to decide, in convention, the question of emancipation. The President having suggested, however, the propriety of putting the negroes into the service, and emancipating them afterward, has aroused the fears and suspicions of many of the people; and but few have confidence in the integrity of the Secretary of State. Hence the universal gloom and despondency of the croakers. There may be difficulty in replenishing the Federal armies, and they may be depleted by spring; and if so, Gen. Lee may be able to make another grand campaign with the men and material now at his command. The issue of the next campaign may inaugurate *real* negotiations. Wilmington may be taken, blockade-running may cease; but we have ammunition and other stores for another campaign.

At last we have a dispatch from Gen. Lee, announcing the fall of Fort Fisher. Most of the garrison, supposed to be 1500, were taken.

Gold was $70 for $1 on Saturday: what will it be to-day or to-morrow?

A voluminous correspondence is going on between Mr. Conrad (secret agent to arrest disloyal men endeavoring to cross the Potomac) and Mr. Secretary Seddon. Mr. Foote, arrested by their great skill, has applied, indignantly, for a writ of *habeas corpus.* Thus the time of our *great* dignitaries is consumed removing molehills, while mountains are looming up everywhere.

The following dispatch was received here at 11 A.M. to-day from Gen. Bragg's A. D. C.: "January 15th, 1865.—Official information from Gen. Whiting, at Fort Fisher, up to 8 o'clock this evening, reports enemy's attack on fort unsuccessful. Fresh troops are being sent to him."

This does not agree with the dispatch from Gen. Lee. It must have been taken *last* night, and after the hour indicated. Gen. Lee certainly says it has fallen. It is gone, and I fear the "reinforcements" also—with Gen. Whiting "to boot."

Alas for Bragg the unfortunate! He seems to be another BOABDIL the Unlucky.

Dr. Woodbridge announced in the Monumental Church, yesterday, that only five ladies had responded to the call to knit socks for the soldiers! A *rich* congregation, too. My daughters (poor) were among the five, and handed him several pairs. They sent one pair to their cousin S. Custis, Clingman's brigade, Hoke's North Carolina division.

Mr. Lewis, disbursing clerk of Post-Office Department, has sent in a communication asking an investigation of the conduct of Mr.

Peck, agent to buy supplies for clerks. What will Mr. Seddon do now?

The Commissary-General says 100,000 bushels corn for Lee's army may be got in Southwest Virginia.

JANUARY 17TH.—Cloudy, and spitting snow.

Mr. Foote's release from custody has been ordered by Congress.

The news of the fall of Wilmington, and the cessation of importations at that port, falls upon the ears of the community with stunning effect.

Again we have a rumor of the retirement of Mr. Seddon.

There are more rumors of revolution, and even of displacement of the President by Congress, and investiture of Gen. Lee. It is said the President has done something, recently, which Congress will not tolerate. Idle talk!

Mr. Foote, when arrested, was accompanied by his wife, who had a passport to Tennessee. He said to the Provost Marshal, Doggett, Fredericksburg, that he intended to accompany his family, passing through Washington, and to endeavor to negotiate a peace. He deposited a resignation of his seat in Congress with a friend, which he withdrew upon being arrested. He was arrested and detained "until further orders," by command of the Secretary of War.

Lieut.-Gen. Hood has been relieved, and ordered to report here.

The rumor gains belief that Gen. Breckinridge has been offered the portfolio of the War Department by the President. This may be the act alluded to which Congress will not agree to, perhaps, on the ground that Gen. B. remained in the United States Senate long after secession. The general is understood to be staying at G. A. Myers's house, which adds strength to the rumor, for Myers has a keen scent for the sources of power and patronage.

The Surgeon-General states that, during the years 1862 and 1863, there were 1,600,000 cases of disease in hospitals and in the field, with only 74,000 deaths. There have been 23,000 discharges from the armies since the war began.

The Provost Marshal at Fredericksburg telegraphs that his scouts report the enemy have arrested Mrs. Foote, and threaten to rescue Mr. Foote. The Secretary and the President concur in ordering his discharge. The President says that will not be permission for him to pass our lines. He will come here, I suppose.

Mentioning to R. Tyler the fact that many of the clerks, etc. of the War Department favored revolution and the overthrow of the President, he replied that it was a known fact, and that some of them would be hung soon. He feared Mr. Hunter was a submissionist.

The Northern papers say Mr. *G. B. Lamar* has applied to take the oath of allegiance, to save his cotton and other property.

The *Examiner* to-day has another article calling for a convention to abolish the Constitution and remove President Davis.

Mr. Seward, United States Secretary of State, escorted Mrs. Foote to her hotel, upon her arrival in Washington.

The following official telegram was received at the War Department last night:

"HEADQUARTERS, January 15th, 1865.

"HON. J. A. SEDDON.

"Gen. Early reports that Gen. Rosser, at the head of three hundred men, surprised and captured the garrison at Beverly, Randolph County, on the 11th instant, killing and wounding a considerable number and taking five hundred and eighty prisoners. His loss slight. R. E. LEE."

JANUARY 18TH.—Cloudy and cool. Cannon heard down the river.

No war news. But blockade-running at Wilmington has ceased; and common calico, now at $25 per yard, will soon be $50.

The stupor in official circles continues, and seems likely to continue.

A secret detective told the Assistant Secretary, yesterday, that a certain member of Congress was uttering treasonable language; and, for his pains, was told that matters of that sort (pertaining to members of Congress) did not fall within his (detective's) jurisdiction. It is the policy now not to *agitate* the matter of disloyalty, but rather to wink at it, and let it die out—if it will; if it *won't*, I suppose the government must take its chances, whatever they may be.

Breckinridge, it is now said, will not be Secretary of War: the position which Mr. Seddon is willing to abandon, cannot be desirable. And Northrop, Commissary-General, is still held by the President, contrary to the wishes of the whole Confederacy.

Flour is $1250 per barrel, to-day.

A detective reports that one of the committee (Mr. Mc———?) selected by Mr. Secretary Seddon to hunt up flour for Gen. Lee's army, has a large number of barrels secreted in his own dwelling! But they must not be touched.

Gen. Lee writes that he thinks the crisis (starvation in the army) past. Good.

In South Carolina we hear of public meetings of submission, etc.

JANUARY 19TH.—Clear and frosty. Among the rumors, it would appear that the Senate in secret session has passed a resolution making Lee generalissimo.

It is again said Mr. Seddon will resign, and be followed by Messrs. Benjamin and Mallory, etc.

The following dispatch was received by the President yesterday:

"TUPELO, MISS., January 17th, 1865.—Roddy's brigade (cav.) is useless as at present located by the War Department. I desire authority to dispose of it to the best advantage, according to circumstances.—G. T. BEAUREGARD, *General*."

The President sends it to the Secretary of War with this indorsement: "On each occasion, when this officer has been sent with his command to distant service, serious calamity to Alabama has followed. It is desirable to know what disposition Gen. Beauregard proposes to make of this force.—J. D."

We have nothing further from Wilmington. Bad enough.

Sherman is said to be marching on Charleston. Bad enough, too!

Our papers have glowing accounts of the good treatment the citizens of Savannah received from the enemy.

Mr. Foote has arrived in the city—and it is said he will take his seat in Congress to-day.

Gen. Whiting and Col. Lamb were taken at Fort Fisher—both wounded, it is said—and 1000 of the garrison.

Mr. Peck paid back to the clerks to-day the unexpended balance of their contributions for supplies, etc. The money is not worth half its value some months ago. But Mr. P. secured ten barrels of flour for himself and as many more for the Assistant Secretary, Mr. Kean, etc. etc.

One o'clock P.M. The day has grown dark and cold, indicating snow, and a dismal gloom rests upon the faces of the increasing party of croakers. We have famine, owing to the incapacity of the government, and the rapacity of speculators. Wood, however, is coming in, but it is only for *military* officers, etc. No one can live on wood. Gold is $70 for $1, and meal about $100 per bushel.

The House of Representatives (in secret session) has passed the Senate joint resolution creating the office of commander-in-chief (for Gen. Lee), and recommending that Gen. Johnston be reinstated, etc. It passed by a vote of 62 to 14.

What will result from this? Is it not a condemnation of the President and the administration that displaced Gen J., etc.? Who will resign? *Nous verrons!*

JANUARY 20TH.—Clear and cold. No news—that is bad news. Nothing has transpired officially of the events and details near Wilmington, but there is a rumor, exaggerated perhaps, of the fall of Wilmington itself. No doubt Sherman is marching on Charleston, and if there be no battle soon, it is feared he will take the city without one.

Mr. Foote made a speech in Congress yesterday—a savage one, I am told. Going home yesterday at 3 o'clock, I met Mr. Foote, and told him what I had heard. He said he could have wished me to hear every word of it. I asked if it would not be printed. He held up a roll of manuscript, saying he had written it in full, and that it would certainly be published. The papers say in their brief reports, that he disavowed all ideas of reconstruction. After he left the House, one of the Missouri members offered a resolution for his expulsion, on the ground that he had, unlawfully, attempted to pass into the enemy's lines, for the purpose of negotiating a peace, etc. It was referred to the Committee on Elections.

After this a resolution was introduced, that a joint committee be appointed to prepare an address, etc., solemnly declaring that the war shall be waged until independence be achieved, etc. Such addresses have been repeatedly made, and at last seem to have a demoralizing effect. People remember how many test votes were taken in the Virginia Convention, showing that the State never would secede—and at length the Convention passed an ordinance of secession! Nothing can save this government long but military successes, and these depend upon having the slave and other property owners in the field. This can never be done without a renovation of the machinery used to fill up the ranks.

The President is calm. Some think him subdued. A few days or weeks will determine.

Gen. Howell Cobb writes his views, etc. Utterly opposed to arming the slaves—better emancipate them at once, conceding to the "*demands of England and France*," and then enlist them. But he thinks a return to the system of volunteering would answer to fill the ranks with white men; also suggests that the President concede something to popular sentiment—restore Gen. J. E. Johnston, etc. He says gloom and despair are fast settling on the people.

J. P. McLean, Greensborough, N. C., in response to the request of Mr. Secretary Seddon, gives information of the existence of many Union men in that section, and suggests sudden death to —— etc. The Secretary *is diligent* in getting such information; but lately it seems he never applies the remedy.

Mr. Secretary Seddon thinks Mr. Peck's explanation of his purchasing satisfactory; the Assistant Secretary, Chief of Bureau of War, and Mr. Seddon's private clerk got an abundance of flour, etc.

Major Harman, Staunton, says provisions cannot be had in that section to feed Early's army, unless one-fourth of all produce be bought at market prices, and the people go on half rations. The *slaves* everywhere are on *full* rations.

JANUARY 21ST.—A dark, cold, sleety day, with rain. Troopers and scouts from the army have icicles hanging from their hats and caps, and their clothes covered with frost, and dripping.

The *Examiner* this morning says very positively that Mr. Secretary Seddon has resigned. Not a word about Messrs. Benjamin and Mallory—yet. The recent action of Congress is certainly a vote of censure, with great unanimity.

It is said Congress, in secret session, has decreed the purchase of all the cotton and tobacco! The stable locked after the horse is gone! If it had been done in 1861——

Mr. Secretary Trenholm is making spasmodic efforts to mend the currency—selling cotton and tobacco to foreign (Yankee) agents for gold and sterling bills, and buying Treasury notes at the market depreciation. For a moment he has reduced the price of gold from $80 to $50 for $1; but the flood will soon overwhelm all opposition, sweeping every obstruction away.

The Federal papers say they got 2500 prisoners at Fort Fisher.

It is said the President refuses to accept Mr. Seddon's resignation.

A rumor has sprung up to the effect that Judge Campbell, Assistant Secretary of War, has also resigned. If this be so, it will soon produce a great commotion among detailed and exempted men all over the country. Rumors fly thick these dark days. It is a good time, however, for some to resign. The President has need even of incompetent men, and may beg them to remain, etc., and thus they are flattered. But if they really feel that the ship is sinking, they will endeavor to jump ashore, notwithstanding the efforts made to retain them. And then, if the ship should *not* sink, manned by different men!

I hear nothing more about Gen. Breckinridge as Mr. Seddon's successor, but he is the guest of the old lawyer, G. A. Myers; and it is not probable he is bestowing his bread and meat, in such times as these, *for nothing*. He has made a fortune, and knows how to increase it—and even Gen. B. would never be the wiser.

We have at last a letter from Gen. Hood, narrating the battle of Franklin, Tenn. He says he lost about 4500 men—enemy's loss not stated. Failure of Gen. Cheatham to execute an order the day before, prevented him from routing the enemy. His account of the battle of Nashville I have not yet seen—but know enough about it.

Both the Secretary and his Assistant have been pretty constantly engaged, for some time past, in granting passports beyond our lines, and generally into those of the enemy.

Congress has passed an act allowing reserve forces to be ordered anywhere. Upon the heels of this, Governor Smith notifies the Secretary of War that the two regiments of second class militia here, acting with the reserves, shall no longer be under the orders of Gen. Kemper. He means to run a tilt against the President, whereby Richmond may be lost! Now "Tray, Blanche, and Sweetheart, bark at him."

JANUARY 22D.—Another day of sleet and gloom. The pavements are almost impassable from the enamel of ice; large icicles hang from the houses, and the trees are bent down with the weight of frost.

The mails have failed, and there is no telegraphic intelligence, the wires being down probably. It rained very fast all day yesterday, and I apprehend the railroad bridges have been destroyed in many places.

The young men (able-bodied) near the Secretary of War and the Assistant Secretary, at the War Department, say, this morning, that both have resigned.

It is said the Kentucky Congressmen oppose the acceptance of the portfolio of war by Gen. Breckinridge.

Whoever accepts it must reform the conscription business and the passport business, else the cause will speedily be lost. Most of our calamities may be traced to these two sources.

JANUARY 23D.—Foggy, and raining. F. P. Blair is here again. If enemies are permitted to exist in the political edifice, there is danger of a crash. This weather, bad news, etc. etc. predispose both the people and the army for *peace*—while the papers are filled with accounts of the *leniency* of Sherman at Savannah, and his forbearance to interfere with the slaves. The enemy cannot take care of the negroes—and to feed them in idleness would produce a famine North and South. Emancipation now is physically impossible. Where is the surplus food to come from to feed 4,000,000 idle non-producers?

It is said by the press that Mr. Seddon resigned because the Virginia Congressmen expressed in some way a want of confidence in the cabinet. But Mr. Hunter was in the Secretary's office early this morning, and may prevail on him to withdraw his resignation again, or to hold on until —— all is accomplished.

Gen. Breckinridge, it is said, requires the removal of Northrop, before his acceptance. Gen. Bragg is also named.

Congress, in creating the office of a commander-in-chief, also aimed a blow at Bragg's staff; and this may decide the President to appoint him Secretary of War.

A long letter came to-day from Governor Brown, dated Macon, Ga., Jan. 6th, 1865, in reply to a long one from the Secretary of War, filled with criminations and recriminations, and a flat refusal to yield the old men and boys in State service, in obedience to the call of the "usurping" and "despotic" demand of the Confederate

States Executive. Georgia trembles, and may topple over any day!

Mr. Blair's return has excited many vague hopes—among the rest, even of recognition by the United States Government! Yet many, very many croakers, weary of the war, would acquiesce in reconstruction, if they might save their property. Vain hopes.

It is rumored that a commissioner (a Louisianian) sailed to-day for England, to make overtures to that government.

The government has ordered the military authorities at Augusta, Ga. (Jan. 21), to remove or burn *all* the cotton in that town if it is likely to be occupied by the enemy.

Senator Hunter sends a letter to Mr. Seddon which he has just received from Randolph Dickinson, Camp 57th Virginia, stating that it is needful to inaugurate negotiations for the best possible terms without delay, as the army, demoralized and crumbling, cannot be relied upon to do more fighting, etc. Mr. Hunter indorses: "My dear sir, will you read the inclosed? I fear there is too much truth in it. Can't the troops be paid?

"Yours most truly, R. M. T. HUNTER."

JANUARY 24TH.—Clear and cool. It is now said Mr. Seddon's resignation has not yet been accepted, and that his friends are urging the President to persuade him to remain. Another rumor says ex-Gov. Letcher is to be his successor, and that Mr. Benjamin has sent in his resignation. Nothing seems to be definitely settled. I wrote the President yesterday that, in my opinion, there was no ground for hope unless communication with the enemy's country were checked, and an entire change in the conscription business speedily ordered. I was sincere, and wrote plain truths, however they might be relished. It is my *birth-right*.

It is said (I doubt it) that Mr. Blair left the city early yesterday.

To add to the confusion and despair of the country, the Secretary of the Treasury is experimenting on the currency, ceasing to issue Treasury notes, with unsettled claims demanding liquidation to the amount of hundreds of millions. Even the clerks, almost in a starving condition, it is said will not be paid at the end of the month; and the troops have not been paid for many months; but they are fed and clothed. Mr. Trenholm will fail to raise our credit in this way; and he may be instrumental in precipitating a *crash* of the government itself. No doubt large amounts of gold have been shipped every month to Europe from Wilmington; and the government may be now selling the money intended to go out from that port. But it will be only a drop to the ocean.

The Northern papers say Mr. Blair is authorized to offer an amnesty, including all persons, with the "Union as it was, the Constitution as it is" (my old motto on the "Southern Monitor," in 1857); but gradual emancipation. No doubt some of the people here would be glad to accept this; but the President will fight more, and desperately yet, still hoping for foreign assistance.

What I fear is *starvation;* and I sincerely wish my family were on the old farm on the Eastern Shore of Virginia until the next campaign is over.

It is believed Gen. Grant meditates an early movement on our left—north side of the river; and many believe we are in no condition to resist him. Still, we have faith in Lee, and the President remains here. If he and the principal members of the government were captured by a sudden surprise, no doubt there would be a clamor in the North for their trial and execution!

Guns have been heard to-day, and there are rumors of fighting below; that Longstreet has marched to this side of the river; that one of our gun-boats has been sunk; that Fort Harrison has been retaken; and, finally, that an armistice of ninety days has been agreed to by both governments.

JANUARY 25TH.—Clear, and very cold. We lost gun-boat Drewry yesterday in an unsuccessful attempt to destroy the enemy's pontoon bridge down the river. Fort Harrison was not taken as reported, nor is it likely to be.

The rumor of an armistice remains, nevertheless, and Mr. Blair dined with the President on *Sunday,* and has had frequent interviews with him. This is published in the papers, and will cause the President to be severely censured.

Congress failed to expel Mr. Foote yesterday (he is off again), not having a two-thirds vote, but censured him by a decided majority. What will it end in?

No successors yet announced to Seddon and Campbell—Secretary and Assistant Secretary of War. Perhaps they can be persuaded to remain.

After all, it appears that our fleet did not return, but remains down the river; and as the enemy's gun-boats have been mostly sent to North Carolina, Gen. Lee may give Grant some trouble. If he destroys the bridges, the Federal troops on this side the river will be cut off from their main army.

It is said the President has signed the bill creating a commander-in-chief.

Rev. W. Spottswood Fontaine writes from Greensborough, N. C., that —— reports that Senator Hunter is in favor of Virginia negotiating a separate peace with the United States, as the other States will probably abandon her to her fate, etc.

I saw Mr. Lyons to-day, who told me Mr. Hunter dined with him yesterday, and that Gen. Lee took tea with him last evening, and seemed in good spirits, hope, etc. Mr. Lyons thinks Gen. Lee was always a thorough emancipationist. He owns no slaves. He (Mr. Lyons) thinks that using the negroes in the war will be equivalent to universal emancipation, that not a slave will remain after the President's idea (which he don't seem to condemn) is expanded and reduced to practice. He favors sending out a commissioner to Europe for aid, on the basis of emancipation, etc., as a dernier ressort. He thinks our cause has received most injury from Congress, of which he is no longer a member.

If it be really so, and if it were generally known, that Gen. Lee is, and always has been opposed to slavery, how soon would his great popularity vanish like the mist of the morning! Can it be possible that *he* has influenced the President's mind on this subject? Did he influence the mind of his father-in-law, G. W. Park Custis, to emancipate his hundreds of slaves? Gen. Lee would have been heir to all, as his wife was an only child. There's some mistake about it.

The Secretary of State (still there!) informs the Secretary of War (still here!) that the gold he wrote about to the President on the 18th inst. for Gen. Hardee and for Mr. Conrad, is ready and subject to his order.

Four steamers have run into Charleston with a large amount of commissary stores. This is providential.

JANUARY 26TH.—Clear and cold. No further news from the iron-clad fleet that went down the river.

Beef is selling at $8 per pound this morning; wood at $150 per cord. Major Maynard, instead of bringing 120, gets in but 30 or

40 cords per day. I am out of wood, and must do my little cooking in the parlor with the coal in the grate. This is famine!

Congress passed a bill a few days ago increasing the number of midshipmen, and allowing *themselves* to appoint a large proportion of them. Yesterday the President vetoed the bill, he alone, by the Constitution, being authorized to make all appointments. But the Senate immediately repassed it over the veto—only three votes in the negative. Thus the war progresses! And Mr. Hunter was one of the three.

The President, in reply to a committee of the State Legislature, says Gen. Lee has always refused to accept the command of all the armies unless he could relinquish the immediate command of the Army of Northern Virginia defending the capital; and that he is and ever has been willing to bestow larger powers on Gen. Lee; but he would not accept them.

This makes me doubt whether the President has signed the bill creating a commander-in-chief.

It is *said again*, that Commissary-General Northrop has resigned. Doubtful.

Still, there are no beggars in the streets, except a few women of foreign or Northern birth. What a people! If our affairs were managed properly, subjugation would be utterly impossible. But all the statesmen of the years preceding the war have been, somehow, "ruled out" of positions, and wield no influence, unless it be a vengeful one in private. Where are the patriots of the decade between 1850 and 1860? "Echo answers where?" Who is responsible for their absence? A fearful responsibility!

Gold is *quoted* at $35 for $1—illusory! Perhaps worse.

The statistics furnished by my son Custis of the military strength of the Confederate States, and ordered by the President to be preserved on file in the department, seems to have attracted the attention of Mr. Assistant Secretary Campbell, and elicited a long indorsement, saying a calculation of the number of casualties of war was not made—all this *after* the paper was sent in by the President. But the estimate *was* made, and included in the reduction from the 800,000, leaving 600,000. Judge C thinks 200,000 have been killed, 50,000 permanently disabled, and 55,000 are prisoners; still 500,000 availables would be left.

Custis has drafted, and will send to the President, a bill establishing a Corps of Honor, with a view to excite emulation and to popularize the service, now sadly needed.

JANUARY 27TH.—Clear, and coldest morning of the winter. None but the rich speculators and quartermaster and commissary peculators have a supply of food and fuel. Much suffering exists in the city; and prices are indeed fabulous, notwithstanding the efforts of the Secretary of the Treasury and the press to bring down the premium on gold. Many fear the high members of the government have turned brokers and speculators, and are robbing the country—making friends of the mammon of unrighteousness, against the day of wrath which they see approaching. The idea that Confederate States notes are improving in value, when every commodity, even wood and coal, daily increases in price, is very absurd!

The iron-clad fleet returned, without accomplishing anything— losing one gun-boat and having some fifteen killed and wounded. The lower house of Congress failed yesterday to pass the Midshipman bill over the President's veto—though a majority was against the President.

It is said, and published in the papers, that Mrs. Davis threw her arms around Mr. Blair and embraced him. This, too, is injurious to the President.

My wood-house was broken into last night, and two (of the nine) sticks of wood taken. Wood is selling at $5 a stick this cold morning; mercury at zero.

A broker told me that he had an order (from government) to sell gold at $35 for $1. But that is not the market price.

It is believed (by some credulous people) that Gen. J. E. Johnston will command the army in Virginia, and that Lee will reside here and be commander-in-chief. I doubt. The clamor for Gen. J. seems to be the result of a *political* combination.

Mr. Hunter came to the department to-day almost in a run. He is excited.

Lieut.-Gen. Hardee, of Charleston, 26th (yesterday), dispatches to the Secretary that he has received an order from Gen. Cooper (Adjutant-General) for the return of the 15th Regiment and 10th Battalion North Carolina troops to North Carolina. He says these are nearly the only regular troops he has to defend the line of the Combahee—the rest being reserves, disaffected at being detained out of their States. The withdrawal may cause the loss of the State line, and great disaster, etc. etc.

Official statement of Gen. Hood's losses shows 66 guns, 13,000 small arms, etc. The report says the army was saved by sacrificing transportation; and but for this the losses would have been nothing.

JANUARY 28TH.—Clear and very cold; can't find a thermometer in the city.

The President *did* sign the bill creating a general-in-chief, and depriving Gen. Bragg of his staff.

Major-Gen. Jno. C. Breckinridge *has* been appointed Secretary of War. May our success be greater hereafter!

Gen. Lee has sent a letter from Gen. Imboden, exposing the wretched management of the Piedmont Railroad, and showing that salt and corn, in "immense quantity," have been daily left piled in the mud and water, and exposed to rain, etc., while the army has been starving. Complaints and representations of this state of things have been made repeatedly.

Gold sold at $47 for one at auction yesterday.

Mr. Hunter was seen early this morning running (almost) toward the President's office, to pick up news. He and Breckinridge were old rivals in the United States.

The *Enquirer* seems in favor of listening to Blair's propositions.

Judge Campbell thinks Gen. Breckinridge will not make a good Secretary of War, as he is not a man of small *details*. I hope he is not going to indulge in so many of them as the judge and Mr. Seddon have done, else all is lost! The judge's successor will be recommended soon to the new Secretary. There will be applicants enough, even if the ship of State were visibly going down.

Although it is understood that Gen. Breckinridge has been confirmed by the Senate, he has not yet taken his seat in the department.

The President has issued a proclamation for the observance of Friday, March 10th, as a day of "fasting, humiliation, and prayer, with thanksgiving," in pursuance of a resolution of Congress.

It seems that Virginia, Georgia, Alabama, and Tennessee will not be represented in the cabinet; this may breed trouble, and we have trouble enough, in all conscience.

It is said Mr. Blair has returned again to Richmond—third visit.

Can there be war brewing between the United States and England or France? We shall know all soon. Or have propositions been made *on our part* for reconstruction? There are many smiling faces in the streets, betokening a profound desire for peace.

JANUARY 29TH.—Clear, and moderating.

To-day at 10 A.M. three commissioners start for Washington on a mission of peace, which may be possibly attained. They are Vice-President Stephens, Senator R. M. T. Hunter, and James A. Campbell, Assistant Secretary of War, and formerly a judge on the bench of the Supreme Court of the United States, all of them heartily sick of war, and languishing for peace. If *they* cannot devise a mode of putting an end to the war, none can. Of course they have the instructions of the President, with his ultimata, etc., but they will strive earnestly for peace.

What terms may be expected? Not independence, unless the United States may be on the eve of embarking in a foreign war, and in that event that government will require all the resources it can command, and they would not be ample if the war should continue to be prosecuted against us. Hence it would be policy to hasten a peace with us, stipulating for valuable commercial advantages, being the first to recognize us over all other powers, hoping to restore the old trade, and *ultimately* to reconstruct the Union. Or it may proceed from intimations of a purpose on the part of France and England to recognize us, which, of itself, would lead inevitably to war. The refusal of the United States to recognize the Empire of Mexico is an offense to France, and the augmentation of the armament of the lakes, etc. is an offense to England. Besides, if it were possible to subjugate us, it would be only killing the goose that lays the golden egg, for the Southern trade would be destroyed, and the Northern people are a race of manufacturers and merchants. If the war goes on, 300,000 men must be immediately detailed in the United States, and their heavy losses heretofore are now sorely felt. We have no alternative but to fight on, they have the option of ceasing hostilities. And we have suffered so much that almost any treaty, granting us independence, will be accepted by the people. All the commissioners must guard against is any appearance of a PROTECTORATE on the part of the United States. If the *honor* of the Southern people be saved, they will not haggle about material losses. If negotiations fail, our people will receive a new impulse for the war, and great will be the slaughter. Every one will feel and know that these commissioners sincerely desired an end of hostilities. Two, perhaps all of them, even look upon eventual reconstruction without much repugnance, so that slavery be preserved.

JANUARY 30TH.—Bright and beautiful, but quite cold; skating in the basin, etc.

The departure of the commissioners has produced much speculation.

The enemy's fleet has gone, it is supposed to Sherman at Charleston.

No doubt the Government of the United States imagines the "rebellion" *in articulo mortis*, and supposes the reconstruction of the Union a very practicable thing, and the men selected as our commissioners may confirm the belief. They can do nothing, of course, if independence is the ultimatum given them.

Among the rumors now current, it is stated that the French Minister at Washington has demanded his passports. Mr. Lincoln's message, in December, certainly gave Napoleon grounds for a quarrel by ignoring his empire erected in Mexico.

Mr. Seddon still awaits his successor. He has removed Col. and Lieut.-Col. Ruffin from office.

Mr. Bruce, M. C. from Kentucky, and brother-in-law to Mr. Seddon, is named as Commissary-General.

The President has vetoed another bill, granting the privilege to soldiers to receive papers free of postage, and the Senate has passed it again by a two-thirds vote. Thus the breach widens.

Some of our sensible men have strong hopes of peace immediately, on terms of alliance against European powers, and commercial advantages to the United States. I hope for even this for the sake of repose and independence, if we come off with honor. We owe nothing to any of the European governments. What has Blair been running backward and forward so often for between the two Presidents? Has it not been clearly stated that independence alone will content us? Blair *must* have understood this, and made it known to *his* President. Then what else but independence, on some terms, could be the basis for *further* conference? I believe our people would, for the sake of independence, agree to an alliance offensive and defensive with the United States, and agree to furnish an army of volunteers in the event of a war with France or England. The President has stigmatized the affected neutrality of those powers in one of his annual messages. Still, such a treaty would be unpopular after a term of peace with the United States. If the United States be upon the eve of war with France and England, or either of them, our commissioners abroad will soon have proposals from those governments, which would be accepted, if the United States did not act speedily.

JANUARY 31ST.—Bright and frosty.

The "peace commissioners" remained Sunday night at Petersburg, and proceeded on their way yesterday morning. As they passed our lines, our troops cheered them very heartily, and when they reached the enemy's lines, they were cheered more vociferously than ever. Is not this an evidence of a mutual desire for peace?

Yesterday, Mr. De Jarnette, of Virginia, introduced in Congress a resolution intimating a disposition on the part of our government to unite with the United States in vindication of the "Monroe doctrine," *i.e.* expulsion of monarchies established on this continent by European powers. This aims at France, and to aid our commissioners in their endeavors to divert the blows of the United States from us to France. The resolution was referred to the Committee on Foreign Relations.

If there be complication with France, the United States may accept our overtures of alliance, and our people and government will acquiesce, but it would soon grow an *unpopular* treaty. At this moment we are hard pressed, pushed to the wall, and prepared to catch at anything affording relief. We pant for a "breathing spell." Sherman is advancing, but the conquest of territory and liberation of slaves, while they injure us, only embarrass the enemy, and add to their burdens. Now is the time for the United States to avert another year of slaughter and expense.

Mr. Foote has been denouncing Mr. Secretary Seddon for selling his wheat at $40 per bushel.

It is rumored that a column of the enemy's cavalry is on a raid somewhere, I suppose sent out from Grant's army. This does not look like peace and independence. An extract from the New York *Tribune* states that peace must come soon, because it has *reliable information* of the exhaustion of our resources. This means that we must submit unconditionally, which may be a fatal mistake.

The raiders are said to be on the Brooke Turnpike and Westhaven Road, northeast of the city, and menacing us in a weak place. Perhaps they are from the Valley. The militia regiments are ordered out, and the locals will follow of course, as when Dahlgren came.

Hon. Mr. Haynes of the Senate gives information of a raid organizing in East Tennessee on Salisbury, N. C., to liberate the prisoners, cut the Piedmont Road, etc.

Half-past two P.M. Nothing definite of the reported raid near the city. False, perhaps.

No papers from the President to-day; he is disabled again by neuralgia, in his *hand*, they say.

CHAPTER XLVII.

Gen. Lee appointed General-in-Chief.—Progress of Sherman.—The markets.—Letter from Gen. Butler.—Return of the Peace Commissioners.—The situation.—From Gen. Lee.—Use of negroes as soldiers.—Patriotism of the women.—Pardon of deserters.—The passport system.—Oh for peace!—Gen. Lee on negro soldiers.—Conventions in Georgia and Mississippi.

FEBRUARY 1ST.—Clear and pleasant; subsequently thawing and foggy. Gen. R. E. Lee has been appointed General-in-Chief by the President, in response to the recent action of Congress and the clamorous demands of the people. It is to be hoped he will, nevertheless, remain in person at the head of the Army of Virginia, else the change may be fraught with disaster, and then his popularity will vanish! He has not been fortunate when not present with the troops under his command, as evidenced by Early's defeat and Jones's disaster in the Valley last year. A general must continue to reap successes if he retains his popularity.

Gen. Lee has called upon the people everywhere to send in any cavalry arms and equipments in their possession—the importation being stopped.

The report of a raid yesterday, grew out of the return to the city of a small body of our own cavalry that had been on detached service. Quite an alarm was raised!

The President was better yesterday; it is neuralgia in the right shoulder, disabling his arm.

Our "commissioners" were delayed until yesterday morning at Petersburg; during which there was a sort of truce, and the troops of the opposing fortifications ventured out, both sides cheering vociferously.

Gen. Lee writes that his army is suffering for want of soap. The Secretary sends the letter to Commissary-General Northrop (neither of their successors being inducted yet) for "prompt attention." The Commissary-General sends it back, saying 800 barrels of soap are now, and have been for *months*, lying at Charlotte, N. C., awaiting transportation! The speculators get from Charlotte that much freight every week. The Commissary-General says 800 barrels of soap ought to last Gen. Lee's army one month. It must be a large army to consume that amount of soap in a month.

Yesterday Congress passed another bill over the President's veto, to allow soldiers to receive letters, etc. free. Thus the war progresses between the executive and the legislative branches of the government.

In future revolutions, never let a "permanent government" be established until independence is achieved!

FEBRUARY 2D. — Bright and beautiful, and pleasantly frosty. Gen. Sherman is advancing as usual in such dubiety as to distract Gen. Hardee, who knows not whether Branchville or Augusta is his objective point. I suppose Sherman will be successful in cutting our communications with the South—and in depreciating Confederate States Treasury notes still more, in spite of Mr. Trenholm's spasmodic efforts to *depreciate* gold.

Yesterday the Senate passed a bill *dropping* all commissaries and quartermasters not in the field, and not in the bureaus in Richmond, and appointing *agents* instead, over 45 years of age. This will make a great fluttering, but the Richmond rascals will probably escape.

Military men here consider Augusta in danger; of course it is! How could it be otherwise?

Information from the United States shows that an effort to obtain "peace" will certainly be made. President Lincoln has appointed ex-Presidents Fillmore and Pierce and Hon. S. P. Chase, commissioners, to treat with ours. The two first are avowed "peace men;" and may God grant that their endeavors may prove successful! Such is the newspaper information.

A kind Providence watches over my family. The disbursing clerk is paying us "half salaries" to-day, as suggested in a note I wrote the Secretary yesterday. And Mr. Price informs me that the flour (Capt. Warner's) so long held at Greensborough has arrived! I shall get my barrel. It cost originally $150; but subsequent expenses may make it cost me, perhaps, $300. The market price is from $800 to $1000. I bought also of Mr. Price one-half bushel of red or "cow-peas" for $30; the market price being $80 per bushel. And Major Maynard says I shall have a load of government wood in a few days!

FEBRUARY 3D.—The report that the United States Government had appointed commissioners to meet ours is contradicted. On the contrary, it is believed that Gen. Grant has been reinforced by 30,000 men from Tennessee; and that we shall soon hear thunder in Richmond.

Gen. Lee writes urgently in behalf of Major Tannahill's traffic for supplies, in Northeastern North Carolina and Southeastern Virginia, for the army. Large amounts of commissary stores are obtained in exchange for cotton, tobacco, etc; but the traffic is in danger of being broken up by the efforts of bureau officials and civilian speculators to participate in it—among them he mentions Major Brower (Commissary-General's office, and formerly a clerk)—and asks such orders as will be likely to avert the danger. The traffic is with the *enemy;* but if conducted under the exclusive control of Gen. Lee, it would be of vast benefit to the army.

The House of Representatives yesterday passed a singular compensation bill, benefiting two disbursing clerks and others already rich enough. I have written a note to Senator Johnson, of Missouri, hoping to head it off there, or to so amend it as to make it equable and just. All the paths of error lead to destruction; and every one seems inclined to be pressing therein.

The freezing of the canal has put up the price of wood to about $500 per cord—judging from the little one-horse loads for which they ask $50.

One o'clock P.M. Dark and dismal; more rain or snow looked for. Certainly we are in a dark period of the war—encompassed by augmenting armies, almost starving in the midst of plenty (hoarded by the speculators), our men deserting—and others skulking duty, while Congress and the Executive seem paralyzed or incapable of thought or action.

The President was better yesterday; but not out. They say it is neuralgia in the shoulder, disabling his right arm. Yet he orders appointments, etc., or forbids others.

Major Noland, Commissary-General, has refused to impress the coffee in the hands of speculators; saying there is no law authorizing it. The speculators rule the hour—for all, nearly, are speculators! God save us! we seem incapable of saving ourselves.

No news to-day from Georgia and South Carolina—which means there is no good news. If it be true that Gen. Thomas has reinforced Grant with 30,000 men, we shall soon *hear* news without seeking it! The enemy will not rest content with their recent series of successes; for system of *easy communication* will enable them to learn all they want to know about our weak points, and our childish dependence on the speculators for subsistence.

After leaving thirty days' supplies in Charleston for 20,000 men—all the rest have been ordered to Richmond.

FEBRUARY 4TH.—Clear, but rained last night. From the South we learn that Sherman is marching on Branchville, and that Beauregard is at Augusta.

The *great struggle* will be in Virginia, south of Richmond, and both sides will gather up their forces for that event. We can probably get men enough, if we can feed them.

The City Council is having green "old field pine" wood brought in on the Fredericksburg railroad, to sell to citizens at $80 per cord—a speculation.

The Quartermaster's Department is also bringing in large quantities of wood, costing the government about $40 per cord. Prior to the 1st inst., the Quartermaster's Department *commuted* officer's (themselves) allowance of wood at $130 per cord!

The President still suffers, but is said to be "better."

Yesterday much of the day was consumed by Congress in displaying a *new flag* for the Confederacy—before the old one is worn out! Idiots!

I have just seen on file a characteristic letter from Major-Gen. Butler, of which this is a literal copy:

"HEADQUARTERS DEPT. VA. AND N. C.,
"ARMY OF THE JAMES IN THE FIELD,
"FORTRESS MONROE, Oct. 9th, 1864.

"HON. ROBT. OULD—SIR:

"An attempt was made this morning by private Roucher, Co. B, 5th Penna. cavalry, to commit a rape upon the persons of Mrs. Minzer and Mrs. Anderson, living on the Darbytown Road.

"On the outrage being discovered, he broke through the picket line, and fled for your lines. Our soldiers chased him, but were unable to overtake him.

"I have therefore the honor to request that you will return him, that I may inflict the punishment which his dastardly offense merits. I cannot be responsible for the good conduct of my soldiers, *if they are to find protection from punishment by entering your lines.*

"I have the honor to be, your obt. servt.,
"(Signed) B. F. BUTLER,
"*Major-Gen. Comd'g and Com. for Exchange.*"

The ladies were Virginians.

I got my barrel (2 bags) flour to-day; 1 bushel meal, ½ bushel peas, ½ bushel potatoes ($50 per bushel); and feel pretty well. Major Maynard, Quartermaster, has promised a load of wood. *Will these last until* ——? I believe I would make a good commissary.

FEBRUARY 5TH.—Clear and cold. Our commissioners are back again! It is said Lincoln and Seward met them at Fortress Monroe, and they proceeded no further. No basis of negotiation but reconstruction could be listened to by the Federal authorities. How could it be otherwise, when their armies are marching without resistance from one triumph to another—while the government "allows" as many emissaries as choose to pass into the enemy's country, with the most solemn assurances that the Union cause is spreading throughout the South with great rapidity—while the President is incapacitated both mentally and physically by disease, disaster, and an inflexible defiance of his opponents—and while Congress wastes its time in discussions on the adoption of a *flag* for future generations!

This fruitless mission, I apprehend, will be fraught with evil, unless the career of Sherman be checked; and in that event the BATTLE for RICHMOND, and Virginia, and the Confederacy, will occur within a few months—perhaps weeks. The sooner the better for us, as delay will only serve to organize the UNION PARTY sure to spring up; for many of the people are not only weary of the war, but they have no longer any faith in the President, his cabinet, Congress, the commissaries, quartermasters, enrolling officers, and most of the generals.

Judge Campbell was closeted for hours last night with Mr. Secretary Seddon at the department. I have not recently seen Mr. Hunter.

We have news from the Eastern Shore of Virginia. My wife's aunt, Miss Sally Parsons, is dead—over 90 years of age. The slaves are free, but remain with their owners—on wages. The people are prosperous, getting fine prices for abundant crops. Only a few hundred Federal troops are in the two counties; but these, under the despotic orders of Butler, levy heavy "war contributions" from the unoffending farmers.

FEBRUARY 6TH.—Bright and frosty. As I supposed, the peace commissioners have returned from their fruitless errand. President Lincoln and Mr. Seward, it appears, had nothing to propose, and would listen to nothing but unconditional submission. The Congress of the United States has just passed, by a two-thirds vote, an amendment to the Constitution *abolishing slavery*.

Now the South will soon be fired up again, perhaps with a new impulse—and WAR will rage with greater fury than ever. Mr. Stephens will go into Georgia, and reanimate his people. Gen. Wise spoke at length for independence at the Capitol on Saturday night amidst applauding listeners, and Governor Smith speaks to-night.

Gen. Breckinridge is here and will take his seat to-morrow. Every effort will be made to popularize the cause again.

Hon. Mr. Foote is at Washington, in *prison*.

Gen. Wise's brigade has sent up resolutions consenting to gradual *emancipation*—but never to reunion with the North.

There is a more cheerful aspect on the countenances of the people in the streets. All hope of peace with independence is extinct—and valor alone is relied upon now for our salvation. Every one thinks the Confederacy will at once gather up its military strength and strike such blows as will astonish the world. There will be desperate conflicts!

Vice-President Stephens is in his seat to-day, and seems determined.

Mr. Hunter is rolling about industriously.

Gen. Lee writes that desertions are caused by the bad management of the Commissary Department, and that there are supplies enough in the country, if the proper means were used to procure them.

Gen. Taylor sends a telegram from Meridian, Miss., stating that he had ordered Stewart's corps to Augusta, Ga., as Sherman's movement rendered a *victory necessary at once*. The dispatch was to the President, and seems to be in response to one from him. So we may expect a battle immediately near Augusta, Ga. Beauregard should have some 20,000 men, besides Hardee's 15,000—which ought to be enough for victory; and then good-by to Sherman!

February 7th.—A snow four inches in depth on the ground, and snowing. Last night Governor Smith, President Davis, Senator Oldham (Texas), Rev. Mr. Duncan, Methodist preacher, and a Yankee Baptist preacher, named Doggell, or Burroughs, I believe, addressed a large meeting in the African Church, on the subject of the Peace Mission, and the ultimatum of the United States authorities. The speakers were very patriotic and much applauded. President Davis (whose health is so feeble he should have remained away) denounced President Lincoln as "His Majesty Abraham the First"—in the language of the press—and said before the campaign was over he and Seward might find "they had been speaking to their masters," when demanding unconditional submission. He promised the people great successes, after our destined reverses had run out, provided they kept from despondency and speculation, and filled the ranks of the army. He denounced the speculators, and intimated that they might yet be called upon to "disgorge their earnings."

A grand assemblage is called for next Thursday, to meet in the Capitol Square.

Congress will soon be likely to vote a negro army, and their emancipation after the war—as Lee favors it.

There was some fighting near Petersburg yesterday and the day before; but the press is reticent—a bad sign.

There is a rumor that Charleston has been evacuated!

Gen. Lee again writes that desertions occur to an alarming extent, for want of sufficient food. And he says there is enough subsistence in the country, but that the Commissary Department is inefficiently administered.

Gen. Breckinridge is in his office to-day.

A scramble is going on by the young politicians for the position of Assistant Secretary of War, and Mr. Kean is supposed to be ahead in the race. When a ship is thought to be sinking, even the cook may be appointed captain! Anything, now, to keep out of the *field*—such is the word among the mere politicians.

It is rumored that Gen. Pegram (since confirmed) was killed in the enemy's attack on our right near Petersburg, and that seven brigades were engaged and repulsed the enemy. Still, there is no official confirmation—and the silence of Gen. Lee is interpreted adversely.

Senator Haynes, of Tennessee, and Senator Wigfall, of Texas, denounced the President yesterday as mediocre and malicious—and that his blunders had caused all our disasters.

Our commissioners were not permitted to land at Fortress Monroe, but Lincoln and Seward came on board.

Judge Campbell is still acting as Assistant Secretary; but he looks very despondent. If Beauregard gains a victory ——.

FEBRUARY 8TH.—Rained all day yesterday—slush—bright this morning and cool—ground still covered with snow. It is reported by Gen. Lee that the losses on both sides on Monday were light, but the enemy have established themselves on Hatcher's Run, and intrenched; still menacing the South Side Railroad. It is also said fighting was going on yesterday afternoon, when the dreadful snow and sleet were enough to subdue an army!

We have nothing from Charleston or Branchville, but the wires are said to be working to Augusta.

A deficiency of between $300,000,000 and $400,000,000 has been discovered in the amount of our indebtedness! the present Secretary being led into the error by the estimates of his predecessor, Memminger. Congress is elaborating a bill, increasing taxation 100 per cent.! An acquaintance, who has 16 acres near the city, says he will sell, to escape a tax of $5000.

Senator Brown, of Mississippi, has introduced a resolution for the employment of 200,000 negroes, giving them their freedom.

Gen. Kemper is strongly recommended as Assistant Secretary of War.

The wounded are still coming in from the fight beyond Petersburg. Horrible weather, yesterday, for fighting—and yet it is said much of it was done.

Vice-President Stephens was in the department to-day. He has a ghostly appearance. He is announced to speak in Richmond to-morrow; but I believe he starts for Georgia *to-day*. He may publish a letter. He had a long interview with Judge Campbell—with locked doors.

Twelve M. The sun is melting the snow rapidly.

The Legislature of Virginia has passed resolutions in favor of the restoration of Gen. J. E. Johnston to a command. What will the President *do*, after *saying* he should never have another command?

Intelligence was received to-day of the sudden death of Brig.-Gen. Winder, in Georgia; from apoplexy, it is supposed. He was in command of the prisons, with his staff of "Plug Uglies" around him, and Cashmeyer, their sutler.

"HEADQUARTERS ARMY OF NORTHERN VIRGINIA,
"February 6th, 1865.
"GENERAL S. COOPER.

"The enemy moved in strong force yesterday to Hatcher's Run. Part of his infantry, with Gregg's cavalry, crossed and proceeded on the Vaughan Road—the infantry to Cattail Creek, the cavalry to Dinwiddie Court House, when its advance encountered a portion of our cavalry, and retreated.

"In the afternoon, parts of Hill's and Gordon's troops demonstrated against the enemy on the left of Hatcher's Run, near Armstrong's Mill. Finding him intrenched, they were withdrawn after dark. During the night, the force that had advanced beyond the creek retired to it, and were reported to be recrossing.

"This morning, Pegram's division moved down the right bank of the creek to reconnoiter, when it was vigorously attacked. The battle was obstinately contested several hours, but Gen. Pegram being killed while bravely encouraging his men, and Col. Hoffman wounded, some confusion occurred, and the division was pressed back to its original position. Evans's division, ordered by Gen. Gordon to support Pegram's, charged the enemy and forced him back, but was, in turn, compelled to retire. Mahone's division arriving, the enemy was driven rapidly to his defenses on Hatcher's Run.

"Our loss is reported to be small; that of the enemy not supposed great. R. E. LEE."

FEBRUARY 9TH.—Bright, frosty, beautiful, after a cold night.

We have nothing more specific from the fight of Tuesday, when we learn another general was killed. It seems that most of Grant's army was in the movement, and they have a lodgment several miles nearer the South Side Railroad—the objective point. Their superior numbers must ultimately prevail in maintaining the *longest line*.

There is to be public speaking in the African Church to-day, or in the Square, to reanimate the people for another carnival of blood. Mr. Hunter, it is said, has been chosen to preside, and no man living has a greater abhorrence of blood! But, perhaps, he cannot decline.

Papers from the United States indicate that the peace epidemic prevails in that country also to an *alarming* extent: for the day (15th instant) of drafting is near at hand; and even the Republican papers hope and pray for peace, and reconstruction without slavery.

Senator Brown's resolution to put 200,000 slaves in the army was voted down in secret session. Now the slave*owners* must go in themselves, or all is lost.

One of the President's pages says the President will make a speech at the meeting to-day. He is a good political speaker, and will leave no stone unturned to disconcert his political enemies in Congress and elsewhere—and their name is legion.

The President has ordered the nomination of ex-Gov. Bonham as brigadier-general of a brigade of South Carolina cavalry, in opposition to *Gen. Cooper's* opinion: a rare occurrence, showing that Mr. Davis can be flexible when necessity urges. Gen. Hampton recommended Bonham.

The day is bright, but the snow is not quite all gone: else the meeting would be very large, and in the Capitol Square. There will be much cheering; but the rich men will be still resolved to keep out of the army themselves.

We have nothing from Charleston for several days. No doubt preparations are being made for its evacuation. The stores will be brought here for Lee's army. What will be the price of gold then?

Mr. Seddon has published a correspondence with the President, showing why he resigned: which was a declaration on the part of Congress of a want of confidence in the cabinet. The President says such a declaration on the part of Congress is extra-official, and subversive of the constitutional jurisdiction of the Executive; and, in short, he would not accept the resignation, if Mr. S. would agree to withdraw it. So, I suppose the other members will hold on, in spite of Congress.

FEBRUARY 10TH.—Bright and cold. It is estimated that the enemy lost 1500 men in the fight near Petersburg, and we 500.

Sherman has got to the railroad near Branchville, and cut communications with Augusta.

At the meeting, yesterday, Mr. Hunter presided, sure enough; and made a carefully prepared patriotic speech. There was no other alternative. And Mr. Benjamin, being a member of the cabinet, made a significant and most extraordinary speech. He said the white fighting men were exhausted, and that black men must recruit the army—and it must be done at once; that Gen. Lee had informed him he must abandon Richmond, if not soon reinforced, and that negroes would answer. The *States* must send them, Congress having no authority. Virginia must lead, and send 20,000 to the trenches in twenty days. Let the negroes volunteer, and be emancipated. It was the only way to save the slaves—the women and children. He also said all who had cotton, tobacco, corn, meat, etc. must *give* them to the government, not sell them. These remarks were not literally reported in the *Dispatch*, but they were uttered. He read resolutions, adopted in certain regiments, indorsing the President and his cabinet—of which Mr. B. said, playfully, he was one.

Yesterday, in the House, upon the passage of a bill revising the Commissary Department, Mr. Miles said the object was to remove Col. Northrop. [His removal *has* been determined.] Mr. Baldwin said the department had been well conducted. Mr. Miles said in these times the test of merit must be success. The bill passed.

Senator Hunter is at the department this morning, calling for the statistics, prepared by my son Custis, of the fighting men in the Southern States. Doubtless Mr. Hunter is averse to using the slaves.

The new Secretary of War is calling for reports of "means and resources" from all the bureaus. This has been done by no other Secretary. The government allowed Lee's army to suffer for months with the *itch*, without knowing there were eight hundred barrels of soap within a few hours' run of it.

From the ordnance report, I see we shall have plenty of powder —making 7000 pounds per day; and 55,000 rifles per annum, besides importations. So, if there must be another carnival of blood, the defense can be maintained at least another year, provided the *right men* have the management.

A violent opposition is likely to spring up against Mr. Benjamin's suggestions. No doubt he is for a desperate stroke for independence, being out of the pale of mercy; but his moral integrity is impugned by the representatives from Louisiana, who believe he has taken bribes for passports, etc., to the injury of the cause. He feels strong, however, in the strength of the President, who still adheres to him.

There is much excitement among the slaveowners, caused by Mr. Benjamin's speech. They must either fight themselves or let the slaves fight. Many would prefer submission to Lincoln; but that would not save their slaves! The Proclamation of Emancipation in the United States may yet free the South of Northern domination.

FEBRUARY 11TH.—Cloudy and cold; froze hard last night.

Yesterday a bill was introduced into both houses of Congress authorizing the enlistment of 200,000 slaves, *with consent of their owners*, which will probably be amended. Mr. Miles, as a test vote, moved the rejection of the bill; and the vote *not* to reject it was more than two to one, an indication that it will pass.

The failure of the peace conference seems to have been made the occasion of inspiring renewed zeal and enthusiasm for the war in the United States, as well as here. So the carnival of blood will be a "success."

The enemy claim an advantage in the late battle on the south side of the James River.

Sherman's movements are still shrouded in mystery, and our generals seem to be *waiting* for a development of his intentions. Meantime he is getting nearer to Charleston, and cutting railroad communications between that city and the interior. The city is doomed, unless Hardee or Beauregard, or both, successfully take the initiative.

Here the price of slaves, men, is about $5000 Confederate States notes, or $100 in specie. A great depreciation. Before the war, they commanded ten times that price.

It is rumored that *hundreds* of the enemy's transports have come into the James River. If it be Thomas's army reinforcing Grant, Richmond is in immediate peril! Information of our numbers, condition, etc. has been, doubtless, communicated to the enemy—and our slumbering government could not be awakened!

Wigfall, of Texas, Graham, of North Carolina, Orr and Miles, of South Carolina, oppose the employment of negro troops, and Gen. Wickham, of this department, openly proclaims such a measure as the end of the Confederacy! We are upon stirring times! Senator Wigfall demands a new cabinet, etc.

Two P.M. The sun has come out; warmer. But it does not disperse the prevailing gloom. It is feared Richmond must be abandoned, and our forces concentrated farther South, where supplies may be more easily had, and where it will be a greater labor and expense for the enemy to subsist his armies.

Assistant Secretary of War, Judge Campbell, is still furloughing, detailing, and discharging men from the army; and yet he thinks the country is pretty nearly exhausted of its fighting population! His successor is not yet appointed; the sooner the better, perhaps.

FEBRUARY 12TH.—Bright, windy, cold, and disagreeable.

There was nothing new at the department this morning. Nothing from below; nothing from South Carolina. Perhaps communications are cut between this and Charleston. All are anxious to hear the result of the anticipated battle with Sherman, for somehow all know that the order to fight him was sent from Richmond more than a week ago.

People's thoughts very naturally now dwell upon the proximate future, and the alternatives likely to be presented in the event of the abandonment of Richmond, and consequently Virginia, by Lee's army. Most of the *male* population would probably (if permitted) elect to remain at their homes, braving the fate that might await them. But the women are more patriotic, and would brave all in following the fortunes of the Confederate States Government. Is this because they do not participate in the hardships and dangers of the field? But many of our men are weary and worn, and languish for repose. These would probably remain quiescent on parole, submitting to the rule of the conqueror; but hoping still for foreign intervention or Confederate victories, and ultimate independence.

Doubtless Lee could protract the war, and, by concentrating farther South, embarrass the enemy by compelling him to maintain a longer line of communication by land and by sea, and at the same time be enabled to fall upon him, as occasion might offer, in heavier force. No doubt many would fall out of the ranks, if Virginia were abandoned; but Lee could have an army of 100,000 effective men for years.

Still, these dire necessities may not come. The slaveowners, speculators, etc., hitherto contriving to evade the service, may take the alarm at the present aspect of affairs, and both recruit and subsist the army sufficiently for victory over both Grant and Sherman; and then Richmond will be held by us, and Virginia and the Cotton States remain in our possession; and we shall have peace, for exhaustion will manifest itself in the United States.

We have dangerous discussions among our leaders, it is true; and there may be convulsions, and possibly expulsion of the men at the head of civil affairs: but the war will not be affected. Such things occurred in France at a time when the armies achieved their greatest triumphs.

One of the greatest blunders of the war was the abandonment of Norfolk; and the then Secretary of War (Randolph) is now safely in Europe. That blunder brought the enemy to the gates of the capital, and relinquished a fertile source of supplies; however, at this moment Lee is deriving some subsistence from that source by connivance with the enemy, who get our cotton and tobacco.

Another blunder was Hood's campaign into Tennessee, allowing Sherman to raid through Georgia.

FEBRUARY 13TH.—Coldest morning of the winter.

My exposure to the cold wind yesterday, when returning from the department, caused an attack of indigestion, and I have suffered much this morning from disordered stomach and bowels.

From Northern papers we learn that Gen. Grant's demonstration last week was a very formidable effort to reach the South Side Railroad, and was, as yet, a decided failure. It seems that his spies informed him that Gen. Lee was evacuating Richmond, and under the supposition of Lee's great weakness, and of great consequent demoralization in the army, the Federal general was induced to make an attempt to intercept what he supposed might be a retreat of the Confederate army. There will be more fighting yet before Richmond is abandoned, probably such a carnival of blood as will make the world start in horror.

The New York *Tribune* still affects to believe that good results may come from the recent peace conference, on the basis of reunion, other basis being out of the question. The new amnesty which it was said President Lincoln intended to proclaim has not appeared, at least our papers make no mention of it.

Gen. Lee has proclaimed a pardon for all soldiers, now absent without leave, who report for duty within 20 days, and he appeals to their patriotism. I copy it.

"HEADQUARTERS ARMIES OF THE CONFEDERATE STATES,
"February 11th, 1865.
"GENERAL ORDERS NO. 2.

"In entering upon the campaign about to open, the general-in-chief feels assured that the soldiers who have so long and so nobly borne the hardships and dangers of the war require no exhortation to respond to the calls of honor and duty.

"With the liberty transmitted by their forefathers they have inherited the spirit to defend it.

"The choice between war and abject submission is before them.

"To such a proposal brave men, with arms in their hands, can have but one answer.

"They cannot barter manhood for peace, nor the right of self-government for life or property.

"But justice to them requires a sterner admonition to those who have abandoned their comrades in the hour of peril

"A last opportunity is offered them to wipe out the disgrace and escape the punishment of their crimes.

"By authority of the President of the Confederate States, a pardon is announced to such deserters and men improperly absent as shall return to the commands to which they belong within the shortest possible time, not exceeding twenty days from the publication of this order, at the headquarters of the department in which they may be.

"Those who may be prevented by interruption of communications, may report within the time specified to the nearest enrolling officer, or other officer on duty, to be forwarded as soon as practicable; and upon presenting a certificate from such officer, showing compliance with this requirement, will receive the pardon hereby offered.

"Those who have deserted to the service of the enemy, or who have deserted after having been once pardoned for the same offense, and those who shall desert, or absent themselves without authority, after the publication of this order, are excluded from its benefits. Nor does the offer of pardon extend to other offenses than desertion and absence without permission.

"By the same authority, it is also declared that no general amnesty will again be granted, and those who refuse to accept the pardon now offered, or who shall hereafter desert or absent themselves without leave, shall suffer such punishment as the courts may impose, and no application for clemency will be entertained.

"Taking new resolution from the fate which our enemies intend for us, let every man devote all his energies to the common defense.

"Our resources, wisely and vigorously employed, are ample, and with a brave army, sustained by a determined and united people, success, with God's assistance, cannot be doubtful.

"The advantages of the enemy will have but little value if we do not permit them to impair our resolution. Let us, then, oppose constancy to adversity, fortitude to suffering, and courage to danger, with the firm assurance that He who gave freedom to our fathers will bless the efforts of their children to preserve it.

"R. E. LEE, *General.*"

The Senate did nothing on Saturday but discuss the policy of abolishing the Bureau of Conscription, the office of provost marshal outside of our military lines.

Gov. Smith's salary is to be increased to $20,000, and he is still exempting young justices, deputy sheriffs, deputy clerks, constables, etc.

FEBRUARY 14TH.—Bright and cold. Very cold, and fuel unattainable.

The papers speak of heavy raids in process of organization: one from Newbern, N. C., against Raleigh, and one from East Tennessee against Salisbury and our communications.

The news from South Carolina is vague, only that the armies are in active motion. So long as Sherman keeps the initiative, of course he will succeed, but if Beauregard should attack, it may be different.

Yesterday some progress was made with the measure of 200,000 negroes for the army. Something must be done—and *soon*.

Gen. Wise sent me a letter of introduction to Gen. Breckinridge yesterday. I sent it in to-day. I want the system of passports changed, and speculation annihilated, else the cause is lost. I expect no action, for impediments will be interposed by others. But my duty is done. I have as little to lose as any of them. The generals all say the system of passports in use has inflicted great detriment to the service, a fact none can deny, and if it be continued, it will be indeed "idiotic suicide," as Gen. Preston says.

The weather is moderating, but it is the most wintry 14th of February I remember to have seen. Yet, as soon as the weather will admit of it, the carnival of blood must begin. At Washington they demand unconditional submission or extermination, the language once applied to the Florida Indians, a few hundred of whom maintained a war of seven years. Our cities may fall into the hands of the enemy, but then the populations will cease to subsist on the Confederacy. There is no prospect of peace on terms of "unconditional submission," and most of the veteran troops of the enemy will return to their homes upon the expiration of their terms of enlistment, leaving mostly raw recruits to prosecute the work of "extermination."

Meantime the war of the factions proceeds with activity, the cabinet and the majority in both Houses of Congress. The President remains immovable in his determination not to yield to the demand for new men in the government, and the country seems to have lost confidence in the old. God help us, or we are lost! The feeble health of the President is supposed to have enfeebled his intellect, and if this be so, of course *he* would not be likely to discover and admit it. Mr. Speaker Bocock signs a communication in behalf of the Virginia delegation in Congress asking the dismissal of the cabinet.

The Northern papers mention a gigantic raid in motion from Tennessee to Selma, Montgomery, and Mobile, Ala., consisting of 40,000 cavalry and mounted infantry, *a la Sherman*. They are resolved to give us no rest, while we are distracted among ourselves, and the President refuses to change his cabinet, etc.

Gen. Grant telegraphed the Secretary of War at Washington, when our commissioners were in his camp, that he understood both Messrs. Stephens and Hunter to say that peace might be restored on the basis of REUNION.

FEBRUARY 15TH.—Moderated last night; this morning sleety and dangerous.

Gen. Lee was in the city yesterday, walking about briskly, as if some great event was imminent. His gray locks and beard have become white, but his countenance is cheerful, and his health vigorous.

The papers say Wheeler has beaten Kilpatrick (Federal cavalry general) back five miles, somewhere between Branchville and Augusta. So he did once or twice when Sherman was marching on Savannah, and he took it while Bragg remained at Augusta. The news of a victory by Beauregard over Sherman would change the face of affairs in that quarter, and nothing less will suffice.

It is surprising that the Federal authorities do not seem to perceive that in the event of a forced reconstruction of the Union, and a war with any European power, the South would rise again and join the latter. Better recognize a separate nationality, secure commercial advantages, and have guarantees of neutrality, etc.

Scouts report Gen. Thomas (Federal), with 30,000 men, encamped in the vicinity of Alexandria, Va., awaiting fair weather to march upon Richmond from that direction. The number is exaggerated no doubt, but that Richmond is to be subjected to renewed perils, while Congress is wasting its time in idle debate, is pretty certain.

The Senate passed a bill yesterday abolishing the Bureau of Conscription, and I think it will pass the House. The President ought to have abolished it months ago—years ago. It may be too late.

Col. St. John, Chief Mining and Niter Bureau, has been nominated as the new Commissary-General.

FEBRUARY 16TH.—Cloudy; rained yesterday and last night.

We have no important news from South Carolina, except the falling back toward Columbia of our troops; I suppose before superior numbers. Branchville is evacuated.

The roads will not admit of much movement in the field for some days. But pretty heavy cannonading is heard down the river.

Congress did nothing yesterday; it is supposed, however, that the bill recruiting negro troops will pass—I fear when it is too late.

Meantime the President is as busy as a bee making appointments and promotions, and many meritorious men are offended, supposing themselves to be overslaughed or neglected.

The published letter taking leave of Mr. Secretary Seddon rasps Congress severely, and is full of professions of esteem, etc. for the retiring Secretary. The members of Congress reply with acrimony.

The quartermaster at Charlotte, N. C., dispatches the Secretary of War that he has there some millions in specie, government funds, besides specie of the banks for safe keeping. He also desires the removal of the "Foreign Legion" there, paroled prisoners taken from the enemy and enlisting in our service. They are committing robberies, etc.

I saw Gen. Lee at the department again this morning. He seems vigorous, his face quite red, and very cheerful. He was in gray uniform, with a blue cloth cape over his shoulders.

Exchange of prisoners has been resumed, and many of our men are returning from captivity. Gen. Grant has the matter under his control.

Gen. Pillow has been appointed commander of prisons in place of Gen. Winder, deceased.

Only $4\frac{5}{8}$ pounds bacon were issued as meat ration to detailed men this month.

I learn that some 2000 of our men, confined at Point Lookout, Md., as prisoners of war, during the last two months, offered to take the oath of allegiance, which was refused, because it would reduce the number to exchange.

By the last flag of truce boat a negro slave returned. His master took the oath, the slave *refused.* He says "Massa had no principles."

FEBRUARY 17TH.—Frosty morning, after a rain last night.

We have no authentic war news this morning, from any quarter.

Congress is at work in both Houses on the Negro bill. It will pass, of course, without some unforeseen obstacle is interposed.

A letter from Gen. Lee to Gen. Wise is published, thanking the latter's brigade for resolutions recently adopted, declaring that they would consent to gradual emancipation for the sake of independence and peace. This is a strong indication (confirmatory) that Gen. Lee is an emancipationist. From all the signs slavery is doomed! But if 200,000 negro recruits can be made to fight, and can be enlisted, Gen. Lee may maintain the war very easily and successfully; and the powers at Washington may soon become disposed to abate the hard terms of peace now exacted.

How our fancies paint the scenes of peace now which were never appreciated before! Sitting by our cheerless fires, we summon up countless blessings that we could enjoy, if this war were only over. We plan and imagine many things that would be bliss to us in comparison with the privations we suffer. Oh, what fine *eating* and comfortable *clothes* we shall have when we enjoy another season of repose! We will hunt, we will "go fishing," we will cultivate nice gardens, etc. Oh for peace once more! Will this generation, with their eyes open, and their memories fresh, ever, ever go to war again?

There is a *dark* rumor that Columbia, S. C., has been taken possession of by the enemy; but I hardly believe it, for Gen. Beauregard would fight for it.

Gen. Beauregard telegraphs from Columbia, S. C., *yesterday*, that Gen. Pillow proposes to gather troops west of that point, and Gen. B. approves it. The President hesitates, and refers to *Gen. Cooper*, etc.

Eleven o'clock A.M. Raining again; wind east.

Mr. Hunter looks rather cadaverous to-day; he does not call

on the new Secretary often. Gen. B. is a formidable rival for the *succession*—if there should be such a thing.

To-day my son Thomas drew his rations. I have also had another load of coal from Lieut. Parker, C. S. N., out of his contract, at $30, a saving of nearly $100! that will take us through the winter and spring. We also bought another bushel of black beans at $65.

Alas! we have news now of the capture of Columbia, S. C., the capital of the State. A dark day, truly! And only this morning—not three short hours ago—the President hesitated to second Beauregard's desire that Gen. Pillow—although not a "red tapist" —should rouse the people to the rescue; but *Gen. Cooper* must be consulted to throw obstacles in the way! This will be a terrible blow; and its consequences may be calamitous beyond calculation. Poor South Carolina! her day of agony has come!

FEBRUARY 18TH.—Rained last night; but this is as lovely a morning as ever dawned on earth. A gentle southern breeze, a cloudless sky, and a glorious morning sun, whose genial warmth dispels the moisture of the late showers in smoky vapors.

But how dark and dismal the aspect of our military affairs! Columbia fallen and Charleston (of course) evacuated. My wife wept, my daughter prayed, upon hearing the news. South Carolina was superior to all the States in the estimation of my wife, and she regarded it as the last stronghold. Now she despairs, and seems reckless of whatever else may happen in Sherman's career of conquest.

A dispatch to Gen. Bragg states that Thomas's army (the ubiquitous) is landing at Newbern, N. C.! This is to cut Lee's communications and strike at Raleigh perhaps.

The people are stunned and sullen; sometimes execrating the President for retaining a cabinet in which the country has no confidence, etc.

One hundred for one is asked for gold.

The President was at work very early this morning making appointments in the army. But that does no good to the cause, I fear. A sufficient number of men must *be* placed in the ranks, or there will be no military success.

The Senate has passed a bill abolishing the "Bureau of Conscription," and it is now before the House. That is one step in the right direction. Hon. J. Goode yesterday made a speech in favor of its abolition, in which he said 150,000 men had been "handled" by the bureau during the last twelve months, and only 13,000 had been sent to the army! But it did not pass—no vote was taken; it is to be hoped it will pass to-day.

It is rumored that the "money-printing machine" was lost at Columbia, including a large amount of "treasure"—if Confederate Treasury notes be worthy that appellation.

FEBRUARY 19TH.—Another bright and glorious morning. I hear of no news whatever from the South—although I know that important events are transpiring—and the reticence of the government is construed very unfavorably. Hence if Beauregard has fought a battle, it is to be apprehended that he did not gain the day; and if this be so, South Carolina lies at the conqueror's feet.

I thought I heard brisk cannonading in the distance (down the river) this morning, but am not certain. I saw Mr. Hunter going briskly toward the Executive department. He does not come often now to the War Office.

The new Secretary has a large audience of members of Congress every morning.

The President and three of his aids rode out this afternoon (past our house), seemingly as cheerful as if each day did not have its calamity! No one who beheld them would have seen anything to suppose that the capital itself was in almost immediate danger of falling into the hands of the enemy; much less that the President himself meditated its abandonment at an early day, and the concentration of all the armies in the Cotton States!

FEBRUARY 20TH.—Another morning of blue skies and glorious sunshine. Sherman is reported to be marching northward, and to have progressed one-third of the way between Columbia and Charlotte, N. C.; where we had "millions of specie" a few days ago.

Some of the lady employees, sent by Mr. Memminger to Columbia last year, have returned to this city, having left and lost their beds, etc.

Grant's campaign seems developed at last. Sherman and Thomas will concentrate on his left, massing 200,000 men between Lee and his supplies, effectually cutting his communications by flanking with superior numbers. It is probable Charleston, Wilmington, and Richmond will fall without a battle; for how can they be held when the enemy stops supplies? and how could the garrisons escape when once cut off from the interior?

And yet Congress has done nothing, and does nothing, but waste the precious time. I fear it is too late now! It is certainly too late to raise recruits for service in the campaign now in *active operation*, a fact which our politician leaders seem to be unconscious of. Even our furloughed troops cannot now rejoin their regiments from their distant homes.

Then, if Lee must evacuate Richmond, where can he go? No one knows!

My belief is that the only chance for Lee—and a desperate one—is to beat Grant *immediately*, before the grand junction can be formed.

Letters are beginning to come in from the South, advocating the abandonment of Richmond, and the march of Lee's army into East Tennessee and Northern Georgia, and so on down to Montgomery, Ala., etc. etc.; concentrating in the Cotton States. What an ugly programme! How many would then follow the fortunes of this government? How many heads of bureaus, etc. would abandon it? How would it be possible for those with families on their hands to get transportation? A great many other questions might be asked, that few could answer at this time.

Charleston was evacuated on Tuesday last—nearly a week ago—so says the *Examiner*, and no one doubts it.

Mr. Hunter seems more depressed to-day than I have ever seen him. He walks with his head down, looking neither to the right nor the left.

I shall expect soon to hear of a battle. Beauregard must have nearly 50,000 men—such as they are, poor fellows! The rich have generally bribed themselves out of the service through the complicated machinery of the "Bureau of Conscription."

Senator Brown, of Mississippi, I am sorry to see, often retards legislation by motions to postpone; and the Senate listens to him, not knowing what to do. Hours now are worth weeks hereafter.

The President has made Wm. M. Browne—one of his aids, an Englishman and a Northern newspaper reporter—a brigadier-general. This does not help the cause. Mr. B. knows no more about war than a cat; while many a scarred colonel, native-born, and participants in a hundred fights, sue in vain for promotion.

Governor Clarke (Mississippi) telegraphs the President that nothing keeps the negroes from going to the enemy but the fear of being put in the Federal army; and that if it be attempted to put them in ours, all will run away, etc.

FEBRUARY 21ST.—Another bright and glorious morning.

Charleston fell on Thursday night last. A large number of heavy guns fell into the hands of the enemy. The *confidential* telegraph operators remained with the enemy. They were Northern men; but it is the policy of those in possession of this government to trust their enemies and neglect their friends.

Congress passed yesterday a bill abolishing the "Bureau of Conscription" in name—nothing more, if I understand it. The bill was manipulated by Judge Campbell, who has really directed the operations of the bureau from the beginning.

The negro bill also passed one House, and will pass the other to-day.

Also a bill (in one House) abolishing provost marshals, except in camps of the army.

These measures may come too late. The enemy is inclosing us on all sides with great vigor and rapidity. A victory by Beauregard would lift up the hearts of the people, now prone in the dust.

Mr. D. H. London (on the street) is smiling this morning. He says there is no doubt but that we shall be speedily recognized by France, and that Gen. Lee has gone South to checkmate Sherman. I fear some one has been deceiving Mr. London, knowing how eager he is for a few grains of comfort. He is a rich man.

A dispatch was sent from the department to Gen. Lee this morning, at his headquarters, supposed to be near Petersburg. Gold was selling at $60 for $1 yesterday. This may be a "dodge" of the brokers, who want to purchase; or it may be the government selling specie.

A gentleman from South Carolina reports that the Georgians (militia and reserves, I suppose) refused to enter South Carolina in obedience to Gen. Beauregard's orders, and that Gen. B. has not exceeding 10,000 reliable men. If this be so, Sherman may march whither he chooses! This is very bad, if it be true, and more and more endangers the capital.

Surgeon-General S. P. Moore's estimates for the year's expenses of his bureau are $46,000,000.

FEBRUARY 22D.—Bright and frosty. A fine February for fruit.

Yesterday the Senate postponed action on the Negro bill. What this means I cannot conjecture, unless there are dispatches from abroad, with assurances of recognition based upon stipulations of emancipation, which cannot be carried into effect without the consent of the States, and a majority of these seem in a fair way of falling into the hands of the Federal generals.

The House passed the bill to abolish quartermasters and commissaries in a modified form, excepting those collecting tax in kind; and this morning those officers in this city under forty-five years of age advertise the location of their places of business as collectors of tax in kind, Capt. Wellford, a kinsman of Mr. Seddon, among the rest, the very men the bill was intended to remove! Alas for Breckinridge and independence!

The following dispatch has just been received from Gen. R. E. Lee:

"HEADQUARTERS, February 22d, 1865.

"From dispatches of Gen. Bragg of 21st, I conclude he has abandoned Cape Fear River. He says he is embarrassed by prisoners. Enemy refuses to receive or entertain propositions. I expect no change will be made by Gen. Grant. It is his policy to delay. Have directed prisoners to be sent to Richmond by rail or highway, as may be most practicable; if wrong, correct it.

"R. E. LEE."

This looks like the speedy fall of Wilmington, but not of Richmond.

To-day is the anniversary of the birth of Washington, and of the inauguration of Davis; but I hear of no holiday. Not much is doing, however, in the departments; simply a waiting for calamities, which come with stunning rapidity. The next news, I suppose, will be the evacuation of Wilmington! Then Raleigh may tremble. Unless there is a speedy turn in the tide of affairs, confusion will reign supreme and universally.

We have here now some 4000 or 5000 paroled prisoners returned by the Federal authorities, without sufficient food for them, and soon there may be 10,000 Federal prisoners from Wilmington, which it seems cannot be exchanged there. Is it the policy of their own government to starve them?

Mr. Burgwyn, of North Carolina, writes to the President (11th inst.) that some 15,000 bales of cotton are locked up in Wilmington, belonging to speculators, awaiting the coming of the enemy, when the city will certainly fall into their hands. He says Gen. Bragg's orders regarding its removal are wholly disregarded; and he implores the President to prevent its falling into the enemy's hands, and disgracing his State as Georgia was disgraced by the cotton taken at Savannah. He says these speculators have an understanding with the enemy. The President indorses, simply, "For attention.—J. D."

I bought quarter ounce early York cabbage-seed to day at $10 per ounce.

FEBRUARY 23D.—Raining; the most inclement February for years.

It is stated that Gen. J. E. Johnston has been replaced in command of the army in front of Sherman; a blunder, for Beauregard's friends will raise a clamor.

Grant's men fired salutes yesterday in honor of the DAY—22d—and had the Richmond papers read to them by order of Gen. Grant—accounts of the fall of Charleston. Our government will continue this fatal policy of allowing easy communication between Richmond and the enemy, begun by Mr. Benjamin, and continued by his successors! It will ruin us, and would destroy any cause. Next, our papers will announce the fall of Wilmington.

Three preachers—Hoge, Burroughs, and Edwards—have sent in a proposition to the President, to take the stump and obtain subscriptions of rations for the troops. The President marks it "special," and refers it to the Secretary "for attention and advice." Humbugged to the end! These men might fight, but they won't. They will speak two words for the soldiers, and one for themselves. I believe two of them are *Northern* men. What idiocy! If they meddle at all in the carnival of blood, I would put them in the ranks.

Gen. Bragg says he is greatly outnumbered by the enemy's two corps near Wilmington. Of course he will evacuate.

There is no money (paper) in the Treasury. Mr. Trenholm, seeing Mr. Memminger abused for issuing too much paper money, seems likely to fall into the opposite error of printing too little, leaving hundreds of millions of indebtedness unpaid. This will soon rouse a hornet's nest about his ears !

Gold is arriving from Charlotte, N. C., and I suppose from other places. Its accumulation here, when known to the enemy, as it certainly will be, only endangers the city more and more.

Mr. Harman, of Staunton, suggests that every house in Virginia be visited, and one third the subsistence for man and beast be bought at market price. He says that would subsist the army.

FEBRUARY 24TH.—Rained all day yesterday; cloudy and cool this morning. We have no news—only rumors that Wilmington has been abandoned, that A. P. Hill's corps (Lee's army) has marched into North Carolina, etc.

Yesterday the Senate voted down the bill to put 200,000 negroes in the army. The papers to-day contain a letter from Gen. Lee, advocating the measure as a *necessity*. Mr. Hunter's vote defeated it. He has many negroes, and will probably lose them ; but the loss of popularity, and fear of forfeiting all chance of the succession, may have operated on him as a politician. What madness ! " Under which King, Benzonian ?"

The President and Gen. Breckinridge rode out to Camp Lee yesterday, and mingled with the returned prisoners, not yet exchanged. They made speeches to them. The President, being chilled, went into a hut and sat down before a fire, looking ill and wan.

The Bureau of Conscription being abolished, the business is to be turned over to the generals of reserves, who will employ the reserves mainly in returning deserters and absentees to the army. The deserters and absentees will be too many for them perhaps, at this late day. The mischief already effected may prove irremediable.

A dispatch from Gen. Lee, this morning, states that Lieut. McNeill, with 30 men, entered Cumberland, Maryland, on the 21st inst., and brought off Gens. Crook and Kelly, etc. This is a little affair, but will make a great noise. We want 300,000 men in the field instead of 30. However, this may be the beginning of a new species of warfare, by detached parties. Our men, of course, have the best knowledge of the country, and small bands may subsist where armies would starve. The war can be prolonged indefinitely, if necessary, and probably will be, unless there should be some relaxation of the stringency of measures on the part of the United States Government.

The markets are now almost abandoned, both by sellers and purchasers. Beef and pork are sold at $7 to $9 per pound, and everything else in proportion. Butter, from $15 to $20.

The President walked down to his office after 11 o'clock this morning, very erect, having heard of Lieut. McNeill's exploit.

Another dispatch from Gen. Lee says detachments of Gen. Vaughan's cavalry a few days ago captured two of the enemy's posts in Tennessee beyond Knoxville, with 60 prisoners, horses, etc.

The following letter from Gen. Lee, on the subject of putting negroes into the army, clearly defines his views on that important subject:

"HEADQUARTERS CONFEDERATE STATES ARMIES,
"February 18th, 1865.

"HON. E. BARKSDALE, HOUSE OF REPRESENTATIVES, RICHMOND.

"SIR:—I have the honor to acknowledge the receipt of your letter of the 12th inst., with reference to the employment of negroes as soldiers. I think the measure not only expedient, but necessary. The enemy will certainly use them against us if he can get possession of them; and as his present numerical superiority will enable him to penetrate many parts of the country, I cannot see the wisdom of the policy of holding them to await his arrival, when we may, by timely action and judicious management, use them to arrest his progress. I do not think that our white population can supply the necessities of a long war without overtaxing its capacity and imposing great suffering upon our people; and I believe we should provide resources for a protracted struggle—not merely for a battle or a campaign.

"In answer to your second question, I can only say that, in my opinion, the negroes, under proper circumstances, will make efficient soldiers. I think we could at least do as well with them as the enemy, and he attaches great importance to their assistance. Under good officers, and good instructions, I do not see why they should not become soldiers. They possess all the physical qualifications, and their habits of obedience constitute a good foundation for discipline. They furnish a more promising material than many armies of which we read in history, which owed their efficiency to discipline alone. I think those who are employed should be freed. It would be neither just nor wise, in my opinion, to require them to serve as slaves. The best course to pursue, it seems to me, would be to call for such as are willing to come with the consent of their owners. An impressment or draft would not be likely to bring out the best class, and the use of coercion would make the measure distasteful to them and to their owners.

"I have no doubt that if Congress would authorize their reception into service, and empower the President to call upon individuals or States for such as they are willing to contribute, with the condition of emancipation to all enrolled, a sufficient number would be forthcoming to enable us to try the experiment. If it proved successful, most of the objections to the measure would disappear, and if individuals still remained unwilling to send their negroes to the army, the force of public opinion in the States would soon bring about such legislation as would remove all obstacles. I think the matter should be left, as far as possible, to the people and to the States, which alone can legislate as the necessities of this particular service may require. As to the mode of organizing them, it should be left as free from restraint as possible. Experience will suggest the best course, and it would be inexpedient to trammel the subject with provisions that might, in the end, prevent the adoption of reforms suggested by actual trial.

"With great respect,
"Your obedient servant,
"R. E. LEE, *General.*"

FEBRUARY 25TH.—Raining. There are more rumors of the evacuation of Wilmington and even *Petersburg*. No doubt that stores, etc. are leaving Petersburg; but I doubt whether it will be evacuated, or Richmond, either. Grant may, and probably will, get the Danville Railroad, but I think Lee will disappoint him in the item of evacuation, nevertheless; for we have some millions in gold—equal to 300,000,000 paper—to purchase subsistence; and it is believed Virginia alone, for *specie,* can feed the army. Then *another* army may arise in Grant's rear.

From the published accounts in the enemy's journals, we learn that Charleston fell on the 18th inst. They say one-third of the city was burned by us. I presume they saw the ruins of the old fire; and that most of the citizens, except the destitute, had left the town. All the cotton was destroyed by the inhabitants. They say an explosion killed several hundred of our people. They boast of capturing 200 guns, and a fine lot of ammunition—the latter, it seems to me, might have been destroyed.

I hear the deep booming of guns occasionally—but still doubt the policy or purpose of evacuating Petersburg.

Mr. Hunter's eyes seem blood-shotten since he voted against Lee's plan of organizing negro troops. He also voted against displacing the brood of quartermasters and commissioners.

The papers are requested to say nothing relative to military operations in South and North Carolina, for they are read by Gen. Grant every morning of their publication. The garrisons of Charleston and Wilmington may add 20,000 men to our force opposing Sherman, and may beat him yet.

FEBRUARY 26TH.—Cloudy and cool; rained all night. No news from the South, this morning. But there is an ugly rumor that Beauregard's men have deserted to a frightful extent, and that the general himself is afflicted with disease of mind, etc.

Mr. Hunter is now reproached by the slaveowners, whom he thought to please, for defeating the Negro bill. They say his vote will make Virginia a free State, inasmuch as Gen. Lee must evacuate it for the want of negro troops.

There is much alarm on the streets. Orders have been given to prepare all the tobacco and cotton, which cannot be removed immediately, for destruction by fire. And it is generally believed that Lieut.-Gen. A. P. Hill's corps has marched away to North Carolina. This would leave some 25,000 men to defend Richmond and Petersburg, against, probably, 60,000.

If Richmond be evacuated, most of the population will remain, not knowing whither to go.

The new Secretary of War was at work quite early this morning.

The "Bureau of Conscription" and the Provost Marshal's office are still "operating," notwithstanding Congress has abolished them both.

FEBRUARY 27TH.—Bright and windy. The Virginia Assembly has passed resolutions *instructing* the Senators to vote for the negro troops bill—so Mr. Hunter must obey or resign.

It is authoritatively announced in the papers that Gen. J. E. Johnston has taken command of the army in front of Sherman (a perilous undertaking), superseding Beauregard.

Grant is said to be massing his troops on our right, to precipitate them upon the South Side Railroad. Has Hill marched his corps away to North Carolina? If so, Richmond is in very great danger.

The *Examiner* to-day labors to show that the evacuation of Richmond would be fatal to the cause. The *Sentinel* says it has authority for saying that Richmond will *not* be given up. "Man proposes—God disposes." It is rumored that Fayetteville, N. C., has fallen into the hands of the enemy.

I saw Col. Northrop, late Commissary-General, to-day. He looks down, dark, and dissatisfied. Lee's army *eats* without him. I see nothing of Lieut.-Col. Ruffin. He always looks down and darkly. Gen. Breckinridge seems to have his heart in the cause— not his soul in his pocket, like most of his predecessors.

I saw Admiral Buchanan to-day, limping a little. He says the enemy tried to shoot away his legs to keep him from dancing at his granddaughter's wedding, but won't succeed.

Robert Tyler told me that it was feared Governor Brown, and probably Stephens and Toombs, were sowing disaffection among the Georgia troops, hoping to get them out of the army; but that if faction can be kept down thirty days, our cause would assume a new phase. He thinks Breckinridge will make a successful Secretary.

The President and Gen. Lee were out at Camp Lee to-day, urging the returned soldiers (from captivity) to forego the usual furlough and enter upon the spring campaign now about to begin. The other day, when the President made a speech to them, he was often interrupted by cries of "furlough!"

The ladies in the Treasury Department are ordered to Lynchburg, whither the process of manufacturing Confederate States notes is to be transferred.

A committee of the Virginia Assembly waited on the President on Saturday, who told them it was no part of his intention to evacuate Richmond. But some construed his words as equivocal. Tobacco, cotton, etc. are leaving the city daily. The city *is* in danger.

FEBRUARY 28TH.—Raining; warm. The Northern papers announce the capture of Wilmington. No doubt the city has fallen, although the sapient dignitaries of this government deem it a matter of policy to withhold such intelligence from the people and the army. And wherefore, since the enemy's papers have a circulation here—at least their items of news are sure to be reproduced immediately.

The Governor of Mississippi has called the Legislature of the State together, for the purpose of summoning a convention of the people. Governor Brown, of Georgia, likewise calls for a convention. One more State calling a convention of all the States may be the consequence—if, indeed, rent by faction, the whole country does not fall a prey to the Federal armies immediately. Governor Brown alleges many bitter things in the conduct of affairs at Richmond, and stigmatizes the President most vehemently. He denounces the President's generalship, the Provost Marshals, the passport system, the "Bureau of Conscription," etc. etc. He says it is attempted to establish a despotism, where the people are sovereigns, and our whole policy should be sanctioned by popular favor. Instead of this it must be admitted that the President's inflexible adherence to obnoxious and incompetent men in his cabinet is too well calculated to produce a depressing effect on the spirits of the people and the army.

T. N. Conrad, one of the government's secret agents, says 35,000 of Thomas's army passed down the Potomac several weeks ago. He says also *that our telegraph operator in Augusta, Ga., sent all the military dispatches to Grant!*

CHAPTER XLVIII

From the North.—Rumored defeat of Gen. Early.—Panic among officials.—Moving the archives.—Lincoln's inaugural.—Victory in North Carolina.—Rumored treaty with France.—Sheridan's movements.—Letter from Lord John Russell.—Sherman's progress.—Desperate condition of the Government.—Disagreement between the President and Congress.—Development of Grant's combination.—Assault at Hare's Hill.—Departure of Mrs. President Davis.

MARCH 1ST.—Cloudy, cold, and dismal. We have no news, except from the North, whence we learn Lieut. Beall, one of our Canada raiders, has been hung; that some little cotton and turpentine were burnt at Wilmington; and that the enemy's columns are approaching us from all directions. They say the rebellion will be crushed very soon, and really seem to have speedy and accurate information from Richmond not only of all movements of our army, but of the intentions of the government. They say Lynchburg and East Tennessee now occupy the mind of Gen. Lee; and they know every disposition of our forces from day to day sooner than our own people! What imbecile stolidity! Will we thus blunder on to the end?

Congress has passed an act organizing the artillery force of Lee's army—submitted by Gen. Pendleton (Episcopal clergyman), who writes the Secretary that Col. Pemberton (Northern man and once lieutenant-general) is making efforts to induce the President to withhold his approval of the bill, which he deprecates and resents, as the bill is sanctioned by the judgment of Gen. Lee. From this letter I learn we have 330 guns and 90 mortars under Lee; enough to make a *great noise* yet!

Lieut.-Gen. Grant has directed Col. Mulford, Agent of Exchange, to say that some 200 prisoners escaped from us, when taken to Wilmington for exchange, and now in his lines, will be held as paroled, and credited in the general exchange. Moreover, all prisoners in transitu for any point of exchange, falling into their hands, will be held as paroled, and exchanged. He states also that all prisoners held by the United States, whether in close confinement, in-irons, or under sentence, are to be exchanged. Surely Gen. Grant is trying to please us in this matter. Yet Lieut. Beall was executed!

MARCH 2D.—Raining. No well-authenticated news; but by many it is believed Staunton is in the hands of the enemy, and Lynchburg menaced. Nevertheless, the government is sending a portion of the archives and stores to Lynchburg!

The clergymen are at work begging supplies for the soldiers; and they say the holding of Richmond and the success of the cause depend upon the success of their efforts, the government being null! A large per cent. of these preachers is of Northern birth—and some of them may possibly betray the cause if they deem it desperate. This is the history of such men in the South so far. But the President trusts them, and we must trust the President.

Hon. Wm. C. Rives has resigned his seat in Congress. Alleged causes, ill health and great age—over 70.

The Negro bill still hangs fire in Congress.

Roger A. Pryor is to be exchanged. He was the guest of Forney in Washington, and had interviews with President Lincoln.

The government is impressing horses in the streets, to collect the tobacco preparatory for its destruction in the event of the city falling into the hands of the enemy. This fact is already known in the North and published in the papers there. A pretty passport and police system, truly!

I saw a paper to-day from Mr. Benjamin, saying it had been determined, in the event of burning the tobacco, to exempt that belonging to other governments—French and Austrian; but that belonging to foreign subjects is not to be spared. This he says is with the concurrence of the British Government. Tobacco is being moved from the city with all possible expedition.

MARCH 3D.—Raining and cold. This morning there was another arrival of our prisoners on parol, and not yet exchanged. Many thousands have arrived this week, and many more are on the way. How shall we feed them? Will *they* compel the evacuation of the city? I hope not. Capt. Warner, Commissary-General, is here again; and if assigned to duty, has sufficient business qualifications to collect supplies.

Thank God, I have some 300 pounds of flour and half that amount of meal—bread rations for my family, seven in number, for more than two months! I have but $7\frac{1}{2}$ pounds of meat; but we can live without it, as we have often done. I have a bushel of peas also, and coal and wood for a month. This is a guarantee against immediate starvation, should the famine become more rigorous, upon which we may felicitate ourselves.

Our nominal income has been increased; amounting now to some $16,000 in paper—less than $300 in specie. But, for the next six months (if we can stay here), our rent will be only $75 per month—a little over one dollar; and servant hire, $40—less than eighty cents.

It is rumored that Gen. Early has been beaten again at Waynesborough, and that the enemy have reached *Charlottesville* for the first time. Thus it seems our downward career continues. We *must* have a victory soon, else Virginia is irretrievably lost.

Two P.M. The wind has shifted to the south; warm showers.

Three P.M. It is said they are fighting at Gordonsville; whether or not the enemy have Charlottesville is therefore uncertain. I presume it is an advance of Sheridan's cavalry whom our troops have engaged at Gordonsville.

MARCH 4TH.—Raining hard, and warm. We have vague reports of Early's defeat in the Valley by an overwhelming force; and the gloom and despondency among the people are in accordance with the hue of the constantly-occurring disasters.

Brig.-Gen. J. Gorgas, Chief of Ordnance, has been rebuked by Gen. Lee for constantly striving to get mechanics out of the service. Gen. Lee says the time has arrived when the necessity of having able-bodied men in the field is paramount to all other considerations.

Brig.-Gen. Preston (Bureau of Conscription) takes issue with Gen. Lee on the best mode of sending back deserters to the field. He says there are at this time 100,000 *deserters!*

C. Lamar, Bath, S. C., writes to the President that ——, a bonded farmer, secretly removed his meat and then burnt his smoke-house, conveying the impression that all his meat was destroyed. The President sends this to the Secretary of War with the following indorsement: "For attention—this example shows the vice of class exemption, as well as the practices resorted to to avoid yielding supplies to the government."

The Legislature of North Carolina has passed resolutions exempting millers, blacksmith, etc.—in contravention of the act of Congress—and directing Gov. Vance to correspond with the Secretary of War on the subject. This bears an ugly aspect.

Gen. Early's little army is scattered to the winds. Charlottesville has been in possession of the enemy, but at last accounts Gen. Rosser, in Sheridan's rear, held it. Sheridan advanced to Scottsville; and is no doubt still advancing. Lynchburg is rendered unsafe; and yet some of the bureaus are packing up and preparing to send the archives thither. They would probably fall into the hands of the enemy.

Gen. Lee is in the city — where there is much confusion of tongues—and impatient, waiting for the next scene of the drama. If there was to be concert of action between Grant and Sheridan, probably the copious rains have prevented it.

Two P.M. There is almost a panic among officials here who have their families with them, under the belief that the city may be suddenly evacuated, and the impossibility of getting transportation. I do not share the belief—that is, that the event is likely to occur immediately; but if it should occur, I know my wife and children will remain—for a season. We must "pray that our flight be not in the winter."

Gen. Lee was closeted with the Secretary of War several hours to-day. It is reported that Gen. L.'s family are preparing to leave the city.

MARCH 5TH.—Bright and cool; some frost this morning.

I saw an officer yesterday from Early's command. He said the enemy entered Charlottesville on Friday at half-past two o'clock P.M., between 2000 and 3000 strong, cavalry, and had made no advance at the latest accounts. He says Gen. Early, when last seen, was flying, and pursued by some fifteen well-mounted Federals, only fifty paces in his rear. The general being a large heavy man, and badly mounted, was undoubtedly captured. He intimated that Early's *army* consisted of only about 1000 men! Whether he had more elsewhere, I was unable to learn. I have not heard of any destruction of property by the enemy.

There is still an accredited rumor of the defeat of Sherman. Perhaps he may have been checked, and turned toward his supplies on the coast.

I learn by a paper from Gen. Gorgas, Chief of Ordnance, that the machinery of the workshops here is being moved to Danville, Salisbury, and other places in North Carolina. He recommends that transportation be given the families of the operatives; and that houses be built for them, with permission to buy subsistence at government prices, for twelve months, that the mechanics may be contented and kept from deserting. This would rid the city of some thousands of its population, and be some measure of relief to those that remain. But how long will we be allowed to remain? All depends upon the operations in the field during the next few weeks—and these may depend upon the wisdom of those in possession of the government, which is now at a discount.

The Secretary of the Treasury is selling gold for Confederate States notes for reissue to meet pressing demands; the machinery for manufacturing paper money having just at present no certain abiding place. The government gives $1 of gold for sixty of its own paper; but were it to cease selling gold, it would command $100 for $1.

MARCH 6TH.—A bright frosty morning.
This day I am fifty-five years of age.

It is now reported that Gen. Early made his escape, and that most of his men have straggled into this city.

One body of Sheridan's men are said to have been at Gordonsville yesterday, coming hitherward, while another were near Scottsville, aiming for the South Side Railroad.

The Adjutant-General, having granted furloughs to the returned prisoners two days ago, to-day revokes them. Will such vacillating policy conciliate the troops, and incite them to heroic deeds?

The President and his wife were at church yesterday; so they have not left the city; but Gen. Lee's family, it is rumored, are packing up to leave.

I bought a quarter of a cord of oak wood this morning to mix with the green pine, and paid $55 for it.

Gen. Early's cavalry, being mostly men of property, were two-thirds of them on furlough or detail, when the enemy advanced on Charlottesville; and the infantry, being poor, with no means either to bribe the authorities, to fee members of Congress, or to aid their suffering families, declined to fight in defense of the property of their rich and *absent* neighbors! We lost four guns beyond Charlottesville, and our forces were completely routed.

There are rumors to-day that a column of the enemy's cavalry has reached Hanover County. Gen. R. E. Lee has ordered Major-Gen. Fitz Lee's cavalry to march against them.

Twelve M. They are bringing boxes to the War Office, to pack up the archives. This certainly indicates a sudden removal in an emergency. It is not understood whether they go to Danville or to Lynchburg; that may depend upon *Grant's* movements. It may, however, be Lee's purpose to *attack* Grant; meantime preparing to fall back in the event of losing the day.

Four days hence we have a day of fasting, etc., appointed by the President; and I understand there are but *three* day's rations for the army—a nice calculation.

Gen. Johnston telegraphs the Secretary that his army must suffer, if not allowed to get commissary stores in the North Carolina depots. The Secretary replies that of course his army must be fed, but hopes he can buy enough, etc., leaving the stores already collected for Lee's army, *which is in great straits.*

MARCH 7TH.—Bright and frosty.

Yesterday we had no certain accounts of the movements of Sheridan. His force was said to be near Charlottesville—at Keswich. Fitz Lee's cavalry and Pickett's infantry were sent in that direction. Not a word has yet appeared in the Richmond papers concerning this movement from the Valley—the papers being read daily in the enemy's camp below. We hear of no corresponding movement on the part of Grant; and perhaps there was none.

Preparations to evacuate the city are still being made with due diligence. If these indications do not suffice to bring the speculators into the ranks to defend their own property (they have no honor, of course), the city and the State are lost; and the property owners will deserve their fate. The extortioners ought to be hung, besides losing their property. This would be a very popular act on the part of the conquerors.

On the 4th inst., the day of inauguration at Washington, the troops (Federal) near Petersburg got drunk, and proposed an hour's truce to have a friendly talk. It was refused.

I met my friend Brooks to-day, just from Georgia, in a pucker. He says the people there are for reunion. Mr. B. rented his house to Secretary Trenholm for $15,000—furnished. It would now bring $30,000. But he is now running after teams to save his tobacco—*he* a speculator!

A letter was received yesterday from ——, Selma accusing the Assistant Secretary of War, Judge Campbell, his brother-in-law, Judge Goldthwait, and Judge Parsons, of Alabama, with disloyalty, and says Judge C. is about to issue passports for delegates to go to the *Chicago* Convention, soon to assemble, etc. etc. He says Judge C. is the Fouche of the South. The letter is dated August 23d, 1864, and the President *now* sends it to the Secretary "for his information."

Judge Campbell has exercised almost exclusive control of the conscription and the passport business of the government since his appointment. The President and Secretary must attach some importance to the communication of Mr. ——, the first for sending over the letter at this juncture—the latter, for having just called in Lieut.-Col. Melton, A. A. G., who is assigned a position in his office, and is now superintending the business of *passports*. This arrangement also cuts the earth under the feet of Mr. Kean, Chief of the Bureau of War.

The raid of Sheridan has caused some speculators to send their surplus flour into the city for sale. Some sold for $700 per barrel to-day, a decline of $50.

D. H. London says the enemy captured the tobacco at Hamilton's Crossing (near Fredericksburg) this morning. I doubt it, but would not deplore it, as it belongs to speculators, sent thither for barter with the enemy. No doubt many articles will decline in price—the owners fearing the coming of the enemy.

The packing up of the archives goes on, with directions to be as quiet as possible, so as "not to alarm the people." A large per cent. of the population would behold the exodus with pleasure!

MARCH 8TH.—Damp and foggy. We have no military news yet—9 A.M.

President Lincoln's short inaugural message, or homily, or sermon, has been received. It is filled with texts from the Bible. He says both sides pray to the same God for aid—one upholding and the other destroying African slavery. If slavery be an offense,—and woe shall fall upon those by whom offenses come,—perhaps not only all the slaves will be lost, but all the accumulated products of their labor be swept away. In short, he "quotes Scripture for the deed" quite as fluently as our President; and since both Presidents resort to religious justification, it may be feared the war is about to assume a more sanguinary aspect and a more cruel nature than ever before. God help us! The history of man, even in the Bible, is but a series of bloody wars. It must be thus to make us appreciate the blessings of peace, and to bow in humble adoration of the great Father of all. The Garden of Eden could not yield contentment to man, nor heaven satisfy all the angels.

It is said the enemy have left Fredericksburg—bought all the tobacco, I suppose.

To-day the *State* made distribution in this city of cotton cloth, three yards to each member of a family, at $5.50 for 7-8 and $6.25 for 4-4 width. The State paid about $3 per yard for it, and the profits make a portion of its revenue, or, perhaps, the revenue of its *officers* and *agents*. Nevertheless, there was a large crowd, and one man fainted. The shops sell at $12 to $15 per yard.

Raining at 12 M. All quiet below.

Another report of the defeat of Sherman is current to-day, and believed by many.

MARCH 9TH.—Rained all night; clearing away this morning. Warm. Nothing positive from Sherman, Grant, or Sheridan. The enemy's papers say Gen. Early and 18,000 men were captured—which is nonsense.

Yesterday the Senate passed the Negro troops bill—Mr. Hunter voting for it under instructions.

The enemy did capture or destroy the tobacco sent to Fredericksburg by the speculators to exchange for bacon—and 31 cars were burned. No one regrets this, so far as the speculators are concerned.

Letters from North Carolina state that the country is swarming with deserters—perhaps many supposed to be deserters are furloughed soldiers just exchanged. It is stated that there are 800 in Randolph County, committing depredations on the *rich* farmers, etc.; and that the quartermaster and commissary stores at Greensborough are threatened.

Meal is selling at $2 per pound, or $100 per bushel, to-day. Bacon, $13 per pound.

Two P.M. Cloudy, and prospect of more rain. It is quite warm.

A great many officers are here on leave from Lee's army—all operations being, probably, interdicted by the mud and swollen streams. Sheridan failed to cross to the south side of James River, it being certainly his intention to cross and form a junction with Grant, cutting the Danville and South Side Roads on his way.

I saw Mr. Benjamin to-day without his usual smile. He is not at ease. The country demands a change of men in the cabinet, and he is the most obnoxious of all.

Again, there is a rumor of peace negotiations. All men know that no peace can be negotiated except for reconstruction—and, I suppose, emancipation.

MARCH 10TH.—Raining and cold. This is the day appointed by the government for prayer, fasting, etc.; and the departments, shops, etc. are closed. The people; notwithstanding the bad weather, pretty generally proceeded to the churches, which will be open morning, noon, and night, for it is a solemn occasion, and thousands will supplicate Almighty God to be pleased to look upon us with compassion, and aid us, in this hour of extremity, to resist the endeavors of our enemies to reduce us to bondage.

The morning papers contain a dispatch from Lee, giving an account of a successful battle in North Carolina. I append it, as the first success chronicled for a great length of time.

"HEADQUARTERS, ETC., March 9th, 1865.
"HON. J. C. BRECKINRIDGE, SECRETARY OF WAR.

"Gen. Bragg reports that he attacked the enemy, yesterday, four miles in front of Kinston, and drove him from his position. He disputed the ground obstinately, and took up a new line three miles from his first.

"We captured 3 pieces of artillery and 1500 prisoners.

"The number of the enemy's dead and wounded left on the field is large. Ours comparatively small.

"The troops behaved most handsomely, and Major-Gens. Hill and Hoke exhibited their usual zeal and energy. R. E. LEE."

MARCH 11TH.—Bright and frosty. From a published correspondence between Gens. Hampton and Sherman, on the subject of retaliatory executions, it is mentioned by the former that the City of Columbia, S. C. was burned by the latter.

Dispatches this morning inform us of some little successes—Hampton over Kilpatrick in the South, and Rosser over a body of the enemy at Harrisonburg, in the North.

Some 1500 prisoners, paroled, arrived this morning—making some 10,000 in the last fortnight. I fear there will soon be a great scarcity of arms, when the negroes are drilled, etc.

Mrs. Hobson, of Goochland County, a relative of my wife, has offered a home to my eldest daughter Anne. Mr. H. is wealthy, and his mansion is magnificent. It is lighted with gas, made on the plantation.

I am often called upon to lend a copy of the "Wild Western Scenes." My copy is lost. I learn that new editions of my works are published in the United States, where the stereotype plates were deposited. *Here*, as in old times in the North, the publishers prefer to issue publications upon which they pay no copyright—and, I believe, most of our publishers are not Southern men by birth, and hence have no care but for the profits of the business.

Congress was to adjourn to-day. But it is said the President has requested them to remain a short time longer, as further legislation will be required *growing out of a treaty with France, about to be consummated.* It is said an alliance has been agreed upon, offensive and defensive, etc. etc. If this should be true! It is but rumor yet—but was first mentioned, gravely, by Judge Campbell, Assistant Secretary of War.

MARCH 12TH.—Bright and frosty. About one o'clock last night, there was an alarm, supposed to be the approach of the enemy from the West—Sheridan's cavalry—and the tocsin sounded until daylight. It was a calm moonlight night, without a cloud in the sky. Couriers reported that the enemy were at the outer fortifications, and had burned Ben Green's house. Corse's brigade and one or two batteries passed through the city in the direction of the menaced point; and all the local organizations were ordered to march early in the morning. Mr. Secretary Mallory and Postmaster-General Reagan were in the saddle; and rumor says the President and the remainder of the cabinet had their horses saddled in readiness for flight. About a year ago we had Dahlgren's raid, and it was then announced that the purpose was to burn the city and put to death the President, the cabinet, and other prominent leaders of the "rebellion." Perhaps our leaders had some apprehension of the fate prepared for them on that occasion, and may have concerted a plan of escape.

As well as I can learn from couriers, it appears that only some 1200 or 1500 of the enemy's cavalry advanced toward the city, and are now (10 A.M.) retiring—or driven back by our cavalry. But it is a little extraordinary that Gen. Lee, with almost unlimited power, has not been able to prevent 1200 Federals riding from Winchester to Richmond, over almost impracticable roads, without even a respectable skirmish wherein 1000 men were opposed to them. It is true Early was routed—but that was more than a week ago, and we have no particulars yet. The enemy's papers will contain them, however.

MARCH 13TH.—Bright and pleasant.

The reports of the army of Sheridan (mostly mounted infantry) being within a few miles of the city were at least premature. Subsequent reports indicate that none of the enemy's cavalry have been in the vicinity of Richmond, but that his force, a pretty strong one, is some 20 miles up the river, with pontoon trains, etc., manifesting a purpose to cross the James and cut the Danville Road. In this they will be disappointed probably.

The President vetoed several bills last week, among them the one legislating out of office most of the able-bodied post-quartermasters and commissaries. There is much anxiety to learn the nature of the communication he intends laying before Congress in a few days, and for the reception of which the session has been prolonged. The prevalent supposition is that it relates to foreign complications. Some think the President means to tender his resignation, but this is absurd, for he would be the last man to yield. To-day it is understood the Secretary of War is to be absent from his office, closeted with the President.

Gen. Johnston is concentrating on the Wilmington and Weldon Railroad, and perhaps a battle will occur near Goldsborough. Its issue will decide the fate of Raleigh, perhaps of Richmond.

The President had the Secretary of War and Mr. Benjamin closeted nearly the entire day yesterday, Sunday. Some important event is in embryo. If Lee's army can be fed—as long as it can be fed—Richmond is safe. Its abandonment will be the loss of Virginia, and perhaps the cause. To save it, therefore, is the problem for those in authority to solve. If we had had competent and honest men always directing the affairs of the Confederacy, Richmond never would have been in danger, and long ere this independence would have been achieved. But passports have been sold, political enemies have been persecuted, conscription has been converted into an engine of vengeance, of cupidity, and has been often made to subserve the ends of the invader, until at last we find ourselves in a deplorable and desperate condition.

Gen. Wise, who has been here a few days on sick furlough, has returned to his command, still coughing distressfully, and distressed at the prospect.

Miers W. Fisher, member of the Virginia Secession Convention, neglected by the government, and racked with disease, is about to return to the Eastern Shore of Virginia. He may submit and die. He might have done good service, but the politicians who controlled the Confederate States Government ignored him because he had once been a supporter of Gov. Wise for the Presidency.

There is a report that Sheridan's force has crossed the James River. If this be so, the Danville Road is in danger, and the President and his cabinet and Congress are all in a predicament. No wonder there is some commotion! But the report may not be true. It is also said Grant is crossing his army to the north side of the river. This may be a feint, but stirring events are casting their shadows before!

MARCH 14TH.—Bright and pleasant, but indications of change.

The papers contain no news from the armies, near or remote. But there was some alarm in the upper portion of the city about 9 P.M. last night, from a signal seen (appended to a balloon) just over the western horizon. It was stationary for ten minutes, a blood-red light, seen through a hazy atmosphere. I thought it was Mars, but my eldest daughter, a better astronomer than I, said it was neither the time nor place for it to be visible. The air was still, and the dismal barking of the ban-dogs conjured up the most direful portents. All my neighbors supposed it to be a signal from Sheridan to Grant, and that the city would certainly be attacked before morning. It was only a camp signal of one of our own detachments awaiting the approach of Sheridan.

Sheridan's passage of the James River has not been confirmed, and so the belief revives that he will assault the city fortifications on the northwest side, while Grant attacks elsewhere.

Yesterday the President vetoed several bills, and sent back others unsigned, suggesting alterations. Among them is the Conscript and Exemption bills, which he has detained *ten days*, as Senators say, on a point of constructive etiquette, insisting that the President and Secretary ought to make certain details and exemptions instead of Congress, etc. It is precious time lost, but perhaps in view of the great calamities immediately threatening the country, Congress may yield. But ten days might be enough time lost to lose the cause.

The communication referred to by the President, in detaining Congress, has not yet been sent in, unless it be one of his qualified vetoes, and conjecture is still busy, some persons going so far as to hint that it relates to a *capitulation*, yielding up Richmond on certain terms. I have not heard of any demands of Grant of that nature.

A dispatch from Gen. R. E. Lee, received this morning, says Fitz Lee's cavalry was at Powhatan C. H. last night (so it was not Fitz's signal), and had been ordered to cross to the north side of the James, which may not be practicable above Richmond. We shall probably see them pass through the city to-day. He says the roads are bad, etc. Sheridan, then, has not crossed the river.

Gen. Lee sends to the department this morning a copy of a fierce letter from Lord John Russell, British Secretary of State, to our commissioners abroad, demanding a discontinuance of expeditions fitted out in Canada, and the building and equipping of cruisers in British ports. It says such practices must cease, for they are not only in violation of British law, but calculated to foment war between Great Britain and the United States, which Lord John is very much averse to. The communication is sent to *Washington, D. C.*, and thence forwarded by Mr. Seward to Lieut.-Gen. Grant, who sends it by flag of truce to Gen. Lee. Great Britain gives us a kick while the Federal generals are pounding us.

The enemy have Fayetteville, N. C. Hardee and Hampton crossed the Cape Fear on the 11th inst. Sherman's army was then within 7 miles of Fayetteville. Bragg, after his fight near Kinston, had to fall back, his rear and right wing being threatened by heavy forces of the enemy coming up from Wilmington.

Some of Sheridan's force did cross the James, but retired to the north side. So telegraphs Gen. Lee.

MARCH 15TH.—Warm and cloudy. My cabbages coming up in the garden.

The papers contain no war news whatever, yet there is great activity in the army.

Sheridan's column is said to be at Ashland, and Grant is reported to be sending swarms of troops to the north side of the river, below, "in countless thousands."

The President's message, for the completion of which Congress was desired to remain, has been sent in. I will preserve this splendidly exordiumed and most extraordinary document. It is a great legal triumph, achieved by the President over his enemies in Congress, and if we are permitted to have more elections, many obnoxious members will be defeated, for the sins of omission and commission. The President strikes them "between wind and water," at a time, too, when no defense would be listened to, for he says the capital was never in such danger before, and shows that without prodigious effort, and perfect co-operation of all branches of the government, the cause is lost, and we shall have negro garrisons to keep us in subjection, commanded by Northern officers. He will have the satisfaction, at least, of having to say a portion of the responsibility rested with his political opponents.

Mr. Benjamin, who is supposed to have written a portion of the message, was very jubilant yesterday, and it is said the President himself was almost jocund as he walked through the Capitol Square, returning home from his office.

It is now rumored that a French agent is in the city, and that the President, besides his message, sent to Congress a secret communication. I doubt—but it may be so.

Gen. Hood is here, on crutches, attracting no attention, for he was not successful.

Judge Campbell, Assistant Secretary of War, said to Mr. Wattles, a clerk, to-day, that we were now arrived at the last days of the Confederacy. Mr. Wattles told me that the judge had been convinced, as far back as 1863, that the cause was nearly hopeless.

Some 1200 of Fitz Lee's cavalry passed through the city at 2 P.M. Gen. Longstreet has been ordered by Gen. Lee to attack Sheridan. He telegraphs back from north of the city that he "cannot find them," and this body of cavalry is ordered to reconnoiter their position. I know not how many more men Fitz Lee has in his division, but fear at least *half* have passed.

MARCH 16TH.—Clouds and sunshine; warm. Splendid rainbow last evening.

We have nothing new in the papers from any quarter. Sheridan's position is not known yet, though it must be within a short distance of the city. There was no battle yesterday. Sheridan reports the killing of Commodore Hollins, and says it was done because he attempted to escape at Gordonsville.

Sherman's march through South Carolina is reported to have been cruel and devastating. Fire and the sword did their worst.

Congress, the House of Representatives rather, yesterday passed a bill suspending the privilege of the writ of *habeas corpus*. The Senate will concur probably. Also the President's suggestion amending the Conscript act has been passed. The President has the reins now, and Congress will be more obedient; but can they save this city? Advertisements for recruiting negro troops are in the papers this morning.

It is rumored that Sheridan has crossed the Chickahominy and got off without hinderance. If this be so, Gen. Lee will be criticised.

One P.M. It is ascertained that Sheridan has withdrawn to the York River, and abandoned any attempt on Richmond.

And it is supposed by high military authority that but for the providential freshet, Sheridan would have succeeded in crossing the James River, and cutting the Danville Railroad, which would have deprived Lee's army of supplies. The freshet rendered his pontoon bridge too short, etc. This may be claimed as a direct interposition of Providence, at a time when we were fasting, praying, etc., in accordance with the recommendation of the government.

MARCH 17TH.—Bright and cool. A violent southeast gale prevailed last evening, with rain. Of course we have no news in the papers from any quarter. Sheridan having retired, all the local troops returned yesterday.

After all, the President does not reap a perfect triumph over Congress. The bill suspending the writ of *habeas corpus* passed the House by only four majority; and in the Senate it was defeated by nine against six for it! So the President cannot enjoy Cromwell's power without the exercise of Cromwell's violence.

We shall have a negro army. Letters are pouring into the department from men of military skill and character, asking authority to raise companies, battalions, and regiments of negro troops. It is the desperate remedy for the very desperate case—and may be successful. If 300,000 efficient soldiers can be made of this material, there is no conjecturing where the next campaign may end. Possibly "over the border," for a little success will elate our spirits extravagantly; and the blackened ruins of our towns, and the moans of women and children bereft of shelter, will appeal strongly to the army for vengeance.

There is a vague rumor of another battle by Bragg, in which he did not gain the victory. This is not authentic; and would be very bad, if true, for then Sherman's army would soon loom up in our vicinity like a portentous cloud.

The Commissary-General, in a communication to the Secretary urging the necessity of keeping the trade for supplies for Lee's army, now going on in Eastern North Carolina, a profound secret, mentions the "miscarriage of the Fredericksburg affair," which proves that the government *did* send cotton and tobacco thither for barter with the enemy.

One reason alleged for the refusal of Congress to suspend the writ of *habeas corpus*, is the continuance of Mr. Benjamin in the cabinet.

MARCH 18TH.—Bright and windy. The following telegram was received this morning from Gen. R. E. Lee: "Gen. Johnston reports that on the 16th Gen. Hardee was repeatedly attacked by four divisions of the enemy a few miles south of Averysborough, but always (cipher). The enemy was reported at night to have crossed Black River, to the east of Varina Point, with the rest of the army. Gen. Hardee is moving to a point twelve miles from Smithfield. Scofield's troops reported at Kinston, repairing railroad. Cheatham's corps not yet up. North Carolina Railroad, with its enormous amount of rolling stock, only conveys about 500 men a day."

There has always been corruption—if not treason—among those having charge of transportation.

Yesterday the President vetoed another bill—to pay certain arrears to the army and navy; but the House resented this by passing it over his head by more than a two-thirds vote. The Senate will probably do the same. We have a spectacle of war among the politicians as well as in the field!

Gen. Whiting, captured at Wilmington, died of his wounds. The government would never listen to his plans for saving Wilmington, and rebuked him for his pertinacity.

It is now said Sheridan has crossed the Pamunky, and is returning toward the Rappahannock, instead of forming a junction with Grant. Senator Hunter's place in Essex will probably be visited, and all that region of country ravaged.

It is rumored that RALEIGH has fallen!

By consulting the map, I perceive that after the battle of Thursday (day before yesterday), Hardee fell back and Sherman advanced, and was within less than thirty miles of Raleigh.

The President, it is understood, favors a great and *decisive* battle.

Judge Campbell said to-day that Mr. Wigfall had sent him Mr. Dejarnette's speech (advocating the Monroe doctrine and alliance with the United States), with a message that he (Mr. W.) intended to read it between his sentence and execution, thinking it would tend to reconcile him to death. The judge said, for his own part, he would postpone reading it until after execution.

MARCH 19TH.—As beautiful a spring morning as ever dawned since the sun spread its glorious light over the Garden of Eden.

Cannon is heard at intervals down the river; and as we have had a few days of wind and sunshine, the surface of the earth is becoming practicable for military operations.

I heard no news at the department; but the belief prevails that Raleigh has fallen, or must speedily fall, and that Richmond is in danger—a danger increasing daily.

Thousands of non-combatants and families, falling weekly within the power of Sherman's army, have succumbed to circumstances and perforce submitted. I suppose most of those remaining in Savannah, Charleston, Wilmington, etc. have taken the oath of allegiance to the United States; and I hear of no censures upon them for doing so. Whether they will be permitted long to enjoy their property—not their slaves, of course—will depend upon the policy adopted at Washington. If it be confiscated, the war will certainly continue for years, even under the direction of President Davis, who is now quite unpopular. If a contrary course be pursued, the struggle may be more speedily terminated—perhaps after the next great battle.

And Mrs. Davis has become unpopular with the ladies belonging to the old families. Her father, Mr. Howell, it is said was of low origin, and this is quite enough to disgust others of "high birth," but yet occupying less exalted positions.

Ladies are now offering their jewels and plate at the Treasury for the subsistence of the army. It is not a general thing, however.

Yesterday bacon was selling at $20 per pound, and meal at $140 per bushel. If Sherman cuts the communication with North Carolina, no one doubts that this city must be abandoned by Lee's army—and yet it may not be so if diligent search be made for food. The soldiers and the people may suffer, but still subsist until harvest; and meantime the God of battles may change the face of affairs, or France may come to our relief.

Four P.M. It is reported that the enemy have taken Weldon. They seem to be closing in on every hand. Lee must soon determine to march away—whether northward or to the southwest, a few weeks, perhaps days, will decide. The unworthy men who have been detained in high civil positions begin now to reap their reward! And the President must reproach himself for his inflexible adherence to a *narrow idea*. He *might* have been successful.

MARCH 20TH.—Sunny and pleasant, but hazy in the south.

Cannon heard, quite briskly, south of the city. The papers report that Gen. Hardee repulsed Sherman on the 16th. But the official dispatch of Gen. Johnston says Hardee retired, and Sherman advanced after the fighting was over.

Congress adjourned *sine die* on Saturday, without passing the measures recommended by the President. On the contrary, a committee of the Senate has reported and published an acrimonious reply to certain allegations in the message, and severely resenting the "admonitions" of the Executive.

When the joint committee waited on the President to inform him that if he had no further communication to make them they would adjourn, he took occasion to fire another broadside, saying that the measures he had just recommended he sincerely deemed essential for the success of the armies, etc., and, since Congress differed with him in opinion, and did not adopt them, he could only hope that the result would prove he was mistaken and that Congress was right. But if the contrary should appear, *he* could not be held responsible, etc. This is the mere *squibbing* of politicians, while the enemy's artillery is thundering at the gates!

The Secretary of War visited Gen. Lee's headquarters on Saturday afternoon, and has not yet returned. Breath is suspended in expectation of some event; and the bickering between the President and the Congress has had a bad effect—demoralizing the community.

Governor Vance writes (17th instant) to the Secretary of War, that he learns an important secret communication had been sent to Congress, concerning probably his State, and asks a copy of it, etc. The Secretary sends this to the President, intimating that the communication referred to was one inclosing a view of our military "situation" by Gen. Lee, in which he concurred. The President returns Gov. V.'s letter, stating that he does not know his purpose, or exactly what he refers to; but [red tape!] until Congress removes the injunction of secrecy, no one can have copies, etc. Yet he suggests that Gov. V. be written to.

Flour is held at $1500 per barrel.

Senator Hunter publishes a card to-day, denying that he is in favor of reconstruction, which has been rumored, he says, to his injury, and might injure the country if not denied.

A correspondence between Generals Lee and Grant is published, showing that Gen. Longstreet has misunderstood Gen. Ord (Federal) in a late conversation, to the effect that Gen. Grant would be willing to meet Gen. Lee to consult on the means of putting an end to the war. The President gave Lee full powers; but Gen. Grant writes Gen. Lee that Gen. Ord must have been misunderstood, and that he (Grant) had no right to settle such matters, etc. Sad delusion!

Assistant Secretary Campbell has given one of his clerks (Cohen, a Jew) a passport to return home—New Orleans—*via* the United States.

The government is still sending away the archives.

MARCH 21ST.—Clear and warm. Apricots in blossom. At last we have reliable information that Johnston has checked one of Sherman's columns, at Bentonville, capturing three guns. This success is a great relief—more as an indication of what is to follow, than for what is accomplished. So Bragg and Johnston have both shown successful fight lately. Beauregard next. Sherman has three full generals in his front, with accumulating forces. A few days more will decide his fate—for immortality or destruction.

There are many red flags displayed this morning in Clay Street, for sales of furniture and renting of houses to the highest bidders. They have postponed it until the last moment to realize the highest possible prices—and they will get them, in consequence of Johnston's success, which revives the conviction that Richmond will not be evacuated. But they have overreached themselves in demanding extortionate prices—such prices depreciating the currency—$1500 being equivalent to one barrel of flour! If it be determined to abandon the city, what will houses rent for then?

Lord Russell's letter, forwarded from Washington some days ago, after much consultation here, was sent back to Gen. Lee by the Secretary of State, declining to receive a communication from a neutral power through a hostile one, and expressing doubts of its *authenticity*. Gen. Lee returns the papers to-day, suggesting that the expression of doubts of the *authenticity* be omitted—but will, at all events, when returned to him again, have it delivered to Gen. Grant. Mr. Benjamin thinks there is some occult diplomatic danger in the papers—at least he is idle, and wants some diplomatic work on his hands, in the regular way. How to avoid doing anything whatever, diplomatically, with this matter before him, is the very quintessence of diplomacy! He can look at it, read it, handle it, and return it to Lord John, and then diplomatically prove that this government never had any knowledge of its existence!

"The following official dispatch, from Gen. Lee, was received yesterday:

"HEADQUARTERS ARMIES CONFEDERATE STATES,
March 20th, 1865.

"HON. JOHN C. BRECKINRIDGE, SECRETARY OF WAR.

"Gen. J. E. Johnston reports that about 5 P.M. on the 19th inst. he attacked the enemy near Bentonsville, routed him, capturing three guns. A mile in rear, the enemy rallied upon fresh troops, but was forced back slowly until 6 o'clock P.M., when, receiving more troops, he apparently assumed the offensive, which movement was resisted without difficulty until dark. This morning he is intrenched.

"Our loss is small. The troops behaved admirably well.

"Dense thickets prevented rapid operations. R. E. LEE."

MARCH 22D.—Rained last night; clear and cool this morning. The report of another battle, since Sunday, in North Carolina, is not confirmed.

The "Bureau of Conscription" still lives, notwithstanding the action of Congress! The President himself, who favored its abolition, yet being displeased with some of the details of the act, seems to have finally withheld his approval; and so Col. G. W. Lay, son-in-law of Judge Campbell, is again acting Superintendent. The great weight (wealth) of Gen. Preston perhaps saved it—and may have lost the cause. However, it is again said Judge Campbell will soon retire from office. He considers the cause already lost—the work quite accomplished.

To-day some of our negro troops will parade in the Capitol Square.

The Texas cavalry in Virginia—originally 5000—now number 180!

Congress adjourned without adopting any plan to reduce the currency, deeming it hopeless, since the discovery of a deficiency, in Mr. Memminger's accounts, of $400,000,000! So the depreciation will go on, since the collection of taxes is rendered quite impracticable by the operations of the enemy. Yet buying and selling, for what they call "dollars," are still extensively indulged; and although the insecurity of slave property is so manifest, yet a negro man will bring $10,000 at auction. This, however, is only equivalent to about $100. Land, when the price is reduced to the gold standard, is similarly diminished in price.

MARCH 23D.—Clear, with high wind. Nothing further from North Carolina. A dispatch from Gen. Lee states that he has directed Gen. Cobb to organize an expedition into *Tennessee*, to cut the enemy's communications. Gen. Wafford, of Kentucky, is in Georgia, with 2000 mounted men, etc.

Beef in market this morning sold at $12 to $15 per pound; bacon at $20, and butter at $20.

The parade of a few companies of negro troops yesterday was rather a ridiculous affair. The owners are opposed to it.

Gen. Rains sends in an indorsement, alleging that owing to the deception of Quartermaster Rhett (not furnishing transportation), he failed to arrest the approach of the enemy on a narrow causeway; and Columbia, S. C., and his shells, etc. fell into the hands of the enemy.

A dispatch from Lee states that Gen. Thomas is at Knoxville, and that the enemy has commenced his advance from *that* direction—is repairing railroads, etc. The same dispatch says Gen. J. E. Johnston is removing his wounded to Smithsville from Bentonville; that the intrenchments of the enemy and greatly superior numbers of Sherman render further offensive operations impracticable.

Grant's grand combination is now developed. Sherman from the Southwest, 70,000; Grant himself from the South, 70,000; Thomas, from the West, 40,000; and Sheridan, with 15,000 cavalry from the North—some 200,000 men converging toward this point. To defend it we shall have 120,000 men, without provisions, and, without some speedy successes, no communications with the regions of supply or transportation! Now is coming the time for the exercise of great generalship!

Gen. Early has been sent to the West—Tennessee.

MARCH 24TH.—Clear and very windy. The fear of utter famine is now assuming form. Those who have the means are laying up stores for the day of siege,—I mean a closer and more rigorous siege,—when all communications with the country shall cease; and this makes the commodities scarcer and the prices higher. There is a project on foot to send away some thousands of useless consumers; but how it is to be effected by the city authorities, and where they will be sent to, are questions I have not heard answered. The population of the city is not less than 100,000, and the markets cannot subsist 70,000. Then there is the army in the vicinity, which *must* be fed. I suppose the poultry and the sheep will be eaten, and something like a pro rata distribution of flour and meal ordered.

There is a rumor of a great victory by Gen. Johnston in North Carolina, the taking of 4500 prisoners, 70 guns, etc.—merely a rumor, I am sure. On the contrary, I apprehend that we shall soon have news of the capture of Raleigh by Sherman. Should this be our fate, we shall soon have three or four different armies encompassing us!

I tried in vain this morning to buy a small fish-hook; but could not find one in the city. None but coarse large ones are in the stores. A friend has promised me one—and I can make *pin-hooks*, that will catch minnows. I am too skillful an angler to starve where water runs; and even minnows can be eaten. Besides, there are eels and catfish in the river. The water is always muddy.

MARCH 25TH.—Clear and cool.

It is reported that Grant is reinforcing Sherman, and that the latter has fallen back upon Goldsborough. This is not yet confirmed by any official statement. A single retrograde movement by Sherman, or even a delay in advancing, would snatch some of his laurels away, and enable Lee to obtain supplies. Yet it may be so. He may have been careering the last month on the unexpended momentum of his recent successes, and really operating on a scale something more than commensurate with the forces of his command. Should this be the case, the moral effect on our people and the army will be prodigious, and a series of triumphs on our side may be the consequence.

The Northern papers chronicle the rise in flour here—to $1500 per barrel—a few days ago, and this affords proof of the fact that every occurrence of military importance in Richmond is immediately made known in Washington. How can success be possible? But our authorities are confirmed in their madness.

There were some movements yesterday. Pickett's division was ordered from this side of the river to the Petersburg depot, to be transported in haste to that town; but it was countermanded, and the troops now (9 A.M.) are marching back, down Main Street. I have not learned what occasioned all this.

The marching and countermarching of troops on this side of the river very much alarmed some of the people, who believed Lee was about to evacuate the city.

Eleven A.M. Gen. Lee attacked the enemy's fort (Battery No. 5) near Petersburg this morning, the one which has so long been shelling the town, and captured it, with 600 prisoners, and several guns. This may interfere with Gen. Grant's projects on his left wing, against the railroad.

It is rumored that Gen. Grant is moving heavy bodies of troops toward Weldon, to reinforce Sherman.

MARCH 26TH.—Frost last night. Cloudy, cold, and windy to-day.

Suffered much yesterday and last night with disordered bowels —from cold. This, however, may relieve me of the distressing cough I have had for months.

After all, I fear Lee's attempt on the enemy's lines yesterday was a failure. We were compelled to relinquish the fort or battery we had taken, with all the guns we had captured. Our men were exposed to an enfilading fire, not being supported by the divisions intended to co-operate in the movement. The 600 prisoners were completely surprised—their pickets supposing our troops to be merely *deserters*. This indicates an awful state of things, the enemy being convinced that we are beaten, demoralized, etc.

There was a communication for the Secretary this morning, from "headquarters;" but being marked "confidential," I did not open it, but sent it to Gen. Breckinridge.

Pickett's division has been marching for Petersburg all the morning.

MARCH 27TH.—Bright, calm, but cold,—my disorder keeping me at home.

The dispatch of Gen. Lee, I fear, indicates that our late attempt to break the enemy's lines was at least prematurely undertaken.

The *Dispatch* newspaper has an article entreating the people not to submit "*too hastily*," as in that event we shall have no benefit of the war between France and the United States—a certain event, the editor thinks.

> "HEADQUARTERS ARMY CONFEDERATE STATES,
> "March 25th, 1865—11.20 P.M.

"HON. J. C. BRECKINRIDGE, SECRETARY OF WAR.

"At daylight this morning, Gen. Gordon assaulted and carried the enemy's works at Hare's Hill, capturing 9 pieces of artillery, 8 mortars, and between 500 and 600 prisoners, among them one brigadier-general and a number of officers of lower grade.

"The lines were swept for a distance of four or five hundred yards to the right and left, and two efforts made to recover the captured works were handsomely repulsed. But it was found that the inclosed works in rear, commanding the enemy's main line, could only be taken at a great sacrifice, and our troops were withdrawn to their original position.

"It being impracticable to bring off the captured guns, owing to the nature of the ground, they were disabled and left.

"Our loss, as reported, is not heavy. Among the wounded are Brig. Gen. Terry, flesh wound, and Brig.-Gen. Phil. Cooke, in the arm.

"All the troops engaged, including two brigades under Brig.-Gen. Ransom, behaved most handsomely. The conduct of the sharpshooters of Gordon's corps, who led the assault, deserves the highest commendation.

"This afternoon there was skirmishing on the right, between the picket lines, with varied success. At dark the enemy held a considerable portion of the line farthest in advance of our main work.

"[Signed] R. E. LEE."

MARCH 28TH.—Cloudy and sunshine; but little wind. Too ill to go to the department, and I get nothing new except what I read in the papers. Some of the editorials are very equivocal, and have a squint toward reconstruction.

The President, and one of his Aids, Col. Lubbock, ex-Governor of Texas, rode by my house, going toward Camp Lee. If driven from this side the Mississippi, no doubt the President would retire into Texas.

And Lee must gain a victory soon, or his communications will be likely to be interrupted. Richmond and Virginia are probably in extreme peril at this moment.

MARCH 29TH.—Slightly overcast, but calm and pleasant.
I am better, after the worst attack for twenty years. The only medicine I took was blue mass—ten grains. My wife had a little tea and loaf-sugar, and a solitary smoked herring—and this I relish; and have nothing else. A chicken, I believe, would cost $50. I must be careful now, and recuperate. Fine weather, and an indulgence of my old passion for angling, would soon build me up again.

The papers give forth an uncertain sound of what is going on in the field, or of what is likely to occur. Unless food and men can be had, Virginia must be lost. The negro experiment will soon be tested. Custis says letters are pouring in at the department from all quarters, asking authority to raise and command negro troops: 100,000 recruits from this source might do wonders.

I think Lee's demonstrations on Grant's front have mainly in view the transportation of subsistence from North Carolina.

Mrs. President Davis has left the city, with her children, for the South. I believe it is her purpose to go no farther at present than Charlotte, N. C.—rear of Sherman. Some of their furniture has been sent to auction. Furniture will soon be *low* again.

It is now believed that the government will be removed with all expedition to Columbus, Ga. But it is said Richmond will still be held by our army. *Said!* Alas! would it not be too expensive—"too much for the whistle?"

Shad are selling at $50 per pair. If Richmond should be left to strictly military rule, I hope it will rule the prices.

It is reported that Gen. Johnston has fallen back on Weldon; some suppose to attack *Grant's* rear, but no doubt it is because he is pressed by Sherman with superior numbers.

A dispatch from Gen. Lee, to-day, states the important fact that Grant's left wing (cavalry and infantry) passed Hatcher's Run this morning, marching to Dinwiddie C. H. The purpose is to cut the South Side and Danville Roads; and it may be accomplished, for we have "here no adequate force of cavalry to oppose Sheridan; and it may be possible, if Sheridan turns his head this way, that shell may be thrown into the city. At all events, he may destroy some bridges—costing him dear." But pontoon bridges were sent up the Danville Road yesterday and to-day, in anticipation, beyond the bridges to be destroyed.

MARCH 30TH.—Raining rapidly, and warm.

Again the sudden change of weather may be an interposition of Providence to defeat the effort of the enemy to destroy Gen. Lee's communications with his Southern depots of supplies. I hope so, for faith in man is growing weaker.

Our loss in the affair of the 25th instant was heavy, and is now admitted to be a disaster; and Lee himself was there! It amounted, probably, to 3000 men. Grant says over 2000 prisoners were registered by his Provost Marshal. It is believed the President advised the desperate undertaking; be that as it may, many such blows cannot follow in quick succession without producing the most deplorable results. The government would soon make its escape—*if it could*. Mrs. Davis, however, soonest informed of our condition, got away in time.

Dispatches from Generalissimo Lee inform the Secretary that large expeditions are on foot in Alabama, Mississippi, etc., and that Thomas's army is rapidly advancing upon Virginia from East Tennessee, while no general has yet been designated to command our troops.

The papers say nothing of the flank movement commenced yesterday by Grant. This reticence cannot be for the purpose of keeping *the enemy* in ignorance of it!

I am convalescent, but too weak to walk to the department to-day. The deathly "sick man," as the Emperor of Russia used to designate the Sultan of Turkey, is our President. His mind has never yet comprehended the magnitude of the crisis.

Custis says letters still flow in asking authority to raise negro troops.

In the North the evacuation of Richmond is looked for between the 1st and 25th of April. They may be fooled. But if we lose the Danville Road, it will only be a question of time. Yet there will remain too great a breadth of territory for subjugation—if the *people* choose to hold out, and soldiers can be made of negroes.

It is reported (believed) that several determined assaults were made on our lines yesterday evening and last night at Petersburg, and repulsed with slaughter; and that the attack has been renewed to-day. Very heavy firing has been heard in that direction. Gen. Lee announces no result yet.

We have 2,000,000 bread rations in the depots in North Carolina.

MARCH 31ST.—Raining; rained all night. My health improving, but prudence requires me to still keep within the house.

The reports of terrific fighting near Peterburg on Wednesday evening have not been confirmed. Although Gen. Lee's dispatch shows they were not quite without foundation, I have no doubt there was a false alarm on both sides, and a large amount of ammunition vainly expended.

"HEADQUARTERS, March 30th, 1865.

"GEN. J. C. BRECKINRIDGE, SECRETARY OF WAR.

"Gen. Gordon reports that the enemy, at 11 A.M. yesterday, advanced against a part of his lines, defended by Brig.-Gen. Lewis, but was repulsed.

"The fire of artillery and mortars continued for several hours with considerable activity.

"No damage on our lines reported. R. E. LEE."

We are sinking our gun-boats at Chaffin's Bluff, to obstruct the passage of the enemy's fleet, expected soon to advance.

Congress passed two acts, and proper ones, to which the Executive has yet paid no attention whatever, viz.: the abolition of the Bureau of Conscription, and of all Provost Marshals, their guards, etc. not attached to armies in the field. If the new Secretary has consented to be burdened with the responsibility of this contumacy and violation of the Constitution, it will break his back, and ruin our already desperate cause.

Four P.M.—Since writing the above, I learn that an order has been published abolishing the "Bureau of Conscription."

Gov. Vance has written to know why the government wants the track of the North Carolina Railroad altered to the width of those in Virginia, and has been answered: 1st, to facilitate the transportation of supplies to Gen. Lee's army from North Carolina; and 2d, in the event of disaster, to enable the government to run all the locomotives, cars, etc. of the Virginia roads into North Carolina.

CHAPTER XLIX.

Rumors of battles.—Excitement in the churches.—The South Side Road captured by the enemy.—Evacuation of Richmond.—Surrender of Gen. Lee.—Occupation of Richmond by Federal forces.—Address to the people of Virginia by J. A. Campbell and others.—Assassination of President Lincoln.

APRIL 1ST.—Clear and pleasant. Walked to the department.

We have vague and incoherent accounts from excited couriers of fighting, without result, in Dinwiddie County, near the South Side Railroad.

It is rumored that a battle will probably occur in that vicinity to-day.

I have leave of absence, to improve my health; and propose accompanying my daughter Anne, next week, to Mr. Hobson's mansion in Goochland County. The Hobsons are opulent, and she will have an excellent asylum there, if the vicissitudes of the war do not spoil her calculations. I shall look for angling streams: and if successful, hope for both sport and better health.

The books at the conscript office show a frightful list of deserters or absentees without leave—60,000—all Virginians. Speculation!

Jno. M. Daniel, editor of the *Examiner*, is dead.

The following dispatch from Gen. Lee is just (10 A.M.) received:

"HEADQUARTERS, April 1st, 1865.

"HIS EXCELLENCY PRESIDENT DAVIS.

"Gen. Beauregard has been ordered to make arrangements to defend the railroad in North Carolina against Stoneman. Generals Echols and Martin are directed to co-operate, and obey his orders. R. E. LEE."

A rumor (perhaps a 1st of April rumor) is current that a treaty has been signed between the Confederate States Government and Maximilian.

APRIL 2D.—Bright and beautiful. The tocsin was sounded this morning at daybreak, and the militia ordered to the fortifications, to relieve some regiments of Longstreet's corps, posted on this side of the river. These latter were hurried off to Petersburg, where a battle is impending, I suppose, if not in progress.

A street rumor says there was bloody fighting yesterday a little beyond Petersburg, near the South Side Road, in which Gen. Pickett's division met with fearful loss, being engaged with superior numbers. It is said the enemy's line of intrenchments was carried once or twice, but was retaken, and remained in their hands.

I hear nothing of all this at the department; but the absence of dispatches there is now interpreted as bad news! Certain it is, the marching of veteran troops from the defenses of Richmond, and replacing them hurriedly with militia, can only indicate an emergency of alarming importance. A decisive struggle is probably at hand—and may possibly be in progress while I write. Or there may be nothing in it—more than a precautionary concentration to preserve our communications.

Mrs. Davis sold nearly all her movables—including presents—before leaving the city. She sent them to different stores.

An intense excitement prevails, at 2 P.M. It pervaded the churches. Dr. Hoge intermitted his services. Gen. Cooper and the President left their respective churches, St. James's and St. Paul's. Dr. Minnegerode, before dismissing his congregation, gave notice that Gen. Ewell desired the local forces to assemble at 3 P.M.—and afternoon services will not be held. The excited women in this neighborhood say they have learned the city is to be evacuated to-night.

No doubt our army sustained a serious blow yesterday; and Gen. Lee may not have troops sufficient to defend both the city and the Danville Road at the same time.

It is true! The enemy have broken through our lines and attained the South Side Road. Gen. Lee has dispatched the Secretary to have everything in readiness to *evacuate the city to-night.* The President told a lady that Lieut.-Gen. Hardee was only twelve miles distant, and might get up in time to save the day. But then Sherman must be in *his* rear. There is no wild excitement—*yet.* Gen. Kemper was at the department looking for Gen.

Ewell, and told me he could find no one to apply to for orders. The banks will move to-night. Eight trains are provided for the transportation of the archives, etc. No provision for civil employees and their families.

At 6 P.M. I saw the Hon. James Lyons, and asked him what he intended to do. He said many of his friends advised him to leave, while his inclination was to remain with his sick family. He said, being an original secessionist, his friends apprehended that the Federals would arrest him the first man, and hang him. I told him I differed with them, and believed his presence here might result in benefit to the population.

Passing down Ninth Street to the department, I observed quite a number of men—some in uniform, and some of them officers—hurrying away with their trunks. I believe they are not allowed to put them in the cars.

The Secretary of War intends to leave at 8 P.M. this evening. The President and the rest of the functionaries, I suppose, will leave at the same time.

I met Judge Campbell in Ninth Street, talking rapidly to himself, with two books under his arm, which he had been using in his office. He told me that the chiefs of bureaus determined which clerks would have transportation—embracing only a small proportion of them, which I found to be correct.

At the department I learned that all who had families were advised to remain. No compulsion is seen anywhere; even the artisans and mechanics of the government shops are left free to choose—to go or to stay.

A few squads of local troops and reserves—guards—may be seen marching here and there. Perhaps they are to burn the tobacco, cotton, etc., if indeed anything is to be burned.

Lee must have met with an awful calamity. The President said to several ladies to-day he had hopes of Hardee coming up in time to save Lee—else Richmond must succumb. He said he had done his best, etc. to save it. Hardee is distant two or three days' march.

The negroes stand about mostly silent, as if wondering what will be their fate. They make no demonstrations of joy.

Several hundred prisoners were brought into the city this afternoon—captured yesterday. Why they were brought here I am at a loss to conjecture. Why were they not paroled and sent into the enemy's lines?

At night. All is yet quiet. No explosion, no conflagration, no riots, etc. How long will this continue? When will the enemy come?

It was after 2 o'clock P.M. before the purpose to evacuate the city was announced; and the government had gone at 8 P.M.! Short notice! and small railroad facilities to get away. All horses were impressed.

There is a report that Lieut.-Gen. A. P. Hill was killed, and that Gen. Lee was wounded. Doubtless it was a battle of great magnitude, wherein both sides had all their forces engaged.

I remain here, broken in health and bankrupt in fortune, awaiting my fate, whatever it may be. I can do no more. If I could, I would.

APRIL 3D.—Another clear and bright morning. It was a quiet night, with its million of stars. And yet how few could sleep, in anticipation of the entrance of the enemy! But no enemy came until 9 A.M., when some 500 were posted at the Capitol Square. They had been waited upon previously by the City Council, and the surrender of the city stipulated—to occur this morning. They were asked to post guards for the protection of property from pillage, etc., and promised to do so.

At dawn there were two tremendous explosions, seeming to startle the very earth, and crashing the glass throughout the western end of the city. One of these was the blowing up of the magazine, near the new almshouse—the other probably the destruction of an iron-clad ram. But subsequently there were others. I was sleeping soundly when awakened by them.

All night long they were burning the papers of the Second Auditor's office in the street—claims of the survivors of deceased soldiers, accounts of contractors, etc.

At 7 A.M. Committees appointed by the city government visited the liquor shops and had the spirits (such as they could find) destroyed. The streets ran with liquor; and women and boys, black and white, were seen filling pitchers and buckets from the gutters.

A lady sold me a bushel of potatoes in Broad Street for $75, Confederate States money—$5 less than the price a few days ago.

I bought them at her request. And some of the shops gave clothing to our last retiring guards.

Goods, etc. at the government depots were distributed to the poor, to a limited extent, there being a limited amount.

A dark volume of smoke rises from the southeastern section of the city, and spreads like a pall over the zenith. It proceeds from the tobacco warehouse, ignited, I suppose, hours ago, and now just bursting forth.

At 8½ A.M. The armory, arsenal, and laboratory (Seventh and Canal Streets), which had been previously fired, gave forth terrific sounds from thousands of bursting shells. This continued for more than an hour. Some fragments of shell fell within a few hundred yards of my house.

The pavements are filled with pulverized glass.

Some of the great flour mills have taken fire from the burning government warehouses, and the flames are spreading through the lower part of the city. A great conflagration is apprehended.

The doors of the government bakery (Clay Street) were thrown open this morning, and flour and crackers were freely distributed, until the little stock was exhausted. I got a barrel of the latter, paying a negro man $5 to wheel it home—a short distance.

Ten A.M. A battery (United States) passed my house, Clay Street, and proceeded toward Camp Lee. Soon after the officers returned, when I asked the one in command if guards would be placed in this part of the city to prevent disturbance, etc. He paused, with his suite, and answered that such was the intention, and that every precaution would be used to preserve order. He said the only disturbances were caused by our people. I asked if there was any disturbance. He pointed to the black columns of smoke rising from the eastern part of the city, and referred to the incessant bursting of shell. I remarked that the storehouses had doubtless been ignited hours previously. To this he assented, and assuring me that *they* did not intend to disturb us, rode on. But immediately meeting two negro women laden with plunder, they wheeled them to the right about, and marched them off, to the manifest chagrin of the newly emancipated citizens.

Eleven A.M. I walked down Brad Street to the Capitol Square. The street was filled with *negro troops*, cavalry and infantry, and were cheered by hundreds of negroes at the corners.

I met Mr. T. Cropper (lawyer from the E. Shore) driving a one-horse wagon containing his bedding and other property of his quarters. He said he had just been burnt out—at Belom's Block —and that St. Paul's Church (Episcopal) was, he thought, on fire. This I found incorrect; but Dr. Reed's (Presbyterian) was in ruins. The leaping and lapping flames were roaring in Main Street up to Ninth; and Goddin's Building (late General Post-Office) was on fire, as well as all the houses in Governor Street up to Franklin.

The grass of Capitol Square is covered with parcels of goods snatched from the raging conflagration, and each parcel guarded by a Federal soldier.

A general officer rode up and asked me what building that was —pointing to the old stone United States Custom House—late Treasury and State Departments, also the President's office. He said, "Then it is fire-proof, and the fire will be arrested in this direction." He said he was sorry to behold such destruction; and regretted that there was not an adequate supply of engines and other apparatus.

Shells are still bursting in the ashes of the armory, etc.

All the stores are closed; most of the largest (in Main Street) have been burned.

There are supposed to be 10,000 negro troops at Camp Lee, west of my dwelling.

An officer told me, 3 P.M., that a white brigade will picket the city to-night; and he assured the ladies standing near that there would not be a particle of danger of molestation. After 9 P.M., all will be required to remain in their houses. Soldiers or citizens, after that hour, will be arrested. He said we had done ourselves great injury by the fire, the lower part of the city being in ashes, and declared that the United States troops had no hand in it. I acquitted them of the deed, and told him that the fire had spread from the tobacco warehouses and military depots, fired by our troops as a military necessity.

Four P.M. Thirty-four guns announced the arrival of President Lincoln. He flitted through the mass of human beings in Capitol Square, his carriage drawn by four horses, preceded by out-riders, motioning the people, etc. out of the way, and followed by a mounted guard of thirty. The cortege passed rapidly, precisely as I had seen royal parties ride in Europe.

APRIL 4TH.—Another bright and beautiful day.

I walked around the burnt district this morning. Some seven hundred houses, from Main Street to the canal, comprising the most valuable stores, and the best business establishments, were consumed. All the bridges across the James were destroyed, the work being done effectually. Shells were placed in all the warehouses where the tobacco was stored, to prevent the saving of any.

The War Department was burned after I returned yesterday; and soon after the flames were arrested, mainly by the efforts of the Federal troops.

Gen. Weitzel commanded the troops that occupied the city upon its abandonment.

The troops do not interfere with the citizens here any more than they do in New York—yet. Last night everything was quiet, and perfect order prevails.

A few thousand negroes (mostly women) are idle in the streets, or lying in the Capitol Square, or crowding about headquarters, at the Capitol.

Gen. Lee's family remain in the city. I saw a Federal guard promenading in front of the door, his breakfast being just sent to him from within.

Brig. Gen. Gorgas's family remain also. They are Northern-born.

It is rumored that another great battle was fought yesterday, at Amelia Court House, on the Danville Road, and that Lee, Johnston and Hardee having come up, defeated Grant. It is only rumor, so far. If it be true, Richmond was evacuated prematurely; for the local defense troops might have held it against the few white troops brought in by Weitzel. The negroes never would have been relied on to take it by assault.

I see many of the civil employees left behind. It was the merest accident (being Sunday) that any were apprised, in time, of the purpose to evacuate the city. It was a shameful *abandonment* on the part of the heads of departments and bureaus.

Confederate money is not taken to-day. However, the shops are still closed.

APRIL 5TH.—Bright and pleasant.

Stayed with my next door neighbors at their request last night—all females. It was quiet; and so far the United States pickets and guards have preserved perfect order.

The cheers that greeted President Lincoln were mostly from the negroes and Federals comprising the great mass of humanity. The white citizens felt annoyed that the city should be held mostly by negro troops. If this measure were not unavoidable, it was impolitic if conciliation be the purpose.

Mr. Lincoln, after driving to the mansion lately occupied by Mr. Davis, Confederate States President, where he rested, returned, I believe, to the fleet at Rocketts.

This morning thousands of negroes and many white females are besieging the public officers for provisions. I do not observe any getting them, and their faces begin to express disappointment.

It is said all the negro men, not entering the army, will be put to work, rebuilding bridges, repairing railroads, etc.

I have seen a *New York Herald* of the 3d, with dispatches of the 1st and 2d inst. from Mr. Lincoln, who was at City Point during the progress of the battle. He sums up with estimate of 12,000 prisoners captured, and 50 guns.

The rumor of a success by Gen. Lee on Monday is still credited. *Per contra*, it is reported that President Davis is not only a captive, but will soon be exhibited in Capitol Square.

The Rev. Mr. Dashiell, who visited us to-day, said it was reported and believed that 6000 South Carolina troops threw down their arms; and that a large number of Mississippians deserted—giving such information to the enemy as betrayed our weak points, etc.

Three P.M. I feel that this Diary is near its end.

The burnt district includes all the banks, money-changers, and principal speculators and extortioners. This seems like a decree from above!

Four P.M. The Square is nearly vacated by the negroes. An officer told me they intended to put them in the army in a few days, and that the Northern people did not really like negro equality any better than we did.

Two rumors prevail: that Lee gained a victory on Monday, and that Lee has capitulated, with 35,000 men.

The policy of the conquerors here, I believe, is still undecided, and occupies the attention of Mr. Lincoln and his cabinet.

APRIL 6TH.—Showery morning.

I perceive no change, except, perhaps, a diminution of troops, which seems to confirm the reports of recent battles, and the probable success of Lee and Johnston. But all is doubt and uncertainty.

The military authorities are still reticent regarding the fate of those remaining in Richmond. We are at their mercy, and prepared for our fate. I except some of our ladies, who are hysterical, and want to set out on foot "for the Confederacy."

APRIL 7TH.—Slight showers.

Wm. Ira Smith, tailor, and part owner of the *Whig*, has continued the publication as a Union paper.

I visited the awful crater of the magazine. One current or stream of fire and bricks knocked down the east wall of the cemetery, and swept away many head and foot stones, demolishing trees, plants, etc.

It is said President Lincoln is still in the city. Dr. Ellison informed me to-day of the prospect of Judge Campbell's conference with Mr. Lincoln. It appears that the judge had prepared statistics of our resources in men and materials, showing them to be utterly inadequate for a prolongation of the contest, and these he exhibited to certain prominent citizens, whom he wished to accompany him. Whether they were designed also for the eye of President Lincoln, or whether he saw them, I did not learn. But one citizen accompanied him—GUSTAVUS A. MYERS, the little old lawyer, who has certainly cultivated the most friendly relations with all the members of President Davis's cabinet, and it is supposed he prosecuted a lucrative business procuring substitutes, obtaining discharges, getting passports, etc.

The ultimatum of President Lincoln was Union, emancipation, disbandment of the Confederate States armies. Then no oath of allegiance would be required, no confiscation exacted, or other penalty; and the Governor and Legislature to assemble and readjust the affairs of Virginia without molestation of any character.

Negotiations are in progress by the clergymen, who are directed to open the churches on Sunday, and it was intimated to the Episcopalians that they should pray for the President of the United

States. To this they demur, being ordered by the Convention to pray for the President of the Confederate States. They are willing to omit the prayer altogether, and await the decision of the military authority on that proposition.

APRIL 8TH.—Bright and pleasant weather.

We are still in uncertainty as to our fate, or whether an oath of allegiance will be demanded.

Efforts by Judge Campbell, Jos. R. Anderson, N. P. Tyler, G. A. Myers and others, are being made to assemble a convention which shall withdraw Virginia from the Confederacy.

Hundreds of civil employees remained, many because they had been required to *volunteer* in the local defense organization or lose their employment, and the fear of being still further perfidiously dealt with, forced into the army, notwithstanding their legal exemptions. Most of them had families whose subsistence depended upon their salaries. It is with governments as with individuals, injustice is sooner or later overtaken by its merited punishment.

The people are kinder to each other, sharing provisions, etc.

A New York paper says Gen. H. A. Wise was killed; we hear nothing of this here.

Roger A. Pryor is said to have remained voluntarily in Petersburg, and announces his abandonment of the Confederate States cause.

APRIL 9TH.—Bright and beautiful. Rev. Mr. Dashiell called, after services. The prayer for the President was omitted, by a previous understanding.

Rev. Dr. Minnegerode, and others, leading clergymen, consider the cause at an end. A letter from Gen. Lee has been found, and its authenticity vouched for (Rev. Dr. M. says) by Judge Campbell, in which he avows his conviction that further resistance will be in vain—but that so long as it is desired, he will do his utmost in the field.

And Dr. M. has information of the capture of three divisions of Longstreet since the battle of Sunday last, with some eight generals—among them Lieut.-Gen. Ewell, Major-Gen. G. W. Custis Lee, etc.

The clergy also seem to favor a convention, and the resumption by Virginia of her old position in the Union—minus slavery. Charlottesville has been named as the place for the assembling of the convention. They also believe that Judge Campbell remained to treat with the United States at the request of the Confederate States Government. I doubt. We shall now have no more interference in Cæsar's affairs by the clergy—may they attend to God's hereafter!

Ten o'clock P.M. A salute fired—100 guns—from the forts across the river, which was succeeded by music from all the bands. The guard promenading in front of the house says a dispatch has been received from Grant announcing the surrender of Lee!

I hear that Gen. Pickett was killed in the recent battle!

APRIL 10TH.—Raining. I was startled in bed by the sound of cannon from the new southside fort again. I suppose another hundred guns were fired; and I learn this morning that the Federals declare, and most people believe, that Lee has really surrendered his army—if not indeed all the armies.

My Diary is surely drawing to a close, and I feel as one about to take leave of some old familiar associate. A *habit* is to be discontinued—and that is no trifling thing to one of my age. But I may find sufficient employment in revising, correcting, etc. what I have written. I never supposed it would end in this way.

Ten A.M. It is true! Yesterday Gen. Lee surrendered the "Army of Northern Virginia." His son, Custis Lee, and other generals, had surrendered a few days previously. The men are paroled by regimental commanders, from the muster rolls, and are permitted to return to their homes and remain undisturbed until exchanged. The officers to take their side-arms and baggage to their homes, on the same conditions, etc. There *were* 290 pieces of artillery belonging to this army a few weeks ago. This army was the pride, the hope, the prop of the Confederate cause, and numbered, I believe, on the rolls, 120,000 men. All is lost! No head can be made by any other general or army—if indeed any other army remains. If Mr. Davis had been present, he never would have consented to it; and I doubt if he will ever forgive Gen. Lee.

APRIL 11TH.—Cloudy and misty. It is reported that Gen. Johnston has surrendered his army in North Carolina, following the example of Gen. Lee. But no salutes have been fired in honor of the event. The President (Davis) is supposed to be flying toward the Mississippi River, but this is merely conjectural. Undoubtedly the war is at an end, and the Confederate States Government will be immediately extinct—its members fugitives. From the tone of leading Northern papers, we have reason to believe President Lincoln will call Congress together, and proclaim an amnesty, etc.

Judge Campbell said to Mr. Hart (clerk in the Confederate States War Department) yesterday that there would be no arrests, and no oath would be required. Yet ex-Captain Warner was arrested yesterday, charged with ill treating Federal prisoners, with registering a false name, and as a dangerous character. I know the contrary of all this; for he has been persecuted by the Confederate States authorities for a year, and forced to resign his commission.

My application to Gen. Shepley for permission to remove my family to the Eastern Shore, where they have relatives and friends, and may find subsistence, still hangs fire. Every day I am told to call the *next* day, as it has not been acted upon.

APRIL 12TH.—Warm and cloudy. Gen. Weitzel publishes an order to-day, requiring all ministers who have prayed for the President of the Confederate States to pray hereafter for the President of the United States. He will not allow them to omit the prayer.

In answer to my application for permission to take my family to the Eastern Shore of Virginia, where among their relations and friends shelter and food may be had, Brevet Brig.-Gen. Ludlow indorsed: "Disallowed—as none but loyal people, who have taken the oath, are permitted to reside on the Eastern Shore of Virginia." This paper I left at Judge Campbell's residence (he was out) for his inspection, being contrary in spirit to the terms he is represented to have said would be imposed on us.

At 1½ P.M. Another 100 guns were fired in Capitol Square, in honor, I suppose, of the surrender of JOHNSTON'S army. I must go and see.

Captain Warner is still in prison, and no one is allowed to visit him, I learn.

Three P.M. Saw Judge Campbell, who will lay my paper before the military authorities for reconsideration to-morrow. He thinks they have acted unwisely. I said to him that a gentleman's *word* was better than an enforced oath—and that if persecution and confiscation are to follow, instead of organized armies we shall have bands of assassins everywhere in the field, and the stiletto and the torch will take the place of the sword and the musket—and there can be no solid reconstruction, etc. He says he told the Confederate States authorities months ago that the cause had failed, but they would not listen. He said he had telegraphed something to Lieut.-Gen. Grant to-day.

The salute some say was in honor of Johnston's surrender—others say it was for Lee's—and others of Clay's birthday.

APRIL 13TH.—Raining. Long trains of "supply" and "ammunition" wagons have been rolling past our dwelling all the morning, indicating a movement of troops southward. I suppose the purpose is to *occupy* the conquered territory. Alas! we know too well what military occupation is. No intelligent person supposes, after Lee's surrender, that there will be found an army anywhere this side of the Mississippi of sufficient numbers to make a stand. No doubt, however, many of the dispersed Confederates will join the trans-Mississippi army under Gen. E. Kirby Smith, if indeed, he too does not yield to the prevalent surrendering epidemic.

Confederate money is valueless, and we have no Federal money. To such extremity are some of the best and wealthiest families reduced, that the ladies are daily engaged making pies and cakes for the Yankee soldiers of all colors, that they may obtain enough "greenbacks" to purchase such articles as are daily required in their housekeeping.

It is said we will be supplied with rations from the Federal commissariat.

APRIL 14TH.—Bright and cool.

Gen. Weitzel and his corps having been ordered away; Major-Gen. Ord has succeeded to the command at Richmond, and his corps has been marching to Camp Lee ever since dawn. I saw no negro troops among them, but presume there are some.

Gen. Weitzel's rule became more and more despotic daily; but it is said the order dictating prayers to be offered by the Episcopal clergy came from Mr. Stanton, at Washington, Secretary of War. One of the clergy, being at my house yesterday, said that unless this order were modified there would be no services on Sunday. To-day, Good Friday, the churches are closed.

The following circular was published a few days ago:

"TO THE PEOPLE OF VIRGINIA.

"The undersigned, members of the Legislature of the State of Virginia, in connection with a number of the citizens of the State, whose names are attached to this paper, in view of the evacuation of the City of Richmond by the Confederate Government, and its occupation by the military authorities of the United States, the surrender of the Army of Northern Virginia, and the suspension of the jurisdiction of the civil power of the State, are of opinion that an immediate meeting of the General Assembly of the State is called for by the exigencies of the situation.

"The consent of the military authorities of the United States to the session of the Legislature in Richmond, in connection with the Governor and Lietenant-Governor, to their free deliberation upon public affairs, and to the ingress and departure of all its members under safe conducts, has been obtained.

"The United States authorities will afford transportation from any point under their control to any of the persons before mentioned.

"The matters to be submitted to the Legislature are the restoration of peace to the State of Virginia, and the adjustment of questions involving life, liberty, and property, that have arisen in the State as a consequence of the war.

"We therefore earnestly request the Governor, Lieutenant-Governor, and members of the Legislature to repair to this city by the 25th April (instant).

"We understand that full protection to persons and property will be afforded in the State, and we recommend to peaceful citizens to remain at their homes and pursue their usual avocations, with confidence that they will not be interrupted.

"We earnestly solicit the attendance in Richmond, on or before the 25th of April (instant), of the following persons, citizens of Virginia, to confer with us as to the best means of restoring peace to the State of Virginia. We have procured safe conduct from the military authorities of the United States for them to enter the city and depart without molestation: Hon. R. M. T. Hunter, A. T. Caperton, Wm. C. Rives, John Letcher, A. H. H. Stuart, R. L. Montague, Fayette McMullen, J. P. Holcombe, Alexander Rives, B. Johnson Barbour, James Barbour, Wm. L. Goggin, J. B. Baldwin, Thomas S. Gholson, Waller Staples, S. D. Miller, Thomas J. Randolph, Wm T. Early, R. A. Claybrook, John Critcher, Wm. Towns, T. H. Eppes, and those other persons for whom passports have been procured and especially forwarded that we consider it to be unnecessary to mention.

"A. J. Marshall, Senator, Fauquier; James Neeson, Senator, Marion; James Venable, Senator elect, Petersburg; David I. Burr, of House of Delegates, Richmond City; David J. Saunders, of House of Delegates, Richmond City; L. S. Hall, of House of Delegates, Wetzel County; J. J. English, of House of Delegates, Henrico County; Wm. Ambers, of House of Delegates, Chesterfield County; A. M. Keily, of House of Delegates, Petersburg; H. W. Thomas, Second Auditor of Virginia; St. L. L. Moncure, Chief Clerk Second Auditor's office; Joseph Mayo, Mayor of City of Richmond; Robert Howard, Clerk of Hustings Court, Richmond City; Thomas U. Dudley, Sergeant Richmond City; Littleton Tazewell, Commonwealth's Attorney, Richmond City; Wm. T. Joynes, Judge of Circuit Court, Petersburg; John A. Meredith, Judge of Circuit Court, Richmond; Wm. H. Lyons, Judge of Hustings Court, Richmond; Wm. C. Wickham, Member of Congress, Richmond District; Benj. S. Ewell, President of William and Mary College; Nat. Tyler, Editor Richmond *Enquirer;* R. F. Walker, Publisher of *Examiner;* J. R. Anderson, Richmond; R. R. Howison, Richmond; W. Goddin, Richmond; P. G. Bayley, Richmond; F. J. Smith, Richmond; Franklin Stearns, Henrico; John Lyons, Petersburg; Thomas B. Fisher, Fauquier; Wm. M. Harrison, Charles City; Cyrus Hall, Ritchie; Thomas W. Garnett, King and Queen; James A. Scott, Richmond.

"I concur in the preceding recommendation.

"J. A. CAMPBELL.

"Approved for publication in the *Whig*, and in handbill form.

"G. WEITZEL, Major-Gen. Commanding.

"RICHMOND, VA., April 11th, 1865."

To-day the following order is published :

"HEADQUARTERS DEPARTMENT OF VIRGINIA,
"RICHMOND, VA., April 13th, 1865.

"Owing to recent events, the permission for the reassembling of the gentlemen recently acting as the Legislature of Virginia is rescinded. Should any of the gentlemen come to the city under the notice of reassembling, already published, they will be furnished passports to return to their homes.

"Any of the persons named in the call signed by J. A. Campbell and others, who are found in the city twelve hours after the publication of this notice, will be subject to arrest, unless they are residents of the city.

"E. O. C. ORD, Major-Gen. Commanding."

Judge Campbell informs me that he saw Gen. Ord yesterday, who promised to grant me permission to take my family to the Eastern Shore of Virginia, and suggesting some omissions and alterations in the application, which I made. Judge C. is to see him again to-day, when I hope the matter will be accomplished.

Judge Campbell left my application with Gen. Ord's youngest adjutant, to whom he said the general had approved it. But the adjutant said it would have to be presented again, as there was no indorsement on it. The judge advised me to follow it up, which I did; and stayed until the adjutant did present it again to Gen. Ord, who again approved it. Then the polite aid accompanied me to Gen. Patrick's office and introduced me to him, and to Lieut.-Col. John Coughlin, "Provost Marshal General Department of Virginia," who indorsed on the paper: "These papers will be granted when called for."

APRIL 17TH.—Bright and clear.

I add a few lines to my Diary. It was whispered, yesterday, that President Lincoln had been assassinated! I met Gen. Duff Green, in the afternoon, who assured me there could be no doubt of it. Still, supposing it might be an April hoax, I inquired at the headquarters of Gen. Ord, and was told it was true. I cautioned those I met to manifest no *feeling*, as the occurrence might be a calamity for the South; and possibly the Federal soldiers, supposing the deed to have been done by a Southern man, might become uncontrollable and perpetrate deeds of horror on the unarmed people.

After agreeing to meet Gen. Green this morning at the Provost Marshal's office, and unite with him in an attempt to procure the liberation of Capt. Warner, I returned home; and saw, on the way, Gen. Ord and his staff riding out toward Camp Lee, with no manifestations of excitement or grief on their countenances.

Upon going down town this morning, every one was speaking of the death of Lincoln, and the *Whig* was in mourning.

President Lincoln was killed by Booth (Jno. Wilkes), an actor. I suppose his purpose is to live in history as the slayer of a tyrant; thinking to make the leading character in a tragedy, and have his performance acted by others on the stage.

I see no grief on the faces of either officers or men of the Federal army.

R. A. Pryor and Judge W. T. Joynes have called a meeting in Petersburg, to lament the calamity entailed by the assassination.

I got passports to-day for myself and family to the Eastern Shore, taking no oath. We know not when we shall leave.

I never swore allegiance to the Confederate States Government, but was true to it.

APRIL 19TH.—Yesterday windy, to-day bright and calm.

It appears that the day of the death of President Lincoln was appointed for illuminations and rejoicings on the surrender of Lee. There is no intelligence of the death of Mr. Seward or his son. It was a dastardly deed—surely the act of a madman.

THE END.

www.ingramcontent.com/pod-product-compliance
Lightning Source LLC
Chambersburg PA
CBHW031227170426
43191CB00030B/305